The Essential Theatre

THE ESSENTIAL THEATRE

SIXTH EDITION

OSCAR G. BROCKETT

THE UNIVERSITY OF TEXAS AT AUSTIN

HARCOURT BRACE COLLEGE PUBLISHERS

Fort Worth Philadelphia San Diego New York Orlando Austin San Antonio
Toronto Montreal London Sydney Tokyo

Publisher	Ted Buchholz
Editor in Chief	Christopher P. Klein
Acquisitions Editor	Barbara J. C. Rosenberg
Developmental Editor	Cathlynn Richard
Project Editor	Laura J. Hanna
Production Manager	Jane Tyndall Ponceti
Art Director	Vicki Whistler

Cover artwork by David Hockney
Parade Curtain after Picasso, 1980
Oil on canvas, 40 × 60 inches
© David Hockney

Address for Editorial Correspondence:
Harcourt Brace College Publishers
301 Commerce Street
Suite 3700
Fort Worth, Texas 76102

Address for Orders:
Harcourt Brace & Company
6277 Sea Harbor Drive
Orlando, Florida 32887
1-800-782-4479, or 1-800-433-0001 (in Florida)

Printed in the United States of America

Library of Congress Catalog Card Number: 95-79644

ISBN: 0-15-501598-2

5 6 7 8 9 0 1 2 3 4   039   9 8 7 6 5 4 3 2 1

Preface

Behind this edition lies more than thirty years of publication—for although *The Essential Theatre* was published first in 1976, it began as an abridged version of *The Theatre: An Introduction,* which first appeared in 1964. *The Essential Theatre* has now taken on an identity of its own, this being the sixth edition.

Like the earlier versions, this edition is still divided into three parts. Within those parts, however, a number of changes have been made. In Part I, the opening chapter, "The Nature of Theatre," has been considerably rewritten to better orientate students to the values of theatrical art. The chapters that make up Part II have been reorganized and reduced by one in number. At the suggestion of many users, the section on Japanese theatre has been eliminated. The final chapter in Part II, Chapter 9, includes extensive new material concerning cultural diversity. It now provides discussions of African American, Asian American, Latino, Native American, Women's, and Gay and Lesbian drama and performance. As part of this discussion, four recent plays are examined at length as examples of contemporary theatre's diversity.

In Part III, material about the playwright's work has been removed from the chapter on the producer and the director and combined with a discussion of the dramaturg's functions to create a new Chapter 11. All the book's chapters have been partially rewritten to sharpen discussions, add new material, and respond to user reactions. Many new illustrations have been added and integrated with the written text, and the number of illustrations in color has been increased. The Bibliography has been updated. Many alterations have been made in the boxed materials scattered throughout the book and used either to give special emphasis to topics or persons thought particularly pertinent or to provide additional concrete details. Several of the boxes have been replaced by new ones; others have been revised or enlarged; and many boxes have been added.

I have assumed that those who use this book will both read plays and attend theatrical performances. Ideally, students should be able to read a script and then see a performance of that script. This is not always possible, but reading a play and seeing a performance, even if both are not of the same script, illustrate the differences between a text on the printed page and the enacted script on the stage—the difference between drama and theatre.

Since students may not have read a wide range of plays, I have selected many of the examples cited in *The Essential Theatre* from fourteen scripts included in a companion anthology, *Plays for the Theatre* (6th Edition), edited by Oscar G. Brockett and published in 1995 by Harcourt Brace College Publishers. These scripts also serve as foundations for discussions in *The Essential Theatre* of various types of theatrical experience. The plays are as follows: Sophocles' *Oedipus the King,* the anonymous *Noah and His Sons,* Shakespeare's *Hamlet,* "The Dentist," (a *commedia dell'arte* scenario), Molière's *Tartuffe,* Ibsen's *A Doll's House,* O'Neill's *"The Hairy Ape,"* Brecht's *The Good Woman of Setzuan,* Williams' *Cat on a Hot Tin Roof,* Beckett's *Happy Days,* Wolfe's *The Colored Museum,* Hwang's *M. Butterfly,* Sanchez-Scott's *Roosters,* and Vogel's *Baltimore Waltz.* Those who prefer to read different but parallel selections may wish to consider *World Drama,* edited by Oscar G. Brockett and Mark Pape, published in 1984 by Harcourt Brace College Publishers. It includes seventeen plays: Sophocles' *Antigone,* Euripides' *Iphigeneia at Aulis,* Aristophanes' *Lysistrata,* Plautus' *Pseudolus,* the anonymous *Everyman,* Kan'ami's *Matsukaze,* Shakespeare's *King Lear,* Molière's *The School for Wives,* Farquhar's *The Recruiting Officer,* Aiken's *Uncle Tom's Cabin,* Ibsen's *A Doll's House,* Shaw's *Major Barbara,* Hellman's *The Little Foxes,* Brecht's *Life of Galileo,* Beckett's *Krapp's Last Tape,* Soyinka's *The Strong Breed,* Baraka's *Slave Ship,* and Shepard's *Buried Child.*

   The Essential Theatre is intended to meet the needs of two kinds of courses: introduction to theatre (an overview serving as a foundation for students who expect to major in theatre—future theatre makers) and theatre appreciation (an overview providing insight into and understanding of theatre for audience members—future theatregoers). Although these two types of courses may treat the same topics, they usually do so with somewhat different emphases. Instructors may of course use the material in ways suited to their needs. I have sought to provide a logically organized, comprehensive overview of the theatre, but instructors need not follow the sequence I have chosen or use all of the material in the book. Some instructors may wish to use only some chapters in Part II, while others may wish to assign Part III prior to or concurrently with Part II. My aim has been to provide helpful discussions of topics pertinent to introductory courses rather than to prescribe how the courses should be organized.

   It is impossible to list all of those to whom I am indebted. The Bibliography indicates most of the sources I have used, and captions indicate those people or organizations who have permitted me to include these illustrations. A few individuals deserve special mention. I want to thank colleagues in the field for insightful and useful comments: Gary Faircloth, East Carolina University; Elizabeth C. Ramírez, University of Oregon; LaLonnie Lehman, Texas Christian University; Ron Thronson, Chapman University; and Julia Allacdice Gagne, Valencia Community College.

   Above all, I wish to acknowledge the contributions of Robert Ball of Vanderbilt University, who not only gave perceptive and ongoing advice based on his extensive experience in teaching the introductory course, but who also devoted countless hours to tracking down and negotiating for illustrations. For his assistance, I am truly grateful. Finally, I thank my developmental editor at Harcourt Brace College Publishers, Cathlynn Richard, for her guidance and encouragement, and my project editor, Laura Hanna, for her help in producing the book.

Contents

The Essential Theatre

PART ONE

Foundations

When we attend the theatre today, we and a few hundred other people come together, usually in the evening, to see a performance that will last approximately two hours on an indoor stage illuminated by artificial light. But theatregoing has not always been this way. Our experience of theatregoing would have seemed strange indeed to Greeks living in the fifth century B.C. They assembled at dawn in an outdoor theatre seating approximately seventeen thousand people to watch a series of plays that lasted all day under the bright sunlight. Our experience would have seemed equally strange to a fifteenth-century A.D. English audience that gathered at various places along a route to watch a series of short biblical plays performed on wagons that moved from one site to the next. These examples by no means exhaust the possibilities, for theatrical experience has been as varied as the cultures in which it has appeared.

Theatre is a complex art with a recorded history going back at least 2,500 years. During such a long span, it has undergone many changes and followed diverse paths. Studying this history encourages us to see the numerous forms theatrical experience can take and leads us to realize that the practices we are familiar with today encompass only a limited range of the theatre's possibilities. Despite its diversity, theatre's long history also invites questions about what its varied manifestations have in common, about their ongoing appeal, and about how we evaluate theatrical performances (why we think one production is better than another).

Let us begin our look at the theatre by examining some basic issues: the nature and function of theatre; the relationship of theatre to other forms of art; criteria for judging theatrical performances; how scripts, the usual starting point of theatrical production, are structured; and other related topics. These initial explorations provide a foundation for a more detailed look at several varieties of theatrical experience (past and present) and the processes of theatrical production in today's theatre.

Scene from the American Repertory Theatre's production of Shakespeare's *A Midsummer Night's Dream.* Oberon is dropping the magic potion into Titania's eyes that will make her fall in love with the first creature she sees. Directed by Alvin Epstein, costumes by Zack Brown. (Photo by Richard Feldman.)

Chapter 1

The Nature of Theatre

Opening scene of Jean-Claude Carrière's adaptation of the Sanskrit epic, *Mahabharata*. The Hindu god, Ganesh (at right), is enlisting the help of the boy to write down the story that is about to unfold on the stage. Directed by Peter Brook; designed by Chloe Oblensky. (Photo © Martha Swope.)

'Theatre' consists in this: in making live representations of reported or invented happenings between human beings, and doing so with a view to entertainment.

—Bertolt Brecht, *A Short Organum for the Theatre*

Just how and when theatre originated is uncertain, but as far back as we can trace human history various kinds of rituals considered vital to the well-being of the tribe were already using the elements needed for theatre: a performance space, performers, masks or makeup, costumes, music, dance, and an audience. The function of these early rites was only incidentally theatrical; they were addressed to supernatural forces thought to control the return of spring, success in hunting and war, the fertility of human beings and the land, and the place of humans in the cosmic scheme. Other activities that contributed to theatre, such as storytelling and mimicry, also were already evident.

Although exactly how it emerged from these beginnings is unclear, theatre achieved its own distinct identity at least twenty-five hundred years ago. During its existence, it has at times been highly developed and highly prized. In ancient Greece, it was performed for the entire community at religious festivals financed by the state and wealthy citizens. At other times, theatre has existed on the fringes of respectability, as it did from the fifth to the tenth century A.D., when small bands of itinerant performers traveled around playing wherever they could for whatever they could collect from those who came to watch. In other times, theatre has been forbidden altogether, as it was in England between 1642 and 1660 when the Puritans then in power considered it not only morally unacceptable but also an activity that tempted people away from more honest work. During its long life, theatre has as often been denounced as praised, and its value—even its right to exist—has frequently been questioned.

Such ambivalent response has been encouraged in part by theatrical terminology (*play*, *show*, *acting*) that suggests theatre is the product of grown-ups who have prolonged their childhood by dressing up and playing games to divert themselves and others. Furthermore, because dramas are fictional, they have at times been denounced as a form of lying, as they were in colonial New England. Because they tend to emphasize human crises (often involving deception, violence, and socially reprehensible behavior), they have been accused of exerting dangerous influence on the young (as many claim much television drama does today). Nevertheless, in almost all periods at least some people have considered theatre not only an acceptable form of entertainment but also a truthful reflection of human behavior.

The theatre, then, has had its detractors and its advocates. Nevertheless, those who value it often find themselves on the defensive against those who question whether it has a valid place in a college curriculum or whether a world dominated by film and television would miss theatre if it disappeared altogether.

The Basic Elements of Theatre

One reason for the varying responses can be found in the theatre's range and diversity, both of which are evident in its three basic elements: what is performed (script, scenario, or plan); the performance (including all the processes involved in the creation and presentation of a production); and the audience (the perceivers). Each is essential, and each affects conceptions of the whole.

What is performed can be extremely varied—from a comic routine performed by a single entertainer to a Shakespearean tragedy performed by a large company of actors. Some people consider such events as street carnivals and parades to be types of theatre. Because of this great range, theatre is not easy to define. The critic Eric Bentley has argued that all the many definitions of theatre can be reduced to: A performs B for C. That is, the most basic definition of theatre is: someone performing something for someone else.

Though theatre is varied, typically it is thought of as the staged performance of a written text. But it is important to remember that theatre does not require a script, dialogue, or even drama (as that term is usually understood). Juggling and tumbling, for example, have often been presented as theatrical entertainments. But even if we restrict our definition of theatre to performances in some degree dramatic, we are still faced with great diversity because improvised scenes, pantomimes, vaudeville sketches, musical plays, and spoken dramas are all dramatic entertainments. Furthermore, they may be brief or lengthy; they may deal with the everyday or the unusual, the comic or the serious. With so much diversity, it is not surprising that some people think of theatre primarily as entertainment while others

---

Bill Irwin

Bill Irwin (1950–   ) is a performer whose career illustrates the many forms that entertainment can take: After studying theatre at UCLA, California Institute of the Arts, and Oberlin College, he attended the Ringling Brothers Clown College, was a busker and street performer, a clown in the Pickle Family Circus, an actor in theatrical productions (including *Waiting for Godot* at Lincoln Center in New York), a dancer, and a developer of his own vaudeville-type acts and full-length productions. He has shown that he can be equally effective in scripted and nonscripted pieces and that he can address intellectual issues while he entertains. Because so much of his work makes use of popular entertainment forms, ranging through circus, vaudeville, commedia dell'arte, and experimental theatre, Irwin is often called a "new vaudevillian." His full-length pieces in this mode have included *In Regard of Flight, Largely New York,* and *Fool Moon,* in all of which he plays a hapless performer beset by various accidents and strange occurrences. Although he often resorts to speech, he depends even more on sleight of hand, pantomime, facial expression, costumes, props, and dance movement. He has stated that he gained much of his most important experience as a street performer. "You can always tell how you're doing when you perform on the street. When you reach people they stand there; when you don't, they leave. . . . Nothing I've ever done since . . . has been without connection to those days."

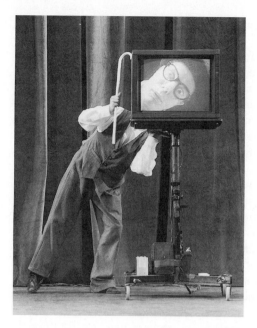

Bill Irwin in *Largely New York*. Here, as in others of his pieces, he becomes the hapless victim of the technology he seeks to use. (Photo by Joan Marcus.)

find the essence of theatre to be its capacity to provoke thought or action about significant issues. If we are to understand the theatre, we must acknowledge its great range and recognize that its potential (like that of most human creations) can be developed in many ways, some of which we may like and some of which we may even consider dangerous.

Theatre's second ingredient, *the performance*, is equally complex. It translates the potential of a script, scenario, or plan into actuality. What the audience usually sees when it goes to the theatre is the fleshing out of a script or plan through the application of theatrical processes. The performance takes place in a space that can vary from a building intended specifically for theatrical performances to a street, park, or nightclub. Spaces may accommodate fewer than a hundred people or (as in ancient Greece) fifteen to twenty thousand. The arrangement of this space may also vary: It may permit spectators to surround the performers, require the audience to sit in rows facing a platform on which the performance occurs, or it may utilize other audience-performer configurations, each of which alters the total theatrical experience. (This subject is explored more fully in Chapter 10.)

Most performances require the creative efforts and cooperation of many people: playwright, director, actors, designers, and technicians. A musical will probably involve even more: composer, instrumentalists, singers, choreographer, and dancers. Any component of production (script, acting, scenery, costumes, lighting, music, dance) can be manipulated to create varied effects. All the components may be so skillfully integrated that the spectator is aware of only a single unified impression; or one or more of the components—such as acting or spectacle—may completely overshadow the others. Today, for example, many people argue that spectacular effects overwhelm the other elements in such popular musicals as *Phantom of the Opera, Les Miserables,* or *Tommy*.

The components may be handled in a way easily understood by almost everyone, or in ways so strange that all but a few are puzzled. A performance may seem to one part of the audience original and entertaining and to another obvious and boring; conversely, what to one group may seem strange and incomprehensible may be judged insightful and brilliant by another. Although the possibilities and results of performance may be infinite, the beginning point of the theatrical experience has been reduced to its essentials by Peter Brook in his book *The Empty Space:* "I can take any empty space and call it a bare stage. A man walks across this empty space whilst someone else is watching him, and this is all that is needed for an act of theatre to be engaged."

The third ingredient of the theatre is *the audience*, because until material is performed and seen by a public, we usually do not call it theatre. Brook has said: "The only thing that all forms of theatre have in common is the need for an audience. This is more than a truism: in the theatre the audience completes the steps of creation." For all the arts, a public is imperative, but for some this public may be thought of as individuals—the reader of a novel or poem, the viewer of a painting or a piece of sculpture—each of whom may experience the work in isolation. But a theatre audience (as well as the audience for music and dance) is assembled as a group at a given time and place to experience a performance.

The audience affects the theatre in many ways, perhaps most clearly through the immediate feedback it provides the performers. Continuous interaction occurs not only between stage and auditorium, but also among spectators involved in a communal experience. For example, if one segment of the audience begins to laugh at what the director intended to be serious, the rest of the audience may come to respond in the same way; in turn, such unexpected response will probably disrupt the actors' concentration and alter their performance. Conversely, the shared enthusiastic laughter of an audience during scenes intended to be comic may lift the actors to greater effectiveness. This live three-way interaction is a distinctive characteristic of theatre and a major cause of variations in performances from night to night.

Audiences also affect the theatre through their expectations and motives for attending. Some members of the audience come to the theatre wanting only to be entertained, to be diverted from personal cares and the problems of their world. This group is likely to consider it the job of the playwright and director to make everything clear; it may see no need to make an effort to understand unfamiliar ideas or conventions. Such spectators may resent or avoid any production that questions conventional moral, political, or social values. Other members of the audience may prefer productions that challenge accepted values, raise provocative issues, advocate action about political or social issues, or use innovative theatrical means. Ultimately, various segments of the public make their preferences felt through attendance or nonattendance. They support what appeals to them and fail to support what they do not like or do not understand. Now that the cost of tickets to many Broadway productions exceeds fifty dollars, audiences understandably hesitate to attend the theatre unless they feel confident that a performance will suit their tastes. In turn, Broadway producers, who need to recover the large sums required to mount a play on Broadway, often avoid controversial subject matter or unfamiliar

Audience and performers at a New York Shakespeare Festival performance in the Delacorte Theatre in New York's Central Park. (Photo by George E. Joseph.)

staging conventions so as to attract as many theatregoers as possible. Off-Broadway and regional theatres, with lower costs and ticket prices, can afford to take greater chances and may seek a more restricted audience than that wooed by Broadway. Audience taste thus significantly influences what is performed, how it is performed, and where it is performed.

These three elements—script, performance, and audience—although they may be treated separately in discussion, interact and modify each other in practice. Playwrights may have specific intentions when they write scripts, but they can seldom control how directors and others involved in production will interpret their scripts. Therefore, different productions of the same playscript can vary drastically. Nor can directors dictate what audiences will get from their productions, and individual members of a single audience may have widely different reactions to the performance they see.

Because what is performed, how it is performed, and audience taste and perception are so diverse, not all theatre will appeal to all segments of the public. Responses to theatre are inescapably varied.

Theatre as a Form of Art

Theatre should entertain. No one seriously questions that. But not everyone finds the same things entertaining. When a performance begins to violate our sense of propriety by presenting things we believe should not be seen on the stage, we may be too offended to be entertained. But theatre is a form of art, and art is not always comfortable or comforting. It often insists on its right to look at the world in unpopular ways and to challenge our ways of looking at ourselves and the standards of the culture that has shaped the way we view the world.

What is art? Probably no term has been discussed so frequently or defined so ambiguously. Until the eighteenth century, *art* always meant the systematic application of known principles to achieve some predetermined result. The word is still used in this sense when we speak of the art of medicine, politics, or persuasion. During the eighteenth century, critics began to divide the arts into two groups, "useful" and "fine." Into the latter category were placed literature (including drama), painting, sculpture, architecture, music, and dance. (In the twentieth century, this list has been extended to include other forms, such as cinema and photography.) The reasoning was that, whereas the useful arts may be taught and mastered, the fine arts, as products of genius, cannot be reduced to rules or principles that, even if learned, would enable just anyone to create significant works of art. As a result, since about 1800 art has often been depicted as too complex to be fully understandable. Many critics have implied that only those with superior sensitivity can fully appreciate art and that the average person often mistakes an inferior product (usually some type of popular entertainment) for authentic artistic expression. Therefore, those who view the theatre as an art form are often contemptuous of those who think of it as "show business." Similarly, in the visual arts, a distinction is usually made between works considered worthy of the museum or gallery and those created for advertisements or as illustrations; and in music, a clear line is usually drawn between compositions considered appropriate to a symphony orchestra and those played by a rock band.

Many people are uneasy at the very mention of "art." Uncertain of what art is or how they should respond to it, they feel inadequate or resentful. This is probably one of the principal reasons why many people do not visit museums or attend concerts or theatrical performances and why they may discount altogether the importance of these types of art. Their reluctance might be overcome if they could be convinced that there are no right or wrong responses to art: One responds as one does. Through multiple experiences we begin to perceive distinctions and patterns that permit us to develop our own standards. But we can never begin this process if we are unwilling to open ourselves to the unfamiliar.

We are faced less with distinctions between art and nonart than with two attitudes about what is worthwhile. All art is "made" (that is, artworks are not produced by nature the way human beings, animals, and plants are). They come into being through the application of certain processes, which are basically the same for all works in the same category. For example, in painting, all works, whether a sunset depicted on black velvet or a nonfigural composition on canvas, utilize the same basic elements: line, mass, color, light, and shadow, all of which are used to create spatial relationships. Unfortunately, in the twentieth century the word *art* has come to be used as a value judgment. Consequently, though both works were created using the same process, artistic status would probably be denied the velvet painting but accorded the nonfigural composition.

Perhaps this will become clearer if we relate the issue to two broad categories used by cultural historians: *popular culture* and *elitist culture*. As the terms imply, popular culture is usually thought to reflect the tastes of a broad, general public,

Musicals have been among the most popular of entertainments in recent times. One of the most successful of these has been *Phantom of the Opera* by Andrew Lloyd Webber, Charles Hart, and Richard Stilgoe. Here the Phantom is rowing the heroine, Christine Daaé, across an underground lake lit by candles. Directed by Harold Prince; sets and costumes by Marie Bjornson; lighting by Andrew Bridge. (Photo by Bob Marshak.)

whereas elitist culture reflects the tastes of a smaller group that applies what it considers to be more demanding standards, often ones with which the general public is unfamiliar. Proponents of each category may speak contemptuously of the other using such terms as "low brow" for those who favor popular culture and "high brow" for those who take the elitist view. Although the boundaries are fluid, popular culture today would probably encompass such forms of expression as rock music, television sitcoms, advertising art, and musical comedy; elitist forms would include those kinds of music usually heard in concert halls, the visual art shown in galleries and museums, and many of the theatrical productions seen in not-for-profit or regional theatres. Nevertheless, no clear-cut distinctions exist between low and high art; they may and often do overlap or intermingle, and what was at one time looked upon as mere popular diversion (such as the plays of Shakespeare or the films of Charlie Chaplin) may later come to be considered significant art. Today the distinctions between high and low art have eroded as elements of each have increasingly been intermingled.

The type of theatre associated with popular culture seeks primarily to provide entertainment for a general audience by telling a story in a way that engages and builds interest. It employs easily recognizable character types, situations, and dramatic conventions, manipulating them with sufficient inventiveness to be entertaining but usually without raising disturbing questions that challenge the audience's values and assumptions. Perhaps the most obvious examples of this kind of entertainment are the prime-time, network-television series which, though they often show characters violating societal values, do so within a framework that ultimately reaffirms those values. These series are certifiably popular because the networks retain only those programs that attract audiences in sufficiently large numbers to please the advertisers who sponsor them. Anything so controversial as to alienate viewers is avoided. Such performances entertain, reaffirm values, divert audiences from their cares, and offer a change from the routine of existence. The majority of people feel most at ease with this type of art.

Popular entertainment is sometimes grouped with games, sports, and other recreational pastimes. Dramatic performances share many characteristics with sports and games because all these forms pit one side against another, build suspense, and reach an outcome. Games and theatre also share a dependence on *conventions*—that is, agreed-upon and understood rules, practices, and procedures. In football, the size and layout of the playing field, the number of downs and players, the uniforms, the system of scoring, and the length of the game are conventions that are understood both by players and spectators.

The theatre, too, depends on conventions, although more flexible ones: the stage as a place where fictional events occur; the use of scenery to suggest locales; the use in some periods of masks, or of males to play female roles; the singing (rather than speaking) of lines in opera. If we introduce new (or alter old) conventions, we are likely to confuse spectators, at least at first, although the changes may be accepted once understood. When Samuel Beckett's *Waiting for Godot* was first performed in the 1950s, many spectators were unable to relate to a play in which there was no discernible story line beyond two tramps waiting for someone who never arrived. The response of many to this innovative play was summed up in one of the play's speeches: "Nobody comes, nobody goes. It's terrible." But the conventions of this play, now considered one of the most important of the twentieth century, have become so familiar as to be commonplace.

Despite the similarities between games and theatre, we usually do not confuse them, not only because of differences in conventions but also because in most scripted drama the outcome is predetermined before the performance begins. For example, Hamlet always avenges the death of his father and dies himself because Shakespeare's text dictates these actions. In addition, the attitudes of audiences to the characters and their struggles are determined by information revealed during the performance, whereas in games, loyalties that existed before the action begins usually determine which side spectators will root for.

While much of the theatre's appeal lies in its ability to entertain, if it does not offer additional challenges, it may be (and often is) dismissed as an easily forgotten, momentary diversion—especially by those who consider the functions of art to include raising disturbing questions, challenging accepted values and assumptions, and searching for new types of theatrical expression, even though these often are the very elements that alienate the general public. Elitists have so fully coopted the term *art* that the general public seldom applies it to the works it admires. Nevertheless, *art* (in the broad sense of something that is made and the process by which it is made) encompasses the whole range of theatre.

If no definition of art is universally accepted, some of its distinguishing characteristics can be explored by comparing it with other approaches to experience. First and most broadly, art is one way whereby human beings seek to understand their world. In this respect, it can be compared with history, philosophy, or science, each of which strives to discover and record patterns in human experience. All of these approaches recognize that human experience is composed of innumerable happenings that have occurred to an infinite number of people through countless generations, and that each person's life is made up of a series of momentary occurrences, many seemingly determined wholly by chance. One question these disciplines seek to answer is: What unifying patterns can be perceived behind the apparent randomness? The questions raised and the methods used to discover possible truths differ in each field, but they are always directed toward finding those relationships that reveal some pattern. As one approach, art shapes perceptions about human experience into forms (or patterned relationships) that help to order our views about humanity and the world in which we live. Many students of contemporary American culture have argued that our notions about love and marriage, for example, are determined much more by what we see on television (both in dramatic programs and advertising) than by our real-life experiences with our own family and acquaintances. One may argue that the notions absorbed from television are inaccurate or harmful, but they suggest nevertheless the power of art to shape perceptions.

The methods used in various approaches to human experience differ significantly. Historians, philosophers, and scientists isolate a limited problem, do their research or experiments, and then set down their conclusions in logical, expository prose; they direct their appeal primarily to the intellect. Artists, on the other hand, work primarily from their own perceptions and seek to involve the audience's emotions, imagination, and intellect directly. A play consequently shows events as though occurring at that moment before our eyes; we absorb them in the way we absorb life itself—through their direct operation on our senses. Art differs from life by stripping away irrelevant details and by organizing and telescoping events so that they compose a connected pattern. Thus a play illuminates and comments (though sometimes indirectly) on human experience even as it creates it. Nevertheless, a play often is not perceived to be a way of knowing and understanding because we are aware that it is fiction.

How, then, can imagined experience be a way of knowing and understanding? Shakespeare offers one answer in *As You Like It* (II, 7): "All the world's a stage, /And all the men and women merely players." This speech states not only that we may think of the world as a stage upon which each person plays a role but also, conversely, that the stage is a symbol of the world where it is possible to see reflected fundamental patterns of human behavior. Such representations, however, need not be realistic; they may represent experience in alternative ways. (For some examples, see the illustrations on pages 4 and 14.) The stage can also serve as a magnifying glass through which we examine some aspect of human experience. What we see onstage, even though not factually real, are embodiments of types of

Some theatre pieces appeal to limited audiences because of unfamiliar staging conventions or nonlinear story lines as in *Nosferatu,* created and staged by the Asian-American director, author, and performance artist Ping Chong. Notice the Playboy Bunny at the head of the chorus line and Uncle Sam at its end. (Photo © Carol Rosegg.)

human beings, situations, motivations, and actions. Thus, though fictional, plays may provide insights about human behavior that are as "truthful" as those obtained from a statistical study of actual human beings. What they show us also reflects basic assumptions of the society from which the play has come. For example, the range of activities and values permitted female characters in the drama of any period reflects (by supporting or challenging) that period's cultural assumptions about women.

Our responses to a play differ from those to an actual event. Just as we do not mistake a statue for a real person, we do not mistake stage action for reality. We usually view a play with what Samuel Taylor Coleridge called a "willing suspension of disbelief"—while we know the events of a play are not real, we agree for the moment not to disbelieve them. We are nevertheless not moved to immediate action by what we see on the stage as we might be by real-life events. We watch one man seemingly kill another, but make no attempt to rescue the victim or to call the police. We are aware that we are watching actors impersonate characters, but we acquiesce in granting them temporary reality. This state, in which we are sufficiently detached to view an artistic event semiobjectively, is sometimes called *esthetic distance.*

At the same time, the distance must not be so great as to induce indifference. While a degree of detachment is necessary, involvement is of equal importance. This feeling of involvement is sometimes called *empathy*. Art lifts us above the everyday fray and gives us something like a "god's-eye" view of experience.

Art, then, is one method of discovering and presenting patterns that provide insights and perceptions or of raising questions about ourselves and our world. Thus, art may be viewed as one form of knowledge or way of knowing. In addition, it is an imaginative reshaping of experience that operates directly on our senses in a way that involves us both esthetically and empathically, allowing us to be simultaneously at a distance from and involved in the experience so that we participate in it emotionally even as we gain insights from it. Art lays claim to being serious (in the sense of having something important to communicate), but because its methods are indirect (it presents experience but does not attempt to explain all of its ramifications), it is often ambiguous and almost always open to alternative interpretations.

Special Qualities of Theatre

Within the fine arts, theatre holds a special place as the art that comes closest to life as it is lived day by day. Shakespeare has Hamlet say (III, 2), "the purpose of playing . . . is to hold . . . the mirror up to nature; to show virtue her own feature, scorn her own image, and the very age and body of the time his form and pressure." Not only is human experience its subject, but theatre also uses live human beings (actors) as its primary means of communicating with an audience. Often the speech of the performers approximates that heard in real life, and the actors may wear costumes that might be seen on the street; they may perform in settings that recall actual places. Not all theatre attempts to be realistic, and at times it may approximate other arts (such as dance, music, or visual arts), but it remains the art (along with film and television) most capable of re-creating everyday human experience.

Such *lifelikeness* is one of the reasons theatre is often insufficiently valued: A play, a setting, and the acting may so resemble what is familiar to spectators that they fail to recognize how difficult it is to produce this lifelikeness skillfully. To a certain degree all people are actors; they vary the roles they play (almost moment by moment) according to the people they encounter and their relationship to them (parent, priest, friend, lover, enemy, and so on). In doing so, they utilize the same tools as the actor does: voice, speech, movement, gesture, psychological motivation. Consequently, many people do not fully recognize or appreciate the problems that actors face.

The theatre further resembles life in being *ephemeral*. As in life, each episode is experienced and then immediately becomes part of the past. When the performance ends, its essence can never be fully recaptured because—unlike a film, novel, painting, or statue, each of which remains relatively unchanged—when a theatrical production ends, it lives only in the script, program, pictures, reviews, and memories of those who were present.

Theatre resembles life also in being the most *objective* of the arts because characteristically it presents both outer and inner experience through speech and action.

As in life, we come to know characters both externally and internally through listening and watching. What we learn about their minds, personalities, and motivations comes from what they say and do and from what others tell us about them. But these are also conditions that make it necessary that each spectator interpret what is seen and heard—and, as in real life, interpretations may differ markedly. Thus, though theatre is objective in its presentation, it demands subjective response.

The theatre can be said to resemble life because of the *complexity of its means*, for like a scene from life itself it is made up of intermingled sound, movement, place, dress, lighting, and so on. Theatre draws on all the other arts: literature in its script; painting, architecture, and sculpture (and sometimes dance) in its spectacle; and speech and music in its audible aspects.

Furthermore, theatre is psychologically the most *immediate* of the arts. Several contemporary critics have argued that the essence of the theatre (what distinguishes it from other dramatic media such as television and film) lies in the simultaneous presence of live actors and spectators in the same room. On the surface, theatre may seem to have several drawbacks compared with other dramatic media. For example, more people often see a filmed or televised show on a single evening than attend the live theatre during an entire year. In fact, the theatre may be likened to a hand-crafted product in an age of mass production, for it must be re-created at each performance and for a relatively small group of spectators. Conversely, thousands of copies of a film may be printed and shown throughout the world simultaneously and year after year, and a televised program may be videotaped and repeated at will. These media may make performers world famous almost overnight, whereas the actor who works only in the theatre may build up an international reputation only over a considerable period of time, if ever.

Nevertheless, the theatre has important attributes that television and film cannot duplicate. The most significant of these are the three-dimensionality of the

Thornton Wilder on the Nature of Theatre

Thornton Wilder, author of *Our Town*, one of the best known and most popular of all American plays, argued that four things distinguish theatre from the other arts:

1. The theatre is an art which reposes upon the work of many collaborators;
2. It is addressed to the group-mind;
3. It is based upon a pretense and its very nature calls out a multiplication of pretenses;
4. Its action takes place in a perpetual present time.

—*"Some Thoughts on Playwriting," in* The Intent of the Artist, *ed. Augusto Centeno*

Might the same be said of television drama and film? What distinguishes dramatic presentations in theatre from those in other media?

theatrical experience and the interactive relationship between performers and spectators. In film and television, the camera is used to select what the audience can see and to ensure that it will see nothing more; the camera can frame the picture to restrict our view to a facial expression, the twitch of a hand, or a small object. In the theatre, the director uses various means to focus the audience's attention on a specific character or object, but—because the full acting area remains visible and close-ups are impossible—the audience may choose to watch something else. Perhaps most important, during a live performance, there is continuous interaction between performer and spectator; the pacing of a scene, for example, affects how the audience responds, and in turn the audience response may stimulate the actors to alter the pace. Because of such interaction, each performance differs in many details. The audience thus plays a far more active role in the theatre than it does in film or television. (Although television and film are now experimenting with interactive devices, the choices a viewer can make are merely already filmed, alternative story lines.) Ultimately, there is an important difference in the psychological responses aroused in the spectator by electronic media and by theatre, because the former present *pictures* of events whereas the latter performs the actual events in the same space as that occupied by the audience. This difference results in one unique characteristic of the theatre: the simultaneous presence of live actors and audience. Film also is much more literal than theatre because it seeks to show every detail of setting and action, whereas theatre requires the audience to imagine what it cannot show. Some critics have charged that film dulls whereas theatre stimulates the imagination.

These special qualities—lifelikeness, ephemerality, objectivity, complexity, and immediacy—define both the weaknesses and strengths of the theatre.

Art and Value

Art is valuable for its capacity to improve the quality of life—by bringing us pleasure, by sharpening our perceptions, by increasing our sensitivity to others and our surroundings, by reminding us that moral and societal concerns should take precedence over materialistic goals. Of all the arts, theatre has perhaps the greatest potential as a humanizing force, for much of it asks us to enter imaginatively into the lives of others so we may understand their aspirations and motivations. Through role-playing (either in daily life or in the theatre), we come to understand who and what we are and see ourselves in relation to others. Perhaps most important, in a world given increasingly to violence and tensions among ethnic and other diverse groups, the value of being able to understand and feel for others as human beings cannot be overestimated, because violence depends on dehumanizing others so that we no longer think of their hopes, aims, and sufferings but treat them as objects to be manipulated or on whom to vent our frustrations. To experience (emotionally, imaginatively, and intellectually) what it means to be human in the broadest sense ought to be one of the primary goals of both education and life; few approaches have greater potential than theatre for reaching this goal because humanity is its subject and human beings its primary medium.

Many plays (such as Greek tragedies) tend to attract primarily elitist audiences. Sophocles' *Oedipus the King,* usually considered one of the world's greatest dramas, is seen here in a production at the State Theater, Darmstadt, Germany. (Courtesy German Information Center.)

Theatre is also valued as a form of cultural expression. Every culture has some types of theatrical expression, the nature of which and the degree to which it is accepted tell us much about the society in which it exists. Greek tragedies and comedies, and the circumstances under which they were presented, tell us much about a culture that considered theatre its highest form of expression. Ancient Rome, whose theatrical activities were far more extensive and varied than those of Greece, favored entertainments such as mimes, chariot races, gladiatorial contests, and animal baiting—strong indicators that Rome valued popular-culture forms more highly than did Greece. We can gain insight into any culture by examining the range, prestige, and relative popularity of its entertainment forms. We can also measure the theatre's value to a culture by studying the relative emphasis it places on the theatre's capacity to provide diversion, recreation, or artistic expression.

Most people probably give little thought to the arts as an integral part of their lives. But try to conceive of life without any music, dance, drama (whether in theatre, television, or film), or visual art of any kind. Without these, the quality of our lives would be greatly diminished. Still, many people think of the arts as expendable "frills" that can be eliminated when financial stress occurs. Many also devalue the arts because they do not yield concrete benefits of the type derived from medicine or engineering. For these reasons, most artists have a difficult time making a living, although a few (including performers) win enormous fame and wealth. Parents typically try to discourage their children, especially as they approach adulthood, from viewing the arts as appropriate career choices. Because of such attitudes, many

Americans by the time they become adults have suppressed whatever artistic inclinations they may have had. They are therefore cut off from, or are only partly utilizing, one of the primary ways of knowing the world and understanding themselves.

Much of this is because many educators and the general public lack an understanding of the nature of intelligence. Until recently human intelligence was treated as a very narrow group of abilities measurable by I.Q. tests. The two clusters of abilities that education has sought to cultivate are the linguistic-verbal and the logical-mathematical, and achievement or ability in these two areas is the only one addressed by the most commonly used standardized tests. In fact, the effectiveness of the educational system is often judged by how well students perform on standardized tests. More recently, psychologists have posited that there are many types of intelligence. Howard Gardner, a professor at Harvard University, argues that there are seven types of intelligence. To (1) linguistic-verbal and (2) logical-mathematical,

The Role of Drama and Theatre

Ideas about the role of drama and theatre in our lives differ widely. John Millington Synge, one of the leading Irish dramatists during the turn of the century, argued in the preface to his play, *The Tinker's Wedding,* that drama is at its best, not when it is dealing with social problems that will soon be forgotten, but when it feeds the imagination:

> The drama is made serious . . . not by the degree in which it is taken up with problems that are serious in themselves, but by the degree in which it gives the nourishment . . . on which our imaginations live. We should not go to the theatre as we go to a [pharmacist's] . . . , but as we go to dinner, where the food we need is taken with pleasure and excitement. . . . [Unfortunately] these days the playhouse is too often stocked with the drugs of many seedy problems. The drama, like the symphony, does not teach or prove anything. Analysts with their problems . . . are soon . . . old-fashioned but the best plays . . . can no more go out of fashion than the blackberries on the hedges.

Peter Brook, one of the world's great directors (writing in the September 1992 issue of *American Theatre*), sees theatre as serving a quite different role:

> . . . the basic function of theatre is to be anti-government, anti-establishment and anti-social. What we all recognize as feeble theatre is the theatre that enters into the public lie of pretending that everything's okay. . . . Social authority wishes for a nice, decent, convenient image to be given to the world. . . . The theatre [can] do something that no politician can do—make a radical transformation so that for a moment the world is seen complete, with all its difficulties, all its riches and all its potentialities.

he adds: (3) musical—sensitivity to melody, rhythm, pitch, and tone; (4) bodily-kinesthetic—the ability to use the body and handle objects; (5) spatial—the ability to envision and manipulate spatial relationships; (6) interpersonal—the ability to understand others and human relationships; and (7) intrapersonal—the ability to use one's own emotions as a key to understanding oneself and others. If Gardner is correct, much education has failed to cultivate five major aspects of intelligence. Of these, most are related to one or more of the arts, especially music, dance, visual arts, and theatre. If education and society are to stimulate and develop the full range of human intelligence, the potential of the arts in this process and the value of the arts in society need to be more fully acknowledged and encouraged.

One purpose of this book is to affirm the value of theatre. The chapters that follow seek to acknowledge and encourage understanding and appreciation of the theatre by providing an overview of its various aspects: how plays are structured; varieties of theatre experience, both past and present; how the theatre functions today; and how each theatre artist makes use of available materials and techniques. Taken together, these discussions should provide a foundation for intelligent and sensitive reactions to the theatre and its role in its culture.

Chapter 2

Performance, Audience, and Critic

Audience at a performance in the Adams Outdoor Theatre at the Utah Shakespearean Festival. (Courtesy of the Utah Shakespearean Festival.)

> The audience is the most revered member of the theatre. Without an audience there is no theatre. Every technique learned by the actor, every curtain and flat on the stage, every careful analysis by the director, every coordinated scene, is for the enjoyment of the audience. . . . They make the performance meaningful.
>
> —Viola Spolin, *Improvisation for the Theatre*

All types of theatrical performance require an audience, for it is in the mind and imagination of the spectator that the final step in the creative process occurs. No matter what the playwright or performers had in mind, audience members observing the theatrical event as it unfolds arrive at their own interpretations of what was intended. There is no guarantee that a spectator's interpretation will accord with the playwright's or director's or that one spectator's interpretation will be the same as that of other spectators. Nevertheless, shaping the theatrical medium to arouse the desired audience response is the primary challenge that playwright, director, and performers seek to meet.

Although not all theatrical performances are based on scripts, this book is concerned primarily with those that translate a play from the medium of words on a page into the concrete language of the stage—acting, costumes, scenery, lighting, sound, and so on. When such a translation is effective, it allows spectators to experience directly and immediately the developing action, the relationships among the characters, the rhythms, the spectacle, and the overall implications of the production as a whole. Thus spectators absorb the play as they would events from real life—through watching and listening—rather than, as in reading, seeking inwardly both to see and to hear everything.

During the theatrical performance, spectators are carried along at the pace that the performers set. The spectator who fails to hear a line or to see a piece of business cannot go back and recover them; there are no instant replays or fast-forwards. Readers of plays may proceed at their own pace, turn back, look ahead, or reread the entire play. The reader may decide that there are several possible interpretations of a line or scene and may leave all these possibilities open, whereas the spectator in the theatre is offered only the one chosen by the director. What the spectator sees is one interpretation, but never the only possible interpretation, of a script. Productions of the same play by other directors may offer drastically different interpretations. Nevertheless, an effective performance can be far more satisfying than a reading because it makes what had been mere words on a page immediate and present in the living flesh and voices of the actors.

Watching a Performance

Attending a play differs in several ways from going to a film. A live performance has more of a sense of special occasion. Except in large cities, live performances are not always readily available. One must usually buy tickets in advance and go to the theatre at a specified time; usually there is only one performance a day, although some theatres offer two afternoon matinees each week. Because tickets for a live performance usually specify the seat in which one is to sit, much more attention is given to such matters as ushering spectators to their seats than at movie theatres. At live performances, spectators are usually provided with programs listing the author, director, designers, cast of actors, and the production staff—much like the on-screen credits shown at the ends of movies. Programs often contain statements or articles about the play or information about the persons involved in the production. Because today the stage is seldom hidden by a curtain, the spectator can usually examine the stage and scenery and gain some idea of the production approach before the performance begins. Music is frequently used to get the audience into the appropriate mood. Most live performances have one or more intermissions, during which audience members may leave their seats, mingle, and discuss what they have seen or what is to come.

There are no rules about how to experience a theatrical performance. Willingness to give one's full attention to what is happening onstage moment by moment

Preparing the Audience

Theatres use various devices to prepare audiences for experiencing performances in an informed and perceptive manner. Some of the most common are advance press releases, articles in newsletters sent to subscribers, lobby displays, and programs (sometimes very elaborate) containing articles and documents that place the production the audience is about to see within an interpretive context.

Many theatres are also concerned with developing new audiences, especially among young people still in school. The theatres usually offer teachers some training and supply them with study guides designed to help them talk to students about the play both before and after they attend a performance. Among the most active of such groups is Theatre for New Audiences, founded in 1979 by Jeffrey Horowitz and based at St. Clement's Church in New York City. It produces two plays each year intended for elementary, middle, and high school students, as well as for adult audiences. Among the plays done in recent years are *The Tempest, As You Like It, Romeo and Juliet, Henry V,* and *Titus Andronicus*, all by Shakespeare. Between 1988 and 1994, some forty-five thousand students were involved in this program. In addition to preparing them to see performances, "teaching artists" employed by Theatre for New Audiences conduct follow-ups out of which students do their own productions, sometimes using scenes from the plays they have seen, sometimes improvising on themes suggested by the plays, and sometimes writing their own plays. The best of the original plays are chosen for presentation at St. Clement's at the end of the school year. The purpose of the total program is to build new and diverse audiences (drawn from a variety of ethnic and economic backgrounds) by challenging the common notion that theatre is inaccessible and that it "exists only for rich white people over 50."

Caliban in Shakespeare's *The Tempest* as produced at the Theatre for New Audiences in New York. The mask, within which Caliban is imprisoned here and because of which he is considered to be a monster, is eventually broken, freeing the man within. Directed and designed by Julie Taymor. (Photo by Richard Feldman.)

is the prime requisite. As a performance unfolds, many questions that a reader can answer only in the imagination are given immediate form, at least in this production of the play: What is the appearance of the stage setting? How are the characters dressed? How do the characters move and relate to each other? Unlike a film, in which the settings are usually realistic (often actual places), a live performance may use little scenery. The spectator may need to imagine much that is merely suggested by a few set pieces, projected images, lighting, or dialogue; and the same basic setting may be used to represent quite different locales. Costumes may be based on the dress of some historical period, or actors may wear ordinary street attire even though the characters are mythical, biblical, or historical personages. The audience may be asked to accept visual styles that alter ordinary modes of perception. These and other conventions may make great demands on the spectator's imagination.

In addition to using imagination, spectators need to concentrate. Unless they let their eyes and ears be carried along by the production, spectators may miss what is significant. More collaboration between director and spectator is required in the theatre than in film because in the theatre, although directors seek to direct audience attention to what is significant at any given moment, they cannot force attention as film directors can through such filmic devices as close-ups and directional shots that deny the audience the possibility of seeing anything other than what the director wishes. In the theatre, the entire stage space is visible, and consequently the spectator may choose what to look at regardless of what the director wishes. Audience response also may be affected by the size and configuration of the auditorium and the stage. A large auditorium may make seeing and hearing difficult, whereas a small auditorium may make it possible to see and hear every detail. How the seating area is related to the acting area can also affect audience response. (The typical arrangements—arena, thrust, proscenium, and flexible stages—are explained at length in Chapter 10.)

The Audience and Critical Perspective

Most of us go to the theatre hoping to be fully caught up in the performance. When this happens, we are too involved to pass judgment on what we are seeing, although our involvement itself is an acknowledgement of the production's power. Only after the performance has ended do we begin to examine our response to it. At an ineffective performance, however, we are likely to pass judgment even as we watch, largely because we are not able to become absorbed in it. Even if we have liked a production, we may have trouble formulating our responses to it when it is over. Most of us restrict ourselves to such generalized responses as "I really enjoyed it" or "I thought the actors did a good job with a weak play." If we are to be more articulate, we must not only examine our overall response but also look more analytically at the elements that went into the production (the script, the directing, acting, scenery, costumes, lighting) and develop criteria for judging the individual elements as well as the overall achievement. This book, taken as a whole, seeks to assist in this process.

Although every member of the audience is in some sense a critic, this title is usually reserved for those who formulate their judgments for publication. Such critics should have had considerable theatregoing experience (an inexperienced theatre critic is comparable to a sports columnist who has never seen a baseball game); they need to understand what goes into a production (the potentials and limitations of the various theatre arts) so they can assess the contributions of each element of a production. Critics need to be aware of the audience for whom they are writing so they can express themselves in terms meaningful to it.

Usually, the critic has a particular type of reader in mind. The production reviews published in daily newspapers are addressed to a general public that may have no extensive knowledge of theatre, whereas the critical articles written for literary quarterlies or scholarly journals are addressed to a more restricted, often an academic, audience. A single piece of criticism seldom serves the needs of all readers.

Critics who write reviews for newspapers often think of themselves as consumer guides, alerting readers to which productions are worth their time and money and which are not. It is often said that an unfavorable review in *The New York Times* is sufficient to close a Broadway production unless the play already has substantial advance sales. In recent years, many television stations have begun reviewing plays (usually in short spots of two to five minutes). Both newspaper and television reviews have had substantial impact on ticket sales.

This chapter includes two complete reviews and parts of another review of Tennessee Williams' *Cat on a Hot Tin Roof.* Reading this play will contribute greatly to your understanding of the reviews, but if you cannot read it you will find a discussion of it on pages 207–211. Two of the reviews are of the original Broadway production. The first is by Walter F. Kerr, who for many years was the highly respected principal critic for *The New York Herald Tribune* and later for *The New York Times.* The second review was written by Eric Bentley, since the 1940s one of America's major drama critics and a professor who has taught at several leading universities. Kerr's review was written immediately after seeing the production; Bentley's was written some time later and was eventually published in a volume of theatrical criticism intended for a relatively sophisticated audience. The third review, by Frank Rich of *The New York Times*, is of the 1990 revival of the play on Broadway. (Reviews of each major production in New York are gathered and published in *New*

Review by Walter F. Kerr (dated March 25, 1955) written for The New York Herald Tribune *immediately after the opening night of the original production of* Cat on a Hot Tin Roof.

"Cat on a Hot Tin Roof" is a beautifully written, perfectly directed, stunningly acted play of evasion: evasion on the part of the principal character, evasion perhaps on the part of its playwright.

In a dimly-lit, significantly shuttered bed-sitting room on a Mississippi plantation, a young and handsome athlete hobbles about on crutches, heads for his private bar with purposeful regularity, and refuses to sleep with his wife.

He has had, in his life, one profound friendship: with a fellow football player. The friend is now dead—dead of drink—and this bitter and sodden Tennessee Williams hero is sure of just one thing. The descent of his friend, and his own as well, began with a half-uttered suspicion on the part of his wife—a suspicion that the close relation of the two men was unnatural. The wife has felt left out; she has pried her way in, in an inno-

Scene from the original production of Tennessee Williams' *Cat on a Hot Tin Roof* in 1955. The actors are Ben Gazzara, Madeleine Sherwood, and Barbara Bel Geddes. Directed by Elia Kazan. (Photo by Bob Golby. Courtesy Harry Ransom Humanities Research Center, University of Texas at Austin.)

cent but ugly and disastrous fashion; her husband cannot now bear the sight of her.

As Barbara Bel Geddes prattles despairingly on about the other men who do desire her; as the young man's parents nag and scratch at him in greedy hope of an heir; as the pressures of sex, alcohol, and family pride mount, the play at the Morosco stretches this tormented soul taut on the rack and then claws at his open "sores."

Brilliant scenes, scenes of sudden and lashing dramatic power, break open. A horde of birthday-partying children pour into the bedroom just as Ben Gazzara, as the anguished Brick, is attempting to silence his wife forever with the head of his crutch. Barbara Bel Geddes, knowing what she has done to this man but fiercely begging credit for telling the truth, pounds out a first-act scene of devastating honesty. Throughout the play images of searing intensity hold you fast to its elusive narrative: a father sending his helpless son crashing to the floor; a mother hanging on a doctor's lapels

and begging for a lie; a terrifying family gathering in which those who should offer love behave like vultures. There is, indeed, no one moment in the evening when the stinging accuracy of Mr. Williams' ear for human speech, or Mr. Kazan's passion for brutal but truthful statement, is not compellingly in evidence.

There is, however, a tantalizing reluctance—beneath all the fire and all the apparent candor—to let the play blurt out its promised secret. This isn't due to the nerve-wracking, extraordinarily prolonged silence of its central figure, to his merely repeating the questions of other people rather than answering them. It is due to the fact that when we do come to a fiery scene of open confession—between a belligerent father and his defiant son—the truth still dodges around verbal corners, slips somewhere between the veranda shutters, refuses to meet us on firm, clear terms.

We do learn, in a faint echo of "The Children's Hour," that there has been something to the accusation—at least on the part of Brick's friend. We learn that Brick himself, in his horror at the discovery, has done the damage he blames on his wife. But we never quite penetrate Brick's own facade, know or share his precise feelings. And when he does turn once more to his wife, taking her hand across the marriage bed, it is not really out of a new relationship with her; it is out of vague admiration for a sturdy lie she has told, and out of merciful affection for his father. In "Cat on a Hot Tin Roof" you will believe every word that is unspoken; you may still long for some that seem not to be spoken.

This is, I think, a flaw in the work. It should not keep you from seeing it. Mr. Williams is the man of our time who comes closest to hurling the actual blood and bone of life onto the stage; he is also the man whose prose comes closest to being an incisive natural poetry. If the new play has not

the staggering clarity of "A Streetcar Named Desire," it is a probing and disturbing stroke from the same pen.

And the production has no flaw. Apart from Barbara Bel Geddes' lashing and altogether luminous performance as the tenacious wife, and Ben Gazzara's steely cold portrait of a man torn by divided loyalties and anguished self-doubt, there is a Rabelaisian contribution from Burl Ives that is apt to be the talk of the town. Mr. Ives is seen as the massive master of the Delta estate, an oracle who exhales profanities with every puff of his cigar and a father who is not above cutting his son's heart open. The performance is not only robust in scale; it is filled with many a courageous nuance. Mildred Dunnock is startlingly fine in an unfamiliar sort of role: the brash, gravel-voiced, outspoken matron of the house. In supporting roles Madeleine Sherwood and Pat Hingle are particularly effective.

York Theatre Critics' Reviews. This publication provides a ready means for comparing reviews of New York productions.)

Although (because of its length) it cannot be reprinted here in its entirety, another important critical view of *Cat on a Hot Tin Roof* is offered by Eric Bentley. It differs from Kerr's review primarily in seeking to place the play in a larger context and seeing the production as exemplary of a performance style—developed by Elia Kazan (as director) and Jo Mielziner (as designer)—that had become dominant in post-World War II American theatre. He writes:

> Jo Mielziner's setting for *Cat on a Hot Tin Roof* consists of a square and sloping platform with one of its corners, not one of its sides, jutting out toward the audience. . . . On the platform are minimum furnishings for a bed-sitting-room. Around the room steps and space suggest the out-of-doors. The whole stage is swathed in ever-changing light and shade. . . . Such is the world of Elia Kazan, as we know it from his work on plays by more authors than one. . . . an exterior that is also an interior—but, more important, a view of *man's* exterior that is also a view of his interior. . . .

Bentley goes on to say that the performance achieves a kind of grandeur that results "from the interaction between formality in the setting, lighting, and grouping and an opposite quality . . . in the individual performances. . . . the actors live their roles with that vigilant, concentrated, uninterrupted nervous intensity which Mr. Kazan always manages to give."

Despite his praise for the production, Bentley found several shortcomings in the play, among them the failure to resolve the question of Brick's relationship to Skipper, the insistence on a happy resolution, and the naturalistic sordidness of its "dirty" humor (a charge that seems quaint today when obscenity and sexual references have become prevalent and explicit in the theatre).

Review by Frank Rich of the revival of Cat on a Hot Tin Roof, *published in* The New York Times, *March 22, 1990.*

It takes nothing away from Kathleen Turner's radiant Maggie in "Cat on a Hot Tin Roof" to say that Broadway's gripping new production of Tennessee Williams' 1955 play will be most remembered for Charles Durning's Big Daddy. The actor's portrayal of a 65-year-old Mississippi plantation owner in festering extremis is an indelible hybrid of red neck cutup and aristocratic tragedian, of grasping capitalist and loving patriarch. While "Cat" is not the American "King Lear" its author hoped, this character in this performance is a cracker-barrel Lear and Falstaff in one.

Just try to get the image of Mr. Durning—a dying volcano in final, sputtering eruption under a Delta moon—out of your mind. I can't. "Cat" is a curiously constructed work in which the central but sullen character of Brick, the all-American jock turned booze hound, clings to the action's periphery while Act I belongs to his wife, Maggie, Act II to his Big Daddy and the anti-climactic Act III (of which the author left several variants) to no one. Such is Mr. Durning's force in the second act at the O'Neill that he obliterates all that comes after, despite the emergence of Polly Holliday's poignant Big Mama in the final stretch.

Mr. Durning's Act II tour de force begins with low comedy: the portly, silver-haired actor, dressed in a sagging white suit and wielding a vaudeville comedian's stogie, angrily dismisses his despised, nattering wife and his bratty grandchildren, those cap-gun-toting "no-neck monsters" who would attempt to lure him into a saccharine birthday party. From that hilarious display of W.C. Fields dyspepsia, it is quite a leap to the act's conclusion. By then, Mr. Durning is white with fear, clutching the back of a chair for support, for he has just learned what the audience has long known: Big Daddy is being eaten away by cancer that "has gone beyond the knife."

In between comes a father-son confrontation that is not only the crux of Mr. Durning's performance but also the troubling heart of a play that is essential, if not first-rank, Williams. Big Daddy loves Brick (Daniel Hugh Kelly) and would like to favor him when dividing his estate of $10 million and "28,000 acres of the richest land this side of the valley Nile." But there are mysteries to be solved before the writing of the will. Why are Brick and Maggie childless? Why is Brick, once a football hero and later a television sports announcer, now, at 27, intent on throwing away his life as if it were "something disgusting you picked up on the street"? How did Brick break his ankle in the wee hours of the night before?

Mr. Durning will have his answers, even if he has to knock Brick off his crutch to get them. But his Big Daddy, while tough as a billy goat, is not a cartoon tyrant. He wants to talk to his son, not to badger him. He offers Brick understanding and tolerance in exchange for the truth, even if that truth might be Brick's closeted homosexual passion for his best friend and football buddy, Skipper, now dead of drink. All Big Daddy wants is freedom from the lies and hypocrisy of life that have so long disgusted him. Yet Brick, while sharing that disgust, won't surrender his illusions without a fight.

"Mendacity is the system we live in," the son announces. "Liquor is one way out and death's the other." When the truth finally does emerge—and for both men it is more devastating than any sexual revelation—liquor and death do remain the only exits. Life without the crutch of pipe dreams or anesthesia is too much to take. As the lights dim on Act II, Mr. Kelly is isolated in a stupor and Mr. Durning, his jaw distorted by revulsion and rage, is howling like Lear on the heath. Advancing relentlessly into the bowels of his mansion, the old man bellows an epic incantation of "Lying! Dying! Liars!" into the tall shadows of the Southern Gothic night.

Along with the high drama and fine acting—Mr. Kelly's pickled Adonis included—what makes the scene so moving is Williams's raw sensitivity to what he called (in his next play, "Orpheus

Descending") man's eternal sentence to solitary confinement. In "Cat," Maggie probably does love Brick, Big Mama probably does love Big Daddy, and Brick loves Skipper and Big Daddy as surely as they have loved him. Yet the lies separating those who would love are not easily vanquished. In this web of familial, fraternal and marital relationships, Williams finds only psychic ruin, as inexorable as the greed that is devouring the romantic Old South.

In his revival, Howard Davies, the English director last represented in New York by "Les Liaisons Dangereuses," keeps his eye on that bigger picture: Williams's compassion for all his trapped characters and his desire to make his play "not the solution of one man's psychological problems" but a "snare for the truth of human experience." With the exception of Mae (Debra Jo Rupp), Brick's conniving sister-in-law, everyone on stage is human. The playwright doesn't blame people for what existence does to them. He has empathy for the defeated and admiration for those like Maggie who continue to fight for life and cling to the hot tin roof "even after the dream of life is all over."

From her salt-cured accent to her unabashed (and entirely warranted) delight in her own body heat, Miss Turner is an accomplished Maggie, mesmerizing to watch, comfortable on stage and robustly good-humored. Merely to see this actress put on her nylons, a ritual of exquisitely prolonged complexity, is a textbook lesson in what makes a star. Miss Turner is so good as far as she goes that one wishes she'd expose her emotions a shade more—without compromising her admirable avoidance of a campy star turn. Her Maggie is almost too stubbornly a survivor of marital wars; she lacks the vulnerability of a woman "eaten up with longing" for the man who shuns her bed.

Though somewhat more can be made of Brick—and was by Ian Charleson, in Mr. Davies's previous staging of "Cat" in London—Mr. Kelly captures the detachment of defeat, and later the rage, of a man who buried hope in his best friend's grave. When Brick is finally provoked to stand up for the "one great good true thing" in his life, the actor gives an impassioned hint of the noble figure who inspired worship from all who knew him. But it's a major flaw of "Cat" that this character is underwritten. Williams defines the physique of his golden boy—and Mr. Kelly fleshes that out, too—but leaves the soul opaque.

Since Brick doesn't pull his weight in any of the playwright's third acts for "Cat," it hardly matters which one is used. Mr. Davies reverts to the unsentimental original draft, which never made it to the stage in Elia Kazan's initial Broadway production. Miss Holliday's Big Mama, an unstrung Amanda Wingfield brought to her own grief by others' mendacity, is a rending figure within the thunderstorm of the denouement. Along with the supporting cast, the designers' vision of a decaying South—from the fading veranda to the intrusion of the latest American inoculation against intimacy, a 1950's console television—thickens the rancid mood of a household where, in Big Mama's words, "such a black thing has come . . . without invitation."

But even in Act III, even offstage, Mr. Durning continues to dominate, and, in a way, he gets the big scene with the star that the script denies him. As Maggie tenaciously clings to her tin roof, Big Daddy can be heard from somewhere deep within, his terrifying screams of pain rattling that roof, threatening even at death's doorstep to blow the lid off life's cruel, incarcerating house of lies.

To many, *criticism* means adverse response, but the true meaning of the word is "the act of making judgments." The best criticism requires attention both to excellence and shortcomings. Not all critics provide balanced discussions, either for lack of space or because they believe a play or a production is so good or so inadequate that nothing of importance can be said on the other side. Kerr's review is almost entirely favorable; Bentley's, while predominantly favorable to both the play and the production, points out significant problems; Rich's concentrates primarily on the actors' performances, which he praises, and secondarily on the script, about which he is generally favorable but not without reservations.

Although these reviews of *Cat on a Hot Tin Roof* are representative of critical approaches, they do not exhaust the possibilities. Other commentaries are almost wholly descriptive. A writer may explain how Williams' (or some other) play is structured, or may provide information about certain aspects of the production (the visual appearance of the costumes, the use of lighting, the innovative conventions, how the production differs from previous ones of the same play, and so on) without passing judgment on these features. Such descriptive pieces can help an audience appreciate a production or play that it might otherwise find baffling because of unfamiliar conventions or a controversial directorial interpretation.

Some reviewers have a tendency to be flippant or condescending. Famous examples of flippancy are Dorothy Parker's remark that Katharine Hepburn ran the gamut of emotion from A to B (in a Broadway production of *The Lake* in 1933) and John Mason Brown's statement, "Tallulah Bankhead barged down the Nile last night and sank" (in his review of her performance in Shakespeare's *Antony and Cleopatra*). Examples of condescension include John Simon's remarks on Jerzy Grotowski's production of *The Constant Prince* ("I was so dumbfounded by the infantilism and coarseness of the proceedings that sheer amazement kept me from even trying [to take notes]") and George Jean Nathan's about a production of Shakespeare's *Richard III*. ("To the multiplicity of the play's murders, Mr. Coulouris and his company added another: that of the play itself.") Such quips may be amusing, but they can be infuriating and discouraging to theatre workers whose efforts are callously dismissed out of hand. Such reviews contribute significantly to the antipathy that often exists between theatre artists and critics.

The Basic Problems of Criticism

The critic is concerned with three basic problems—understanding, effectiveness, and ultimate worth: What were the playwright, director, and other theatre artists trying to do? How well did they do it? Was it worth doing?

Critics follow any of several paths to understanding. If the script is available, they may study it carefully prior to attending the production. They may find out more about the author's life and other works and about what other critics have said about the dramatist's plays. They may refresh their memory of previous work by the director and production team or of previous productions of the same play. Note in the reviews of *Cat on a Hot Tin Roof* the references to previous work by the playwright, director, and designer. Some reviewers avoid any preparation for viewing a production because they wish to attend it much as any other spectator might, so that they may react without any preconceptions about the play or how it should be performed.

By choice or necessity, many reviewers write about plays that they have not read and that they know only from a single performance. In such circumstances, reviewers

Shakespeare's *Hamlet* is a play so well known and so complex that it is often considered a touchstone for judging actors and directors. Seen here is a scene from the play at the Guthrie Theatre, Minneapolis. Zelijko Ivanek (center) as Hamlet. Directed by Garland Wright; set by Doug Stein; costumes by Ann Hould-Ward; lighting by James Ingalls. (Photo by Joe Giannetti. Courtesy of the Guthrie Theatre.)

are often guilty of damning a play rather than its inadequate production, or a performance rather than its inadequate script, because of the difficulty in sorting out the sources of strengths and weaknesses based on a single viewing or without any prior knowledge of the script.

In dealing with effectiveness—how successful were the playwright, director, and other theatre artists in accomplishing what they set out to do?—the critic may focus on the play's intention or the director's interpretation. Rarely do playwrights state their intentions directly. Intention is indicated by the way conflicts, characters, and ideas are handled, and by the look and sound of the production. Evidence of the director's interpretation usually comes from what the critic sees and hears during the performance, although sometimes the director explains his or her approach in notes printed in the program, in interviews before the opening, or in publicity releases. Many directors try to embody the play's intention as faithfully as possible. But no one can require a director to remain true to a script, and some directors use the script (somewhat like acting, scenery, and lighting) as raw material to be shaped according to the director's vision. Contemporary directors often interpret scripts in ways that are at variance with the author's apparent intentions on the grounds that by doing so one gains a new perspective on the issues dealt with in the play, or that a close examination of the play reveals unconscious motives or biases that need to be brought out, or that certain changes make a play from the past more relevant to today's world. For example, Peter Sellars moved the action of Mozart's *Don Giovanni*, an opera dealing with an amoral, compulsive womanizer in seventeenth-century Spain, to present-day New York, and used drug addiction and street violence to clarify the characters' behavior. (For a look at the final scene of this production, see the photo on page 321.) In evaluating such productions, the critic may assess how the director's interpretation is related to, or differs from, the play's apparent intention. Although the critic may think the director is misguided, this belief is irrelevant in the critic's assessment of whether the director has achieved what he or she set out to do.

Even though a play or production is understandable and effective, a critic may still consider it unsatisfactory when seeking to answer the third basic question: Was it worth doing? Any response to this question assumes some standard against which worth can be measured. Unfortunately, there are no universally accepted standards of worth, and no standard can be proven incontestably better than another. Often we are puzzled by other people's pronouncements because we do not know what criteria have been used in making them. Why do friends detest a play or movie we have greatly admired? If we discuss our conflicting responses, we often find that each of us is looking at the same work from a different perspective. One of us may praise a production's comic inventiveness, while another may find the work's treatment of women (or some other element) so appalling that nothing can compensate for this shortcoming.

Many contexts are used in evaluating the worth of plays or productions. Some critics consider the only meaningful context to be other plays or productions of the same type. Each critic may value a production for a different reason: its emotional power, its relevance to contemporary issues, its insights into human behavior, its innovations, its embodiment of the script, its ability to entertain. At times, critics seem to damn productions for failing to satisfy criteria that the playwright or director never intended to meet. Furthermore, critics do not necessarily adhere to a single context in making their judgments and often shift their ground within a single review.

Examine carefully the reviews of *Cat on a Hot Tin Roof* and note the stated or implied criteria that underlie the various value judgments expressed. For example, Kerr seems to believe that excellence demands that the action seem uncontrived, that the characters be treated with compassion, and that the work arouse powerful emotions, whereas Bentley is more concerned about clarity of intention and unity in execution, and Rich is concerned above all with effective acting. A detailed examination should uncover still other criteria.

Most of us are probably not aware of the preconceptions and prejudices that underlie our own judgments. Therefore, we should define what for us makes a production satisfying or unsatisfying. Many believe that the most satisfying production is one that so fully absorbs their attention that they completely forget themselves. Others have argued that to enter so fully into a production makes it impossible to watch critically or to be aware of the ideology or prejudices implied by the action.

In assessing our own critical stance, here are some questions that may be helpful:

- Am I open to unfamiliar subjects, ideas, or conventions?
- In the theatre, am I uncomfortable with moral stances that differ from my own?

Working-Class and Middle-Class Audiences

John McGrath, director of England's 7:84 Theatre, argues that there are clearly recognizable differences in the way working-class and middle-class audiences respond to theatre. In "The Practice of Political Theatre," he argues:

> A working-class audience likes to know exactly what you are trying to do or say to it. A middle-class audience prefers obliqueness and innuendo— it likes to feel the superiority of exercising its perception, which has been so expensively acquired, thus opening up areas of ambiguity and avoiding any stark choice of attitude. . . . Working-class audiences demand more moment-by-moment effect from their entertainers. . . . They like clear, worked-for results—laughs, respectful silence, rapt attention to a song, tears, thunderous applause. Middle-class audiences have been trained to sit still in the theatre for long periods, not talk, and bear with a slow build-up to great dramatic moments, or slow build-ups to nothing at all.

McGrath clearly favors the working-class (or popular) audience because he thinks its responses are more spontaneous and uncalculated than those of the middle-class (or elitist) audience, whose responses he sees as conditioned and concerned with showing superiority. One could, of course, make quite contrary points by viewing the working-class audience's responses as having been conditioned by television and those of elitist audiences as being more discriminating because of experience with a wider range of performance. Either view is an oversimplification, but together they alert us to the dangers of generalizing about audiences.

- Are there subjects that I think should not be treated on the stage? If so, which?
- What standards do I use in judging a play or performance? Why?

Such questions suggest the need for each of us to understand our own convictions and biases because these influence (usually quite unconsciously) our critical judgments.

Critical responses, whether those of the casual spectator or the professional critic, ultimately involve the three major questions already posed:

- What was attempted?
- How fully was it accomplished?
- Was it worth doing?

In addition, an informed and perceptive reviewer usually deals with elaborations on the following major questions:

- What play was performed? Who is the author? What information about the author or script is important for understanding the production?
- Where and when did the performance take place? Will there be additional performances?

- Who was involved in the production—producer, director, actors, designers? (Not everyone need be named, and comments about those who are may be scattered throughout the review.)
- What were the apparent goals of the script or production?
- How effectively and fully were the goals realized (in the directing, acting, design elements)?
- Should others see it? Why?

As is demonstrated by the reviews of *Cat on a Hot Tin Roof,* a critic may not deal with all of these questions or in this order, and answers to each question may vary in length and complexity.

Qualities Needed by the Critic

Because the theatre is a composite art and because each of us is subject to many influences, it is difficult to become a good theatre critic. A reliable critic usually has had years of theatregoing on which to draw, as well as a firm foundation of study and reading about the theatre, its processes, and its cultural context.

A critic should strive:

- to be sensitive to feelings, images, and ideas
- to become as well acquainted as possible with the theatre of all periods and of all types
- to be willing to explore plays and production processes
- to be tolerant of innovation
- to be aware of his or her own prejudices and values
- to be articulate and clear in expressing judgments and their bases.

Perhaps most important, the critic should avoid becoming dogmatic or unwilling to consider alternative views. The theatre is constantly changing, and critics must be willing to reassess their standards in light of innovations even as they seek to evaluate the changes.

Chapter 3

The Playscript

Scene from the Pulitzer-Prize-winning play, *Fences,* by August Wilson, one of today's foremost African-American playwrights. Produced at the Yale Repertory Theatre. Directed by Lloyd Richards; set by James D. Sandefur; costumes by Candice Donnelly; lighting by Dianne Mizzy. (Photo by William B. Carter.)

The manuscript, the words on the page, was what you started with and what you have left. The production is of great importance, has given the play the life it will know, but it is gone, in the end, and the pages are the only wall against which to throw the future or measure the past.

—Lillian Hellman, *Pentimento*

The playscript is both the typical starting point for a theatrical production and the most common residue of production, because it usually remains intact after its performance ends. Because the same script may serve as a basis for many different productions, it has greater permanence than its theatrical representations and may come to be considered a literary work. Drama is consequently often taught apart from theatre; many people who read plays have never seen a live dramatic performance, and most students get their first glimpse of theatre through reading plays in literature classes. But a script may seem unsatisfactory or puzzling, for it is essentially a blueprint demanding from both reader and performer the imaginative creation of much that is only implied on the printed page. Learning to read, understand, and fill out the script (either in the mind or on the stage) is essential if the power of a play is to be fully realized.

On Reading a Play

There are no rules about how one should read a play. Nevertheless, some observations may be helpful to those for whom play reading is a new experience. First, one must accept that the ability to read imaginatively and perceptively is a basic skill needed by everyone, for without this skill much of human experience is lost, and intellectually we suffer from historical and cultural amnesia.

Because all writers do not express themselves in the same form, all written works cannot be read in the same way. Each form has its own characteristics, and each makes distinctive demands on the reader. We cannot read a play in the same way we read a historical treatise, an essay, a biography, a novel, or a poem. To read a play adequately, we must adjust our minds to the dramatic form. A play is distinctive in part because it is made up primarily of dialogue constructed with great care to convey its intentions and to create the sense of spontaneous oral utterance by characters involved in a developing action. A play is both a highly controlled structure and a simulated spontaneous reflection of human experience.

Drama requires the reader to contribute more than most other forms of fiction do. Not only must readers see and understand what is explicitly said and done, but they must also be aware of all that is implied. The dramatist may use stage directions to clarify setting, situation, or tone, but usually conveys intentions through dialogue. In reading a play, we should assume that what is written is what the writer wished to say. But because the dramatist must convey intentions through a likeness of conversation, we must be sensitive—as in life—to what is left unspoken. The reader must be alert to the nuances of interactions among characters. Although inwardly and imaginatively seeing and hearing a script is not a simple undertaking, we can become adept at it with practice. Perhaps the best way to begin is by looking at how plays are constructed and how structure is related to dramatic effectiveness and meaning.

Dramatic Action

Broadly speaking, a play is (as the ancient Greek philosopher Aristotle wrote in his *Poetics*) a representation of human beings "in action." By "action" he did not mean mere physical movement. Rather, he was concerned not only with *what* characters do but also with *why* they do it. In turn, the actions of the individual characters relate to some question, problem, or theme that forms the central focus, or *dramatic action,* of the play as a whole. A play's dramatic action can often be summed up in a brief statement about the major thrust of the events and the ultimate goal. Thus, we might sum up the dramatic action of Sophocles' *Oedipus the King* as "to find and expel the murderer of Laius in order to cleanse the city." Or we might formulate the dramatic action of *A Doll's House* as "to conceal the forgery from Torvald in order to preserve the status quo." Statements of dramatic action are most helpful when they sum up what is actively done and the purpose for which it is done because such a statement exposes the skeleton (what the great Russian actor-director Constantin Stanislavsky called the "spine") around which the events are built.

Francis Fergusson, a twentieth-century American critic, has argued that a dramatic action builds through three steps: purpose, passion, and perception. By *purpose* he means awareness of some desire or goal; by *passion* he means the strength of desire or suffering that makes characters act to fulfill their goals, along with the emotional turmoil they undergo while doing so; and by *perception* he means the understanding that eventually comes from the struggle. In *A Doll's House* we see Nora seeking desperately to conceal that she has borrowed money without her husband's knowledge, the increasing anguish into which this attempt leads her, and her eventual discovery that her marriage has been a lie based on a misunderstanding of her husband's character.

The range of human motivation and behavior is so great that a single play can depict only a small part of the totality. Because each playwright's view of the human condition differs, each drama is in some respects unique. Still, all plays share certain qualities that allow us to draw some conclusions about the characteristics of effective dramatic action. Aristotle stated that a dramatic action should have a beginning, middle, and end. On the surface, this statement seems obvious, but it summarizes a fundamental principle: A dramatic action should be *complete and self-contained* (that is, everything essential for understanding it should be in or implied in the play). If this principle is not observed, the action will probably seem incomplete or unsatisfying. Effective dramatic action is *deliberately shaped* or organized to reveal its purpose and goal and to evoke from the audience specific responses (pity, fear, laughter, ridicule, and so on). Effective dramatic action, in addition to having purpose, must also have *variety* (in story, characterization, idea, mood, spectacle) to avoid monotony. Effective dramatic action *engages and maintains interest.* The situ-

Aristotle

Probably no one has exerted greater influence on ideas about the nature of drama, dramatic structure, and dramatic form than the Greek philosopher Aristotle (384–322 B.C.). The son of a physician, he was sent to Athens at the age of eighteen to study at the Academy, the school headed by Plato, another of the great Greek philosophers. Aristotle remained for twenty years, becoming a teacher there. Beginning in 343, he was for the next seven years tutor to the future Alexander the Great. When Alexander succeeded to the throne in 336, Aristotle returned to Athens, where he founded his own school, the Lyceum. When Alexander died in 323, a reaction against those who had been associated with the ruler made it prudent for Aristotle to flee Athens. Aristotle died the next year at the age of sixty-two or sixty-three.

Aristotle was a biologist by training, but he studied and wrote in a number of other fields. His study of drama led to *Poetics* (c. 335–323), the oldest surviving treatise on drama. After it was rediscovered in the fifteenth century A.D., it came to be considered authoritative on drama, especially tragedy. Although its influence began to decline in the nineteenth century, it continues to be one of the works most frequently referred to in discussions of the nature and structure of drama. It seems likely that only a part of *Poetics* has survived, for although it divides drama into two basic types—tragedy and comedy—and promises to treat both, it discusses only tragedy at length. While describing tragedy, it outlines several principles of dramatic writing. It recommends the cause-to-effect arrangement of incidents, progressing through complications and resolution, as the most effective means of unifying action. It also considers internal consistency to be the basis of believability. *Poetics* is too complex to summarize briefly, especially because the meaning of almost every line has been heatedly debated. Because it has been so influential, it is a work with which most serious students of drama should be familiar.

ation must be sufficiently compelling to arouse curiosity, the characters interesting enough to awaken sympathy or antipathy, the issues vital enough to provoke concern, or the spectacle and sound novel enough to attract attention. Effective dramatic action is *internally consistent*. Even if the events might be impossible in real life, they should be consistent with the "rules of the game" established in the opening section of the play. For example, when during the opening speech of Eugene Ionesco's *The Bald Soprano* the clock strikes seventeen times and a character announces that it is nine o'clock, we are warned that in this play we should be prepared for things to deviate from normal modes of perception—and they do. It is consistency within the framework of the particular play, not whether the events would have happened this way in real life, that leads us to accept events in drama as believable.

Methods of Organizing Dramatic Action

A play is composed of incidents organized to accomplish a purpose. This organization directs attention to relationships that create a meaningful and unified pattern. In analyzing a play, it is helpful to pinpoint the source of unity; otherwise, the play may seem a collection of unrelated happenings rather than a whole. The most common sources of unity are: cause-to-effect arrangement of events; character; and thought. (To understand the following discussion most fully, the reader should be familiar with Sophocles' *Oedipus the King,* Henrik Ibsen's *A Doll's House* and Samuel Beckett's *Happy Days.* A discussion of *Oedipus* can be found on pages 68–75, of *A Doll's House* on pages 163–167, and of *Happy Days* on pages 216–219.)

The majority of plays from the past are organized through *cause-to-effect* arrangement of events. This is the organizational principle used in *A Doll's House.* Using this method, in the opening scenes the playwright sets up the necessary conditions—the situation, the desires and motivations of the characters—out of which later events develop. The goals of one character come into conflict with those of another, or two conflicting desires within the same character lead to a crisis. Attempts to surmount the obstacles make up the substance of the play, each scene growing logically out of those that precede it. Any organizational pattern other than cause-to-effect is likely to seem loose, often giving the effect of randomness.

Less often, a dramatist uses a *character* as the source of unity. Such a play is held together primarily because all the events focus on one person. Few plays are unified predominantly through character, however, because, to create a sense of

Samuel Beckett's *Happy Days* at Stage West, Springfield, MA. Ellen Laurie as Winnie. Directed by Gregory Boyd. (Photo by Peter Gould. Courtesy of Stage West.)

purpose, more is required than that all the incidents involve one person. They must also either tell a connected story or embody a theme. Beckett's *Happy Days* is unified in part because Winnie creates the action, but ultimately the play's unity comes from its theme. Similarly, *A Doll's House* gains much of its sense of purpose from Nora Helmer, but the play is organized mainly through the structure of its incidents. Plays with primary emphasis on character are usually biographical, as is Robert Sherwood's *Abe Lincoln in Illinois,* which gains its primary interest from incidents in the early life of Abraham Lincoln.

Many twentieth-century dramatists have organized plays around *thought,* with scenes linked through a central theme or set of ideas. Beckett's *Happy Days* shows its central character, buried up to the waist in the first act and up to the chin in the second act, trying cheerfully to fill her days as if her situation were perfectly normal. It is organized somewhat like a musical composition, in which a theme or motif is introduced and then elaborated upon in a series of variations; ultimately, these variations fuse to create a vision of human existence as an attempt to make the best of the senseless circumstances in which we are trapped. Beckett does not tell a story so much as embroider upon a central idea. Like much contemporary drama, Beckett's is nonlinear, composed more of fragments than of causally related incidents.

Although a play usually has one major source of unity, it also uses secondary sources, because every script involves a sequence of incidents, uses characters, and implies a theme or set of ideas. Other sources of unity are a dominant mood, visual style, or distinctive use of language.

The organization of dramatic action may also be approached through the parts of drama—which, according to Aristotle, are plot, character, thought, diction, music, and spectacle.

Plot

Plot is often considered merely the summary of a play's incidents, but it also refers to the organization of all the elements into a meaningful pattern. Thus, plot is the overall structure of a play.

The Beginning

The beginning of a play establishes some or all of these: the place, the occasion, the characters, the mood, the theme, and the internal logic (the rules of the game) to be followed. Viewing a play is like coming upon previously unknown places and persons. Initially, the novelty may excite interest, but as the facts about the place and people are established, interest either wanes or increases. The playwright is faced with a double problem: to give essential information and at the same time make the audience want to stay and see more.

The beginning of a play involves *exposition,* or the setting forth of information— about earlier events, the identity and relationship of the characters, and the present situation. While exposition is a necessary part of the opening scenes, it is not confined to those scenes, for information is gradually revealed throughout most plays.

The amount of exposition required about past events is partly determined by the *point of attack:* the moment at which the story is taken up. Shakespeare typically uses an early point of attack (that is, he begins the play near the beginning of the story and tells it chronologically). Thus, he needs relatively little exposition. Greek tragic dramatists, on the other hand, use later points, which require that many previous events be summarized for the audience's benefit. Thus, Greek tragedies actually show only the final parts of their stories. In *Oedipus the King,* all the action seems to take place in one day, but to uncover the truth on which the action turns, we must be told about events that begin before Oedipus' birth. Arthur Miller's *Death of a Salesman* is unusual in having a late point of attack (beginning only one day before Willy's death) but still showing, in flashbacks, events that range through many years. The point of attack in *Happy Days* can be called middle because Winnie's situation in Act I has long existed but in Act II is far more advanced; the implication is that her situation would be similar no matter the moment in time.

Playwrights motivate the giving of exposition in many ways. Ibsen, as in *A Doll's House,* frequently introduces a character who has returned after a long absence; questions about happenings while the character was away motivate the giving of background information needed by the audience to understand the situation. On the other hand, some plays offer exposition without attempting to make it seem natural. Many of Euripides' Greek tragedies open with a monologue-prologue that summarizes events up to this time. In a musical play, exposition may be given in song and dance.

In most plays, attention is focused early on a question, potential conflict, or theme. The beginning of such plays includes what may be called an *inciting incident,* an occurrence that sets the main action in motion. In Sophocles' *Oedipus the King,* a plague is destroying the city of Thebes; the oracle at Delphi declares that the murderer of the former king, Laius, must be found and punished before the plague can end. This is the event (introduced in the prologue) that sets the action in motion.

The inciting incident usually leads directly to a *major dramatic question* around which the play is organized, although this question may change as the play progresses. For example, the question first raised in *Oedipus the King* is: Will the murderer of Laius be found and the city saved? Later, this question changes as interest shifts to Oedipus' involvement in the crime. *A Doll's House* asks: Can Nora conceal her criminal act from Torvald and, if not, what will he do?

Not all plays include inciting incidents or clearly identifiable major dramatic questions. All have focal points, nevertheless, frequently a theme or controlling idea around which the action is centered. *Happy Days* is a good example of this alternative pattern as Winnie seeks to cope with the meaninglessness of her daily existence.

The Middle

The middle of a play is normally composed of a series of complications. A *complication* is any new element that changes the direction of the action—the discovery of new information, for example, or the arrival of a character. The substance of most complications is *discovery* (any new information of sufficient importance to alter the direction of action). Discoveries may involve objects (a wife discovers in her husband's pocket a weapon of the kind used in a murder), persons (a young man discovers that his rival in love is his father), facts (a young man about to leave home discovers that his mother has cancer), values (a woman discovers that self-esteem is more important than marriage), or self (a man discovers that he has been acting from purely selfish motives when he thought he was acting out of love for his children). Each complication normally has a beginning, middle, and end—its own development, climax, and resolution—just as the play as a whole does.

Means other than discoveries can be used to precipitate complications. Natural or mechanical disasters (earthquakes, storms, airplane crashes, automobile accidents) are sometimes used, but these are likely to seem contrived if they resolve the problem (for example, if the villain is killed in an automobile accident and as a result the struggle automatically ends).

The series of complications culminates in the *climax,* the highest point of interest or suspense. It is often accompanied by the *crisis,* that discovery or event that determines the outcome of the action. For example, the title character in *Oedipus the King* sets out to discover the murderer of Laius; the interest steadily grows as events increasingly focus attention on Oedipus, and the turning point comes when Oedipus realizes that he himself is the guilty person and becomes the pursued rather than the pursuer. Not all plays have a clear-cut series of complications leading to climax and crisis. *Happy Days,* for example, is less concerned with a progressing action than with a static condition. Nevertheless, interest is maintained by the frequent introduction of new elements and an ongoing pattern of tension and relaxation. One way of analyzing such plays (and all others as well) is to divide them into *units,* the beginnings and endings of which are indicated by shifts in motivation, topic, or the introduction of some new element. One can then examine the function of each of these units both at that point in the action and in the overall development of the play.

The End

The final portion of a play, the *resolution* or *dénouement* (unraveling or untying), extends from the crisis to the final curtain. It ties up the various strands of action, answers the questions raised earlier, or solidifies the theme. It returns the situation to a state of balance and satisfies audience expectations.

Plays may also have *subplots,* in which events or actions of secondary interest are developed, often providing contrast to or commentary on the main plot. In *A Doll's House,* the relationship of Krogstad and Mrs. Linde contrasts sharply with that of Nora and Torvald. Often a subplot becomes a major factor in resolving the main plot, as in *Hamlet,* when Laertes, a morally upright character, is provoked by the death of his father Polonius and the madness of his sister Ophelia to agree to help Claudius in his plan to kill Hamlet.

Henrik Ibsen's *A Doll's House* as produced by the
Hartford Stage. Gerry Bamman as Torvald, Mary
McDonnell as Nora. Directed by Emily Mann.
(Photo © T. Charles Erickson.)

Character and Characterization

Character is the primary material from which plots are created, for incidents are developed through the speech and behavior of dramatic personages. *Characterization* is
anything that delineates a person or differentiates that person from others. It operates
on four levels.

The first level of characterization is *physical* or *biological,* defining gender, age,
size, coloration, and general appearance. Sometimes a dramatist does not supply all
of this information, but when the play is produced, actors necessarily give physical
presence to the characters.

The second level is *societal.* It includes a character's economic status, profession
or trade, religion, family relationships—all the factors that place a character in a
particular social environment.

The third level is *psychological.* It reveals a character's habitual responses, desires, motivations, likes, and dislikes—the inner workings of the mind. Because
drama most often arises from conflicting desires, the psychological is the most essential level of characterization.

The fourth level is *moral.* It reveals what characters are willing to do to get what
they want. It also shows what characters actually do when faced with making a
difficult choice (as opposed to what they have said they or others should do in such

situations). Moral decisions differentiate characters more fully than any other type because deliberating about such decisions causes characters to examine their values and motives, in the process of which their true natures are revealed both to themselves and to the audience. The moral level is developed most fully in serious plays. (Analyzing Nora in *A Doll's House* and Winnie in *Happy Days* in terms of the four levels will reveal much about these characters and the plays in which they appear.)

A playwright may emphasize one or more of these levels and may develop many or few traits, depending on *how the character functions in the play*. For example, the audience needs to know very little about a maid who appears only to announce dinner, whereas the principal characters need to be drawn in considerable depth.

A character is revealed in several ways: through *descriptions in stage directions, prefaces, or other explanatory material* not part of the dialogue; through *what the character says;* through *what others in the play say about the character;* and, most important, through *what the character does.*

Dramatic characters are usually both *typified* and *individualized.* On the one hand, spectators would be unable to relate to a character who was totally unlike any person they had ever known. Therefore, characters can usually be placed in one of several large categories of people. On the other hand, the audience may be dissatisfied unless the playwright goes beyond this typification to give characters individualizing traits that set them apart from other characters of the same type. The most satisfactory dramatic characters are usually easily recognizable types with some unusual or complex qualities.

A playwright may be concerned with making characters *sympathetic* or *unsympathetic.* Normally, sympathetic characters are given major virtues and lesser foibles, while the reverse is true of unsympathetic characters. A character who is either completely good or bad is likely to seem unconvincing as a reflection of human behavior. Acceptability varies, however, with the type of play. Melodrama, for example, oversimplifies human psychology and clearly divides characters into good or evil. Tragedy, on the other hand, normally depicts more complex forces at work both within and without characters and requires greater depth and range of characterization.

Thought

The third basic element of a play is *thought.* It includes the themes, arguments, and overall meaning of the action. It is present in all plays, even the most lighthearted farce, for a playwright cannot avoid expressing some attitudes, for events and characterization always imply some view of human behavior. As we have already seen, thought may also be used to unify a play's dramatic action.

Meaning in drama is usually implied rather than stated directly. It is suggested by the relationships among characters, by the ideas associated with unsympathetic and sympathetic characters, by the conflicts and their resolution, and by such devices as spectacle, music, and song. Sometimes the author's intention is clearly stated in the script, as when characters advocate a certain line of action, point of view, or specific social reform.

Dramatists in different periods have used various devices to project ideas. Greek playwrights made extensive use of the *chorus,* just as those of later periods employed such devices as *soliloquies, asides,* and other forms of statement made directly to the audience. Other tools for projecting meaning are *allegory* and *symbol.* In allegory, characters are personifications of abstract qualities (mercy, greed, and so on), as in the medieval play *Everyman.* A symbol is an object, event, or image that, while meaningful in itself, also suggests a concept or set of relationships. In *Happy Days,* the mound in which Winnie is trapped and which progressively rises around her serves as a symbol of the human condition and visually sums up the play's thought.

Just because plays imply or state meaning we should not conclude that there is a single correct interpretation for each play. Most plays permit multiple interpretations, as different productions of, and critical essays about, the same play clearly indicate. Nevertheless, each interpretation should be supported by evidence found in the script.

Diction

Plot, character, and thought are the basic subjects of drama. To convey these to an audience, playwrights have at their disposal two means: sound and spectacle. Sound includes language, music, and other aural effects; *spectacle* refers to the visual elements of a production (the physical appearance and movement of performers, the costumes, scenery, properties, and lighting).

Language is the playwright's primary means of expression. When a play is performed, other expressive means (music, sound effects, and spectacle) may be added; but to convey intentions to others, the dramatist depends almost entirely on dialogue and stage directions. Thus, language (diction) is the playwright's primary tool.

Diction serves many purposes. It is used to *impart information,* to *characterize,* to *direct attention* to important plot elements, to *reveal the themes and ideas* of a play, to *establish tone or mood and internal logic,* and to *establish tempo and rhythm.*

The diction of every play, no matter how realistic, is more abstract and formal than that of normal conversation. A dramatist always selects, arranges, and heightens language. In a realistic play, although the dialogue is modeled after and may retain the rhythms and basic vocabulary of everyday usage, the characters are usually more articulate and state their ideas and feelings more precisely than their real-life counterparts would.

The dialogue of nonrealistic plays (such as Greek and Shakespearean tragedies) deviates markedly from everyday speech. It employs a larger vocabulary, abandons the rhythms of conversation, and makes extensive use of imagery and meter. Other types of nonrealistic plays may emphasize the clichés and repetitiveness of conversation to comment on the mechanical quality and meaninglessness of exchanges that pass for communication.

The basic criterion for judging diction is its *appropriateness* to characters, situation, internal logic, and type of play.

Music

Music, as we ordinarily understand the term, does not occur in every play. But if the term is extended to include all patterned sound, it is an important ingredient in every production, except those that are wholly silent.

Language has been described as the playwright's principal means of expression. But a written script, like a musical score, is not fully realized until the performers—through the elements of pitch, stress, volume, tempo, duration, and quality—transform print into sound. It is through these elements that meaning is conveyed. For example, though the words of a sentence may remain constant, its meaning can be varied by manipulating emphasis or tone ("You say *he* told her?" as contrasted with "You say he told *her?*" or the differences that result if the tone in the same speech is shifted from joy to sarcasm). Because written language is imprecise in emphasis or tone, actors and directors may interpret a passage in ways the playwright did not intend.

The spoken aspect of language varies in its formal qualities. In some plays, among them *A Doll's House,* it simulates the loose rhythms of everyday speech; in others, such as Shakespeare's *Hamlet,* it is shaped into formalized metrical patterns.

In addition to the sound of the actors' voices, a play may also use music in the form of incidental songs and background music, or—as in musical comedy and opera—it may utilize song and instrumental accompaniment as integral structural means. Music (especially in combination with lyrics) may serve many functions. It may *establish mood,* it may *characterize,* it may *suggest ideas,* it may *compress* characterization or exposition (by presenting information, feelings, or motivations in a song), it may *lend variety,* and it is *pleasurable* in itself.

Spectacle

Spectacle encompasses all the visual elements of a production: the movement and spatial relations of characters, the lighting, settings, costumes, and properties. Because others normally supply these elements, the playwright does not have full control over them; and because the script seldom describes the spectacle precisely, the other theatre artists must discover the play's intentions through careful study of the text. Similarly, the reader of a script must try to envision the spectacle in order to grasp a play's full power. The visual picture of Winnie embedded in the mound is essential to *Happy Days.*

Some scripts give the reader more help than others do. Many older plays (including Greek and Shakespearean tragedies) contain almost no stage directions, and most clues to spectacle must be sought in the dialogue. When place or action is important, such plays usually have a character describe them. Beginning in the nineteenth century, when visual elements were given added prominence, stage directions became usual. Since that time, the printed texts of plays have typically included many aids designed to help the reader visualize the action. In evaluating spectacle, the characteristics we should be most concerned with are *appropriateness* and *distinctiveness.* (The process of transferring the written script to the stage is treated more fully in later chapters.)

Striking music and spectacle are major features of Lee Breuer's and Bob Telson's *The Gospel at Colonus*, a retelling of Sophocles' *Oedipus at Colonus* through American gospel music and preaching. Here in a production at the Goodman Theatre (Chicago), Martin Jacob (a member of the gospel group the Soul Stirrers) separates the Balladeer (Sam Butler, Jr.) and Polyneices (Terrence A. Carson). (Courtesy of the Goodman Theatre.)

Analyzing Scripts

The structure of drama can best be understood by analyzing specific plays. Following is a list of questions useful in play analysis. Applying these to *A Doll's House* and *Happy Days* should further clarify the preceding discussion of dramatic structure.

1. How is the dramatic action unified? Through cause-to-effect relationship of incidents? Character? Theme/motif/idea?
2. What are the given circumstances? (Geographical location? Period? Time of day? Socioeconomic environment? Attitudes and relationships of characters at the beginning of the play? Previous action?) How is this information conveyed?
3. At what point in the total story does the play begin (that is, where is the point of attack)? What sets the dramatic action in motion (the inciting incident)?
4. What is the major conflict, dramatic question, or unifying theme? What is the climactic scene? How is the action resolved? Are there subplots? If so, how is each related to the main plot?

5. What is the dominant tone of the play? Serious? Comic? Ironic? Is the tone consistent throughout or does it change often? How is tone established?

6. For each character, list the biological, social, psychological, and moral traits indicated in the script. Which traits of each character are most important to the dramatic action? What is each character willing to do to achieve his/her desires?

7. What are the major ideas/themes/implications of the dramatic action? Is there a clear-cut message? If not, how is significance conveyed? Are there a number of possible interpretations of the play? If so, which seems most defensible based on the play's action, characterizations, and other elements in the script?

8. To what extent do the vocabulary, rhythm, and tempo of speeches follow or deviate from everyday colloquial usage? What information is given or implied about sound? Music? Is this information significant to the dramatic action? If so, how?

9. What information is given or implied in the script about settings? Costumes and makeup? Lighting? Is this information significant to the dramatic action? If so, how?

10. For what kind of theatrical space was the play written? What characteristics of the script are explained by the theatrical or dramatic conventions in use at the time the play was written?

Not all of these questions need be answered for each script. Additional questions may be needed for some scripts or for specialized interests (to meet the needs of actors, designers, and others) or for atypical scripts.

Form in Drama

Scripts are frequently classified according to form: tragedy, comedy, tragicomedy, melodrama, farce, and so on. Considerable emphasis is sometimes placed on understanding the essential qualities of each dramatic form and the proper classification of each script. Arthur Miller's *Death of a Salesman* (1949), for example, provoked a lengthy controversy over whether it was a true tragedy. Since the 1960s concern over dramatic form has lessened, in part because much recent drama defies formal classification. Nevertheless, one cannot read plays without encountering formal labels. Consequently, some understanding of dramatic form is helpful.

Basically, *form* means the shape given something for a particular purpose. A sentence is a form created by words arranged in a particular order to convey a thought. Similarly, a play is a form created by arranging incidents in a particular order to create a dramatic action. Most plays have in common certain formal elements that permit us to recognize them as plays rather than as novels, epic poems, or essays. Still, those works we recognize as plays are not all alike. Critics have divided them into a number of dramatic forms on the basis of certain characteristics, the most important of which are type of action, overall tone, and basic emotional appeals. Throughout much of history, *tragedy* and *comedy* have been considered the two basic forms.

Tragedy

The oldest known form of drama, tragedy, presents a genuinely serious action and maintains a serious tone throughout, although there may be moments of comic relief. It raises significant issues about the nature of human existence, morality, or human relationships. The protagonist, or leading character, of tragedy is usually someone who arouses our sympathy and admiration but who encounters disaster through the pursuit of some goal, worthy in itself, that conflicts with another goal or principle. The emotional effect of tragedy is the arousal of a strong empathy for those who strive for integrity and dignity.

Tragedy is a form associated especially with ancient Greece and Elizabethan England. (In later chapters, two of the world's greatest tragedies, Sophocles' *Oedipus*

The Possibility of Writing Tragedy in the Twentieth Century

Is it still possible to write tragedy? This question has frequently been debated in the twentieth century. Few dramatists since the mid-nineteenth century have called their serious plays tragedies, and today, though we still study tragedy and talk about tragic form, when we do so we usually look back to the Greeks or to Shakespeare for our examples. Joseph Wood Krutch, a university professor and critic, argued in his essay "The Tragic Fallacy" that it is impossible to write tragedy in the twentieth century because we consider human beings too petty to be capable of tragic action:

> the idea of nobility is inseparable from the idea of tragedy, which cannot exist without it. . . . [A] tragedy . . . must . . . have a hero, and from the universe as we see it both the Glory of God and the Glory of Man have departed. Our cosmos may be farcical or it may be pathetic but it has not the dignity of tragedy. . . . The death of tragedy is, like the death of love, one of those emotional fatalities as the result of which the human as distinguished from the natural world grows more and more a desert.

Not everyone agrees with Krutch's conclusions. Arthur Miller was driven to offer a different point of view when *Death of a Salesman*, following its original production, became the subject of a lengthy debate over whether it could be considered a "true tragedy." Miller responded in an essay entitled "Tragedy and the Common Man":

> For one reason or another, we are often held to be below tragedy—or tragedy above us. . . . I believe that the common man is as apt a subject for tragedy in its highest sense as kings were. . . . [T]he tragic feeling is evoked in us when we are in the presence of a character who is ready to lay down his life, if need be, to secure one thing—his sense of personal dignity. . . .

the King and Shakespeare's *Hamlet* will be discussed in detail.) Few plays in the twentieth century have been called tragedies, perhaps because, as some critics have argued, we no longer consider human beings capable of the kind of heroic action associated with the great tragic heroes.

Comedy

A dramatic form that had its origins in ancient Greece, comedy is based on some deviation from normality in action, character, or thought. It must not pose a serious threat, and an "in-fun" tone is usually maintained. Comedy demands that an audience view the situation objectively. Henri Bergson argues that comedy requires "an anesthesia of the heart," because it is difficult to laugh at anything about which we feel deeply. We may find it funny to see someone slip on a banana peel, but if we discover that it is a close relative who is just recovering from a serious operation, our concern will destroy the laughter. Similarly, we may dislike some things so intensely that we cannot see their ridiculous qualities. Nevertheless, any subject, however trivial or important, can become the subject of comedy if we place it in the right framework and distance ourselves sufficiently from its serious implications. Comedy arouses emotions ranging between joy and scorn, with laughter as their common response.

Other Forms

Not all plays are wholly serious or comic. The two are often intermingled to create mixed effects, as in tragicomedy. Perhaps the best known of the mixed types is *melodrama*, the favorite form of the nineteenth century and still the dominant form among television dramas dealing with crime and danger. A melodrama develops a temporarily serious action that is initiated and kept in motion by the malicious designs of a villain; a happy resolution is made possible by destroying the villain's power. Melodrama depicts a world in which good and evil are sharply differentiated; there is seldom any question where the audience's sympathies should lie. The appeals are strong and basic, creating a desire to see the "good guys" triumph and the "bad guys" punished. This desire is usually met in a double ending, one outcome for the good, another for the bad. Melodrama is related to tragedy through its serious action and to comedy through its happy ending. It is a popular form, perhaps because it assures audiences that good triumphs over evil.

During the twentieth century, concern for giving formal labels to plays has greatly diminished, probably because we no longer consider it possible to categorize situations and people precisely. Boundaries have come to seem so fluid that a single event may be viewed almost simultaneously as serious, comic, threatening, or grotesque. Thus, tone may shift rapidly; elements that in the past were associated with tragedy or comedy may be intermingled or be transformed into their opposites. As a result, the old formal categories have lost much of their significance. Since World War II, plays have been labeled "tragic farce," "anti-play," "tragedy for the music hall," and a variety of other names that suggest how elements from earlier categories and from popular culture have been intermingled.

Despite all the changes, we need to recognize that each play has a form; otherwise, we would not be able to read or comprehend it. It is perhaps best to remember that the form of each play is in some respects unique—no two plays are exactly alike—but that there are sufficient similarities among certain plays to group them into a common category. Whether or not we have precise notions about tragedy, comedy, or other forms, we are aware of distinctions between the serious and the funny, and most of us freely use "tragic," "comic," and "melodramatic" to describe events in the world around us. Basic awareness of dramatic form will be helpful in many of the subsequent discussions in this book.

Style in Drama

Even plays of the same form vary considerably. One reason for this variety is *style*. Like *form*, the word *style* is difficult to define because it has been used to designate many things. Basically, however, style results from a distinctive mode of expression or method of presentation. For example, style may stem from traits attributable to a period, a nation, a movement, or an author. In most periods, the drama of all Western nations has certain common qualities caused by prevailing cultural concepts

Differing styles of production applied to the same script.
Hamlet as directed by Garland Wright at the Guthrie Theatre (left) on a modern thrust stage using costumes of differing periods, mostly from the nineteenth century. Costumes by Ann Hould-Ward. (Photo by Joe Giannetti. Courtesy Guthrie Theatre.)

Hamlet (right, above) as directed by B. Iden Payne on a simulated Elizabethan public stage and using Elizabethan costumes. (Courtesy Department of Theatre and Dance, University of Texas at Austin.)

Hamlet as directed by Mark Lamos at the Hartford Stage (right, below) in costumes and sets that reflect today's world. Richard Thomas, at center, as Hamlet. (Photo by T. Charles Erickson. Courtesy Hartford Stage.)

(religious, philosophical, psychological, economic) and by then-current theatrical conventions. Thus, we may speak of an eighteenth-century style. Within a period, national differences permit us to distinguish a French from an English style. Furthermore, the dramas written by neoclassicists have qualities that distinguish them from those written by romantics, expressionists, or absurdists. Finally, the plays of individual authors have distinctive qualities that set them off from the work of all other writers. Thus, we may speak of Shakespeare's or Sophocles' style.

Style in theatre results from three basic influences. First, it is grounded in assumptions about what is truthful and valuable. Dramatists of all movements or periods have sought to convey truthful pictures of humanity, but they have differed widely in their answers to the following questions: What is ultimate truth? Where is it to be found? How can we perceive reality? Some have argued that surface appearances only disguise truth, which is to be found in some inner or spiritual realm. Others have maintained that truth can be discovered only by objective study of things that can be felt, tasted, seen, heard, or smelled. To advocates of the latter view, observable details hold the key to truth; to advocates of the former view, the same details only hide the truth. Although all writers attempt to depict the truth as they see it, the individual playwright's conception of truth is determined by basic temperament and talent and by the culture in which he or she lives.

Second, style results from the manner in which a playwright manipulates the means of expression. All dramatists have at their disposal the same means—sound and spectacle. Nevertheless, the work of each playwright is distinctive, for each perceives the human condition from a different point of view, and these perceptions are reflected in situations, characters, and ideas; in manipulation of language; and in suggestions for the use of spectacle. In the process of writing, playwrights set their distinctive stamp (or style) on their plays.

Third, style results from the manner in which the play is presented in the theatre. The directing, acting, scenery, costumes, and lighting used to translate the play from the written script to the stage may each be manipulated in many ways; the distinctive manner in which these elements are handled in a production characterizes its style. Because so many people are involved in producing a play, it is not unusual to find conflicting or inconsistent styles in a single production. Typically, unity is a primary artistic goal. Each theatre artist usually seeks to create qualities analogous to those found in the written text, and the director then coordinates all of the parts into a unified whole. In recent times, postmodernism has intermingled different styles, although this intermingling may itself be considered a style. Ultimately, style results from the way in which means are adapted to ends.

Discussions of dramatic action, structure, form, and style remain abstract, however, until applied to specific examples. The chapters that follow explore how these elements have been employed, both in the past and in our own time.

PART TWO

Varieties of Theatrical Experience

Some form of theatrical activity has doubtless existed since the very earliest times, although surviving records permit us to trace it back with any certainty for only about twenty-five hundred years. When we look at today's theatre, we see only a small part of what the theatre is capable of, and we are given insufficient clues about what it has been or might be. If we are to appreciate the full range of theatre, we need to be aware of its multiple possibilities and some of the transformations it has undergone. This is true not merely for the sake of knowing the theatre's past but because awareness of differing types of theatrical expression can alert us to possibilities for reshaping theatre in the present and the future. Creative artists do not merely repeat old forms, they also reshape them by exploring alternative possibilities.

In the theatre, awareness of the past is important for other reasons as well. Many plays from the past are still performed regularly. Each of these plays was written with a particular kind of theatre structure, set of theatrical conventions, and audience in mind. They also reflect the cultural assumptions and values of their time. Although plays may transcend the conditions of time and place (otherwise they would not communicate with us today) we can perhaps understand them most fully in the context within which they originated. Plays are among the best indicators we have of the culture out of which they came. They are simultaneously specific to a particular context and universal in their ability to speak to us in the much broader context of human experience in general.

In a book of this length, it is impossible to treat every form that the theatre has taken in the past and present. Therefore, only representative types of theatrical experience will be discussed. Those chosen do not provide a comprehensive survey of the theatre's development, but they do touch on most major periods in Western theatre. Taken all together, these discussions should contribute to a fuller understanding of today's theatre.

Scene from the Hartford Stage's production of Corneille's seventeenth-century play, *The Illusion*, which has gained popularity in recent years after three hundred years of neglect. Adapted by Tony Kushner; directed by Mark Lamos. (Photo by T. Charles Erickson.)

Chapter 4

Festival Theatre:
Greek, Roman, and
Medieval Theatre Experiences

Sophocles' *Oedipus the King* at the St. Louis Black Repertory Company. Directed by Ben Halley, Jr. (Courtesy of the St. Louis Black Repertory Company.)

The second phase [in the development of theatre brings it] to as elaborate a scale of great festival performance as one can reach, but still acted under the . . . open sky. . . . [The offerings] are performed only on special, ritual occasions in the year. There is still a dominating . . . religious element. There is no, or very little, professionalism. . . .

—Richard Southern, *The Seven Ages of the Theatre*

During the first two thousand years of its existence, Western theatre was markedly different from the professional and commercial theatre that we know today and that has flourished only during the past four hundred years. Until the sixteenth century A.D., theatre in the Western world was performed primarily as part of festivals. Financed by the community and performed for the community, it was available only for brief periods each year when theatrical performances were presented as offerings to a god and for the enjoyment of the general populace. This type of theatre flourished in ancient Greece, Rome, and medieval Europe, although in each the differences were as important as the similarities.

The Theatre of Ancient Greece

Theatre in the Western world can be traced back to ancient Greece, and especially to Athens, usually considered the cradle of Western civilization. The Athenians, inventors of democracy, were the first to have sufficient faith in humanity to let citizens be responsible for making the laws that governed their lives. Nevertheless, the Greeks did not consider everyone equal: Their economy depended on slave labor, and women were permitted no public role. The belief in the ability of human beings to make significant decisions contrasted sharply with the belief of earlier societies that people are pawns of supernatural forces or all-powerful tyrants. This new attitude may have been a major factor in the development of Greek drama, which usually emphasized the attempts of human characters to control their own destinies. The Greeks nevertheless considered happiness to depend on harmony between human and supernatural forces and believed that this harmony could easily be broken. Greek tragedy often shows the results of human attempts to escape fate or the will of the gods.

From the beginning, Greek drama was presented exclusively at festivals honoring Dionysus, one of the many gods worshiped by the Greeks, who conceived of their gods essentially as immortal human beings. Each god had power over a limited sphere of activity. Like human beings, these gods had many failings: They were jealous of each other, bickered among themselves, were vindictive when slighted, took sides in both human and divine quarrels, indulged frequently in adulterous affairs, and in general made human existence unpredictable. The Greeks did not observe a holy day comparable to the Sabbath but had a series of religious festivals throughout the year, one or more dedicated to each of the gods.

Dionysus, the god in whose honor plays were presented, was the god of wine (one of the principal products of Greece) and fertility. His blessing was sought in order to ensure fertility of both human beings and the land. Supposedly the son of

Zeus (the greatest of Greek gods) and Semele (a mortal), Dionysus was killed (allegedly at the behest of Zeus' jealous wife Hera), dismembered, resurrected, and deified. The myths associated with him were closely related to the life cycle and seasonal changes: birth, growth, decay, death, and rebirth; summer, fall, winter, and especially spring, the season of rebirth and the return of fertility. As the god of wine and revelry, he was also associated with a number of irrational forces. By the fifth century B.C., Athens held four festivals in honor of Dionysus each year, at three of which theatrical performances were offered. Plays were not presented at the festivals of other gods.

The major Dionysian festival in Athens was the City Dionysia. Extending over several days near the end of March, it was one of the most important occasions of the year and a major showcase for Athenian wealth and power. The festival was both a religious and a civic celebration under the supervision of the principal state official. Theatrical performances were viewed in a radically different light than they are today. They were offerings of the city to a god. At the same time, they were expressions of civic pride—indications of the cultural superiority of Athens over the other Greek states, which only later developed their own theatres. (Eventually there were theatres throughout the eastern Mediterranean in areas that are now parts of Turkey, Lebanon, Syria, Israel, southern Italy, and elsewhere.)

Our first record of a theatrical event in Athens is the establishment in 534 B.C. of a contest for the best tragedy, a form that also originated in Athens. The first winner was Thespis, the earliest playwright and actor whose name has come down to us. From his name we derive the term *thespian,* still used in reference to actors. During the fifth century, three tragic dramatists competed at each City Dionysia, each writer presenting a group of four plays: three tragedies and one satyr play.

A satyr play was short, comic or satiric in tone, poked fun at some Greek myth, used a chorus of satyrs (half-man, half-goat), and was presented following the

Actors of a satyr play as depicted on a Greek vase of the late fifth century B.C. The embroidered robes resemble those thought to have been worn by tragic actors. Notice at bottom center the flute player, who provided the musical accompaniment for dramatic performances. (From Baumeister, *Denkmaler des Klassischens Altertums* [1888].)

Greek Satyr Plays

Although in the fifth century B.C. each dramatist competing in the contests at the City Dionysia had to present a satyr play in addition to three tragedies, we know little about this comic form, largely because only one complete example—*The Cyclops* by Euripides—has survived. It is an adaptation of an incident in Homer's *Odyssey*, in which Odysseus and his crew, on their way home from the Trojan War, are captured by a cyclops (a giant with one eye in the middle of his forehead).

When the play opens, Silenus and his satyr sons have been enslaved by the cyclops Polyphemus. Odysseus arrives looking for water and provisions, which Silenus is eager to give him in exchange for wine. Arriving unexpectedly, Polyphemus captures the Greeks and eats two of them. Odysseus then gets Polyphemus drunk, sharpens a tree trunk, with which he blinds the cyclops, and escapes with his crew and the satyrs. While the events sound grim, they are given a humorous turn by Silenus' attempts to get as much wine for himself as possible, by various tricks played on Polyphemus, and by a considerable number of jokes. Satyr plays were comic in part because of the antics of the satyrs, who wore masks with shaggy hair and beards, pointed ears, and snub noses. The satyr costume consisted of only a loincloth made of fur, with a horselike tail in the rear and prominent *phallus* in front. The satyr play apparently was considered a happy note on which to end a performance that had included three tragedies.

tragedies. Thus, nine tragedies were produced at each City Dionysia, a total of nine hundred during the fifth century. Of these, only thirty-two have survived, all written by three dramatists—Aeschylus (523–456 B.C.), Sophocles (496–406 B.C.), and Euripides (480–406 B.C.), who are ranked among the world's greatest playwrights.

Of the surviving tragedies, *Oedipus the King* by Sophocles is often considered the finest. Performed about 430 B.C.—approximately a hundred years after the establishment of the contest for tragedy—it continues to be produced frequently. Before we look more closely at this play and its performance, let us examine some features of the Greek theatre building and other conventions that affected staging.

The Theatre of Dionysus

Plays were performed in the Theatre of Dionysus, on the slope of the hill just beneath the Athenian Acropolis (a fortified area including the Parthenon, the city treasury, and other buildings considered essential to the city's survival). The theatre was located within a compound that included a temple and a large outdoor altar dedicated to the worship of Dionysus. Originally, the slope (without any seating) served as the *theatron* ("seeing place," the origin of our word *theatre*). A flat terrace

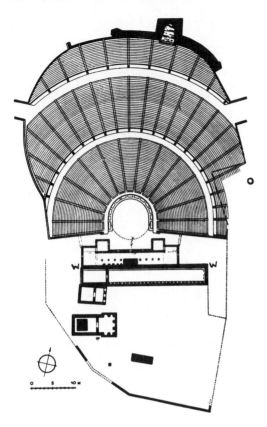

Plan of the precinct devoted to the worship of Dionysus in Athens: at bottom, the temple and altar; at top, the theatre. Notice the scene house below the circular orchestra and the *paradoi* (passages) between the ends of the scene house and the auditorium. (From Dörpfeld-Reisch, *Das Griechische Theater* [1896].)

below the slope served as the *orchestra* ("dancing place"), in the middle of which was placed an altar (*thymele*) dedicated to Dionysus.

This arrangement was gradually converted into a permanent structure. The auditorium eventually became a semicircle of stadiumlike stone seats extending up the hill to the retaining walls of the Acropolis (the structure was not fully completed until the late fourth century B.C.). It held at least fourteen thousand and perhaps as many as seventeen thousand spectators. This seating curved about halfway around a circular orchestra, measuring about sixty-five feet in diameter, that was used as performance space, especially for the chorus. On the side of the orchestra opposite the audience was the *skene* ("hut" or "tent," the origin of our word *scene*). The term suggests that the original structure was used as a place to which the actors could retire or where they could change costumes. Once its possibilities as a background for the action were recognized, the *skene* was elaborated into a structure seventy-five to a hundred feet long and probably two stories high. It is thought that this scene house had three doors—a large central doorway flanked on either side by smaller doors—all opening onto the acting area. The roof of this structure could be used as an acting area to represent high places or for the appearance of gods. The scene house was not architecturally joined to the auditorium; the spaces (called *paradoi*) at either side between the *skene* and the auditorium were used as entrances and exits for performers (especially the chorus) and perhaps by spectators before and after performances. Because the original scene house has long disappeared, no one knows exactly how it looked. (Some possibilities are shown in the illustrations on page 64.)

The scene house (as later in Shakespeare's theatre) probably served as a formalized architectural background for all plays, even those set in woods, on seashores, or outside caves. This convention meant that locale was probably established by the dialogue, not by representational scenery. The action in Greek plays usually took place outdoors, but occasionally the outcome of events that occurred indoors was shown. Most of the latter scenes involved the corpses (effigies) of characters slain offstage that had to be shown onstage. To show the corpses, the large central doorway was probably opened and a wheeled platform (the *eccyclema*) pushed out. Another common occurrence in Greek plays was the appearance of a god. Sometimes the roof was used, but in many plays the god had to descend to ground level or to be lifted from the orchestra to roof level. For this purpose, a cranelike device (the *machina*) was used. (The overuse of gods to resolve difficult dramatic situations led to any contrived ending being labeled a *deus ex machina*—god from the machine—ending.) Probably nothing better illustrates the nonrepresentational conventions of the Greek theatre than the machine, for its fulcrum arm, ropes, and pulleys were visible to the audience. It was not intended to fool anyone;

The theatre at Epidaurus, the best preserved of all ancient Greek theatres, is still used for festival performances. The scene house, at left, is a temporary structure erected on the ruins of the original. A tragic chorus of fifteen is performing in the orchestra. Notice the large size of the theatre and the audience-performer relationship. For another photo of this theatre, see color plate 1. (Courtesy of the Embassy of Greece.)

The scene house of the Theatre of Dionysus in the fifth century B.C. No one knows precisely the appearance of the scene house; these drawings show four possibilities. (From Ernst Fiechter, *Antike Griechische Theaterbauten*, 1936. Courtesy of Dr. Charlotte Fiechter.)

rather, it was used to suggest the *idea* of flying, a power possessed by the gods and denied to human beings (except for a few who had been granted special powers by the gods).

From our standpoint, one of the most remarkable things about the Theatre of Dionysus is its size. Today, a theatre with an audience capacity of even three thousand is considered almost unusable for drama because of the difficulty of seeing and hearing. We expect realistic visual effects and acting, and we feel cheated if we cannot see every detail as we do on the movie or television screen. Obviously, the Greeks had expectations that differed from ours, as is clear from the conventions they developed and accepted. The structures today that most resemble Greek theatres are sports arenas. (Keeping in mind the scale of such structures will help us understand many other conventions of the Greek theatre.)

The Performers

Performers in the Greek theatre may be divided into four categories: actors, chorus, supernumeraries, and musicians. All were male.

By the time *Oedipus the King* was produced, around 430 B.C., the rules of the contests restricted the number of speaking actors to three for each author. This rule did not restrict the number of roles to three; rather, all speaking parts had to be assumed by three actors, which meant that the same actor might have to play several roles, and that the same three actors appeared in all three of the tragedies presented by a competing dramatist. Supernumeraries (extras) could be used, but they were not permitted to speak lines. This convention probably developed to ensure fairness in the competition. A principal actor was assigned by lot to playwrights, who usually staged their own plays. The playwright and the leading actor then probably chose the other two. A prize was offered for the best tragic actor at each festival, but only the leading actors were eligible to win.

The tragic chorus was composed of fifteen men. A playwright wishing to present his plays at the City Dionysia had to apply to the principal government official for a chorus. We do not know how this official decided which playwrights would be granted choruses, but it is clear that being granted a chorus was the mark that a playwright had been accepted as a competitor. This official also paired the dramatist with a *choregus,* a wealthy citizen who bore the expense of training and costuming that dramatist's choruses and of paying the musicians who accompanied the choruses during their training and during performances. The well-to-do citizens of Athens were required to take turns serving as *choregoi,* and most seem to have done so willingly. Thus, the financing of productions was undertaken by the state and a few wealthy citizens. The prize awarded for the best group of plays was shared by the playwright and his *choregus.* We are not sure what the prizes consisted of; they may have included money, but the honor of winning seems to have mattered most, just as winning an Oscar or an Olympic medal does today.

Choruses were assigned approximately eleven months prior to the next festival. How much time was spent in training is unknown, but apparently the routine was not unlike that today in training athletes. Exercises and diets were controlled, and

Statuette of a tragic actor showing mask, headdress, and long robe. This figure is from a period later than the fifth century B.C. and is more exaggerated in appearance than would have been typical in Sophocles' time. The projections below the statuette are pegs used to anchor it in a base. (From *Monumenti Inediti*, 2 [1879].)

the chorus worked under the strict and strenuous supervision of a trainer. A great deal of emphasis was placed on singing and dancing because the fifteen members both sang and danced the choral passages. Thus, much of their training resembled that of opera singers and dancers. Usually they performed in unison, but at times they were divided into semichoruses of seven members. The chorus leader sometimes had solo lines, but the rest of the chorus usually responded as a group or as two subgroups that performed and responded to each other alternately.

The chorus was one of the distinctive conventions of the Greek theatre. It usually made its entrance following the prologue and was present thereafter until the end of the play. The choral odes, performed between episodes, divided the action into segments something like the acts of a modern play. The chorus served several functions in Greek drama. First, it was treated as a group character who expressed opinions, gave advice, and occasionally threatened to interfere in the action. Second, it often seemed to express the author's point of view and to establish a standard against which the actions of the characters could be judged. Third, it frequently served as the ideal spectator, reacting to events and characters as the author would like the audience to react. Fourth, it helped to establish mood and heighten dramatic effects. Fifth, it added color, movement, and spectacle as it sang and danced the choral interludes.

The principal musical accompaniment in Greek tragedy was provided by a flute player, who preceded the chorus as it made its entrance and then (like the chorus) remained onstage throughout. The source of the musical accompaniment was thus visible to the audience and not kept offstage, as in most modern productions. The flute player wore sandals, one with a clapper on its sole for beating time. Both percussionist and flutist, he also seems to have composed the music he played.

Although much music was used in Greek theatrical performances, almost none of it has survived; the texts of Greek plays do little to make us aware that we should be hearing certain passages sung or recited to musical accompaniment. (Attempts to unite music and text as they had been in Greek tragedy gave rise to opera in Italy during the late sixteenth and early seventeenth centuries.) Greek music had a great variety of musical modes, each with a particular tonal quality that was thought appropriate to certain kinds of subjects or emotions. It probably more nearly approximated the sounds of present-day music of the Near East than that of Western Europe or America. In Greek theatre, music may have had much in common with film music, enhancing the mood and emotion of the action it accompanied.

All of the performers, except the musician, wore masks of lightweight wood, cork, or linen. The use of masks, another of the Greek theatre's distinctive conventions, served several purposes: It facilitated the rapid change of roles when three actors had to play all the parts; it made it easier for male performers to embody female roles; it helped the actor in assuming roles that differed widely in age or character type; and it assisted communication in the large theatres by capturing and emphasizing the essential qualities of each character. Because each mask covered the entire head and included the appropriate hair and headdress, the actor's appearance could be changed instantaneously with a change of mask.

A variety of clothing was used for stage purposes. A long-sleeved heavily embroidered tunic was worn by some characters, but, because there are references in the plays to characters in rags, in mourning, and in Greek or in foreign dress, it seems unlikely that all characters were dressed alike. The selection of costume was probably determined by its appropriateness to the role. The sleeved, embroidered tunic, which was not a garment worn in Greek daily life, may have been reserved for supernatural or non-Greek characters, while native dress was used for Greeks. The usual dress in Greece was an ankle-length or knee-length garment called a *chiton*. On his feet the tragic actor wore soft, flexible, high-topped boots in common use at that time.

These conventions suggest that performance in the Greek theatre was highly formalized. When we remember that the same actor often played several roles in the same play, that men played both male and female roles, that the performers wore masks, that much of the text was sung and danced, and that the scale of the theatre prevented small details from being seen, we are faced with a performance mode quite different from that of the present day. That this mode was pleasing to the Greeks emphasizes a simple truth: What any group accepts as effective theatrical performance depends to a great extent upon the group's familiarity with, and acceptance of, a particular set of conventions and upon the skill with which those conventions are handled.

Oedipus the King and Its Performance

Among the many events at the City Dionysia was the reenactment of Dionysus' arrival in Athens in a procession whose participants included the major officials of

Greek Tragic Dramatists

Aeschylus, Sophocles, and Euripides are the only tragic authors whose plays have survived. Aeschylus (523–456 B.C.), a member of the Athenian nobility who distinguished himself in the wars against Persia, wrote approximately eighty plays, of which seven survive: *The Persians, Seven Against Thebes, The Suppliants, Prometheus Bound,* and the *Oresteia* (a trilogy of plays: *Agamemnon, The Libation Bearers,* and *The Furies*). Some scholars believe that all of Aeschylus' surviving plays were parts of trilogies (three plays based on a single story or theme) treating philosophical issues. The *Oresteia,* for example, shows the evolution of the concept of justice as personal revenge is replaced by the impersonal judgment of the state. Aeschylus' plays, the oldest that have survived, are somewhat crude in comparison with Sophocles' but they show heroic figures wrestling with significant philosophical issues.

Sophocles (495–406 B.C.) was from a wealthy family, well educated, handsome, and popular. For a time, he served as one of ten generals, the highest elective office of the Athenian state. Sophocles wrote more than one hundred twenty plays and won twenty-four contests, more than any other Greek dramatist. Of his plays, only seven have survived: *Ajax, Antigone, Oedipus the King, Electra, Trachiniae, Philoctetes,* and *Oedipus at Colonnus.* Sophocles' final play, *Oedipus at Colonnus,* written when he was almost ninety years old, was produced the year after his death. His reputation as one of the world's great dramatists has remained constant since his own lifetime, probably because of his masterful dramatic structure, moving stories, complex characters, beautiful poetry, and universal themes.

Euripides (480–406 B.C.), the last of the great Greek tragic dramatists, wrote about ninety plays, of which eighteen have survived. The best known are *Alcestis, Medea, Hippolytus, The Trojan Women, Electra, The Bacchae,* and *Iphigenia in Aulis.* He is also author of *Cyclops,* the only surviving satyr play. Because he questioned many Athenian beliefs and customs, he was rarely honored during his lifetime but later became the most popular of tragic writers. Often denounced for writing about subjects considered unfit for the stage (such as Medea killing her children and Phaedra falling in love with her stepson), he was also disliked for suggesting that the gods of Greek myth are morally corrupt. Writing at the end of the fifth century, Euripides raised doubts about many of the values that Aeschylus had championed at the beginning of that century.

Athens, the actors and others associated with the performances, and many citizens who carried gifts for the god. This procession wound through much of Athens, stopped for dances and ceremonies at various altars, and ended at the precinct dedicated to Dionysus, where a bull was sacrificed on the main altar. Five days of performances followed. In addition to the tragedies, there were comedies and dithyrambs (hymns to Dionysus sung and danced by groups of fifty men or boys). At the end of the festival, prizes were awarded. The performance of *Oedipus the King* was thus embedded within a much larger festival framework.

The performances were open to everyone—even prisoners, who were released during the festival. Seats at the front of the auditorium were reserved for public officials and special guests, and the center seat in the front row was reserved for the head priest of the Dionysian cult. The audience was composed primarily of men and boys, although some accounts suggest that women, children, and even slaves attended. Officials were responsible for keeping order, and violence in the theatre was punishable by death. Performances probably lasted all day because several plays were presented. There must have been considerable coming and going and much eating and drinking in the theatre. The audience at times expressed itself noisily and occasionally hissed actors off the stage. The atmosphere probably resembled a mixture of religious festival and athletic event.

Performances seem to have begun at dawn. There was no artificial lighting in the theatre, no proscenium arch or curtain. The auditorium rose sharply up the hill, so that most of the spectators looked down on the acting areas and could see over the stage house across a plain to the sea. The total visual context was immense.

The beginning of *Oedipus the King* was signaled by the entrance through one of the *paradoi* of a group of people of all ages carrying branches, the symbol of the suppliant. Oedipus, masked and in full-length *chiton,* appeared through the central doorway of the stage house (which in this play represented a palace) to hear their petition that something be done to end the plague that had been ravishing Thebes for some time. Then Creon, returning from Delphi, where he had been sent to consult the oracle about how to end the plague, arrived through the other *parados.* After the suppliants left, the chorus of fifteen elderly Thebans, all as nearly identical in appearance as possible and preceded by the flute player, marched into the orchestra and performed the first choral song while moving in stately patterns. As this description of the performance's opening suggests, spectacle played an important role throughout.

Let us look more closely at the script. The skill with which *Oedipus the King* is constructed can be appreciated if we compare the complex story (which actually begins with a prophecy prior to the birth of Oedipus) to Sophocles' ordering of the events. In the play, there is a simultaneous movement backward and forward in time during which the revelation of the past moves Oedipus ever nearer to his doom in the present.

The division of the play into a prologue and five episodes separated by choral passages is typical of Greek tragedy. The prologue is devoted principally to exposition: A plague is destroying the city of Thebes; Creon returns from Delphi with a command from the oracle to find and punish the murderer of Laius, the former king; Oedipus promises to obey the command. All of the necessary information is

Oedipus the King as produced at the Wilma Theatre, Philadelphia. Note the use of a mixed chorus of men and women (such mixing was not done when producing tragic drama in ancient Greece). Note also the human figures impressed in the walls at rear. Directed by Blanka Zizka. (Photograph © T. Charles Erickson.)

given in this very brief scene, and the first important question—Who is the murderer of Laius?—is raised. The prologue is followed by the *parodos,* or entry of the chorus, and the first choral song, which offers prayers to the gods for deliverance from the plague.

The first episode begins with Oedipus' proclamation demanding that anyone with knowledge of the crime come forward and placing a curse on the murderer. This proclamation has great dramatic power because Oedipus is unknowingly pronouncing a curse on himself. Then Tiresias, the blind seer, enters. His refusal to answer questions about the past provokes Oedipus' anger, the first display of a response that is developed forcefully throughout the first four episodes. Oedipus' quick temper, we later discover, has caused him to kill Laius. When Tiresias, having been forced to answer, suggests that the truth is too painful to reveal, Oedipus suspects some trickery. The scene ends in a stalemate of accusations.

It is interesting to note that while the first four episodes move forward in the present, they go successively further back in time. This first episode reveals only that part of the past immediately preceding Oedipus' arrival at Thebes. The choral passage that follows the first episode reflects upon the previous scene, stating the confusion that Sophocles probably wished the audience to feel.

The second episode builds logically upon the first. Creon comes to defend himself against Oedipus' accusation that he is involved in a conspiracy with Tiresias. Queen Jocasta is drawn to the scene by the quarrel, and she and the chorus persuade Oedipus to let his anger cool. This quarrel illustrates Oedipus' complete faith in his own righteousness. In spite of Tiresias' hints, Oedipus has no suspicion of his own guilt. Ironically, Jocasta's attempt to placate Oedipus leads to his first suspicion about himself. She tells him that oracles are not to be believed and as evidence points to Laius' death, which did not come in the manner prophesied. But her description of how Laius was killed recalls to Oedipus the circumstances under which he killed a man. He insists that Jocasta send for the one survivor of Laius' party. This scene continues the backward exploration of the past because in it Oedipus tells of his life in Corinth, his visit to the oracle of Delphi, and his killing of the man who is later discovered to have been Laius. The choral song that follows is concerned with the questions Jocasta has raised about oracles. The chorus concludes that if oracles are proven untrue, then the gods themselves are to be doubted.

Though Jocasta has called oracles into question, she obviously does not disbelieve in the gods, for at the beginning of the third episode she makes offerings to them. She is interrupted by the entrance of the Messenger from Corinth, who brings news of the death of Oedipus' supposed father, Polybus. But this news, rather than arousing grief, as one would expect, is greeted with rejoicing, for it seems to disprove the oracle's prediction that Oedipus would kill his father. This seeming reversal serves only to heighten the effect of the following events. Oedipus still fears returning to Corinth because the oracle also has prophesied that Oedipus will marry his own mother. Thinking that he will set Oedipus' mind at ease, the Messenger reveals that he himself brought Oedipus as an infant to Polybus. The circumstances under which the Messenger acquired the child bring home the truth to Jocasta. This discovery leads to a complete reversal for Jocasta, for the oracles she has cast doubt upon in the preceding scene have suddenly been vindicated. She strives to stop Oedipus from making further inquiries, but he interprets her entreaties as fear that he may be of humble birth. Jocasta goes into the palace; it is the last we see of her.

The scene not only has revealed the truth to Jocasta, but it has also diverted attention from the murder of Laius to the birth of Oedipus. The scene goes backward in time to the infancy of Oedipus. The choral song that follows is filled with romantic hopes, as the chorus speculates on Oedipus' parentage and suggests such possibilities as the god Apollo and the nymphs. The truth is deliberately kept at a distance here in order to make the following scene more powerful.

This choral song is followed by the entrance of the Herdsman (the sole survivor of Laius' party at the time of the killing and the person from whom the Corinthian Messenger had acquired the infant). The Herdsman does not wish to speak, but he is tortured by Oedipus' servants into doing so. In this very rapid scene, everything that has gone before is brought to a climax. We are taken back to the beginning of the story (Oedipus' birth), and we learn that Oedipus is the son of Laius and Jocasta, that Oedipus killed Laius, and that Oedipus is married to his mother. The climax is reached in Oedipus' cry of despair and disgust as he rushes into the palace. The brief choral song that follows comments upon the fickleness of fate and points to Oedipus' life as an example.

The final episode is divided into two parts. A Messenger enters and describes what has happened offstage. The "messenger scene" is a standard part of Greek drama because Greek sensibilities dictated that scenes of extreme violence take place offstage, although the results of the violence (the bodies of the dead, or in this case Oedipus' self-inflicted blindness) might be shown. Following the messenger scene, Oedipus returns to the stage and seeks to prepare himself for the future.

Oedipus the King is structurally unusual, for the resolution scene is the longest in the play. Sophocles was not solely concerned with discovering the murderer of Laius, for in this lengthy final scene interest shifts to the question: What will Oedipus do now that he knows the truth? Up to this scene, the play has concentrated upon Oedipus as the ruler of Thebes, but in the resolution, Oedipus as a man and a father becomes the center of interest. At this point, he has ceased to be the ruler of Thebes and has become the lowest of its citizens, and much of the intense pathos results from this change in status. An audience may feel for Oedipus the outcast as it never could feel for the self-righteous ruler shown in the prologue.

Oedipus' act of blinding himself grows believably out of his character, for his very uprightness and deep sense of moral outrage cause him to punish himself by thrusting pins into his eyes. Although he is innocent of intentional sin, he considers the deeds themselves (killing a blood relative and incest) to be so horrible that ignorance cannot wipe away the moral stigma. Part of the play's power resides in the revulsion with which people in all ages have viewed patricide and incest. That they are committed by an essentially good man makes them even more terrible.

In drawing his characters, Sophocles pays little attention to the physical level. The principal characters—Oedipus, Creon, and Jocasta—are mature persons, but Sophocles says almost nothing about their age or appearance. One factor that is likely to distract modern readers—the relative ages of Jocasta and Oedipus—is not even mentioned by Sophocles. When Oedipus answered the riddle of the Sphinx, his reward, being made king, carried the stipulation that he marry the queen, Jocasta. Sophocles never questions the suitability of the marriage on the grounds of disparity in age.

Sophocles does give brief indications of age for other roles. The Priest of the prologue is spoken of as being old; the chorus is made up of Theban elders; Tiresias is old and blind; the Herdsman is an old man. In almost every case, age is associated with wisdom, experience, or knowledge of the past. On the other hand, there are a number of young characters, none of whom speaks: The band of suppliants in the prologue includes children, and Oedipus' daughters, Antigone and Ismene, are young. Here the innocence of childhood is used to arouse pity.

On the sociological level of characterization, Sophocles again indicates little. Oedipus, Creon, and Jocasta hold joint authority in Thebes, although the power has

Oedipus the King at the Stratford Shakespearean Festival (Canada). Oedipus (at center, played by Douglas Campbell) surrounded by the Chorus; Jocasta (Eleanor Stuart) and Creon (Robert Goodier) in background. Directed by Tyrone Guthrie; designed by Tanya Moiseiwitch. (Photo by Donald McKague. Courtesy of the Stratford Shakespearean Festival Foundation of Canada.)

been delegated to Oedipus. Vocational designations—priest, seer, herdsman, servants—are used for some of the characters.

Sophocles is principally concerned with psychological and ethical characteristics. He emphasizes Oedipus' moral uprightness, his reputation for wisdom, his quick temper, his insistence on discovering truth, his suspicion, his love for his children, and his strength in the face of disaster. These qualities make us understand Oedipus, although a limited number of traits are used.

Creon is given even fewer characteristics. He has been Oedipus' trusted friend and brother-in-law. He is quick to defend his honor and is a man of common sense and uprightness who acts as honorably and compassionately as he can when the truth is discovered. Jocasta is similarly restricted. She strives to make life run smoothly for Oedipus: She tries to comfort him, to mediate between him and Creon, to stop Oedipus in his quest. She commits suicide when the truth becomes clear. We know nothing of her as a mother, and the existence of the children is not mentioned until after her death.

Unlike a modern play, then, in which characterization is usually built from numerous realistic details, here the characterization is drawn with a few bold strokes; the most important traits are psychological and moral. Everything is pared to its essentials and then enlarged and formalized, in part because of the scale of the theatre, but also to emphasize the seemingly inevitable fate that overwhelms the characters.

All of the speaking roles had to be played by three actors. Discovering which actor played which roles is revealing. The first actor played Oedipus throughout because he is present in every scene. The second actor probably played Creon and the Messenger from Corinth; the third actor probably played the Priest, Tiresias, Jocasta, the Herdsman, and the second Messenger. The greatest range is required of the third actor, while the greatest individual power is required of the first.

In addition to the three speaking actors, a great many supernumeraries are required, many of whom no doubt appeared in more than one scene. For example, the band of suppliants in the prologue includes children, two of whom could later appear as Antigone and Ismene. Some who portrayed suppliants probably also later appeared as servants and attendants. To the actors must be added the chorus of fifteen members. The total number in the cast of *Oedipus the King* was probably no fewer than thirty-five.

In reading the play, it is sometimes difficult to perceive that there were so many participants and that the visual and aural appeals were so numerous and continuous. The power of the play and of the production was so great that *Oedipus the King* became one of the most admired plays in ancient Greece. Aristotle (384–322 B.C.), author of *Poetics,* the oldest surviving treatise on drama, thought it the finest of all Greek tragedies, and his opinion has been echoed to the present. It is still among the most frequently performed Greek plays. Today, productions of *Oedipus the King* inevitably deviate markedly from the original because the occasion, theatre structure, conventions, and audiences are unlike those of classical Greece. A director now must search the text for those features that remain vital despite the passage of twenty-four centuries. As some of the illustrations included in this chapter indicate, Greek conventions (especially masks and treatments of the chorus) may be used today, but they are almost always adapted to make them acceptable to modern sensibilities.

Why has *Oedipus the King* continued to attract audiences? We have already looked at its skillful construction and its concern with moral taboos of incest and patricide. In addition, it develops themes of universal relevance. The fall of Oedipus from the place of highest honor to that of an outcast demonstrates the uncertainty of human destiny. This is related to another theme: the limited ability of human beings to control their fate. Oedipus has done everything he can to avoid the oracle's prediction that he will kill his father and marry his mother but, in doing so, he unknowingly fulfills the oracle. The contrast between human beings seeking to control their destiny and external forces shaping destiny is clearly depicted.

It is significant that no attempt is made in the play to explain why destruction comes to Oedipus. It is implied that human beings must submit to fate and that in struggling to avoid it, they become only more entangled. An irrational, or at least an unknowable, force apparently is at work. No one in the play asks who or what has determined Oedipus' fate. The truth of the oracle is established, but the purpose is unclear. The Greek concept of the gods did not assume that all the gods were benevolent—all supernatural forces were deified, whether good or evil. It is possible to interpret this play as suggesting that the gods, rather than having decreed the characters' fates, have merely foreseen and foretold what will happen. Such an interpretation shifts the emphasis, but it does not contradict the picture of humanity as a victim of forces beyond its control.

Another motif—blindness versus sight—is emphasized in poetic images and in various comparisons. A contrast is repeatedly drawn between physical sight and the inner sight of understanding. For example, Tiresias, though blind, can see the truth that escapes Oedipus, while Oedipus, who has penetrated the riddle of the Sphinx, cannot solve the puzzle of his own life. When it is revealed to him, he blinds himself in an act of retribution.

Another theme, of which Sophocles may not have been conscious, is that of Oedipus as scapegoat. The city of Thebes will be saved if the one guilty man can be found and punished. In a sense, then, Oedipus takes the troubles of the city upon himself, and in his punishment lies the salvation of others.

Greek Comedy

In addition to tragedy and satyr plays, Athens developed a distinctive comic drama. Comedy became an official part of the Dionysian festivals about fifty years later than tragedy. Although comedy was performed at the City Dionysia with the tragedies, it eventually found its most sympathetic home at another Dionysian festival, the Lenaia, which was held during the winter, when few outsiders were present and at which the playwrights were allowed to ridicule Athenian events more pointedly.

Five comic dramatists competed each year at the Lenaia, but each presented only one play. The conventions of comedy differed significantly from those of tragedy. Greek comedy was usually concerned with current issues in politics or art, with questions of war and peace, or with persons or practices disliked by the author. Occasionally playwrights used mythological material as a framework for satire, but usually they invented their own stories. Comedy used a chorus of twenty-four members, not always identical in appearance or all of the same sex. Sometimes the choruses were depicted as everyday citizens but often as nonhuman (birds, wasps, frogs, clouds). Many of the male characters wore a very tight, too-short *chiton* over flesh-colored tights, creating a ludicrous effect of partial nakedness. This effect was emphasized by an enormous phallus attached to the costumes of most male characters. This was not only a source of humor but was also a constant reminder of the purpose of the Dionysian festival: the celebration of fertility. Masks contributed to the ridiculous appearance of the characters.

Numerous authors wrote Old Comedy, as the plays written prior to 400 B.C. are called, but only eleven comedies have survived, and all of these are by Aristophanes

A figure from Old Comedy. (From Robert, *Die Masken der Neueren Attischen Komodie* [1911].)

(448–380 B.C.). His plays mingle slapstick, fantasy, lyrical poetry, personal abuse, literary and musical parody, and serious commentary on contemporary affairs. The plot of an Old Comedy revolves around a "happy idea" and the results of putting it into practice. For example, in *Lysistrata,* probably the best known of all Greek comedies, the women of Greece successfully use a sex strike to end a war. Old Comedy has several typical features: a *prologue*, during which the happy idea is introduced; a *parados*, or entrance of the chorus; an *agon,* or debate over the merits of the happy idea, ending in its adoption; a *parabasis*, or choral passage addressed to the audience, most frequently filled with advice on civic or other contemporary problems; a series of *episodes* showing the happy idea in practice; and a *komos*, or exit to feasting and revelry. The unity of Old Comedy is found in its ruling idea rather than in a series of causally related events. Sometimes days or weeks are assumed to have passed during one or two speeches, and place may change often. Stage illusion is broken frequently as characters make comments about or to the audience.

After the fifth century B.C., Greek drama declined in quality, although not in quantity. During the fourth century B.C., especially after Alexander the Great conquered most of the Middle East and Egypt, Greek theatres were built throughout the eastern Mediterranean areas, and plays began to be performed at festivals other than those in honor of Dionysus. Comedy underwent the most drastic change, no longer treating major political, artistic, or social issues, turning instead to the intrigues of everyday domestic life. Although Old Comedy (the type written by Aristophanes) is now considered superior to the New Comedy that replaced it, Old Comedy exerted little influence after its own time. New Comedy, especially after it

Aristophanes' The Frogs

Aristophanes' *The Frogs* (405 B.C.) was presented in the year following the deaths of Sophocles and Euripides. Dionysus, fearing that his festivals will suffer, hits on the idea of going down to Hades and bringing Euripides back to Athens. The play's title comes from the chorus of frogs that inhabits the swamps through which Dionysus and his servant Xanthias must pass before reaching Hades. The cowardly Dionysus decides to disguise himself as Heracles, the greatest of Greek heroes, who in myth had once entered and returned from Hades, a supposedly impossible task. But this disguise backfires when Dionysus (accepted as Heracles) is threatened with a beating for having left on his earlier visit without paying his bill at an inn. Seeking to save himself, Dionysus makes Xanthias change disguises with him, only to regret it when the maid declares her desire to resume her sexual relationship with Heracles. Disguises are switched back and forth and eventually both Dionysus and Xanthias are beaten.

All this precedes the major focus of the play. Although Dionysus has come to take Euripides back with him, an argument rapidly develops over the relative merits of the tragic playwrights now in Hades. Sophocles refuses to be involved in such an argument, and the play settles into a debate between Aeschylus and Euripides, during which they deride each other's work and defend their own. (The more familiar one is with the plays of Aeschylus and Euripides, the more comic the debate is because passages from the plays are quoted and ridiculed.) Dionysus, declaring that he will choose the writer who gives the wisest counsel to the citizens of Athens, eventually chooses Aeschylus, and the play ends in revelry and feasting.

The Frogs, though comic throughout, ultimately is concerned with the responsibility of dramatists. Aristophanes seems to conclude that the best playwright is the one who holds up ideals that citizens can aspire to, rather than merely reflecting everyday commonplace behavior.

was taken over, adapted, and expanded by the Romans, set the pattern followed by most popular comic drama down to the present.

The Roman Theatre Experience

Around two hundred years after the first performance of *Oedipus the King,* Rome became a major power, eventually gaining control of Greece, the entire eastern Mediterranean, and most of Western Europe and North Africa. For seven hundred years, the Romans reigned over an extensive empire.

As in Greece, theatrical performances were part of religious festivals, although in Rome they might be for any of several gods. The Roman term for these festivals was *ludi* ("games"). At the *ludi,* in addition to religious ceremonies and sacrifices, many other activities were offered for the pleasure of the god being honored—as well as for the diversion of the Roman people, whose tastes were considered to coincide with those of the gods. Such attitudes led increasingly to theatrical offerings that appealed to the greatest common denominator. The activities (other than the ceremonies and sacrifices) varied from festival to festival and from year to year, but all involved tests of skill, frequently with prizes for the most skillful or popular competitors. The theatrical company that won the greatest favor with the audience received extra payments, as did the winners of chariot races, horse races, animal baitings, acrobatic feats, and other activities. The Romans apparently placed their theatrical performances in the same category as sports and other forms of diversion.

The Romans were great assimilators, accepting, borrowing, or changing those things that seemed useful or desirable. When they encountered Greek drama in the mid-third century B.C., they imported a Greek writer, Livius Andronicus, to adapt Greek drama to Roman tastes. The first of his plays was produced in 240 B.C., and soon native Romans began to write plays. But the taste for this Greek-style drama seems to have peaked quickly because the major period of this type of Roman drama was over by about 150 B.C. When Greek-style plays were introduced in 240 B.C., they were novelties to be elaborated and exploited. When their appeal faded, they were displaced by other kinds of entertainment, although they did not disappear altogether.

Although the taste for full-length scripted drama sharply declined after the mid-second century B.C., the demand for theatrical entertainment actually increased steadily. Roman taste favored variety entertainment: short comic plays of various sorts, dancing, singing, juggling, tightrope-walking, acrobatics, trained animals, gladiatorial contests, animal baiting, water ballets, mock sea fights, and a host of other events. From just one day given over to theatrical entertainments in 240 B.C., the number had grown to 101 by A.D. 354. Because playscripts survive and artifacts relating to other kinds of theatrical entertainment often do not, accounts of theatrical activities usually emphasize performances based on full-length written scripts. Accounts of Roman theatre typically concentrate on theatrical production between 205 and 159 B.C., when Plautus (c. 254–184 B.C.) and Terence (195–159 B.C.) wrote the twenty-six surviving Roman comedies. Nine tragedies by Seneca (5 B.C.–A.D. 65) have survived, but they apparently were not intended for public performance. Let us look at the theatrical experience in the age of Plautus and Terence.

The Roman Theatrical Context

The Roman theatre resembled that of Greece in many ways, but it also differed in significant ways. The Romans were ambivalent about anything derived from Greece, which they considered to be decadent. This ambivalence about drama is probably reflected in Roman comedy, all surviving examples of which are adapted from Greek plays. In these adaptations, the setting and characters remain Greek, even though, as many critics have pointed out, the manners and customs depicted in the plays are far more Roman than Greek. In the period when the Roman comedies were written, Rome placed great emphasis on "gravity" (*gravitas*, seriousness of purpose) in its citizens. Historians have suggested that the Greek setting was

Theatre at Ostia, near Rome. A conjectural reconstruction of one of the oldest permanent Roman theatres, built between 30 and 12 B.C. (D'Espouy, *Fragments d'Architecture Antique,* 1 [1901].)

retained in the comedies so as not to offend the Roman authorities who controlled the festivals and their contents.

As in Greece, the expenses of theatrical production were assumed by the state. The government made an appropriation for each festival as a whole; the officials in charge, usually wealthy citizens who often used the occasion to curry favor with the Roman populace, frequently contributed additional funds. Rather than choose the plays, as seems to have been the rule in Greece, these officials contracted with the heads of theatrical companies for productions. The officials probably viewed the productions before they were presented, more for the sake of guarding against unacceptable material than for judging artistic merit.

In addition to underwriting production expenses, the Roman state also supplied the theatre in which the plays were presented. In the time of Plautus and Terence, all theatres were temporary structures (no permanent theatre was built in Rome until 55 B.C.). We cannot be certain about the appearance of these temporary structures, but it is usually assumed that they were less elaborate versions of the one depicted in the illustration above. Tiered seating for several thousand people apparently surrounded a semicircular orchestra (half of the Greek full-circle orchestra). A long stage (probably more than one hundred feet long and twenty or more feet deep) rose five feet above the orchestra; it was enclosed at either end and across the back by a facade (*scaenae frons*). This facade apparently had three doors in the back wall and one at either end. In comedy, the stage was treated as a street, with the doors in the back wall serving as entrances to houses fronting on the street, and the doors at the ends serving as continuations of the street. The facade also had windows and a second story that could be used as needed by the action. Roman comedies took place outdoors, most frequently in a street in front of one or more houses. The orchestra area seems never to have been used in the comedies, which did not include a chorus.

The scale of the Roman theatre was comparable to that of the Greek. It, too, was an outdoor structure, but the stage house and the auditorium were joined and of the same height, and consequently the audience could not see over the stage house. The individual performer was also much more prominent because of the raised stage and the absence of a chorus.

Admission to this theatre was free, seats were not reserved, and audiences were often unruly. In the prologue to his *The Carthaginian,* Plautus lists several types of behavior that apparently were common among Roman audiences: "Let no worn out prostitutes sit in the front part of the auditorium, nor the guards make any noise with their weapons, nor the ushers move about in front of spectators or show anyone to seats while the actors are onstage. . . . Don't let slaves take up seats meant for free men . . . , let nursemaids keep little children at home. . . . Let matrons . . . refrain from gossiping." Guards were present to enforce order, but, because a series of plays was presented each day, coming and going was frequent. The plays had to compete with other attractions, and consequently the actors had to provide entertainment that would satisfy a mass audience. Terence states in the prologue to one of his plays that it is the third attempt to present the play; the earlier two attempts had been abandoned because once the audience left to see rope dancers and another time to see gladiators. The total context of attractions was akin to the multiple channels on our television sets, which permit us to move from one attraction to another, seeking the most entertaining.

By the time of Plautus and Terence, there seem to have been a number of theatre companies. We do not know what they did when they were not performing at the festivals, but probably they traveled about or gave private performances for wealthy Romans. In any case, more than one company was hired to give performances at the festivals. Once hired, they were responsible for all details of production: finding scripts, providing the actors, costumes, musicians, and so on. Each company was assured a certain payment, but special incentives were offered in the form of prizes to those companies receiving the most favorable response from the audiences.

The characters wore Greek costumes similar to those of daily life, although there may have been some exaggeration for comic purposes. Because most of the characters were types, certain colors came to be associated with particular groups, such as red with slaves and yellow with courtesans. This conventional use of color extended to wigs as well, making distinctions among the types of characters instantly visible to audiences All of the performers were male and wore masks.

Roman comedy does not deal with political or social issues but with everyday domestic affairs. Almost invariably, the plots turn on misunderstandings of one sort or another: mistaken identity (frequently involving long-lost children), misunderstood motives, or deliberate deception. They show the well-to-do middle class (the older man concerned with his wealth or children; the young man who rebels against authority) and those around them (slaves, slave dealers, hangers-on, courtesans, cowardly soldiers). Of all the characters, the most famous is perhaps the "clever

Roman Dramatists

Plays by only three Roman dramatists have survived: Plautus and Terence (both of whom wrote comedies) and Seneca (who wrote tragedies). Titus Maccius Plautus was born in 254 B.C. and apparently had worked at several trades, including that of baker and perhaps actor, before turning to playwriting in 205 when he was almost fifty years old. Thereafter, he was a prolific author up to the time of his death in 184 B.C. After his death, as many as 130 plays were attributed to him, but only 21, all of which have survived, are considered certainly his. *The Braggart Warrior, Pot of Gold, Pseudolus, The Captives,* and *The Menaechmi* are among his best-known works. Owing to his witty dialogue, distinctive characters, and farcical plots, Plautus was extremely popular in his own day and for long after his death.

Publius Terentius Afer (195– or 185–159 B.C.) is said to have been born in Carthage, brought to Rome as a slave, educated, and freed. He wrote six plays, all of which have survived: *Andria, Mother-in-Law, Self-Tormentor, Eunuch, Phormio,* and *The Brothers.* The chief interest in his plays lies in character and the double plots that provided him opportunities for showing contrasts in human behavior. In the Renaissance, Plautus and Terence were major influences on comic writing, in part because their plays were among the few that had survived from the classical era.

Lucius Annaeus Seneca (c. 4 B.C.–A.D. 65) was born in Spain but came to Rome at an early age. A philosopher, he was tutor to the future emperor Nero, who, coming to distrust and fear him, forced Seneca to commit suicide. Nine of his tragedies have survived, among them *Medea, Oedipus,* and *Phaedra.* Though Seneca wrote about many of the same subjects treated by Greek dramatists, his plays differ markedly from theirs, most notably in the amount of violence they include. Seneca's *Oedipus,* for example, dramatizes the same story as Sophocles' *Oedipus the King,* but Seneca graphically depicts the horrors of the plague; a bull is sacrificed on stage so that the prophet Tiresias can read the entrails. In the final scene, Jocasta rips open her womb onstage with Oedipus' sword. In part because of such onstage actions, scholars believe that Seneca's plays were written to be read rather than performed. Seneca's were the tragedies from the classical world with which most Renaissance writers were most familiar because most of them could read Latin but not Greek. The many bloodthirsty scenes in the English plays of Shakespeare's time owe much to Seneca.

slave" who, to help his master, devises all sorts of schemes, most of which go awry and lead to further complications. Very few respectable women appear in Roman plays, and while love affairs may be the source of a play's intrigues, the women involved seldom appear onstage.

While reading a Roman play, we should try to remember the musical element. In Plautus' plays, about two-thirds of the lines were accompanied by the flute. The flute player remained on stage throughout the play, although his presence was ignored by the actors. There were a number of songs by the characters (rather than by the chorus, as had been the practice in Greek drama). In performance, a Roman comedy closely resembled a modern musical.

The Menaechmi

Of all Roman comedies, Plautus' *The Menaechmi* has perhaps been the most popular. It served as the basis for Shakespeare's *Comedy of Errors* as well as for a number of others, including the American musical *The Boys from Syracuse* by Richard Rodgers.

Plautus' *The Menaechmi*. Directed by Harrold Shiffler; designed by Richard Baschky. (Courtesy of the University of Iowa Theatre.)

As in most of Plautus' plays, *The Menaechmi* begins with a prologue that carefully lays out the background of the action and goes over important points more than once. By the time the play begins, the audience has been given a summary of the prior action: twin brothers were separated when very young, and one, who has been looking for the other, arrives in Epidamnus without knowing that this is where his twin now is. Because the prologue has given the audience this information, the introductory scenes are used to establish the present conditions out of which the comedy will grow: the dispute between Menaechmus I and his wife; the visit of Menaechmus I to the courtesan Erotium, his gift to her of a dress stolen from his wife, their plans for an elaborate meal and party later in the day, and the departure of Menaechmus I to the Forum; the entrance of Menaechmus II and his slave, Messenio. When Menaechmus II is addressed by name by Erotium and her servants, he and Messenio assume that they are being set up for some con game by people who have learned Menaechmus' name at the dock where their ship has just put in. The remainder of the play presents a series of scenes in which the two Menaechmi are in turn mistaken

---

Roman Paratheatrical Entertainments

Roman religious festivals included entertainments—many of them quite violent and bloodthirsty—that extended far beyond theatrical performances. The oldest and most popular of these was chariot racing, for which structures (circuses) were built that allowed twelve chariots to race abreast of each other. One of these, the Circus Maximus, held sixty thousand people. The circuses also were used for other forms of entertainment: horse racing (sometimes with trick riding), cavalry battles, footraces, acrobatics, prizefighting, wrestling, exhibitions of wild and trained animals, and fights between animals or between animals and men.

Another popular form of entertainment was gladiatorial contests. Originally, gladiatorial combat was confined to funeral games and did not become part of state religious festivals until 105 B.C. The number of combatants steadily increased. In A.D. 109, five thousand pairs were featured at one festival. It was primarily as a place for gladiatorial contests and animal fights that amphitheatres were built, the most famous of which is the Colosseum (seating fifty thousand), which opened in A.D. 80 when nine thousand animals were killed during the 100-day inaugural program. It was also here that Christians were placed in the arena with lions, for which they became prey, as a form of entertainment and religious persecution.

Among the most spectacular of all the entertainments were the *naumachiae* or sea battles. Sometimes these were staged on lakes, but amphitheatres also were sometimes flooded for such events. The largest of the *naumachiae* was given in A.D. 52 on the Fucine Lake east of Rome; it involved nineteen thousand participants, many of whom perished in the battles.

Although our own entertainments are not always as bloody, they match the Roman in their variety, especially as made available by television.

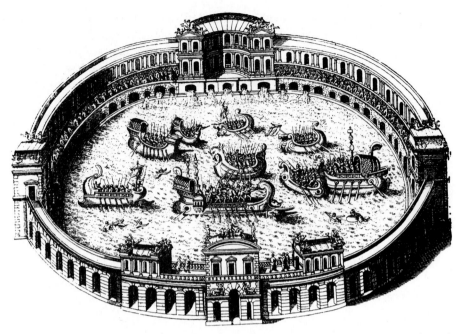

A Roman *naumachia* of the late first century A.D. A conjectural reconstruction made in the Renaissance. (From Laumann, *La Machinerie au Théâtre* [1897].)

for each other, and each is mystified and maddened by being accused of doing things that the other has done. The two are kept apart until the final scene, when their meeting solves the mystery and resolves the complications.

Although Plautus' comic sense is everywhere evident, it may be seen at work especially in the reunion, which might have concluded the play on a sentimental note. Instead, the final lines give the story a twist in keeping with the cynical tone of earlier scenes: Menaechmus I, intending to go away with his twin, offers all of his goods for sale—including his wife, if anyone is foolish enough to buy her.

Plautus has little interest in social satire. Instead, he concentrates on the ridiculous situation growing out of mistaken identity. Consequently, when his characters indulge in adultery, stealing, or deception, they merely contribute to the overall tone of good-humored cynicism—with a considerable touch of misogyny.

As in most Roman comedy, the characters in *The Menaechmi* are types rather than individuals. Some roles are summed up in their names: Peniculus ("Brush") suggests the parasite's (or flattering sponger's) ability to sweep the table clean; the cook is called Cylindrus ("Roller"); and the courtesan is named Erotium ("Lovey"). Each character has a restricted number of motivations: The twins wish to satisfy their physical appetites; the wife wants to reform her husband; the father-in-law desires to keep peace in the family; and the quack doctor, who is sent for when the wife decides that Menaechmus I has gone mad, is seeking a patient on whom he can practice a lengthy and costly treatment.

The ten speaking roles of *The Menaechmi* could easily be performed by a company of six. Doubling of roles was common in the Roman theatre, and in changing roles all of the actors had the advantage of masks and conventionalized costumes and colors of garments and wigs. The play does not require actors who are skilled in the subtle portrayal of a wide range of emotions; rather, they need that highly developed comic technique that produces precision in the timing of business and dialogue. The scenes of quarreling, drunkenness, and simulated madness indicate that physical nimbleness is essential. Most of the actors also must be skilled singers because the main characters have "entering songs" when they first appear and sometimes additional songs later in the action. The musical accompaniment was played on a flute with two pipes, each about twenty inches long. Sometimes it was bound to the player's head to free his hands for playing the instrument. Its sound resembled that of a modern oboe.

Some sense of the overall stage conventions can be derived from the illustration below, although it does not give an adequate sense of the size of the stage.

Other Roman Drama and Theatre

By the beginning of the Christian era, Rome seemed to have forgotten its earlier emphasis on gravity. As power came to rest almost wholly with emperors and armies, the people were offered increasing numbers of public entertainments, many of them bloodthirsty. During this time, theatres and amphitheatres were built

A scene, supposedly from Greek New Comedy, on which Roman comedy was based. At left, two old men; at center, the flute player; at right, a young man and a slave. A bas-relief from southern Italy. (From Robert, *Die Masken der Neueren Attischen Komodie* [1911].)

Christian Opposition to Theatre

Early Christians in Rome came to oppose the theatre for several reasons, perhaps most clearly because the performances were given at festivals for pagan gods, whose existence the Christians did not deny but whom they considered to be demons, as is made clear in *On the Spectacles*, written by Tertullian (c. A.D. 155–c. 220), an early church leader:

> . . . as regards the arts . . . demons, predetermining in their own interests from the first, . . . with the object of drawing man away from his Lord and binding him to their own service, carried out their purpose by bestowing on him the artistic gifts which the shows require. . . . [God] hates all the false; He regards as adultery all that is unreal. . . . He never will approve any putting on of voice, or sex, or age; He never will approve pretended loves, and wraths, and groans, and tears. Then, too, as in His law it is declared that the man is cursed who attires himself in female garments, what must be His judgment of the pantomime, who is even brought up to play the woman!

Many of Tertullian's arguments have resurfaced often in subsequent attacks on the theatre.

throughout the empire, which included most of Western Europe, northern Africa, and the Middle East.

In addition to comedy, the Romans also wrote tragedy. The only surviving examples of Roman tragedy, nine plays by Seneca, are from this period, but were probably not intended for production. Like Greek tragedies, Seneca's are based on myths but emphasize exaggerated emotions and onstage violence, features that centuries later would influence the tragic writers of Shakespeare's age.

The Roman preference for variety entertainment and short plays drove regular comedy and tragedy from the stage. The favorite form in late Rome was the *mime*, a short, topical, usually comic, often improvised playlet. (It was not silent, as today's mime is.) In the mime, female roles were played by women, mime apparently being the first form in which female performers were permitted to appear. None of the mime actors seems to have worn masks. Mime used more realistic conventions than tragedy or comedy did. The dramatic action of mimes in late Rome often centered around sexual encounters, and the dialogue was often obscene. As Christianity grew, its sacraments and beliefs were frequently ridiculed in the mimes.

In addition to the mimes, late Roman festivals increasingly emphasized blood sports, which, along with mimes and variety entertainment, remained integral parts of religious festivals until around A.D. 400. Perhaps not surprisingly, the emerging Christian church became a strong opponent of the theatre—not only because of what was performed but also because it was associated with the worship of pagan gods.

A Funny Thing Happened on the Way to the Forum, a musical adaptation of Roman comedy by Burt Shevelove, Larry Gelbart, and Stephen Sondheim as produced at the Williamstown Theatre Festival. George Wendt (at left) in the role of Pseudolus. Directed by Peter Hunt; costumes by Jess Goldstein. (Photo by Richard Feldman.)

The Roman Empire rapidly disintegrated after it was overrun by invaders in A.D. 476. One consequence was the loss of the official and financial support that had sustained the theatre for more than a thousand years. During the following five hundred years, theatrical activity in Western Europe was reduced to small bands of players or individuals who traveled about performing wherever they could. These performers were often denounced by the Christian church (by then the dominant and most stable institution) and denied its sacraments. It is ironic, therefore, that the revival of the theatre owed most to the church's discovery (during the last half of the tenth century) that the dramatization of biblical episodes was an effective means of teaching.

The Revival of Drama in the Middle Ages

Historians usually divide the Middle Ages (or medieval period) into phases: early (c. A.D. 900 to A.D. 1050), high (c. A.D. 1050 to A.D. 1300), and late (c. A.D. 1300 to A.D. 1500). Although these divisions are indicative of changes in society, all three

Interior of a church such as those in which plays may have been performed in the Middle Ages. Notice the absence of fixed seating, which would have left space for scenic units, performers, and spectators. In the background is the raised apse that might be used for scenes in Heaven or high places, and beneath it the crypt which might be used to represent the descent into the grave or Hell. (From *Romanesque Art in Italy* [1913].)

phases shared a relatively stable set of beliefs and values that permits them to be grouped together and labeled "medieval." During the first two phases, drama was performed primarily within churches or monasteries; it is usually called liturgical drama. During the third, it flourished in elaborate outdoor productions, some of which continued even after 1500 (when the Middle Ages are usually said to have ended). This type is usually referred to as vernacular drama. Most of the plays and productions discussed here are from the late Middle Ages. But before we turn to them, we need briefly to consider drama in the church.

The earliest known example of a liturgical play (one incorporated into the church service, or liturgy) dates from about A.D. 970. It dramatized the arrival of three women at the tomb of Christ, the announcement by an angel that Christ has risen, and the subsequent rejoicing. This short play (only four lines of sung dialogue) was performed as part of Easter services. Subsequently, many other biblical episodes were dramatized, but all remained short so as not to interfere with the regular services. These short plays were written in Latin (the language of the church throughout Western Europe), were chanted or sung, and were performed by choirboys or members of the clergy.

Around A.D. 1200, some religious plays began to be performed outside the church, and by around 1375 a religious drama had developed independent of the liturgy. Plays of this new type were performed throughout most of Western Europe until the sixteenth century, when controversy over religious beliefs and practices (exemplified in the Protestant secessions from the Roman Catholic church) led to

The First Female Dramatist

The first female dramatist of whom we have any record wrote her plays at about the same time liturgical plays began to be performed. Hrosvitha (c. A.D. 935–c. 975), canoness of a nunnery at Gandersheim (Germany), was, according to her own account, drawn to the comedies of the Roman playwright Terence but, fearing their adverse influence, decided to write others that would show Christian virgins and martyrs triumphing over earthly temptations. It is unclear whether her six plays, *Pafnutius, Dulcitius, Gallicanus, Abraham, Callimachus,* and *Sapientia,* all written in rhymed Latin, were performed during her lifetime. Most of these plays deal with characters martyred for their Christian faith or with young women who overcome the temptations of the flesh. After they were published in 1501, they exerted considerable influence on the didactic drama written during the sixteenth century for performance in schools. Hrosvitha, the first dramatist of the postclassical period whose name we know, is a figure of special interest to those seeking to recover the history of women in theatre.

Hrosvitha's uniqueness also reminds us that the theatre prior to the Renaissance was essentially a male preserve. The plays, even those that focus on female characters, not only were written by men but also acted by them. In general, the attitude seems to have been that only a man truly understands what a woman is or should be. In the Christian era, women were usually viewed as daughters of Eve—weak, easily tempted, and themselves temptresses—requiring guidance and discipline from a father or husband. The Virgin Mary was, of course, always treated as an exception.

the suppression of the plays almost everywhere. But by that time these religious plays had for almost two hundred years been the major theatrical expression of Western Europe. They differed from liturgical drama in being written in the vernacular language of a region rather than in Latin, in being spoken rather than chanted or sung, and in being acted primarily by laymen rather than clergy. They were financed by the community rather than by the church.

This medieval religious theatre in some ways resembled that of Greece and Rome. Like those earlier theatres, it was part of religious festivals in which the entire community was invited to participate. But, though similar in purpose, medieval festivals differed from those of Greece and Rome in how they were organized, financed, and presented.

Trade Guilds and the Corpus Christi Festival

The production of the outdoor religious dramas in England is usually associated with trade guilds that flourished beginning in the thirteenth century. The return of relative stability after centuries of warfare and general uncertainty had by around

1200 encouraged increased trade among various parts of Europe, which in turn encouraged an increase in manufactured goods to satisfy the growing demand. Eventually, the need to regulate working conditions, wages, the quality of products, and other matters led craftsmen in various trades—bakers, brewers, goldsmiths, tailors, and so on—to establish guilds to promote the common good of those in each trade. Guilds were organized hierarchically: Each was governed by a council of masters (those who owned their shops and supervised the work of others); under each master were a number of journeymen (those who were skilled in the trade but who worked for wages) and apprentices (boys or young men who received room and board while learning a trade, usually over a period of seven years). The forces that gave rise to the guilds also encouraged the growth of towns. As the towns and guilds grew, power within each town came to rest primarily with the guilds because they usually elected the mayor and the council from among their members.

The increased prominence of secular groups seems also to have been at least partially responsible for the church's desire to incorporate ordinary people more fully into its activities. One result was the creation of a new feast day, Corpus Christi. This festival, officially approved in 1311 and observed throughout Europe by about 1350, celebrates the redemptive power of the sacraments of bread and wine (the body and blood of Christ), the mystery that, to the medieval mind, gave meaning to existence: the union of the human and divine in the person of Christ and the promise of redemption through his sacrifice. All biblical events could be related to this festival, and eventually Corpus Christi became the occasion for dramas encompassing everything from the Creation to the Last Judgment. (Previously, plays about the birth of Christ had been done at Christmas, about his resurrection at Easter, and so on according to the church calendar.) Corpus Christi, observed sixty days after Easter, fell variously from May 23 to June 24. Coming during warm weather and when the days were near their longest, it was favorable to outdoor performance.

The central feature of the Corpus Christi festival was a procession through the town with the consecrated bread and wine. The church sought to involve everyone in the festival by including in the procession representatives from every rank and profession (churchmen, nobles, merchants, craftsmen). This cooperative venture marked the beginning of an association that would eventually lead to the guilds' assumption of a dominant role in the staging of outdoor religious plays. The procession may also be the forerunner of the type of staging eventually adopted in several English towns: mounting plays on wagons and performing them at various stops—a combination of procession and performance.

In the British Isles, plays were produced by about 125 different towns at some time during the Middle Ages. Nevertheless, only a few plays have survived. Most of these are parts of cycles (a number of short plays that, taken together, dramatize the Bible from Creation to Doomsday). The surviving cycles come from four towns: York (whose cycle includes forty-eight plays), Chester (twenty-four plays), Wakefield (thirty-two plays), and an unidentifiable town (forty-two plays). All of these date originally from about 1375 and were performed at intervals (that is, regularly but not every year) over the next two centuries. During that time, the cycles underwent many changes as individual plays were rewritten, new ones added, others dropped. The surviving texts show the cycles as they existed near the end of their active production life. All of the plays dealt with the same basic subject: God's ordering of existence as revealed in the Bible. Regardless of where they were written, they had many common characteristics and shared conventions.

Conventions of Medieval Theatre

A major convention of medieval drama involves the way time was handled. Throughout the Middle Ages, humanity was thought to participate in two kinds of time, eternal and earthly. God, Satan, and human souls exist in eternity—which, unlike physical being, has neither beginning nor end. Thus, earthly existence is a short interlude during which human beings must make choices that will determine how they will spend eternity—in Heaven or Hell. Medieval staging often made the human dilemma visible by using a stage that depicted Heaven at one end of a long platform and Hell at the other end (see the illustration below.). The plays illustrated this situation, especially in the Doomsday (or Last Judgment) play. Because earthly time and place were relatively unimportant, the historical period or geographical location of an event was insignificant. There was little sense of historicity in the plays: Ancient Israelites were dressed in medieval garments, and Old Testament characters referred to Christian saints.

The fluidity of time was also reflected in the structure of the cycles. Rather than treating one of many myths or a restricted story (as the Greeks and Romans did), the medieval cycles encompassed the biblical story of humanity from Creation to Doomsday. Seldom was any causal relationship established among the various plays of a cycle or even among the incidents of a single play. Events were thought

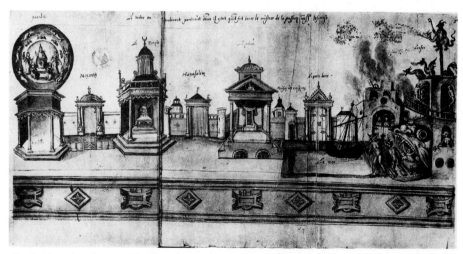

Outdoor stage used for a religious drama at Valenciennes (France). At far left, the mansion representing Heaven; at far right, the Hell mansion (including a "hell mouth"). The mansions between Hell and Heaven represent various earthly locations. This play required twenty-five days to perform. Scenes from the play are depicted in color plate 3. (Courtesy of the Bibliothèque Nationale, Paris.)

Special Effects in Religious Plays

Far greater marvels could be shown on fixed stages than on pageant wagons. Miraculous events proliferated because they reinforced belief in biblical accounts of the life of Christ. One of the most elaborate of these fixed-stage productions was mounted at Valenciennes, France, in 1547. An account (by H. d'Outreman) published almost one hundred years later gives many details, of which the following are only a few:

> The production lasted 25 days, and on each we saw strange and wonderful things. . . . we saw Truth, angels, and others descend from very high up, sometimes by visible and sometimes by invisible means. Lucifer flew out of Hell on a dragon without anyone being able to tell how. . . . Jesus was carried to the top of a wall forty feet high by the Devil. . . . The fig tree, when cursed by Our Lord, dried up and its leaves withered in a minute. Other marvels shown at the death of Our Lord included the eclipse, the earthquake, and the splitting of rocks.

An account of another play staged at Mons in 1501 tells how water was stored in wine barrels on the roofs of buildings so that during a Noah play the flood could be represented by channeling water through perforated pipes (mounted above the playing area) to create five minutes of continuous rain.

to happen simply because God willed them. Both time and place were telescoped or expanded as needed by an incident rather than according to realistic standards.

Staging also involved a number of conventions. There were no permanent theatres, so theatrical spaces were improvised. The principal requirement was that there be sufficient open space to accommodate a large audience. The stages might be either fixed or movable. Fixed stages were most typically set against buildings on one side of a town square or large courtyard, but they sometimes extended down the middle of a square (and were viewed from two or three sides) or were set up in the ruins of a Roman amphitheatre or other circular space (and were viewed in the round). A movable stage was a wagon that could be moved from one location to another.

Regardless of the type of stage or location, the staging conventions were the same everywhere. There were two parts to the stage space: *mansions* and *platea*. Mansions, used to represent locales, were scenic structures, sufficient to indicate place but not meant to do so fully. A single play might require more than one mansion, and an entire cycle might require as many as seventy. The platea was undifferentiated stage space. After the location of the action was established by relating it to a mansion, the actors could move out and appropriate as much of the adjacent stage space as the action required; this appropriated space then was considered to be part of the place represented by the mansion. Thus the same space might change its identity merely by associating it with a different mansion. Place, then, was almost as fluid as time. There was no proscenium arch or other framing device. The overall setting ultimately symbolized (as the total cycle indicates) the entire universe—human and earthly existence framed by Heaven and Hell.

Costumes were used to distinguish among the inhabitants of Earth, Heaven, and Hell. Secular, earthly characters (no matter the period or place of the action) wore contemporary medieval garments appropriate to their rank, profession, or gender because no attempt was made to achieve historical accuracy. God, the angels, the saints, and certain biblical characters wore church garments, usually differentiated by adding accessories: Angels wore church robes with wings attached, while God was dressed as a high church dignitary and often had his face gilded. Many saints and biblical personages were associated with specific symbols. For example, St. Peter carried the "keys to the Kingdom of Heaven," and the Archangel Michael wielded a flaming sword. Because such visual symbolism was common and well understood in the Middle Ages, it quickly identified characters for the audience. The greatest design imagination went into the costumes of devils, who were fancifully conceived with wings, claws, beaks, horns, or tails. The devils also often wore masks to emphasize their deformities.

There were frequently a number of spectacular special effects. Hell with its horrors was depicted with great care to make it as gruesome as possible. The entrance to Hell was often represented as the mouth of a fire-breathing monster (the "Hell mouth"). Many miracles described in the Bible were staged as convincingly as possible to reinforce faith. Nevertheless, the illusion of actuality was not always a goal, because several widely separated places were usually juxtaposed within a limited stage space and represented by fragmentary scenery. Thus, medieval staging ranged between illusionistic and symbolic devices. Overall, conventions permitted rapid switches from broad outline to specific detail, asking the audience to use its eyes in a way analogous to present-day cinematography—focusing in, pulling back, cutting from one locale to another. Much in medieval staging may now seem naive, but in its time it made efficient use of conventions that evoked the human condition as the medieval mind understood it.

The Wakefield Cycle

Let us look at the English cycle staged at Wakefield, a town in central England. The surviving manuscript of this cycle contains thirty-two plays, beginning with the Creation and extending through the Last Judgment. As with all the cycles, the authors (there appear to have been several) are anonymous. Most medieval artists did not strive for individual glory and recognition, but contented themselves with serving God, the church, and the community. Some of the Wakefield plays are borrowed from other cycles, while others have qualities suggesting varied origins. Five of the plays are by the same unknown author, usually referred to as "the Wakefield Master." His plays are noted for their details of everyday life and their comic scenes. One of these, *Noah and His Sons,* will be examined more fully later.

The production of the Wakefield cycle was a community effort involving the town council, the church, and the guilds. The council decided if the plays were to be performed in a particular year, but the church had to agree to this decision, because

Pageant wagon showing the Nativity. Mary, Joseph, and the Christ child are between the two columns at center. (From a painting by Denis van Alsloot of a celebration in Brussels in honor of a visiting ruler in 1615. Courtesy of the Victoria and Albert Museum, London.)

the plays were part of a church festival. The church also had to approve the play texts to ensure that they did not distort church doctrine. There was an official copy of the cycle, which had to be adhered to in performance. The usual rationale for presenting the plays was "to honor God, to edify man, and to glorify the city." Most of the actual work of production was undertaken by the guilds.

The decision to perform the plays apparently was made several months prior to Corpus Christi. One official document is dated September 29, thus permitting nine months of preparation, although it is not certain how much of this time was devoted to preparation. Individual plays apparently were assigned according to a perceived relationship between a guild's specialty and the events of a play. The assignments at Wakefield have not survived, but we know that at other places the shipwrights, fishers, or mariners were assigned plays dealing with Noah (the ark and the Flood), while the goldsmiths were usually given the play in which the Three Kings bring gifts to the Christ child. Sometimes the connections are not immediately apparent. At Chester, the shepherds' play was assigned to the painters, while at York it was assigned to the candlemakers (perhaps because they used tallow from sheep in making candles). Each guild was expected to assume the costs of producing its play, and the city council levied fines against those who failed to fulfill their obligations adequately.

At Wakefield, processional staging appears to have been used. Each play was mounted on a pageant wagon (similar to a modern float in a Rose Bowl parade) and drawn through the streets from one playing place to another in the order indicated in the script. No reliable description of a pageant wagon has survived. The wagons were probably as large as the narrow streets would accommodate and were probably designed to meet the requirements of specific plays. Because the same guild always produced the same play, its pageant wagon and scenery could be designed and built to meet the specific requirements of its play. The wagons could be stored and refurbished as needed for subsequent festivals. Each wagon usually had to carry one or more mansions and might require some machinery for special effects. It seems probable that at each playing place the wagon was drawn up alongside a stationary platform that served as the platea. The actors sometimes performed scenes in the street. (See the illustrations on pages 94 and 95 for conjectures about how the performance space was arranged.)

In addition to providing the pageant wagon and its equipment, each guild had to supply performers and someone to oversee the production. All of the personnel involved in production were amateurs, but as time went by some became quite skilled and seem to have approached the status of professionals. Surviving records sometimes show that one actor was paid much more than the others; thus it seems likely that he was in charge of the total production (that is, served as director). Some guilds put the same person under contract for several years to stage their part of the cycle. Actors were recruited from the local populace and were not restricted

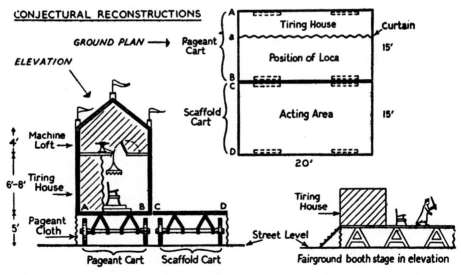

At left, a pageant wagon alongside a wheeled platform stage; above, a floor plan of this arrangement; below right, plan of a booth stage, used to show its similarity to the pageant wagon arrangement of the other two drawings. Reconstructions by Glynne Wickham. (From Wickham, *Early English Stages*, 1 [1959]. Courtesy of Routledge Publishers.)

to members of the guild producing that play. We do not know how many rehearsals were held, but the plays were relatively short, and often the same actor played the same role at many different festivals. All of the actors were male, female roles being played by boys or young men.

Costumes, for the most part, consisted of clothing in common use in medieval England and were usually supplied by the actors or borrowed. Church robes, the starting point for ecclesiastical and angel costumes, could be borrowed or rented from the church, but the costumes of devils had to be made.

Each guild rehearsed and prepared its play separately from the others. No dress rehearsal of the entire cycle was needed because coordinating the individual plays merely required that the pageant wagons be lined up in the correct order.

The council specified the places at which the plays would be performed; at Wakefield there probably were two or three. Actors were required to be in their pageant wagons by 5:00 A.M., presumably the starting time. When all was ready, the first wagon moved to the first performance place, where the actors performed the play, and then moved on to the next. Thus, all of the plays were performed in the prescribed order at each of the designated places.

On the day of performances, all normal work was suspended; most of the town's residents must have crowded into the places designated for the performances. Word about the performances was usually sent to neighboring towns, and a large number of spectators probably came from outside Wakefield. Provisions for the audience were not extensive, other than choosing sites that permitted a crowd to assemble. The majority of spectators stood, although some seating may have been erected. The windows and roofs of houses overlooking the performance place were in great demand and probably were rented. The council's proclamation provided that sizable fines were to be levied against anyone who disturbed the plays or hindered their procession; carrying weapons was forbidden. Even if the performances began at 5:00 A.M., they probably required all the daylight hours (at that time of the year in central England until around 10:00 P.M.) to complete the full cycle at all the prescribed stops. That would have made for a very long day, but spectators were as mobile as the wagons and could move from one viewing place to another, watch only some of the plays, move forward or back along the route, choose how long they wanted to stay. The atmosphere must have been as festive as it was reverential. It was both a holiday and a holy day.

It is impossible here to examine in detail a performance of the entire Wakefield cycle. Therefore, we will look at one play, considered by many to be one of the best of all the English cycle plays. It is the cycle's third play, *Noah and His Sons*.

Noah and His Sons

Before the spectators saw *Noah and His Sons* they had already viewed two others, *The Creation* and *The Killing of Abel*. *Noah*, then, comes very early in the overall cycle of thirty-two plays. This 558-line play is an elaboration of biblical passages from Genesis (chapters 6 through 10).

Noah, one part of *The Mystery Plays* as performed at the Hartford Stage. Adapted by John Russell Brown; directed by Mary B. Robinson. (Photo by Lanny Nagler. Courtesy of the Hartford Stage Company.)

The play begins with Noah praying to God and contrasting God's goodness toward all creatures with the ungrateful responses of those He has created, not only human beings but also Lucifer, whose rebelliousness has caused him to be cast out of Heaven. God, unseen by Noah, continues this lamentation, condemning the wickedness of human beings and promising to destroy them all—except faithful Noah and his family. He then appears to Noah and orders him to build a ship, giving him precise directions about its size and layout. He also orders Noah to take his family and a pair of every known beast into the ship so they may be saved from a flood that will destroy all creatures not on the ship.

The solemn tone of this opening expository scene, which takes up approximately one-third of the play, is abruptly broken when Noah returns home to his wife, who immediately begins to berate him for being an incompetent provider. Their dispute rapidly escalates into an exchange of blows, in which both participate equally. This scene redirects the play's tone toward domestic comedy and relocates the biblical action within the familiar world of the English audience.

Noah then turns to carrying out God's orders and, without any assistance and within a space of twenty-five lines, builds the ship. There follows a lengthy segment during which Noah's three sons and their wives board the ship and seek to persuade Noah's wife to do likewise. Another fight occurs between husband and wife, during which they seemingly beat each other thoroughly, before the wife agrees to come aboard (and then only because the water is rising around her). The remainder of the play takes place on the ship, where a year of domestic harmony passes in the midst of anxiety about their plight, as they measure the depth of the water and send out birds in search of signs that land has reappeared. Eventually, the waters recede, and the play ends with prayers that human beings will profit from Noah's example and reconcile themselves to the will of God.

The action of the play is divided almost equally among three parts: One-third is devoted to the opening expository scene; one-third to the two scenes of bickering between Noah and his wife; and one third to the shipbuilding and on-board scenes. Time is severely telescoped in the third part. No clues are given as to how much time elapses during the building of the ship, but in the final scene Noah speaks of forty days of rain and of having been on board for 350 days.

There are nine roles, of which six are very minor—those of Noah's sons and their wives. They seem to be there only because the biblical source includes them. Their lines are very few. They do not help build the ship; they figure primarily in the scene in which they assist Noah in coaxing his wife on board; they have no lines again until the end of the play. Characterization of the three main roles is simple. God magisterially voices feelings of having been betrayed by his ungrateful creations and announces his decision to destroy them. His benevolence is seen only in his attitude toward Noah and his family. Noah, who claims to be more than six hundred years old, is pious and obedient. His life apparently has been tranquil except where it involves his wife. Despite his wife's claim that Noah is incompetent, he seems unusually efficient in building the ship and carrying out God's instructions. Nevertheless, he would have seemed comical to medieval audiences because of his inability to control his wife. Noah's wife is clearly very headstrong and independent. She resists being bossed about by anyone and insists on her right to gossip with her friends. She apparently is an industrious housewife, always spinning, and once on board shares responsibility equally with Noah. All of the roles would have been played by men; having Noah's wife played by a man probably contributed to making the quarrelling and fighting more acceptably comic. The realistic bickering and highly physical fights help to balance the necessarily nonrealistic scenes—building the ship, the forty days of rain, and the year of floating on the floodwaters.

The script seems to demand stylized speech. It is written in sixty-two nine-line stanzas, each using the same structure. The first four lines use a double rhyme scheme: The final words of the lines rhyme, as do words halfway through those lines. The fifth and ninth lines are short and rhyme, while lines six through eight, somewhat longer than five and nine, also rhyme. Thus, rhythmical speech is a basic structural element.

Only one mansion is required—the ship. It seems likely that a pageant wagon was fitted out to represent a ship and that the ship was initially concealed by a cloth that was gradually removed during the short scene in which Noah supposedly

Noah, from *The Mystery Cycle,* adapted by Bernard Sahlins, as performed at the Court Theatre (Chicago). Noah is shown steering the ark. Directed by Nicholas Rudall and Bernard Sahlins. (Photo © Matthew Gilson; courtesy Court Theatre.)

builds it. It also seems likely that the ship was supplied with cutouts or painted cloths representing animals because only one line mentions getting "gear, cattle, and company" on board. The initial scene and the scenes with Noah's wife required no mansions. The opening scene probably was played with God standing atop the ship with Noah on the platform adjacent to the pageant wagon. The scenes with the wife also probably were played on the platform. When Noah leaves to build the ship, he declares that he must take his tools along—the only stage property that is mentioned in the script other than the spinning wheel, straps that figure in the beating scenes, and a plumb line that is lowered to measure the depth of the water. The raven and doves sent out to search for signs of life may have been actual birds. The costuming was simple. All the characters except God would have worn contemporary working-class dress. God would have been costumed in garments associated with the pope or some other high church official.

Because the spectators crowded around the performance space, the actors were seen at close range by many, and the total configuration of the playing places meant that the performance was viewed from a variety of angles. Thus, the spatial relationship between audience and performer and the overall scale differed markedly from those of the Greek and Roman theatres. In addition, the degree of formalization apparently was less than in classical theatres, for most elements of performance in *Noah*, though perhaps somewhat exaggerated, were variations on things familiar to the audience.

As the play ended, the wagon moved on to another site and was replaced by the next wagon, bearing a play about Abraham and Isaac. Twenty-nine more short plays would be performed before the day ended.

Other Medieval Theatre and Drama

In addition to religious plays, several other dramatic types were popular during the Middle Ages, among them moralities, farces, and interludes. *Morality plays* flourished between 1400 and 1550. Unlike the religious plays, which treated biblical or saintly characters, morality plays treated the spiritual trials of ordinary persons. They were allegories about the moral temptations that beset all human beings. The protagonist (often called Everyman or Mankind) was advised and cajoled by personifications of good and evil; most frequently the protagonist succumbed to temptation but was eventually recalled to the path of righteousness by a character called Faith or Mercy or by the grace of God. The most famous morality play is *Everyman*, in which God orders Death to summon the title character. Everyman, who has been too busy leading a carefree existence to think about death, now seeks among his companions (Kindred, Knowledge, Five Wits, Beauty, Strength, and so on) for one that will accompany him on his journey, but once they know his destination, they decline his invitation. Ultimately only Good Deeds goes into the grave

A booth stage used by traveling players in Europe during the Middle Ages. Redrawing of an illustration from a fifteenth-century manuscript. (From *L'Ancienne France: Le Théâtre . . .* [1887].)

Everyman. An illustration published in the edition of 1530. At left, Everyman; at right, Death. The entrance to the tomb is seen at lower right.

with him. Through this search, Everyman comes to understand the relationship of his earthly life to salvation.

During the sixteenth century, the morality play was gradually secularized, as its original moral concerns were replaced by new ones such as the ideal training of rulers and the content of a proper education. Then, when religious controversies erupted, moralities were used to attack one's opponents, Protestants or Catholics, by associating one's own side with good and one's enemies with evil. Such changes moved the morality play increasingly toward a wholly secular drama; thus it served as a transition between the medieval religious drama and the secular drama of Shakespeare's time.

A comic secular drama, *farce* began to emerge around the thirteenth century, but, because the form was not officially encouraged, it remained a minor though highly entertaining type, emphasizing the ridiculous and comically depraved aspects of human behavior. One of the best examples is *Pierre Patelin,* an anonymous French farce of the fifteenth century that dramatizes the story of an impoverished lawyer who buys a piece of cloth from a merchant, whom he invites to dinner to receive his payment. When the merchant arrives, Patelin is in bed and his wife swears he has not been out of the house. Patelin pretends madness, beats the merchant, and drives him away without payment for the cloth. This story is loosely joined to a second in which Patelin agrees to defend a shepherd against a charge of stealing sheep. He counsels the shepherd that during the trial he should answer only "Baa" no matter what anyone says to him. The accuser turns out to be the cloth merchant, who creates total confusion during the proceedings by his alternating charges against the shepherd and Patelin. In view of this confusion and the shepherd's seeming feeblemindedness, the judge dismisses the case, but when Patelin tries to

An interlude performed during a medieval banquet. In the background St. George is on his horse; he will fight and slay the dragon (center right). The ruler's table is at center back. Notice the spectators in the gallery (upper left). (From Pougin, *Dictionnaire . . . du Théâtre* [1885].)

collect his fee, the shepherd runs away, calling "Baa." Like many farces, *Pierre Patelin* shows clever knaves outwitting each other, but it adds a comic twist by having the seemingly stupid shepherd outwit the experienced lawyer.

The *interlude* was a nonreligious serious or comic play so called because it was performed between the parts of a celebration (such as between the courses of a banquet, usually for some festival or special occasion). It was associated with the rise of professional performers, who developed their art in the specialized entertainments presented in the households of kings and nobles. Eventually these servants were permitted, when not needed at home, to travel about and perform for pay. Thus the interlude is associated with the rise of both the professional actor and the professional theatre.

In addition to those discussed here, many other celebrations utilized theatrical elements, for the Middle Ages were a time when religious and secular ceremony played an important role in people's lives. Amidst the diversity, the religious drama was the most important and characteristic. More than any other type, it appealed to (and actively involved) the largest cross section of the populace and most fully embodied those concerns that the age idealized—the biblical vision of human history and destiny.

Comparing Greek, Roman, and Medieval Theatre

The Greek, Roman, and medieval theatre experiences, then, were alike in some ways and quite unlike in others. For the most part, they were occasional (that is, performances were given on special occasions and not on a continuing, everyday basis as in modern times); ceremonial (performances were part of religious festivals and considered offerings to gods); financed by the state, religious or secular organizations, or wealthy citizens; and open to all. They also used many similar conventions: male performers only, musical accompaniment, large audience spaces, and formalized scenic backgrounds. Greek and Roman theatre used masks for all characters (except in mime); medieval theatre used masks for devils and sometimes for allegorical characters.

There were many differences. In Greek theatre, the chorus played a large role, as did dance. In Roman theatre, the musical element was more equally distributed throughout the play and was associated with the actors more than with the chorus. In medieval theatre, music was plentiful but followed no fixed plan. The theatre structures also differed. But the most important differences were those reflecting basic values. The Greeks seem to have placed great emphasis on moral values and significant issues, whereas the Romans were more concerned with popular entertainment, and medieval theatre was tied to Christian teaching.

Creating a Professional Theatre: Elizabethan England, Italian Commedia dell'Arte, and Seventeenth-Century France

Shakespeare's *Cymbeline* as produced by the Huntington Theatre Company (Boston). Directed by Larry Carpenter; scenery by John Falabella; costumes by David Murin; and lighting by Marcia Madeira. (Photo by Richard Feldman.)

[The third phase in the development of theatre brings] an incursion of the secular; the shows decrease in scale, the performers decrease in number, . . . but a more specialized note creeps in. Professionalism begins. The seasonal element recedes; the religious gives place to the satirical or the philosophical. . . . And the show is designed for a far smaller and more particular audience, an audience which is sometimes indoors.

—Richard Southern, *The Seven Ages of the Theatre*

The theatrical experiences we have examined so far were parts of festivals sponsored by governmental or religious authorities, performed on special occasions, and financed by the state or wealthy citizens. Although there were other types of performance, they were considered inferior. Then, during the sixteenth and seventeenth centuries, the role of theatre in European society was redefined.

Among the forces that brought about change was a growing secularization of thought as people became more interested in life here and now and less preoccupied with preparing for the life hereafter. As interest in earthly concerns increased, a rebirth of learning occurred in many fields that had long been neglected. This period of rebirth is often referred to as the Renaissance. Scholars, artists, and others turned their attention once more to Greece and Rome, both of which had played a relatively minor role during the Middle Ages, in part because so many classical works had been lost or destroyed and others were ignored because, as pagan creations, they were considered to be dangerous. Those that had continued to be used were interpreted in ways that obscured their pagan origins. Elements of the classical world that received revived interest included Greek and Roman plays and theatrical practices, even though during the Renaissance understanding of the classical theatre was severely limited and often distorted. Nevertheless, educated people began to perceive alternatives to medieval practices, and playwrights began to write plays that imitated or adapted classical subjects and forms or that mingled medieval and classical elements.

The Renaissance spirit of inquiry also extended to religion. During the sixteenth century disputes over church doctrine and practice led to secessions from the Roman Catholic church and the formation of several Protestant sects. Various factions soon found theatrical performance a good propaganda medium (especially because the majority of the audience could not read), and they exploited it in plays that ridiculed their opponents and upheld their own views. Disputes often erupted into violence, even wars. Rulers were forced to choose sides in religious controversies. In England, the official state religion changed four times during the sixteenth century, and each time many people were executed because of their refusal to accept the changes. These struggles served to shift the center of power to the state and away from the church, which had been the dominant force throughout the Middle Ages.

Under these circumstances, it is not surprising that by 1550 both church and state had begun to look for ways to reduce disturbances. Shortly after Elizabeth I succeeded to the English throne in 1558, she decreed that no plays dealing with religious or political subjects were to be performed. This decree, in effect, was the death knell for the cycle plays. By 1600, they had all but disappeared, not only in England but throughout Europe, where similar prohibitions existed. A type of theatrical experience—the outdoor religious play—that had enjoyed enormous popularity for more than two hundred years was now forbidden by the same institutions (church and state) that had encouraged and supported it.

Forbidden to perform plays on religious subjects, the theatre had to become secular, and for its subjects it turned to classical literature, historical chronicles, and legends. In part out of necessity, a new kind of drama was born. Perhaps more important, an alternative kind of theatre had to be invented. Because the state, church, and wealthy individuals had withdrawn or curtailed their patronage, other kinds of support had to be found. The theatre was forced to become a commercial enterprise. Rather than remaining occasional (part of a religious festival), officially supported, and free, it became continuous, self-supporting, and sufficiently entertaining to keep a paying public coming back.

Those who had been the most enthusiastic supporters of the religious cycles were the most vehement opponents of a professional theatre. To them, the presentation of plays for the glory of God, the honor of the city, and the edification of citizens seemed a worthy goal, but devoting one's life to performing plays for money was considered wasteful and sinful. The guilds that had produced many of the cycle plays in England sought to have the professional theatre banned on the grounds that it took people away from work, encouraged immoral behavior, spread diseases, and offered cover for seditious activities. Guilds saw the professional theatre in a different light than they had viewed the largely amateur theatre of the Middle Ages.

To survive, professional groups had to be able to play often, had to have a stock of plays sufficiently large and varied to keep the limited available audience coming back, had to have a performance space large enough to accommodate a sizable number of paying customers and sufficiently enclosed to permit the company to control access and collect entrance fees. They also had to own or control their own costumes, scenery, and other production elements, and had to assemble a company of actors and production personnel that could devote full time to theatrical production and performance.

Accomplishing these tasks was difficult because in the sixteenth century acting was not an accepted profession, and did not fit into the then-dominant trade-guild scheme under which there was a clear-cut hierarchy of responsibility under which each master was held responsible for the journeymen and apprentices who worked for him. Because actors did not belong to a guild, they were considered "masterless men," meaning that no one was considered to be responsible for them; they fell into the category of vagrants who, because of their threat to the social order, were subject to arrest and punishment. To get around this difficulty, acting companies petitioned noblemen to serve as their patrons; technically, actors became "servants" of these patrons and therefore were no longer masterless. For this reason, during Shakespeare's time the acting companies had such titles as the Lord Admiral's Men, the Lord Chamberlain's Men, and the King's Men as indications of their legal status. Without the patronage of rulers and noblemen, the professional theatre would have had difficulty surviving. Nevertheless, patronage brought little financial support.

If this system protected the companies, it also imposed restrictions because rulers insisted that every company have a license from the crown and that every play be approved before being performed. Such licensing made it possible for the ruler to ensure that the companies did not perform plays that might stir up political or religious controversy. Despite the legal status that acting companies achieved through the patronage of nobles and the licenses issued by the crown, the London city council (composed of guild members who opposed theatre) sought to forbid performances within the city. Consequently, when permanent theatres were built, they were erected outside the city limits.

Despite these problems, by 1600 English acting companies were creating what many consider the greatest theatrical era the world has known.

Shakespeare and the Globe Theatre

The reputation of the Elizabethan theatre rests above all on the work of William Shakespeare (1564–1616), perhaps the greatest playwright of all time, and the company of which he was a member (the Lord Chamberlain's Men, later the King's Men). Shakespeare was only one of many significant dramatists of his time. Others included Thomas Kyd, Christopher Marlowe, Ben Jonson, John Fletcher, and John Webster, all of whom contributed to making the years between 1585 and 1642 exceptionally effective.

Theatrical conditions favored the development of playwriting. From the 1580s until 1642, there were always at least two (and sometimes as many as four) companies playing in or around London. Because they performed six times a week (every day except Sunday) in the afternoon (beginning around 2:00 P.M.) during normal working hours, and because London was still a relatively small city of around two hundred thousand, the companies were in strong competition for audiences. They

The Swan Theatre, London, 1596. This is the only surviving drawing made of an English public theatre during Shakespeare's lifetime. It shows three levels of seating in galleries, a stage jutting to the middle of an unroofed yard, a roof canopy over part of the stage, and two doors at the rear of the stage (but no "discovery space" between the doors.) (Bapst, *Essai sur l'Histoire du Théâtre* [1893].)

could not rely on long runs; normally, they changed the bill every day. New plays were performed once and then at intervals from time to time thereafter until they lost their appeal. In the 1590s, a London company produced a new play about every seventeen days. The average life of a play was ten performances (that is, the total number of times played—spread over one or more seasons—before it was dropped from the repertory). New plays were in constant demand, a situation obviously favorable to playwrights. This situation has certain parallels in present-day television, where new episodes of series are offered each week in an attempt to keep audiences tuning in to the same channel. This parallel can be extended further in that Shakespeare and his contemporaries, like the writers of television series, did not consider their plays literary works; Shakespeare, like today's television writers, did not seek publication of his plays. Not until 1616, when Ben Jonson collected and published all of his own dramas, did plays begin to gain the status of literature. Shakespeare's plays were not collected and published until several years after his death.

Playwrights had an incentive to be prolific. After a company had paid the dramatist for a play, it belonged to the company, and the author received no further income from it. A writer who depended entirely on plays for a living had to sell four or five a year. Shakespeare seems to have written about two a year, but he was also an actor and a major shareholder in his company (that is, he was a part owner of the company's assets and was involved in running the company) and after 1599 was part owner of the Globe theatre, in which the company performed. Thus he was involved in almost every aspect of the theatre and became wealthier than most of his fellow dramatists.

In addition to a steady supply of new plays, a company needed a performance space. After the professional theatre began to establish a foothold, buildings intended specifically for theatrical performances began to be erected in Europe for the first time since the fall of Rome. In England, the first was the Red Lion (built in 1567), but the best known of the early playhouses was The Theatre (built in 1576). Others soon followed. While the English public theatres varied in details, all had similar features that drew on medieval conventions but transformed them.

Let us look at the Globe, the theatre used by Shakespeare's company after 1599 and of which Shakespeare was part owner. Basically round with an exterior diameter of approximately ninety-nine feet, the Globe had three levels of roofed galleries, each about twelve and one-half feet deep. These galleries enclosed an unroofed open space (the yard) approximately seventy-four feet in diameter. The stage extended to the middle of the yard. Approximately forty-one feet three inches wide and twenty-four feet nine inches deep and raised five to six feet above the yard, the stage was viewed from three sides by spectators seated in the galleries or standing in the yard. The stage was sheltered by a roof ("the heavens" or "the shadow") supported by two posts near the front of the stage platform. At the back of the stage platform was a multilevel facade. On the stage level, at least two large doors permitted exits and entrances and served as openings through which stage properties could be moved onto and off the stage. These doors were the most essential part of the background. Changes of locale were often indicated by the exit of characters through one door, followed by the entrance of different characters through another door. Usually, the doors remained unlocalized, but at times they were used to

Conjectural reconstruction of the interior of the Globe. Drawing by C. Walter Hodges. (From *The Third Globe: Symposium for the Reconstruction of the Globe Playhouse* [1981]. Courtesy Wayne State University Press.)

represent houses, city gates, castles, or other places (what they represented, if important, was indicated in the dialogue). There may have been a larger space between the doors that could be used to make "discoveries" (reveal objects or persons hidden until the crucial moment), common occurrences in the plays of Shakespeare and other dramatists of the time. Some believe that the stage doors were used for this purpose, but others argue that there was something like a small inner stage that could be concealed or revealed by a curtain. The second level of the facade included an acting space used to represent balconies (as in *Romeo and Juliet*), windows, battlements, or other high places. There may have been a playing area on the third level as well, but this has not been verified.

Overall, then, this stage was an adaptation of medieval conventions. The facade served the function of mansions in the medieval stage, while the stage platform served as platea. Stage properties, such as tables, thrones, tents, beds, altars, and scaffolds, were sometimes brought onto the stage, usually because the action demanded them rather than to localize a scene. This stage also had some things in common with those of Greece and Rome. The background for all scenes was the formalized facade, and the specific location of a scene was established primarily through dialogue. When place was important, the characters named or described it. This conventional way of establishing the setting is sometimes called "spoken decor." This Elizabethan structure and the conventions governing its use greatly facilitated staging because one scene could flow into another without a pause for changing scenery. The playwright had almost unlimited freedom in handling time and place.

The conventions that governed costuming and lighting also resembled those of the medieval theatre. Most characters, regardless of the historical era of the action, were clothed in Elizabethan garments appropriate to their rank, age, and profession. Other kinds of costumes were used sparingly: Greek and Roman characters

Sketch (supposedly made in 1595) showing characters from Shakespeare's *Titus Andronicus*. Notice the variety of costumes. The male character standing at center wears drapery suggesting Roman times; the character at extreme right also has some features suggesting the classical era. The others wear Elizabethan costumes. Some scholars consider this drawing a forgery. (Reproduced by permission of the Marquess of Bath, Longleat House, Warminster, Wiltshire, England.)

were often identified by drapery superimposed on Elizabethan dress; ghosts, witches, fairies, and allegorical figures were dressed in fanciful garments corresponding to accepted ideas of the appearance of such creatures; sometimes racial or national stereotypes (Jews, Moors, Turks) were indicated by dress. Costumes and banners accounted for much of the color and pageantry of Elizabethan theatre, because there were many processions, battles, and celebrations. Maintaining an adequate wardrobe was one of a company's greatest expenses. Lighting was not a major problem because performances took place in unroofed structures during daylight hours. Darkness was indicated either in dialogue or by torches, lanterns, or candles carried by characters.

Most important was the acting company itself. It was made up of about twenty-five persons, of whom about half were shareholders (part owners of the company's assets). The shareholders made all important decisions, played most of the major roles, and shared any profit. A number of hired men were paid weekly wages as actors, prompters, musicians, stagehands, or wardrobe-keepers. There were also four to six apprentices—boys who played female roles. All members of the company were male. (There were no English actresses until 1661.) Because the plays often included a large number of characters, there was much double casting, and, because a company usually performed a different play each day, each actor was responsible for a large number of roles. Although the overall performance style was probably not realistic in the modern sense, it was considerably closer to everyday behavior and appearance than a Greek performance. Elizabethan actors did not wear masks (except as disguises), all lines were spoken, and behavior was based on that familiar to the audience. The conventions that most removed the performances from realism were the verse in which much of the dialogue was written, the use of males to play female roles, and the formalized background.

Elizabethan theatre included a considerable musical element. Trumpets sounded flourishes to mark the entrances of kings, to call attention to important announcements, and to serve as signals in the numerous battles. Music accompanied songs and dances in many plays; most performances concluded with a jig (a short, lively music-and-dance piece).

Shakespeare's Actors

Shakespeare's company included many skilled actors. Among these, the most accomplished apparently was Richard Burbage (c. 1569–1619), for whom Shakespeare wrote many of his most challenging roles. Burbage created not only the role of Hamlet but also those of Romeo, King Lear, Othello, Richard III, Henry V, and Shylock. Son of James Burbage, an actor and builder of theatres, he acted from an early age until his death. He was noted for his natural, sensitive, and refined performances. The following funeral elegy was written about him at the time of his death:

> He's gone and with him what a world are dead!
> No more young Hamlet, old Hieronymo,
> King Lear, the grieved Moor, and more beside
> That lived in him have now forever died.
> Oft have I seen him leap into a grave,
> Suiting the person (which he used to have)
> Of a mad lover with so true an eye
> That there I would have sworn he meant to die.
> Oft have I seen him play his part in jest
> So lively that spectators and the rest
> Of his crews, whilst he did but seem to bleed,
> Amazed, thought he had been dead indeed.

—*Reprinted in* Gentleman's Magazine, *June 1826*

Shakespeare wrote his female roles for boy actors. Although we are inclined to think that the playgoer of Shakespeare's day must have regretted not seeing female roles played by actresses, the English not only considered it immoral for women to appear on a public stage, but also apparently believed that boys played female roles more effectively than women could. Thomas Coryat, an Englishman who witnessed some theatrical performances in Venice in 1608, recorded in *Coryat's Crudities* his wonder both at seeing actresses and at their skill: "I saw women act, a thing that I never saw before, . . . and they performed it with as good a grace, action, gesture, and whatsoever convenient for a Player, as ever I saw any masculine Actor."

The Oregon Shakespeare Festival stage during a performance of *The Taming of the Shrew*. This stage attempts to recreate the features of an English public theatre. (Photo by Hank Kranzler. Courtesy Oregon Shakespeare Festival.)

Elizabethan acting companies learned quickly how to make the theatre fully professional and sufficiently attractive and remunerative to support a large number of persons. The other important ingredient was the paying audience, among whom backgrounds and tastes varied considerably. The plays usually included something for everyone. Shakespeare's plays have plots as complex as a modern soap opera and often have as much violence as a television police series, but they also use poetic language and other devices that direct attention to the significance of events and provide insights into human behavior so profound that the plays have retained their appeal.

A small general-admission fee permitted one to stand in the yard. Those who wished to sit had to pay a larger fee for admission to the galleries. Entry to the few private boxes in the galleries ("lords' rooms") required a still larger fee. The Globe probably held about three thousand persons, although seldom did that many attend. The configuration of the theatre (with the stage jutting to the middle of the yard) meant that no one was very far from the stage. There were no intermissions, and wine, beer, ale, nuts, and playing cards were sold in the theatres by vendors who circulated during performances. The atmosphere must have been somewhat like that of a modern sports event. Keeping the audience quiet and attentive depended on the power of the play and the skill of the performers.

Let us look at *Hamlet,* one of the thirty-eight plays by Shakespeare that has come down to us. It is representative of Elizabethan drama in its story, structure, and conventions, but, one of the world's great tragedies, it is superior to most plays of its time.

Hamlet

Like *Oedipus the King, Hamlet* concerns a man charged with the duty of punishing the murderer of a king. But Shakespeare uses a broader canvas than Sophocles and includes within his drama more facets of the story, more characters, and a wider sweep of time and place.

Shakespeare organizes his action with great skill. The opening scene, in which the Ghost of Hamlet's father appears at midnight on the castle ramparts, quickly captures attention and establishes a mood of mystery as well as expectation of revelations to come. The remainder of Act I introduces the main characters and establishes the dramatic situation—that Hamlet's father, the former king, has been murdered by his brother Claudius, the present king and new husband to Hamlet's mother, but that no one—other than the Ghost, Claudius, and Hamlet—knows this. The revelation of the murder to Hamlet by the Ghost and the Ghost's demand

Hamlet as produced at the American Repertory Theatre (Cambridge, MA). Directed by Ron Daniels; scenery and costumes by Antony McDonald; lighting by Frances Aronson. (Photo by Richard Feldman.)

Freud on Hamlet

Sigmund Freud (1856–1939), the pioneer of psychoanalysis, often turned to drama for examples of behavior that exemplified psychological conditions. According to Freud, "falling in love with one parent and hating the other forms part of the permanent stock of the psychic impulses which arise in early childhood." He used the story of Oedipus as an example of the male child's desire to kill his father and marry his mother. Freud declared that Hamlet also suffers from an Oedipus complex, and that this explains why Hamlet cannot bring himself to kill Claudius, because Claudius has done what Hamlet would have liked to do. "Hamlet is able to do anything but take vengeance upon the man who did away with his father and has taken his father's place with his mother—the man who shows him in realization the repressed desires of his own childhood."

—*"On Oedipus and Hamlet"*

that Hamlet revenge his death is the inciting incident that sets the central action of the play in motion. Hamlet, though he wishes to believe the Ghost's charge, cannot be certain that the Ghost has not been sent by the Devil to tempt him into a deed that will damn his soul. Therefore he seeks confirmation of the Ghost's accusations. He is so torn that in Act II others question whether he has lost his sanity, and he is so disillusioned by his mother's behavior that he rejects Ophelia, the woman he loves. Hamlet's search for confirmation of the Ghost's charge reaches its climax in Act III, Scene 2, when Claudius' response to a play, whose action parallels the murder of Hamlet's father, establishes his guilt. But this scene also reveals to Claudius that Hamlet is aware of the murder; consequently, Hamlet—who until this point has been the pursuer—now becomes the pursued. The remainder of the play shows Claudius intriguing to have Hamlet killed in ways that will not draw suspicion to himself. Hamlet kills Polonius, thinking it is Claudius eavesdropping on him and his mother; Claudius uses this as an excuse to send Hamlet to England, accompanied by Hamlet's supposed friends Rosencrantz and Guildenstern, with a letter commanding the ruler there to kill Hamlet. But Hamlet escapes and returns to Denmark just in time for Ophelia's funeral.

Shakespeare skillfully interweaves this main plot with the subplot concerning Polonius and his family. The two strands of action are related through Hamlet's love for Polonius' daughter, Ophelia, Polonius' relation to the king as his principal advisor, and Laertes' wish to revenge his father's death after Hamlet kills Polonius and Ophelia goes mad. The final scene, during which Claudius' plan to have Hamlet killed by Laertes (in a fencing match for which Laertes uses a poisoned foil), ends not only in Hamlet's death but also in that of Gertrude, Laertes, and Claudius, thereby resolving both the main plot and the subplot.

All of the main characters in *Hamlet* are drawn from the nobility or aristocracy. Shakespeare does not tell us the age of his characters or reveal much about their physical appearance. Nevertheless, age and contrast are important. The young and innocent—Hamlet, Ophelia, and Laertes—suffer most.

Many people consider Hamlet to be among the most demanding roles ever written for a tragic actor, in part because the actor must project one set of attitudes and responses to the characters and another to the audience. So carefully balanced are the demands that an ongoing controversy has developed over whether Hamlet feigns madness in Acts II and III or whether for a time he actually is mad. Another controversy concerns whether Hamlet procrastinates unduly. Some critics have argued that Hamlet is so sensitive that he cannot at first bring himself to kill Claudius; others argue that it is not Hamlet's sensitivity but his desire to be certain of Claudius' guilt that causes him to delay, and that he acts as quickly as circumstances permit. Hamlet is a sensitive young man who, faced with a series of disillusioning revelations, procrastinates until the final scenes, when—recognizing Claudius' villainy not only against the dead king but also against others—he acts decisively. The actor playing this role is faced with a range of complex emotional responses, ambiguous speeches and actions, and with keeping energy under great restraint until the final scenes, when it bursts forth.

Like Hamlet, Ophelia is sensitive; having little knowledge of the world, she is easily led by her father, Polonius. Hamlet's seeming rejection of her and his killing of her father come as such shocks that she becomes truly mad (rather than feigning madness, as Hamlet apparently does). Her brother, Laertes, who is near Hamlet in age, rushes into action instead of hesitating when faced with a situation comparable to that with which Hamlet must deal. Claudius, playing on Laertes' impulsiveness, is able to talk him into a deception (the use of the poisoned foil) contrary to his nature—which he repents, although too late. One may conclude that, while Claudius, Gertrude, and Polonius deserve their fates, the young people are victims of their elders' weaknesses.

Claudius is doubtless suave and charming; otherwise it would be difficult to understand how he is able to deceive so many people. He has won the support of the court, he has seduced Gertrude (who apparently is unaware that he has murdered her husband), and he easily takes in Laertes. Not until the final scene do most of the characters perceive Claudius' villainy. Claudius' surface respectability also provides an explanation for Hamlet's hesitation to act hastily or openly because Hamlet probably would not have been believed had he accused Claudius of murder (his knowledge of the murder depends on a Ghost whose accusations only Hamlet has heard).

Hamlet's mother, Gertrude, is still relatively young (she need be no more than forty); she is a weak and sensuous woman who has been seduced by Claudius and has married him hastily following her husband's death, perhaps to prove to herself that she has sinned out of love. Polonius is a pompous, self-important, verbose politician who gives unsolicited advice and reaches unwarranted conclusions. He is often played as a buffoon, but there is danger in exaggerating his ridiculousness, as this diminishes the obstacles that Hamlet must overcome.

Shakespeare's dramatic poetry is generally recognized as the finest in the English language. The usual medium is blank verse, which retains much of the flexibility of ordinary speech while elevating and formalizing it. But many passages are

Hamlet at the Hartford Stage. Richard Thomas (at center) as Hamlet. The other actors are Sheridan Crist and Nick Bakay. Directed by Mark Lamos. (Photo by T. Charles Erickson. Courtesy of the Hartford Stage.)

in prose, especially those involving such lower-class characters as the gravediggers and the actors; because these passages often play on words or use slang, the prose is often more difficult to comprehend than the poetry.

Probably the most important element in Shakespeare's dialogue is figurative language. The principal purpose of a figure of speech in dramatic poetry is to set up either direct or indirect comparisons. Shakespeare's superiority over other writers of dramatic poetry lies in his use of comparisons that enlarge the significance without distracting attention from the dramatic situation. His poetic devices partially fulfill the same function as the visual representation of Heaven and Hell on the medieval stage: They relate human actions to the divine and demonic forces of the universe and treat human affairs as significant to all creation.

Shakespeare's language makes special demands on the actor. Figures of speech are likely to seem contrived and bombastic if the actor does not appear to be experiencing feelings strong enough to call forth such language spontaneously. Shakespeare's plays may be damaged in performance if actors do not rise to the emotional demands of the poetry. Therefore, the very richness of expression can be a stumbling block for both performer and reader.

The action of *Hamlet* occurs in many places, but Shakespeare envisioned them all in terms of stage properties, costumes, and the movement of the actors. Scenery was not important, but change of place was. The main stage, discovery space, and upper stage facilitated the flow of one scene into the next. The relatively bare stage was constantly varied by such scenes as the sentry patrols and the appearance of the Ghost in the opening scenes, the elaborate procession and court ceremony in Act I, the play-within-the-play in Act III, the burial of Ophelia and the fight between Hamlet and Laertes in her open grave (a trapdoor in the stage floor) in Act V, and the fencing match that leaves the stage littered with corpses at the end of Act V.

Costumes added to the visual effect. Though most of the characters were probably dressed in the garments of Shakespeare's own time, Hamlet was set off from the others by his black mourning clothes amid the bright colors the others wore, the period of mourning for the dead king having been replaced by rejoicing at the marriage of Claudius and Gertrude.

Sounds also added to the overall effect. They included trumpet flourishes, cannons, and, in Act IV, the offstage crowd. But most important was the sound of the actors' voices speaking Shakespeare's poetry.

Hamlet is rich in implications, the most important of which concern the shock of betrayal by those whom one has most trusted. The betrayals are pervasive— brother of brother, wife of husband, parent of child, friend of friend. After an

Hamlet (the fencing match between Hamlet and Laertes in Act V). Directed by Ingmar Bergman; performed at the Brooklyn Academy of Music. (Photo by Martha Swope.)

The Continuing Popularity of Shakespeare

Shakespeare's plays today are produced throughout the world and command great critical acclaim almost everywhere. But wide knowledge of the plays also encourages using them in parodies or in constructing pieces that borrow from or comment on the originals. In the fall of 1993, the Nada Theatre (New York) staged a *Hamlet* festival during which twenty-six different "Hamlet" plays were performed. They included: the rap *The Trage-D of Prince Hammy T; Hamster* ("the first production of *Hamlet* to cast animals in human roles"); *Hamlet on the Beach* (a double parody—of *Hamlet* and *Einstein on the Beach* by Robert Wilson and Philip Glass); *Hamlet: Satanic Sentinel of the Suburbs;* Heinar Müller's *Hamletmachine* (in four different versions); and a solo rendition.

For several years the three-actor Reduced Shakespeare Company has been presenting a performance piece that condenses all of Shakespeare's thirty-eight plays, plus his sonnets, into the two-hour *The Complete Works of William Shakespeare.* The history plays dealing with the War of the Roses become a game using a crown as football; *Titus Andronicus* is presented as a cooking show with body parts as primary ingredients; *Othello* is reduced to a rap song. The greatest amount of time (about thirty minutes) is devoted to *Hamlet,* which ends with a brief summation played backward rapidly "so you can hear the subliminal satanic messages." This enormously popular company is concerned primarily with getting laughs as an antidote to overly solemn reverence for Shakespeare.

apparently uneventful youth, Hamlet is suddenly faced with a series of shocking revelations: His father has been murdered by his uncle; his mother has been unfaithful to his father; his mother has accepted his uncle's usurpation of the throne that should have been Hamlet's; and his supposed friends (Rosencrantz and Guildenstern) have become his uncle's spies. It is not surprising that these discoveries make Hamlet suspicious of almost everyone, even of Ophelia, the woman he loves. Considering the nature of the betrayals and the rapidity with which they come, it also is not surprising that both Hamlet and others wonder if he has gone mad. A second theme is the opposing demands made on Hamlet—to avenge his father's death (which seemingly requires him to murder his uncle) and to adhere to Christian teaching (under which the murder of his uncle would be a deadly sin). A third theme concerns the way one crime sets off a chain of evil as the wrongdoer tries to conceal the crime. Everything in *Hamlet* can be traced to Claudius' murder of his brother and the series of deceptions he devises to hide it. It is this deed that leads to the total destruction of two families.

Another set of implications concerns the nature of kingship and the need to rule oneself before attempting to rule others. This motif is seen especially in the conduct of Claudius and is suggested through the contrasts drawn between Claudius and his dead brother, and between Hamlet and Fortinbras (the forceful, uncomplicated prince who is left to return order to the state). These are some implications of the dramatic action, but many others could be suggested, for a play as rich as *Hamlet* cannot be wholly exhausted. Perhaps for that reason, *Hamlet* has transcended its time and place and has appealed to all succeeding generations. It is one of the few plays that has never been out of the active performance repertory.

The English public theatre continued most of the practices of Shakespeare's day until 1642, when civil war forced the closure of all theatres until 1660. When performances resumed, practices drastically different from those of Shakespeare's time were adopted. Thereafter, English theatre reflected practices developed in France during the seventeenth century more than it did those of Elizabethan England.

The Theatre Experience in Renaissance Italy

Another of the theatre's great eras occurred in Italy during the Renaissance. It represents a different kind of experience using conventions that would eventually displace those of Shakespeare's theatre and dominate Western theatrical practices until the nineteenth century. The reawakened interest in Greek and Roman thought, literature, and art, which began in the fourteenth century, had by the late fifteenth century led to occasional performances of Roman comedies at the courts of the many small states into which Italy was then divided. In the early sixteenth century, plays imitating classical forms began to be written in Italian. To present such plays was considered a mark of a ruler's cultural enlightenment, and theatrical entertainments soon became standard features of court festivals given to celebrate betrothals, weddings, births of royal children, visits of emissaries from other states, and similar events. Thus, theatre played a role somewhat like that in Greece, Rome, and the Middle Ages, although the occasions were secular and were intended to reflect glory on the ruler. The subject matter of plays and the themes developed in the many events of a festival were usually drawn from classical mythology.

In mounting these festivals, the Italians drew on classical sources, especially *De Architectura* by Vitruvius (a Roman architect of the first century B.C.), who described how a theatre is laid out as well as the settings appropriate to three kinds of plays: tragedy, comedy, and pastoral. Italian artists sought to re-create what they found in Vitruvius' treatise, but in doing so they transformed it radically, thereby creating the theatre structure and scenic practices that would dominate the European theatre into the twentieth century.

Because they had no permanent theatres, the Italians at first set up temporary performance spaces, usually in large halls of state (comparable in size and shape to the ballrooms of modern hotels). In 1545, Sebastiano Serlio published *Architettura*, in which he showed how to create a performance space within an existing room. He included drawings showing his version of Vitruvius' tragic, comic, and pastoral settings (see the illustrations on page 120). These drawings fuse classical theatre architecture with Renaissance perspective painting.

The principles of perspective drawing had been developed during the fifteenth century. It is difficult today to appreciate the Renaissance excitement over perspective, which was sometimes viewed almost as a form of magic because with it the

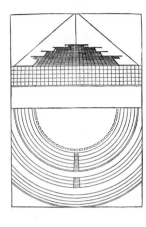

Serlio's floor plan for a theatre set up within an existing hall. The stage is shown at top, the seating arrangement at bottom. (Serlio, *Architectura* [1545].)

Serlio's design for the comic scene. The squares on the raked stage, diminishing in size from front to back, help create apparent depth, as does the downward slope of the upper portions of buildings. (Serlio, *Architectura* [1545].)

artist seemed to create space and distance on a two-dimensional surface. Given this enthusiasm, it is not surprising that by the sixteenth century perspective had been adapted to stage use.

The acceptance of perspective scenery is of profound importance, for it signaled a movement away from the formal and architectural stage to the representational and pictorial stage. The Greek, Roman, and Elizabethan stages all had in common a formalized architectural facade as the basic background for all plays; in these theatres, the facade could be modified by the addition of small elements, but no stage property or pictorial element could ever disguise the fixed facade. Any added elements merely identified (rather than represented realistically) a scene's locale. The mansions of the medieval theatre lay somewhere between the formal and pictorial traditions because semirepresentational structures were often used to represent two or more places simultaneously. Still, no place was represented in its entirety, and the gaps between places were telescoped. With the coming of perspective, each place was represented in its entirety as seen from a fixed eyepoint. If two or more places were involved, they were shown sequentially, not simultaneously. During the seventeenth century, pictorial representation of place would become the standard for stage scenery throughout Europe, remaining so into the twentieth century.

How to transform a two-dimensional drawing into a stage setting that occupies three-dimensional space was a problem that Renaissance artists had to solve. The solution eventually accepted everywhere was to break up the picture and paint the parts on one of three scenic elements: side wings, back drops, and overhead borders. Everything painted on the wings, drops, and borders was drawn as seen from a fixed eyepoint located somewhere in the auditorium (originally the seat of the ruler). The floor of the stage raked upward toward the back, giving us our terms *upstage* and *downstage,* and the height of the side wings diminished as they receded from the audience; both of these features helped perspective achieve apparent depth within a restricted space. The goal was to create a complete and convincing picture.

A pictorialized setting demanded a frame because otherwise spectators would see around or over the setting, and the apparent scale would be negated. From this need came the proscenium arch, used to frame the stage opening (the "picture-frame stage"). Originally, the frame was a temporary structure like the scenery itself, but eventually the advantage of a permanent architectural frame was recognized. The oldest surviving theatre with a permanent proscenium arch is the Teatro Farnese, built in 1618 in Parma, Italy. The proscenium arch soon became a standard feature of theatres and remained so until recently; even today, the picture-frame stage is the most common type.

A setting that depicted a single place in its entirety created another problem: how to move from one locale to another. The solution eventually arrived at used two-dimensional wings set up parallel to the front of the stage and in a series from front to back. At each wing position, as many different flats were used (one immediately in back of another) as there were scenes to be depicted during the performance. To change from one set to the next, the visible wings were pulled offstage, revealing others that represented the next scene. The set was enclosed at the back by painted flats, which met at the center of the stage. Several back-scenes (or shutters) could be set up and shifted in the same way as the side wings. (Eventually, drops that could be lowered and raised replaced the back-scenes.) Borders (two-dimensional

The oldest surviving proscenium theatre, the Teatro Farnese, Parma, Italy, built in 1618. (Streit, *Das Theater* [1903].)

Italian Intermezzi and English Masques

The English developed their own variation on the Italian intermezzi—"masques," which were first performed at the court of Henry VIII. They were most fully developed under the Stuart rulers James I and Charles I between 1605 and 1640. Masques, performed solely for court audiences, were similar in all important respects to Italian intermezzi, except that masques were independent productions, not being inserted between the acts of plays. Like the Italian intermezzi, Stuart masques took their subjects primarily from classical mythology or historical legend; the subjects were developed to draw parallels between some mythical or legendary character and the person who was being honored by the performance. Masques developed an idealized vision of monarchy and nobility because within the masques the action moved from disorder to order, usually with the ruler or a noble as the transforming agent. Thus, masques served not only as an entertainment but also as a justification of the political system.

These spectacular pieces, requiring enormous sums to mount, emphasized music, dance, costumes, scenery, and elaborate special effects. The principal performers were courtiers. The majority of the English masques, which were short and served primarily to establish the mythical framework, were written by Ben Jonson, a major playwright of the day. But the principal appeal of the pieces lay in the spectacle created by Inigo Jones, the court architect, who had studied in Italy, where he observed the staging of intermezzi. It is primarily through Jones' work that Italian scenic practices were brought to England, although they were confined to court productions until after 1660.

cloths, most often representing clouds or the sky) hung above each set of wings and enclosed the scene overhead. Until the nineteenth century, scene changes were usually made in full view of the audience. The front curtain was raised at the beginning of a performance and not lowered until the end. Thus scene shifts were part of the overall visual experience.

The desire to shift scenery was inspired by the love of spectacle and special effects, which the Italians exploited primarily in *intermezzi* (interludes) between the acts of regular plays (which usually did not require any changes of place or special effects). Intermezzi were elaborate compliments that suggested parallels between some mythological figure and the person in whose honor the festival was being given; usually the mythic protagonist routed the forces of chaos through magical feats involving elaborate special effects. Music and dance were major features. More effort usually went into the staging of intermezzi than the plays they accompanied.

The appeals of intermezzi were eventually absorbed into *opera*, a new form that originated in the 1590s out of attempts to re-create the relationship between music and speech found in Greek tragedy. Opera soon became a popular form, combining drama, music, dance, spectacle, and special effects. Opera became the primary medium for popularizing perspective scenery and the picture-frame stage, both of which had developed in the rarefied atmosphere of the Italian courts, where performances were not open to the general public. In 1637, a public opera house in Venice made the pleasures of the court theatres available to the general Italian public for the first time. It was so successful that soon there were four public opera houses in Venice.

The Venetian opera houses were in many ways the prototypes of subsequent theatres, not only for opera but also for drama because they not only incorporated the proscenium arch and perspective scenery but also divided and arranged auditoriums in the way that would remain typical until the late nineteenth century. The division of the auditorium into box, pit, and gallery reflected the class structure of Europe; it permitted each class to attend the theatre without having to mingle with another class. The auditorium was surrounded by two or more levels of boxes (which permitted well-to-do or snobbish spectators to be more or less private while in a crowded place); on the ground floor was the pit (today's orchestra), less expensive than the boxes and favored by those unconcerned about reputation; above the

Setting by Giacomo Torelli for *Bellerophon,* produced at an opera house in Venice in 1642. (Courtesy of the French Cultural Services.)

boxes was the gallery, housing the least desirable and cheapest seats, usually inhabited by working-class patrons. The popularity of opera, which burgeoned during the seventeenth century, spread throughout Europe, bringing with it the staging practices of Italy.

Commedia dell'Arte

Although much of the theatrical activity in Renaissance Italy was neither professional nor open to the public, one form—*commedia dell'arte*—was both. *Commedia dell'arte* ("comedy of professional artists") and *commedia all'improviso* ("improvised comedy") are terms used to distinguish the plays performed by certain professional troupes from those presented by the amateur actors at court (*commedia erudita* or "learned drama"). No one knows precisely how or when commedia dell'arte came into being. Some trace it to the mimes and other entertainers of Roman times, whose traditions were supposedly continued thereafter by small wandering troupes. Others see the form as evolving out of improvisations based on the Roman comedies of Plautus and Terence. There are still other theories. Whatever its origin, commedia dell'arte is first mentioned in historical records in the 1560s. By 1600 companies were playing not only throughout Italy but also in France, Spain, and other European countries. Wherever they went, they easily found audiences both among the common people and the ruling classes.

The actor was the heart of commedia dell'arte and almost the only essential element. The commedia companies could play almost anywhere: in town squares or at court; indoors or out; on improvised stages or in permanent theatres. If elaborate scenery was available, they used it, but they could function as well against the background of a simple curtain (with slits for entrances and exits). Adaptability was one of their major assets.

The script was a scenario merely summarizing the situations, complications, and outcome. The actors improvised the dialogue and fleshed out the action. Although the broad outlines of a script remained the same, the details differed at each performance, depending on the inspiration of the moment and the response of the audience. Many scenarios have survived. A few are tragic, melodramatic, or musical, but the greatest number are comic, revolving around love affairs, intrigues, disguises, and cross-purposes.

Improvisation, a distinguishing feature of commedia, was facilitated by the use of the same characters in all the plays performed by the same troupe, and by the same actor always playing the same role with its fixed attributes and costume. Over the years, the actors must have developed surefire dialogue and stage business that they could call on as needed. Some pieces of comic business (*lazzi*) became sufficiently standardized to be indicated in the plot outlines as lazzi of fear, sack lazzi, fight lazzi, and so on. In addition, actors who played the fashionable young men and women were encouraged to keep notebooks in which to record appropriate sentiments from poetry and popular literature, and many lines and actions were probably repeated in various plays. Nevertheless, performances created the impression of spontaneity because no actor could be certain what the others would say or do, and

Preparing a Commedia Performance

When we read about commedia dell'arte, we can easily get the impression that the performers made everything up as they went along. Indeed, much of what they did was improvised, but improvisation occurred within a rehearsed framework. For the improvisation to be effective, the performers had always to keep in mind where each scene was headed and what had to be done to make the plot as a whole work. They had to know the outline of the action and, when they inserted *lazzi* (extended bits of comic business), they had to make sure they didn't let the pieces of business get so out of hand as to obscure the plot line.

In 1699, Andrea Perrucci wrote a description of how commedia dell'arte companies operated. A first-hand account, it is one of our most reliable sources of information. Here are some of its comments on rehearsal practices:

> The scenario is merely the outline of scenes . . . which are to be acted extemporaneously. . . . The manager or most experienced actor rehearses the scenario . . . until the actors are familiar with the content . . . so they can discover . . . where new *lazzi* can be introduced. . . . [The actors must note] the things that will be needed in the performance, such as letters, purses, daggers, and other properties. . . . After the actors are familiar with what they must do . . . they will be able to run through the scenes and . . . rehearse new material of their own invention. It is wise, however, [when improvising] not to deviate from the plot to such an extent that . . . the audience . . . loses the thread of the plot.

> —Dell'arte rappresentativa, premeditata ad all'improvviso *(1699)*

each had to concentrate moment by moment on the unfolding action and respond appropriately.

The stock characters, commedia's best-known feature, can be divided into three categories: lovers, masters, and servants. The lovers' roles were the most realistic. Young and handsome, they did not wear masks and were usually dressed in the latest fashions. Each company had at least one pair of lovers, and most had two. The lovers were often the children of those characters who fell into the category of masters, and their love affairs were typically opposed by their fathers and aided by their servants.

Three masters recurred most often: Pantalone, Dottore, and Capitano. Pantalone was an elderly Venetian merchant, often the father of one or more of the young lovers or a would-be lover himself. His costume consisted of a tight-fitting red vest, red breeches and stockings, soft slippers, a black ankle-length coat, a soft brimless cap, a brown mask with a large hooked nose, and scraggly gray beard. Dottore, usually Pantalone's friend or rival, was a lawyer or doctor who loved to show off his spurious learning in speeches filled with Latin (often ludicrously incorrect).

Lazzi

The actors inserted many diverse bits of stage business (*lazzi*) into commedia dell'arte performances. Most were usable in a variety of plays and could be curtailed or extended as the particular dramatic situation allowed or as the audience's response seemed to justify. Lazzi were often used to enliven a performance when audience interest lagged, to create a change of pace, to embroider on a situation, or to fill a gap in the action. Actors often worked out their own variations on established, surefire lazzi. Here are a few lazzi, each of which might be elaborated in various ways:

Two servants loudly threaten each other but are visibly relieved to be held back by others. A Capitano enters and officiously orders them to stop the quarrel. The servants are released and, under the pretense of striking at each other, give the Capitano a beating.

A character (often Pantalone) who has been threatened with physical harm by a bully is persuaded by a servant to hide in a sack, which the servant will carry to safety; the servant then assumes the voice of the bully, frightens, and eventually beats the sack's occupant. (This lazzo was often used in plays showing servants getting even with masters who have unjustly punished them.) There were many variations on the sack routine. It could be used as a means of gaining entry to a mistress' house or to a storeroom filled with food or treasure. The person in the sack always got punished, usually without discovering who did it.

Lazzi involving extreme fear were also common, although the causes for the fear varied widely. In these lazzi, characters sometimes think they see a ghost; or a character comes upon what he takes to be a dead body and, trying to flee, is grabbed around the ankle by the supposed corpse; or while a character's attention is distracted, someone repeatedly removes or deposits objects. In all these cases, the events are usually magnified by some prior event that suggests to the character that something mysterious is going on or that danger is near; his response usually builds until it reaches a climax.

Despite his supposed wisdom, he was credulous and easily tricked. His dress was the academic cap and gown of the time. Originally the Capitano was one of the lovers, but eventually he was transformed into a braggart and coward who boasted of his prowess in love and war, only to be discredited in both. He usually wore a cape, sword, and feathered headdress, often greatly exaggerated to indicate his braggadocio. He typically was an unwelcome suitor to one of the young women.

The most varied of the commedia types were the servants (the *zanni*—the origin of the English word *zany*). Most companies included at least two—one clever and one stupid—but there might be as many as four. They figured prominently in the action; their machinations kept the plots moving as they sought to help or thwart their masters. Most of the servants were male, but there might be one or

Bill Irwin, wearing a Harlequin suit and bowler hat, performing a lazzo involving spaghetti, one of his "Clown Bagatelles." (Photo by Joan Marcus.)

more maids (*fantesca*) who served the young women. Typically young, coarsely witty, and ready for intrigue, the female servants carried on their own love affairs with the male servants while helping their mistresses. Occasionally, one was older and served as hostess of an inn, or the object of the older men's affections.

Of the *zanni,* Arlecchino (Harlequin) eventually became the most popular, although originally he was of minor importance. A mixture of cunning and stupidity and an accomplished acrobat and dancer, he was usually at the center of any intrigue. His costume, which began as a suit with irregularly placed multicolored patches, evolved into one with a diamond-shaped red, green, and blue pattern. He wore a rakish hat above a black mask and carried a wooden sword or slapstick (so called because it was slit down the middle so it would make a sharp sound when struck against someone; it is the source of our term *slapstick comedy*). The slapstick figured prominently in the many fights and beatings. While each company had a Harlequinlike character, not every company used that name for the character. Name variations include Truffaldino and Trivellino.

Harlequin's most frequent companion was a cynically witty, libidinous, and sometimes cruel servant. His mask had a hooked nose and moustache, and his jacket and trousers were ornamented with green braid. He was variously called Brighella, Scapino, Mezzetino, and Flautino. Another character, Pulcinello, was always a

The young lover of commedia dell'arte. Etching by Jacques Callot, 1618–19. Notice the stage and audience in the background.

Pantalone, Capitano, and Arlecchino (Harlequin) of the commedia dell'arte. (Maurice Sand, *Masques et Bouffons* [1859].)

Neapolitan, but his function in the scripts varied. Sometimes he was a servant, but he also might be the host of an inn or a merchant. He had an enormous hooked nose, a humped back, and wore a pointed cap. He was the ancestor of the English puppet character, Punch. There were many variations, both in name and attributes, on these zanni because each company developed its own version of these types.

A commedia troupe averaged ten to twelve members (seven or eight men and three or four women). Most companies were organized on the sharing plan, although some of the younger actors and assistants may have been salaried. Most troupes traveled frequently, but some were able to settle in one place for considerable periods of time. Let us examine a commedia scenario.

A Commedia Scenario

The earliest scenarios that have survived are fifty that were published in Venice in 1611 by Flaminio Scala, an actor who performed the role of Flavio, an *inamorato* (male lover). The scripts apparently came from the Gelosi ("jealous") company, the most famous members of which were Isabella Andreini (who played Isabella, an *inamorata* or female lover) and her husband Francesco (who played the Capitano). These scenarios are from the early years of commedia when Arlecchino was still a relatively minor character. Pedrolino was the principal servant in this troupe. In these scenarios, the number of characters varies but some appear in almost every script: Pantalone, Dottore, Capitano Spavento, Oratio and Flavio (the male lovers), Isabella and Flaminia (the female lovers), Pedrolino and Arlecchino (male servants), and Franceschina (female servant). Other characters are introduced much less often. This suggests that the company included ten principal actors, plus a few hired assistants. The fifty scenarios are varied: forty comedies, eight operas, one pastoral, and one tragedy. Comedy was clearly the mainstay of the company, with musical pieces a distant second.

Of these pieces, *The Dentist* may be taken as representative. The action takes place outdoors in a space onto which two houses front: one, that of Pantalone (who has two children—Flaminia and Oratio—and a servant—Pedrolino), the other, that of Flavio (who has a widowed sister—Isabella—and two servants—Arlecchino and Franceschina). In the first scene we learn that both Pantalone and his son Oratio are in love with Isabella and that Pantalone, in order to remove his son, has decided to send him away to school in another city. Pedrolino's objections lead to a fight between Pantalone and Pedrolino, during which Pantalone bites Pedrolino. Pedrolino and Franceschina (Isabella's maid with whom Pedrolino is in love) decide to be revenged on Pantalone. They soon secure the help of almost all the other characters in a trick to be played on Pantalone. Each in turn expresses disgust at Pantalone's bad breath; he decides that the source of his problem is his bad teeth. Arlecchino, disguised as a dentist, extracts four good teeth before Pantalone discovers that the dentist is Arlecchino. Reactions to Pantalone's breath and the tooth-pulling provide many opportunities for lazzi.

This part of the action, which takes up the first act, is only loosely connected to the remainder of the play, which focuses on the intrigues of lovers. Pantalone, Oratio, and the Capitano all want to marry Isabella; Flavio wants to marry

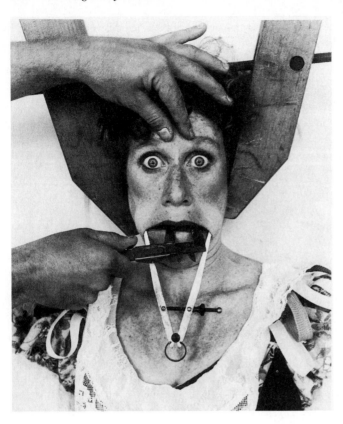

Scene from *Malpractice or Love's the Best Doctor* as performed by the Dell'Arte Players Company. The actress is Joan Mankin. (Courtesy the Dell'Arte Players Company.)

Flaminia, who wants the Capitano, who spurns her. The two main intriguers seeking to resolve the impasses are Isabella and Pedrolino. Isabella learns that an old woman, Pasquela, has two kinds of magic candy—one makes those who eat it insane, the other cures the insanity. Isabella acquires some of both with the goal of making Oratio insane until Pantalone agrees not to send him away. Meanwhile, Flavio, the Capitano, and Dottore (who is not involved in the love plots but is trying to recover money that Pantalone owes him) all seek help from Pedrolino. Pedrolino's schemes involve disguises that will get each person inside the house of the person he wishes to see. Flavio, who wants to see Flaminia, is told to disguise himself as a dentist; the Capitano is told to disguise himself as Pantalone; and Dottore is told to disguise himself as a woman (in a dress secured from Flaminia). Flavio, of course, gets beaten up by Pantalone (who thinks he is the trickster who has pulled his teeth), and Flavio then beats up the Capitano (mistaking him for Pantalone) to get revenge for his earlier beating; and Dottore is beaten up by Pantalone and Pedrolino for supposedly stealing the dress. All of this occurs in the second act.

In the third and final act, Isabella asks Arlecchino to give the doctored candy to Oratio from her, but Arlecchino passes this errand to Pedrolino, who does so but keeps some of the candy for himself. Both Oratio and Pedrolino eat the candy and both lose their wits. The Capitano and Dottore arrive bent on revenge against Pedrolino but he acts so strangely that they abandon their plans. Pantalone is advised

Scene from the Addison Centre Theatre's production of *The Three Cuckolds,* adapted from a commedia dell'arte scenario by Leon Katz; further adapted by Bill Irwin and Michael Greif. Directed by Raphael Parry; setting by Robert Winn; costumes by Giva Taylor; lighting by Robert McVay. (Photo by Susan Kandell.)

that only Isabella has the means of curing Oratio, but she insists that if she does so, Pantalone must allow Flaminia to marry Flavio and Oratio to marry whomever Isabella chooses. Pantalone agrees, and she cures Oratio and Pedrolino with the restorative candy. When Isabella says that Oratio must marry her, Pantalone reluctantly acquiesces. Finally, Pedrolino reveals to Pantalone his part in the tooth-extraction conspiracy, begs forgiveness, and all ends happily.

This scenario is, of course, a bare outline that the actors, playing the same character they did in each of the company's productions, filled out with improvised dialogue, movement, and stage business.

Commedia was most vigorous and popular in the years between 1575 and 1650, but it continued into the last half of the eighteenth century. Its last stronghold was Venice, where two playwrights seeking to reform and preserve it contributed to its destruction. Carlo Goldoni (1707–1793), Italy's most famous comic dramatist, began writing scenarios for commedia companies in Venice around 1734. Because he believed the situations in commedia had become hackneyed and vulgar, he refined and sentimentalized the characters and situations. He also thought the usual level of improvisation was inadequate, and he was able to persuade companies to accept scripts with most of the dialogue written out. In addition, he campaigned for the abandonment of masks because he thought they handicapped the actors by

Carlo Goldoni's *The Servant of Two Masters* at the Piccolo Teatro, Milan, Italy. This production is so popular that it has been in the company's repertory continuously since 1947. Directed by Giorgio Strehler. (Photo by Luigi Ciminaghi. Courtesy of the Piccolo Teatro.)

hiding facial expression. Had all the changes he championed been implemented, they would have done away with most of the basic conventions of commedia. Goldoni wrote a number of plays using commedia characters, the best known of which is *The Servant of Two Masters* (1745), still frequently performed.

Goldoni was bitterly opposed by another dramatist, Carlo Gozzi (1720–1806), who emphasized fairy-tale stories and improvisation in his scripts. His best-known plays include *Turandot, The Love for Three Oranges,* and *King Stag.* For a time their battle aroused new interest in commedia, but by about 1775, this theatrical mode largely ceased to be a living form, perhaps because of overfamiliarity after two hundred years or because its rather broad, often coarse, farcical humor had lost its appeal in the more refined atmosphere of the eighteenth century.

The French Background

The development of the French theatre had been interrupted by the civil wars that grew out of religious controversy in the sixteenth century and recurred in the seventeenth. Stability did not return until around 1625, by which time Cardinal Richelieu, Louis XIII's prime minister, having secured absolute power for the king, set out to make France the cultural center of Europe. Up to that time, France's theatre had remained under medieval influence. Although religious plays were outlawed in Paris in 1548, the theatre had continued to use simultaneous settings for its plays, most of which required numerous locales. (See the illustration on page 133 for a typical stage setting around 1630.) Richelieu believed that the French stage needed drastic reform and looked to Italy for guidance. He advocated adoption of the proscenium stage and perspective scenery and a drama that would adhere to theoretical principles articulated in Italy during the sixteenth century. These principles make up what came to be called the neoclassical ideal.

Design by Laurent Mahelot for *La Prise de Marsilly.* Notice the simultaneous locales. (Courtesy Bibliothèque Nationale, Paris.)

The first proscenium arch theatre in France, built by Cardinal Richelieu in his palace in 1641. Seated in the foreground (from right to left) are Cardinal Richelieu, Louis XIII, and the Queen. After Richelieu's death, this theatre was called the Palais Royal. It was used by Molière's company from 1660 until his death in 1673. (A contemporary engraving.)

Onstage Audiences

From the 1630s until around 1760, some members of Parisian audiences were seated on stage during performances. This practice apparently originated during the controversy over Corneille's *The Cid,* when the demand to see that play was so great that spectators were allowed to sit or stand in the wings. Sitting on stage soon became fashionable for those who came to the theatre to be seen, and the actors permitted it because they could charge more for onstage seats than for seats in the boxes. That some onstage spectators were determined to give their own performances is indicated in this speech from Molière's *The Bores:*

> I was seated on the stage waiting to hear the play, which I had heard praised by several persons. The actors began and everybody was silent when, with a blustering air . . . in rushes a man . . . crying out for a chair, surprising the audience with his great noise which interrupted one of the most beautiful passages in the play. . . . The actors were willing to go on with their parts, but the fellow in seating himself made a new disturbance, and crossing the stage . . . he planted his chair in the middle of the front . . . hiding the actors from three fourths of the house. The yells this aroused would have shamed another man, but he, steady and firm, did not mind at all. [The speech goes on to say that the man moved only so he could talk to another onstage spectator, to whom he insisted on explaining in a loud voice what was coming next.] He got up a good while before the play ended, for these fine fellows, to prove their gentility, are careful above all not to hear the conclusion.

Eventually five rows of benches were permanently installed on either side of the Comédie Française's stage and were not removed until 1759, when the premiere of a tragedy by Voltaire was ruined when a ghost could not make its entrance because the stage was so crowded with spectators. When someone among the spectators shouted, "Make way for the ghost," the audience began laughing and never recovered, thus turning a tragedy into an unexpected comedy. This fiasco supposedly motivated the permanent removal of spectators from the stage, allowing it thereafter to be devoted entirely to the dramatic action for the first time since 1636.

The neoclassicists recognized only two forms of drama, tragedy and comedy, as legitimate and argued that the two should never be mixed. They believed that tragedy could be written only about kings and nobles, while comedy should deal with the middle or lower classes. They thought that all plays should be written in five acts, that plays should observe the unities of time (all the action should occur within twenty-four hours), place (all the action should occur in the same place), and action (there should be only one plot), and that the endings of plays should uphold "poetic justice" (that is, punish the wicked and reward the good). There were other demands, but these were the most important.

Although Richelieu and others favored them, these rules were not widely known or accepted in France until 1636, when *The Cid* by Pierre Corneille (1606–1684) became the most popular play yet written in France. Despite its popularity, the play was viciously attacked because it failed to adhere to some of the neoclassical rules. This controversy, which was heated and dragged on for some time, focused attention in France on the neoclassical rules. Richelieu asked the recently formed French Academy (whose membership was restricted to the forty most eminent literary figures of the day) to deliver a verdict on the play. The Academy praised the play for many of its qualities, but faulted it wherever it deviated from the rules. The Academy was especially unhappy because, though the unity of time had been observed, too many events, including an entire war, had occurred within a twenty-four-hour period. The play, unlike tragedy, ended happily because the heroine agreed to marry the man who had killed her father a few hours earlier. This controversy is a watershed event in French theatre, for it effectively legitimized the neoclassical view. After 1640, Corneille adopted the new mode, which was later perfected by Jean Racine (1639–1699), especially in his *Phaedra*. The tragedies of Corneille and Racine were to set the standard for serious playwriting throughout Europe until the nineteenth century. On the European continent, these French tragedies were, until around 1800, thought superior to those of Shakespeare.

The transition to the new ideal also required that the theatre structure be altered. To set an example, Richelieu in 1641 had the first theatre in France with a proscenium arch erected in his own palace. By 1650, all the Parisian public and court theatres had been transformed into picture-frame stages of the Italian type. Thus, by the mid-seventeenth century, the Italian order had replaced the medieval heritage.

Molière and Seventeenth-Century French Theatre Practice

Just as Corneille and Racine set the standard for tragedy, Molière (1622–1673) set the standard for comedy. Molière began his career as an actor in 1643. Meeting little success in Paris, his company toured the provinces for some thirteen years, often competing with commedia companies, from which he learned much about playwriting and how to please an audience. Upon returning to Paris, his company performed in the theatre that Richelieu had built and that had become the property of the crown upon the cardinal's death. Usually referred to as the Palais Royal, this theatre had a picture-frame stage and an auditorium of box, pit, and gallery. Thus, Molière performed in a theatre owned by the king but open to the general public. He also shared this theatre (alternating playing days) with a commedia company.

Like Shakespeare, Molière was involved in every aspect of the theatre. He was head of his own company, its principal actor, and its principal playwright. He was not part owner of a theatre, however. Despite the differences between the Elizabethan and French stages, their acting companies had many features in common. French companies, like the English, were organized on the sharing plan. They usually included ten to fifteen sharing members, but others were employed as actors, musicians, stage assistants, and so on. A major difference was that French companies included women, who had equal rights with the men and received comparable pay. At the end of each performance, the costs of production were deducted from the receipts, and the remainder was divided among the shareholders. All the leading companies in Paris (usually two or three) received a subsidy from the crown, but the sum was not sufficient to guarantee them against loss.

Plays were selected by a vote of the shareholders after hearing a reading of the play. A play might be bought outright, but the more usual method of payment was to give the author a percentage of the receipts for a limited number of performances, after which the play belonged to the company. An acting company usually had in its active repertory fifty or more plays, which were alternated in order to keep the audience coming back.

Casting was simplified because each actor played a limited range of roles. By the eighteenth century, actors were being hired according to "lines of business" (according to the type of characters they played) and remained in those lines throughout their careers. A new actor in the company usually learned roles from the person he or she was understudying or replacing, and therefore many roles came to be played in a traditional manner handed down from one generation to the next. Such practices continued well into the nineteenth century, not just in France but throughout Europe.

In France, actors were expected to furnish their own costumes, a major expense for the actors. As on the Elizabethan stage, most costumes were contemporary garments, although there were exceptions, especially for Near Eastern, Moorish, and classical characters. Because so many French plays were based on classical myth or history, the costumes for classical characters were of special concern. The typical dress for classical heroes was the *habit à la romaine* (Roman costume), an adaptation of Roman armor, tunic, and boots, which by the late seventeenth century had become highly stylized. (See the illustration on page 137.) Classical female characters, however, wore the fashionable dress of France but with such added exotic touches as ostrich-feather headdresses.

The scenic demands of regular comedy and tragedy were simple. Ordinarily, in compliance with the neoclassical rules, the plays were set in one place and required no scene changes. (Opera and other "irregular" forms were permitted many scene changes and elaborate effects.) Most settings were so generalized in their features (appropriate to a particular kind of play but without individualizing details) that the same set could be used for several different plays. The setting was removed from specificity by using only those stage properties (chairs, tables, beds, and the like) absolutely demanded by the action; thus the stage was largely bare. This emphasis on generalized place served as well to keep down the costs of both scenery and costumes.

Because the theatre was now indoors, lighting was a concern. The available illuminants were candles and oil lamps. The auditorium was usually lighted by chandeliers, those hung just forward of the stage being of special importance because they, along with a row of footlights at the forward edge of the stage, were the primary

The *habit à la romaine*, the costume worn by actors playing the heroes of tragedies set in ancient Greece or Rome. Originally based on Roman armor, it became increasingly stylized and ornate, as in this engraving based on a painting by Watteau. (Gillaumont, *Costumes de la Comédie Française* [1884].)

lighting sources for the actors, who usually played near the front of the stage. Audiences as well as actors were lighted throughout performances, promoting considerable interaction between auditorium and stage. Sometimes chandeliers were also hung above the stage, but more often the onstage lighting sources were concealed by overhead or side masking. Along the sides, behind the proscenium arch and each wing position, were vertical poles on which oil lamps were mounted, one lamp above the other. Lamps could also be mounted on horizontal pipes above the proscenium and behind the overhead borders. Reflectors were sometimes used to increase the amount of light that reached the stage. At least three methods were used to darken the stage: Lights were extinguished (although this was awkward if they had to brighten again); open cylinders were suspended above the lamps and lowered over them to darken the stage, then raised to brighten it; or lamps were mounted on rotating poles that could be turned either toward or away from the visible portions of the stage. Because the intensity of lamps and candles was so limited, providing an adequate level of illumination took precedence over all other functions of stage lighting. By modern standards, the level of illumination was very low.

These were the prevailing practices during the years 1658–1673, when Molière performed in Paris. Molière wrote several kinds of plays, many of them resembling commedia and using commedia characters. But his best-known works are comedies of character, among which the most popular is *Tartuffe*.

Molière

Molière, born Jean-Baptiste Poquelin (1622–1673), was the son of a prosperous upholsterer and furniture maker. After receiving an excellent education, he abandoned a promising future with his father at the age of twenty-one to join nine other young people in founding the Théâtre Illustre. At this time he took the stage name Molière. After the company failed in Paris, they toured the provinces for thirteen years, polishing their skills and learning to please audiences, often in competition with commedia dell'arte companies. In 1658, the company was invited to play for the king, who was sufficiently pleased to let them use a court theatre for public performances. Molière remained in Paris thereafter, often stirring up controversy with plays that satirized obsessive behavior and repressive customs, but enjoying the favor of the king, for whose festivals he wrote entertainments and who awarded the company an annual subsidy. Molière's enemies were often vicious, even spreading the rumor that his wife, some twenty years younger than he, was actually his illegitimate daughter. Molière virtually died on stage, having taken ill while performing the title role in his *The Imaginary Invalid* and surviving only a few hours. Initially denied a Christian burial because he was an actor, only after the king intervened was he permitted minimal ceremony and burial in consecrated ground.

Tartuffe

Tartuffe is concerned with religious hypocrisy. The most likely target of Molière's satire was the Company of the Holy Sacrament, a secret society of the time, one of whose purposes was the improvement of morals through "spiritual police" who spied on the private lives of others. Molière read *Tartuffe* to several persons before it was produced in 1664, and the Company immediately organized an attack upon it. The controversy became so heated that Louis XIV forbade further performances. Molière revised the play in 1667, only to have it withdrawn again. But by 1669, the opposition was largely gone.

Whether or not Molière had the Company in mind, he was clearly thinking of groups like the Company, who feel that they alone can discern true piety from false, creating conditions under which hypocrites flourish. As in all of Molière's works, in *Tartuffe* the balanced view of life is upheld. To Molière, true piety demands not the abandonment of pleasure but the right use of it. The truly devout try to reform the world by actions that set a good example rather than by pious speeches.

The conflict in *Tartuffe* is established quickly in the opening scene, as Madame Pernelle, Orgon's mother, storms out of the house while denouncing the entire household for failing to appreciate Tartuffe's piety. The conflict is further clarified when Orgon, the head of the household, returning home after an absence, demonstrates more concern for the welfare of Tartuffe than for his own wife. When Orgon's brother-in-law, Cleante, tries to reason with him, Orgon asserts his power by announcing his intention of marrying his daughter, Mariane, to Tartuffe, even though he has promised her to Valère. The news of this proposed marriage leads to a quarrel between Mariane and Valère, who assumes that Mariane has not opposed the plan; the rift is finally healed through the intervention of Dorine, the outspoken maid. Orgon's son, Damis, also tries to bring his father to his senses by reporting that he has witnessed Tartuffe trying to seduce Orgon's wife, Elmire. When Tartuffe, with an air of injured humility, refuses to defend himself, Orgon denounces Damis and, to protect Tartuffe from such attacks in the future, signs over all his property to Tartuffe.

Elmire, at last recognizing how deceived Orgon is, seeks to show him his mistake by hiding him under a table to witness Tartuffe's assault on her virtue. Finally convinced, Orgon orders Tartuffe from the house, but Tartuffe, now the owner of the property, declares that, rather than moving out, he will have the family evicted. Just as Tartuffe seems triumphant, officers arrest him as a notorious deceiver on whom the king has been keeping watch and return the property to Orgon.

The plot of *Tartuffe* can be divided into five stages: the demonstration of Tartuffe's complete hold over Orgon; the unmasking of Tartuffe; Tartuffe's attempted revenge; the foiling of Tartuffe's plan; and the happy resolution. There are

Tartuffe as performed at the McCarter Theatre. Here Orgon (Jim Baker, kneeling) comforts Tartuffe (Richard Risso). Directed by Nagle Jackson. (Photo by Randall Hagadorn. Courtesy of the McCarter Theatre Center for the Performing Arts, Princeton, NJ.)

Orgon and Elmire, following her attempted seduction by Tartuffe, in a production at the Hartford Stage. Directed by Mark Lamos; set by Christine Jones; lighting by Scott Zielinski; costumes by Tom Broecker. (Photo © T. Charles Erickson.)

three important reversals. The first (the unmasking of Tartuffe) brings all of the characters to an awareness of the true situation. The resulting happiness is quickly dispelled, however, when Orgon is shown to be at the mercy of Tartuffe. The first two reversals (Orgon turning the tables on Tartuffe; Tartuffe turning the tables on Orgon) have been carefully foreshadowed, but the final one and the play's resolution have not. The contrived (deus ex machina) ending (in which Tartuffe is discovered to be a notorious criminal) is emotionally satisfying in the sense that justice triumphs, but the contrivance is totally unprepared for in the preceding dramatic action.

To prevent any confusion about Tartuffe's nature, Molière uses two acts to prepare for his entrance. The first act includes a lengthy argument by Cleante, the character who apparently represents Molière's point of view, in which true piety is distinguished from false.

The structure of *Tartuffe* may be clarified by examining the use of various characters. Cleante appears in Act I, where he performs his principal function: to present the commonsense point of view. He does not appear again until Act IV, in which, as well as in Act V, he merely reinforces the ideas he set forth in Act I. Cleante does not influence the action, he clarifies the theme.

Although Dorine, the maid, appears in each act, her role is virtually completed after the beginning of Act III, though she has been a major character up to that point. Her frankness and outspokenness serve to show up Orgon's credulity, the lovers' petulance, and Tartuffe's false piety. Her wit and common sense put the exaggerated behavior of others in proper perspective.

Even Tartuffe is given strange treatment when he finally makes his appearance after two acts of preparation. Most of his time on stage is given over to his two "love scenes" with Elmire. Molière seems to take it for granted that the audience will accept the picture of Tartuffe painted by the other characters and that the play need emphasize only one aspect of his hypocrisy. Tartuffe displays his wiles most fully when he is denounced by Damis. Rather than defend himself, he endures the accusations with apparent humility. This scene, more than any other, shows how Orgon has been taken in by Tartuffe.

The lovers, Valère and Mariane, first appear in Act II and are unimportant thereafter. They serve merely to show the depth of Orgon's credulity because he plans to marry his daughter to Tartuffe. The lovers' quarrel that ensues is a source of amusement largely unrelated to the rest of the play.

Elmire appears in Act III (in which Tartuffe first tries to seduce her), but she has only a few lines, and most of these treat Tartuffe's suggestions with an air of frivolity. Most of her lines come in Act IV, where she serves as the instrument for unmasking Tartuffe. This uneven distribution of the role has led some critics to argue that Elmire's moral character is questionable because she originally seems undisturbed by Tartuffe's advances. Molière probably meant to show Elmire as a reasonably worldly but upright woman who is capable of defending herself without making a fuss about it.

Orgon's role is the one most evenly distributed throughout the play. While the Tartuffes of the world are dangerous, they can exist only because of the Orgons because the success of the wicked depends on the gullibility of the foolish. Just as Molière emphasizes Tartuffe's calculated piety, so, too, he emphasizes Orgon's impulsiveness and stubbornness. Orgon errs largely because he acts without considering sufficient aspects of a question. When Tartuffe is finally unmasked, Orgon's character remains consistent; failing to see the difference between hypocrisy and piety, he says: "I'm through with pious men: Henceforth I'll hate the whole false brotherhood." Instead of returning to middle ground, he assumes an equally exaggerated (though opposite) position.

Little indication is given of the age or physical appearance of the characters. Because Molière wrote with his own company in mind and directed the play, he did not need to specify every detail in his script. The role of Tartuffe was written for DuCroisy, a large man with a ruddy complexion. No doubt this was one of the sources of humor. All of Tartuffe's talk about scourges and fasting was contradicted by his obvious plumpness and lecherousness. Orgon was played by Molière, noted for his expressive face and body; Elmire was acted by Molière's wife, who was twenty-seven years old in 1669. As was often the case with comic old women, Mme. Pernelle was played by a man; thus the character was no doubt intended to be seen as ridiculous in her denunciation of pleasure. All of the characters were drawn from the middle or lower classes (in accordance with neoclassical theories of comedy).

In *Tartuffe,* Molière uses the verse form that by that time had become standard in French drama, the alexandrine (twelve-syllable lines, with each pair of adjacent

A radical reinterpretation of *Tartuffe* as directed by the Romanian director Lucian Pintilie at the Guthrie Theatre, Minneapolis. In this production the action progresses through various periods. In the final act, the rescuers arrive in an automobile. Set by Radu Boruzescu; costumes by Marina Boruzescu; lighting by Beverly Emmons. (Photo by Joe Giannetti. Courtesy the Guthrie Theatre.)

lines rhyming). The nearest equivalent in English is the rhymed couplet, although this form seems far more unnatural than the French alexandrine because English verse, unlike French, uses repeated heavy-stress patterns within lines, and these, in combination with rhymed line endings, encourage a singsong quality in English. In French verse, in which these internal stress patterns are absent, rhymed endings are far less intrusive. Molière, like most French dramatists until modern times, started a new scene each time a character entered or exited in order to indicate an alteration in motivations or focus created by the change of characters on stage. Thus, though the action may be continuous, the printed text is divided into numerous scenes. (Such divisions are usually referred to as "French scenes.")

The unities of time and place are strictly observed in *Tartuffe*. Only a single room is used, and even that requires only a table, under which Orgon can be concealed, and a closet, in which Damis can hide, both used to witness Tartuffe trying to seduce Elmire. No specific use is made of the setting except in these two instances. The action is continuous, or nearly so, and occurs in a single day. All of the episodes, with the possible exception of the lovers' quarrel, are directly related to the main theme of the play. *Tartuffe* is clearly within the neoclassical tradition. It has remained in the repertory almost continuously and has been performed more often than any other play by Molière.

The Elizabethan, Italian, and French Traditions

Although Shakespeare and Molière are among the world's great dramatists and were separated in time by only a few years, they worked within different theatrical traditions. Shakespeare's offered greater flexibility, but before the end of the seventeenth century, it had been replaced by Molière's, probably because the tide of taste was moving steadily toward a preference for representationalism. When the English theatres reopened in 1660, after having been closed for eighteen years, they accepted actresses for the first time in England and adopted the picture-frame stage, perspective scenery, and the neoclassical vision (although never so completely as elsewhere in Europe). During the Restoration several of Shakespeare's plays were adapted to make them conform more nearly to the neoclassical ideal. For example, at the end of Nahum Tate's adaptation of *King Lear* only the wicked people died; Lear, Gloucester, and Kent retired to the country, and Cordelia and Edgar married and became the rulers of England. This is the version of *King Lear* that was performed in English theatres until the 1840s.

English theatre between 1660 and 1700, usually referred to as the Restoration, was noted principally for its comedy of manners, which focused on the amoral behavior and witty verbal exchanges of the rich and idle upper class. Restoration comedy was concerned above all with sexual conquests, advantageous marriages (in which love played little part), the latest fashions, and a seeming determination to be shocked at nothing. The butts of ridicule included the fop, the old man who marries a young wife, the old woman who tries to appear young, the pretender at wit and sophistication, and the self-deceived. The moral tone of these plays has made them controversial ever since they were written. Restoration comedy originated with such works as Sir George Etherege's *The Man of Mode* (1676) and *She Would if She Could* (1668), reaching its peak in the plays of William Congreve, especially *Love for Love* (1695) and *The Way of the World* (1700).

Commedia dell'arte influenced many European playwrights. The degree of its influence on English writers of Shakespeare's day is still debated, but it was clearly evident in eighteenth-century English theatre, especially in pantomimes. Commedia's influence on Molière and other French playwrights is undeniable, and this influence continued throughout the eighteenth and into the nineteenth centuries, even after commedia had ceased to be a separate form.

By 1700, while there were still obvious differences among the theatres of various European countries, they shared the same basic conventions. The theatre had made the transition from festival offerings to professional, secular entertainment.

Chapter 6

From Melodrama to Realism

Chekhov's *The Three Sisters* as produced at the Gorki Theater, Berlin. (Courtesy Gorki Theater.)

> The formal and stylistic markers of realistic drama in this period [the mid-nineteenth century] are familiar: prosaic dialogue, bourgeois setting and subject matter . . . , a conflict between internal psychological motives and external economic or social pressures, a rigorously 'causal' plotting, predominance of incident, and so on.
>
> —William Worthen, *Modern Drama and the Rhetoric of Theater*

Study of the arts has typically concentrated on "high art" (the best as determined by elitist taste) and ignored what popular taste favored and supported. When we study the theatre of the past, we usually concentrate on those periods that have left behind scripts we consider to be great literature. We pay more attention to Greece than to Rome, for example, though the theatre of Rome was far more extensive and varied than that of Greece. This is true partly because scripts survive and performances do not and because we assume that the value of a theatre is determined by the quality of the scripts it produces. But what critics consider the best is not always the most popular. In almost every period, the gap between elitist and popular taste can tell us much about the culture because popular art is a more immediate barometer of the general public's preferences than elitist art is. Today, television is the dominant caterer to popular taste and, as with comparable media in the past, its offerings are frequently dismissed as inferior by those who apply elitist standards to them.

Prior to the twentieth century, the theatre was the usual medium of popular entertainment because there was no radio, film, or television and because there were virtually no professional spectator sports (which today draw many who formerly looked to the theatre for diversion). The theatre does not require a literate public because the actors "read" the script to the audience. Thus, the theatre has probably served as popular entertainment more often than as provider of profound insights into human behavior—though, at its best, it has done both simultaneously.

Popular entertainment has existed since the beginning of human history. The Greeks enjoyed mimes (brief comic skits about everyday life), and to mimes the Romans added many variety acts involving acrobats, trained animals, and hand-to-hand combatants. During the Middle Ages, small troupes traveled about performing wherever they could find an audience. From earliest times, numerous seasonal festivals also offered diverting spectacles. In the Renaissance, commedia dell'arte achieved almost universal appeal.

Among later theatrical forms, *melodrama* was one of the most popular (especially during the nineteenth century). Today, nineteenth-century melodrama is usually dismissed as the naive entertainment of an unsophisticated audience, even though melodrama, in crime and police television series, is still a major popular form. Let us look more closely at melodrama as a type of popular entertainment.

The Emergence of Melodrama

The term *melodrama* first came into regular use in France around 1800, and was soon adopted almost everywhere as a label for a form of drama that had evolved during the eighteenth century.

The popularity of melodrama was in part a reaction against the neoclassical rules that had dominated dramatic writing since the mid-seventeenth century. These rules, although not always followed, had attempted to restrict the action of each drama to a span of twenty-four hours, to one place (additional places were permitted as long as they could be reached without stretching the twenty-four-hour limit), and to one plot (subplots were tolerated only if they were clearly offshoots of the main plot). Neoclassicism also sought to rule out fantasy and supernatural elements. And, because it was grounded in the belief that human nature is the same in all times and all places, it sought to depict universal (rather than historically accurate or individualized) traits, behavior, and visual elements. Settings were so generalized that they could be used in many different productions. For example, if the place of action was a prison, the goal was to depict the *essence* of a prison rather than any particular prison; therefore, the same set could be used for any prison scene. Similarly, characters were usually dressed in clothing of the period of the performance, no matter what the historical period of the action, because to place characters in a specific historical milieu might suggest that the play's depiction of human behavior was true only for that earlier time and place. Therefore, in the

Macbeth as costumed c. 1775. Macbeth (played by David Garrick, one of England's greatest actors) is dressed as an eighteenth-century British general, while Lady Macbeth (played by Mrs. Pritchard) wears the fashionable dress of that time. In this scene, Lady Macbeth holds the daggers with which she urges Macbeth to kill King Duncan. (*English Illustrated Magazine*, 1776.)

eighteenth century Hamlet wore fashionable eighteenth-century dress and Macbeth was dressed in the uniform of a British general.

Most of the strictures of neoclassicism were applied only to "regular" drama (that is, comedy and tragedy written in five acts). Perhaps for this reason a number of "irregular" forms gained popularity during the eighteenth century. Many were probably influenced by opera, which had never been subjected to the rules and included numerous special effects, changes of scene, music, dance, and other appeals denied regular drama. But by the eighteenth century opera had become an elitist entertainment in most of Europe because of high ticket prices. Consequently, many of its features, in modified form, were brought into the popular theatre through new types of musical drama. England developed the *ballad opera*, which incorporated in an otherwise spoken drama numerous lyrics set to the tunes of well-known popular songs or ballads. The most famous example is John Gay's *The Beggar's Opera* (1728). In France, comparable pieces were called *opéra comique* and in Germany and Austria *Singspiele* (of which Mozart's *The Magic Flute* is the best-known example, though it is now performed as an opera). Another popular form was *pantomime*, in which Harlequin was usually the main character. Harlequin's slapstick became a magic wand, permitting spectacular transformations of people and places; the action was accompanied throughout by music, and there were usually several dances. Thus, "irregular" pieces overcame the restrictions imposed by the neoclassical rules, although they were considered inferior to the "regular" dramas.

Toward the end of the eighteenth century, the attitudes that had supported neoclassicism began to change, and by the early nineteenth century, they had undergone almost complete reversal, coalescing to create *romanticism*. The earlier belief that truth is to be found in "norms" gave way to the conviction that truth is to be found in the infinite variety of creation. According to the romantics, the universe has been created by God out of himself so that he may contemplate himself. Therefore, everything has a common origin and is part of a greater whole. Thus, rather than eliminate details to arrive at norms, one should welcome them in all their variety. Romantics also believed that the more unspoiled a thing is—the less it deviates from its natural state—the more truthful it is; writers showed a marked preference for poetry about nature and for drama about unspoiled human beings living in primitive times or in rebellion against restraints imposed by society. Romantics glorified the writer-genius, who, grasping intuitively the complexity of the universe, rejected the strictures imposed by neoclassicism.

Perhaps the changes in critical attitudes are best summed up in relation to Shakespeare. Although Shakespeare had always been popular in England, where many of his plays held a firm place in the repertory, they were not performed in any other European country until the late eighteenth century. Except in England, Shakespeare was considered barbarous because his plays were at odds with the neoclassical rules. Even in England, many of his plays were subjected to rewriting intended to bring them more nearly into accord with neoclassical demands. English critics tried to explain Shakespeare's appeal by labeling him a natural genius who, despite his ignorance of the rules, had managed to write effective though flawed dramas. Nevertheless, they implied, he would have been even better had he known and followed the rules.

During the last quarter of the eighteenth century, Shakespeare's plays began to be translated into other European languages and staged, although at first only in heavily adapted versions. As Shakespeare's reputation grew, the plays were altered less and less, and by the early nineteenth century his works were becoming the standard against which plays were judged throughout Europe. During the nineteenth century, Shakespeare achieved the reputation he has been accorded ever since as the greatest dramatist of all time. Because he had written without regard for the neoclassical rules, he became an argument for ignoring them, and the unities of time, place, and action gave way to actions occurring over many years, in numerous places, and through a tangle of plots. Variety often took precedence over unity. The mysterious and supernatural, which had been deplored by the neoclassicists, became common occurrences in the new drama, as did concern for the characteristic features of specific times and places. Historical accuracy in settings and costumes began to be favored, although it was not consistently realized until around 1850. In sum, the theatre underwent major alterations during the early nineteenth century. In this new climate, melodrama flourished, becoming to the general public what Shakespeare was to elitist audiences (although Shakespeare was not without appeal to the masses). Melodrama was the popular-culture manifestation of romanticism, the artistic movement that dominated the first half of the nineteenth century.

Melodrama emphasized clear and suspenseful plots in which a virtuous protagonist was hounded by a villain and rescued from seemingly insurmountable difficulties after undergoing a series of threats to life, reputation, or happiness. All important events occurred on stage; typically, there was at least one elaborate spectacular happening (earthquake, burning building, explosion, or the like) and/or scene of local color (festivals or dances using the picturesque customs or conditions of a specific country or city). Typical plot devices included concealed or mistaken identity, abductions, strange coincidences, and hidden documents. Comic relief was often provided by a servant, ally, or companion of one of the principal characters. Perhaps most important, strict poetic justice was meted out: The evil people were

A frontier theatre in Cheyenne, Wyoming. During the nineteenth century, the number of theatres mushroomed as population steadily increased and created a demand for entertainment everywhere. When people moved westward in the United States, the theatre followed. (*Frank Leslie's Illustrated Newspaper,* 13 October 1877.)

Audience Behavior

It has often been said that the influx of working-class spectators into the nineteenth-century theatre, and their behavior once there, drove away the more refined segment of the audience. This conclusion is supported by a German visitor's account of his experience in London's theatres:

> The most striking thing to a foreigner in English theatres is the unheard-of coarseness and brutality of the audiences. The consequence of this is that the higher and more civilized classes go only to the Italian Opera, and very rarely visit their national theatre. . . . English freedom here degenerates into the rudest license, and it is not uncommon in the midst of the most affecting part of a tragedy . . . to hear some coarse expression shouted from the galleries in a stentorian voice. This is followed, according to the taste of the bystanders, either by loud laughter and approbation, or by the castigation and expulsion of the offender. Whichever turn the thing takes, you can hear nothing of what is passing on the stage. . . . And such things happen not once, but sometimes twenty times, in the course of a performance, and amuse many in the audience. . . .

> *—Hermann Pücker-Muskau,*
> Tour in England, Ireland, and France, in the Years 1826, 1827, 1828, and 1829

punished, and the good were rewarded. The villain might seem triumphant until the final scene, but ultimately he was unmasked and defeated.

Melodrama had a large musical element, as suggested by its name, which literally means "music drama." Originally, there were a number of songs in each play but, more important, the action was accompanied by a musical score (every theatre in the nineteenth century employed a pit orchestra) that enhanced the action and the emotional tone of scenes. With its simple, powerful stories, unequivocal moral tone, spectacle, and music, melodrama offered compelling and popular entertainment to the mass audiences of the nineteenth century. Many of melodrama's features were taken over by film in the twentieth century. (Perhaps the best recent examples of continuity with nineteenth-century melodrama are the Indiana Jones films.)

The popularity of melodrama in the nineteenth century is explained in part by fundamental changes in social and economic conditions stemming from the industrial revolution. As inventions such as the steam engine, power loom, steamship, and locomotive were exploited, the factory system of mass production gradually replaced individual craftsmen, who had been the major producers of goods since medieval times. Because workers had to live near the factories, urbanization accelerated rapidly and created large potential audiences for theatrical entertainment. The largest city in Europe, London, had supported only two or three theatres during the eighteenth century, but between 1800 and 1850, its population doubled and the number of its theatres grew to more than twenty. Its population and number of theatres continued to grow through the remainder of the century. As in television

The Octoroon, a melodrama by Dion
Boucicault, first performed in 1859. Here
a man is seeking to save the mixed-blood
woman he loves from being sold to the
highest bidder at a slave auction. (A
contemporary engraving.)

programming today, theatres sought to attract the largest possible audiences. Melodrama and variety entertainment proved to be the answer. Many critics argue that
catering to mass taste led to a decline in the quality of theatrical offerings. But
eventually theatre managers discovered that they did not have to appeal to everyone
and, during the last half of the nineteenth century, each theatre began to aim its
programming at a specific segment of the population or a particular taste.

A publicity poster for Augustin Daly's *Under the Gaslight,* the first of many plays to place a
character in imminent danger of destruction by an oncoming locomotive.

Scenes of Suspense and Spectacle in Melodrama

Much of the appeal of melodrama during the nineteenth century lay in the suspense created by placing sympathetic characters in great physical danger and by rescuing them at the last minute. These scenes were made even more attractive by spectacular scenic contrivances that made the danger seem real and present. One of these occurs in *Uncle Tom's Cabin,* the most popular melodrama of the nineteenth century. The enslaved Eliza, learning that her child, Harry, is to be taken from her and sold, runs away with him. She finds someone who will help her but she must first get out of Kentucky (where slavery is legal) across the Ohio River (to territory free from slavery). While Eliza waits at an inn for the ferry that will take her across the river, villainous bounty hunters arrive, unaware of her presence. Overhearing their plan to capture her, she slips out through a window, but they see her and give chase. (In some productions, Eliza's pursuers used bloodhounds to track her.) The Ohio River has been frozen over, but the ice has broken into pieces. In desperation, Eliza, clutching Harry, leaps onto a large piece of ice and, as her pursuers look on helplessly, floats across the river, where the man who will rescue her is seen waiting. This scene was so popular and well known that it became legendary. Even in the twentieth century, it was not uncommon for people, when circumstances seemed to be closing in on them, to say they felt like Eliza fleeing the bloodhounds.

Because the pattern of melodrama is always the same (good threatened by evil, with the eventual triumph of good), variety was gained through such novelties as exotic locales, ever-more-spectacular effects, increased realism, incorporation into the action of the latest inventions, and dramatizations of popular novels or notorious crimes. A few melodrama theatres included facilities for horseback riding and featured plays with spectacular feats of horsemanship and last-minute rescues by mounted riders. Others installed water tanks to accommodate "aquatic" melodramas. The first important writer of melodramas, the Frenchman Guilbert de Pixérécourt, resolved one of his plays by having the villain destroyed as lava from a volcanic eruption inundated the stage. Dion Boucicault, one of the most popular playwrights of the English-speaking stage between 1840 and 1890, in 1859 used the newly invented camera to reveal the identity of a murderer in *The Octoroon;* and Augustin Daly, an American playwright, in *Under the Gaslight* (1867) was the first to tie a character to a railroad track in the path of an oncoming locomotive and to rescue the character at the last moment.

After electricity became common in the 1880s, electric motors were coupled with treadmills to stage horse or chariot races. To make the race realistic, moving panoramas (long cloths on which a continuous scene was painted) were suspended at the rear of the stage in overhead tracks and ran between upright spools on either side of the stage. The movement of these panoramas was synchronized with that of

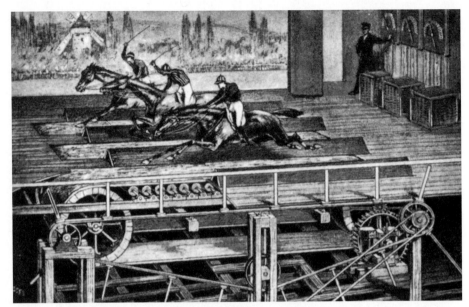

A drawing showing an onstage horse race in *The County Fair*, staged at the Union Square Theatre, New York, 1889, using a moving panorama and treadmills connected to electric motors, the speed of which was controlled by the man at upper right. (*Scientific American*, 1889.)

the treadmills so that the horses were kept onstage by the treadmills while the scene painted on the panorama rushed by behind them, creating the effect that the horses were racing around a track. (See the illustration above.) *Ben Hur's* chariot race had been seen in many theatres by 1900. The trend was toward ever-more-realistic effects. In the early twentieth century, film inherited this tradition and continued to exploit it. After the potential of film was established, the theatre largely abandoned such productions.

Realistic spectacle, thrilling effects, novelty, suspense, and the vindication of virtue were the major appeals of melodrama. Melodrama encouraged the development of realism in the visual aspects of theatre while clinging to recognizable and comforting stereotypes in characterization and morality. Let us look more closely at an example of nineteenth-century melodrama.

Monte Cristo

Monte Cristo is a dramatization of Alexandre Dumas *père's* *The Count of Monte Cristo* (1845), one of the world's most popular novels. Dumas himself dramatized the work in 1848, but it was in twenty acts and required two evenings to perform. Several other dramatizations were made, but the one that eventually held the stage was by Charles Fechter, a French actor who had a long and distinguished career on the stages of France, England, and America. In 1885, the rights to this version were purchased by James O'Neill (1847–1920), who subsequently made numerous revisions. The text as it now stands is the work of several persons. O'Neill became so identified with the role of Edmund Dantès that the public would go to see him in no other play; he toured the United States off and on for thirty years in the production. His plight was like that of many actors of recent times who have become so identified with their roles in television series that they have no subsequent careers or are always cast in the same type of role. O'Neill's sense of being trapped by the role is forcefully stated in *Long Day's Journey into Night* (written by his son, Eugene O'Neill, often considered the greatest dramatist America has produced).

Reducing Dumas' novel of several hundred pages to a play that could be performed in two or three hours was a formidable task, but not unusual in the nineteenth century because popular novels were typically dramatized quickly following their publication. Almost all of Charles Dickens' novels were adapted for the stage, and *Uncle Tom's Cabin,* adapted from Harriet Beecher Stowe's novel, became the most popular play of the nineteenth century. Film and television have continued this practice in the twentieth century.

The sweep of *Monte Cristo* is nearer to that of Shakespeare's plays than to those of Sophocles or Molière. There are many incidents, though the basic pattern is relatively simple. The hero, a ship's officer named Edmund Dantès, returns from a voyage prepared to marry his fiancée, Mercedes. He runs afoul of three villains: Danglars (the ship's cargo officer), Fernand (who loves Mercedes), and Villefort (a

Uncle Tom's Cabin as produced by William Brady in 1901. Eliza (right rear) is about to cross the Ohio River on a piece of ice. The use of dogs and horses by Eliza's pursuers had become common by this time. (Courtesy of the Harvard Theatre Collection.)

government prosecutor who fears that his brother, Noirtier, will ruin his career if he obtains a letter Edmund is bringing from the deposed emperor Napoleon). These three arrange for Dantès' arrest as a traitor, and he is imprisoned on the notorious penal island, the Chateau d'If. Edmund remains in prison for eighteen years, but during that time an elderly prisoner, Faria, befriends him and reveals the location of his family's vast fortune—the island of Monte Cristo. When Faria dies, Edmund takes the corpse's place in the sack which—in the prison's burial practice—will be thrown into the sea. Through this ruse, Edmund escapes, recovers the Faria fortune, and sets out to punish those who have wronged him. While Edmund has been in prison, his betrayers have prospered: Villefort has become minister of justice, Danglars a major financier, and Fernand a general, a peer of France, and Mercedes' husband (after she had been persuaded that Edmund is dead). As the count of Monte Cristo, Edmund relentlessly tracks down his persecutors and punishes each in turn. By the story's end, all the villains have been publicly disgraced and are dead.

Like other melodramas, *Monte Cristo* shows goodness victimized and evil triumphant for a time, but ultimately evil is exposed and punished and goodness is vindicated. It differs from most melodramas in rescuing the hero early from danger (at the end of Act II) and in the great amount of time devoted to punishing the villains. By actual time, of course, the hero languishes in prison for eighteen years, but in the play, those years are passed over in the interval between Acts I and II. Edmund

The Count of Monte Cristo, a revival of James O'Neill's *Monte Cristo*, at the Kennedy Center, Washington, D.C. The performers are (from the left) Anne Beresford Clarke, Patti LuPone, Joaquim de Almeida, Roscoe Lee Browne, Brian McCue, and Tony Azito. Directed by Peter Sellars. (Photo by Joan Marcus.)

is actually seen in prison in only one scene (whereas the novel devotes many chapters to his sufferings). The play omits showing Edmund's recovery of Faria's treasure and his intricate preparations for revenge. Many of the events (especially the way in which Villefort is punished) and character relationships (most importantly in making Albert the son of Edmund and Mercedes rather than of Fernand and Mercedes) differ from those in the novel.

The result of the omissions and alterations is to impose an almost symmetrical pattern on the action. The potential for happiness and harmony in the opening scenes is thwarted by a series of betrayers (Danglars, Fernand, and Villefort), who then prosper from Edmund's downfall. The turning point, Edmund's escape, has a miraculous quality both in the event itself and in Faria's legacy of enormous wealth, which makes Edmund's revenge possible. In this scene, Edmund proclaims himself an instrument of revenge. Reading the script fails to convey the effect created in performance by Edmund rising from the sea, climbing onto a rock, and proclaiming, "The world is mine." This scene became one of the best-loved moments of nineteenth-century theatre. Following this powerful scene, the villains are punished in the reverse order of their betrayals (Villefort first, then Fernand, and finally Danglars). As each is punished, Edmund announces the score—"One," "Two," "Three"—an accounting so satisfying to O'Neill's audiences that they often counted aloud with him. At the end, the play achieves additional symmetry by implying the possibility of achieving the happiness promised in the opening scene. Though the plot is intricate, the underlying pattern is simple—and deeply reassuring in its inexorable meting out of just rewards and punishments.

Characterization is far simpler than plot in *Monte Cristo*. The characters can be divided into three categories: good (Edmund, Mercedes, Noirtier, Albert), evil (Danglars, Fernand, Villefort), and functional (sailors, fishermen, policemen, servants). A drunken and henpecked innkeeper, Caderousse, serves as comic relief. The main characters are types with minimal individualizing traits. Edmund seems almost entirely good. He has only one moment of doubt: when he discovers that Albert, whom he has intended to kill, is his son and not Fernand's as he had thought. Most of the characters are at some point torn briefly between truth and self-interest, but the bad always choose self-interest, and the good, truth. Melodrama seldom suggests that moral choices are determined by environmental forces; rather, awareness of good and evil is innate, and each character is free to choose right or wrong. Values are viewed as absolute rather than relative (as they are in most twentieth-century drama).

The characters are always wholly conscious of their motives and feelings and state them to the audience. To prevent any misperception, they use asides to inform the audience (or another character) of reactions that they do not wish to share with all those onstage. (The *aside*, a convention almost as old as drama itself, came under attack in the late nineteenth century as being unrealistic and was eventually abandoned except in self-consciously nonrealistic plays.)

Next to suspenseful and morally satisfying plots, melodrama owed its appeal most to spectacle. By the 1880s, when O'Neill achieved his triumph in *Monte Cristo*, producers were priding themselves on the realism and authenticity of their costumes and settings. The first act of *Monte Cristo* takes place in 1815 (when

A late-nineteenth-century stage. Notice how the stage floor is divided; notice also the sinking trap, the strong beam of light (either a limelight or carbon arc) and the footlights (lower right corner).

Napoleon was in exile on Elba), while the other acts occur in the 1830s. Costumes played a major role in marking both passage of time and alteration in the economic and social status of the characters. Much of the "local color" of time and place was created through the dress of sailors, policemen, tavern patrons, and partygoers. Disguises were also important to both Noirtier and Edmund.

Monte Cristo requires eight sets, two of which were probably simple and very shallow, permitting more complex sets to be erected behind them while a scene was in progress. The shallow scenes are those for Villefort's office and a room in Fernand's house. These occur in the only acts (I and II) with multiple scenes. The scene in Villefort's office takes place between two others set in taverns overlooking the harbor. Both tavern sets probably shared a number of elements, and the necessary alterations and changes could easily have been made during the scene in Villefort's office. The Act II scene in Fernand's house involves only a few characters and no unusual physical action. It was probably set up in front of the Chateau d'If setting, the most elaborate of the play, involving two levels, one of which sinks, concealing the prisoners' cells and revealing the water into which Edmund's body is thrown and the rock onto which he climbs triumphantly.

The demands of the Chateau d'If scene illustrate the changes that had occurred in scenic practices by the late nineteenth century. O'Neill first played his version of *Monte Cristo* at Booth's Theatre in New York. This theatre, opened in 1869, had been built by one of America's greatest actors, Edwin Booth, and probably was the first stage in modern times to have a flat floor and to eliminate the traditional arrangement of wings. Its stage embodied a recognition that new ways of handling scenery were required by the growing emphasis on creating three-dimensional practicable pieces and on including furniture and other details found in real-life places. Wings had become increasingly unsatisfactory because they were two-dimensional, parallel to the front of the stage, and arranged in symmetrical pairs from front to back. In combination with the raked stage floor, wings made it difficult to move large three-dimensional pieces on and off the stage. The flat floor and the absence of wing positions in Booth's theatre permitted scenery to be erected wherever desired and to be moved on and off without hindrance. This theatre also had a number of elevator traps that raised and lowered heavy set pieces hydraulically.

By the late nineteenth century, the stage floor in most theatres was divided into sections a few feet wide, any of which could be removed to create an opening ("bridge") extending completely across the stage. In the second act of *Monte Cristo*, the sinking of one part of the setting probably utilized one or more bridges. Upstage was the sea and the rock, both of which became visible as the cells sank. The sea was represented by a painted cloth moved up and down rhythmically by ropes attached to the underside. The sack (containing a dummy) was thrown into the water (no doubt with accompanying splash), and then, after a time, a soaked Edmund rose, probably through a trapdoor, climbed onto the rock, and uttered his triumphant "The world is mine." Such complex spectacle was typical of melodrama. The sets for the final three acts (an inn, ballroom, and forest), though elaborate, could be changed during the intervals between acts. The settings, which provided great variety, had to be designed and constructed with care, for O'Neill toured this production throughout the country beginning in the 1880s and for the next thirty years.

Touring such complex productions was made possible by the development of dependable transportation, which became a reality with the spread of railroads. The first transcontinental line in the United States was completed in the 1860s; by the late 1870s, it was possible to reach almost any area of the country by rail, and numerous theatrical productions were touring with sets, costumes, properties, and actors. Such companies soon became the major purveyors of theatrical entertainment in most of America and remained so until displaced by sound motion pictures in the 1930s.

Melodrama's visual appeal was further enhanced by lighting, the potential of which had increased greatly after gas replaced candles and oil during the first half of the nineteenth century. For the first time, the stage could be lighted as brightly as desired. Equally important, control over intensity became possible through a "gas table"—a central location from which all the gas lines ran and from which the supply of gas to any part of the theatre could be controlled. Lights could be dimmed or brightened as desired by one person operating the gas table. It was now possible to darken the auditorium and brighten it again when needed. These improvements encouraged increased concern for atmosphere and mood in stage lighting. Gas also made possible the development and exploitation of the "limelight," a type of spotlight (from which we get our expression "being in the limelight"). The limelight was made by placing a column of calcium (lime) inside a hood equipped with reflector

The final scene of James O'Neill's production of *Monte Cristo*. The acting area is very shallow, but the set is made to seem deep by the use of cut drops—that is, by cutting away portions of each drop so another can be seen through the openings. (Albert Davis Collection, Hoblitzelle Theatre Arts Library, Harry Ransom Humanities Research Center, University of Texas at Austin.)

and lens; onto the lime were directed compressed hydrogen and oxygen along with a gas flame; the lime was heated to incandescence until it gave off an extremely bright light used to create such atmospheric effects as rays of moonlight or sunlight or to focus attention on a character or object. At the end of Act II in *Monte Cristo*, the stage direction reads: "The moon breaks out, lighting up a projecting rock. Edmund rises from the sea, he is dripping, a knife in his hand, some shreds of sack adhering to it." The effectiveness of this scene was greatly enhanced by the limelight.

O'Neill's production of *Monte Cristo* calls attention to another change then under way: Long runs of single plays performed by actors hired for that production only were replacing a repertory of plays performed in rotation by a permanent company (the system that had prevailed since Shakespeare's day). The theatre had begun to adopt those practices that have been typical since the late nineteenth century.

With melodrama, the theatre in the nineteenth and early twentieth centuries achieved its greatest mass appeal. It developed the audience and many of the conventions taken over by film, which displaced it as the prime medium of popular en-

The Appeal of Melodrama

Melodrama may have been artistically crude and its supporters often boisterous, but it was a form well suited to an age in which democracy was struggling to establish itself. Melodrama validated the claim of ordinary people to a kind of aristocracy based on virtue and personal integrity rather than wealth and power.

It took the lives of common people seriously and paid much respect to their superior purity and wisdom. . . . it held up ideals and promised rewards, particularly that of the paradise of the happy home based on female purity, that were available to all. And its moral parable struggled to reconcile social fears and life's awesomeness with the period's confidence in absolute moral standards, man's upward progress, and a benevolent providence that insured the triumph of the pure.

—*David Grimsted*, Melodrama Unveiled: American Theater and Culture, 1800–1850

tertainment, especially after sound was added around 1930. And through film this legacy was subsequently passed on to television. Film forced theatre to reassess what it could do most effectively; as a result theatre largely abandoned attempts to create the kind of realistic spectacle seen in *Monte Cristo*, which can be achieved much more convincingly by film. With their capacity to replicate their products endlessly, film and television were analogous in their effects on theatre to the effects of factories on individual craftsmen in the nineteenth century, making theatre the equivalent of a handcrafted product, one that has difficulty competing in a world attuned to mass production. Theatre had tried to meet the nineteenth-century demand for mass production by mounting elaborate productions and sending them throughout the country by the most efficient means of transportation then available. But theatre ultimately is not a medium adapted to mass production. Film is. The popular entertainment of the late nineteenth and early twentieth centuries, especially melodrama, was the meeting ground for theatre and film and was crucial in the subsequent history of both.

The Advent of Realism

Even as James O'Neill was achieving his great popular success in *Monte Cristo*, other theories and beliefs were undermining the absolutist moral values on which melodrama depended. While unanimity of belief was never an actuality, Western civilization throughout the Christian era had looked to the Bible as the ultimate authority on values and moral principles. The biblical version of Creation and subsequent events was often accepted literally. Until the late nineteenth century, the Earth was thought to be about six thousand years old, the date of the Creation having been calculated by counting back through the generations that, according to the Bible, had preceded the birth of Christ.

In the late nineteenth century, a number of intellectual and scientific developments (especially in the fields of geology and anthropology) called many biblical passages into question. When geologists began to suggest that the Earth is millions (or even billions) of years old, and when anthropologists began to discover animal and human remains thousands of years older than the supposed date of the world's creation, heated controversies resulted. The greatest controversy was provoked by Charles Darwin's *Origin of Species* (1859), in which he argued (1) that all forms of life have developed gradually from a common ancestry, and (2) that this evolution of species can be explained by the "survival of the fittest"—those most capable of adapting to specific environmental conditions. This theory was, and remains, anathema to those who interpret literally the biblical account of the Creation.

Darwin's theories have many implications. First, they suggest that heredity and environment are the primary causes of everything human beings are or do. Second, they suggest that, because human beings have no control over their individual heredity (it is fixed at birth) and little control over their environment (especially during the early years, when an individual's personality and values are being formed), people cannot be held fully responsible for what they do; if blame is to be assigned, it must be shared by the society that has countenanced undesirable hereditary and environmental forces. (Indecisiveness over how responsibility is to be apportioned is the primary cause of contemporary arguments over such issues as the leniency or harshness of court decisions.) Third, Darwin's theories strengthened the idea of progress because if humanity evolved from an atom of being to its present complexity, improvement must be inevitable. (Many of Darwin's contemporaries believed that progress, even though inevitable, could be hastened with the help of science and technology.) Darwin's theories also contradicted the biblical account of the deliberate, instantaneous creation of humanity with its implication that human beings have been the same (at least biologically) since the time of Adam and Eve. Fourth, Darwin's theories absorbed humanity into nature. Prior to Darwin, human beings, because of their awareness of right and wrong, had always been set apart from and considered superior to the rest of nature. With Darwin, human beings, like other animals, became merely a species to be studied scientifically.

These implications were crucial in the development of the modern temperament, for they suggested that change (rather than fixity) is the norm. Late-nineteenth-century thought began increasingly to support the belief that moral standards are relative to each culture and that concepts of right and wrong may vary widely from one society to another.

The new ideas about human conscience were stated most fully in the writings of Sigmund Freud (1856–1939), the most influential psychologist of the twentieth century. Freud argued that the basic human instincts are aggression and sexuality—self-preservation and procreation. Left alone, human beings would seek to satisfy their instincts without regard for others; if they are to be integrated into a community, they must undergo socialization. Through rewards and punishments, they learn early what is acceptable and what is unacceptable, and in this process they develop a superego (an interior, subconscious censor or judge), what had previously been called a conscience. Throughout the Christian era, most people had believed that conscience is innate—that human beings have an instinctive grasp of the difference between right and wrong. (Melodrama was built on this premise.) With Freud, a sense of right and wrong is not absolute and does not come from God; it is relative to the individual, family, and societal environment that has produced it. Freud further argued that the process of socialization causes us to suppress many desires and urges (bury them in the unconscious mind) and find socially acceptable substitutes that the conscious mind can openly acknowledge. Freud's view of human psychology implies that not only can we never fully understand others but also that we can never be certain of our own motives. To assess people and situations, in addition to noting what is consciously said and done, we must also be aware of the subtext—what is not consciously said and done. According to this view, then, not only are moral values relative, but language and behavior are only partially reliable indicators of a person's state of mind and motives.

Relativity eventually affected every area of thought and action. It initially entered the theatre through *realism* and *naturalism,* even though these movements were seeking objective, scientific explanations of human behavior.

Realism and Naturalism

Realism was first recognized during the 1850s, *naturalism* (a more extreme version of realism) during the 1870s. In the theatre, these movements seemed in some ways extensions of already common practices, especially in the area of spectacle. Since around 1800, emphasis on visual accuracy in scenery and costumes had steadily increased and one type of realism had already been achieved. Nevertheless, this realism, as is demonstrated by *Monte Cristo,* was exploited primarily as spectacular or picturesque background. In contrast to all preceding movements, realism and naturalism believed that character is determined in large part by environment, and they demanded that settings play an enlarged role—as representations of the environmental forces that have shaped the characters and (consequently) the dramatic action. In other words, setting was conceived of as environment and not merely as appropriate or impressive background. One consequence was the belief that each play's scenic needs are unique because each play's environment is unlike that of any other. Perhaps more important, this approach to setting implies that what a character is and does is relative to specific environmental forces.

The views of realists and naturalists were grounded in the scientific outlook: the need to understand human behavior in terms of natural cause and effect. They restricted their pursuit of truth to knowledge that can be verified through the five senses. They argued that because we can know the real world only through direct observation, playwrights should write about the society around them and should do so as objectively as possible. Given these premises, it was logical that realists and naturalists would write primarily about contemporary subjects (unlike earlier serious dramatists who usually chose historical or mythical subjects) and introduce behavior not previously seen on the stage. Because many of the plays dealt with unsavory social conditions such as poverty, disease, prostitution, and the plight of

An early example of realistic drama, Alexandre Dumas *fils' The Demi-Monde* as staged at the Théâtre du Gymnase in Paris in 1855.

illegitimate children, conservative critics charged that the theatre had become little better than a sewer, but realists replied that because they were depicting conditions truthfully, they were acting morally, truth being the highest form of morality. Furthermore, the realists argued, what their critics were demanding was an idealized, nonexistent vision of truth; instead, they declared, if audiences did not like the life portrayed on stage, they should change the society that furnished the models rather than denounce the playwrights who had the courage to portray life truthfully. The real issue was the role of art in society: Should art, as in melodrama, always show good triumphant? If art shows deviations from accepted morality and behavior, should it reaffirm traditional values even though they have not triumphed in this instance? Or should art, as the realists and naturalists argued, follow truth wherever it leads without concern for conformity to social codes and moral values? Ultimately, it was a controversy over absolute versus relative values.

These issues were brought into focus about 1880 by Henrik Ibsen (1828–1906), a Norwegian playwright often called the founder of modern drama. Ibsen had begun his playwriting career around 1850 with verse dramas about Scandinavian

Critical Reaction to Ibsen

It is difficult for us to understand how violent a response Ibsen's plays evoked when they first appeared. The reaction to *Ghosts* was extreme because, although the disease is never named in the play, both the husband and son of the principal character, Mrs. Alving, are victims of syphilis, a subject considered not only wholly inappropriate in the theatre but also unmentionable in polite society. In addition, the play suggests that her son might have escaped this curse had Mrs. Alving been permitted to leave her husband, as she wished. To many, Ibsen, in introducing into his play both syphilis and divorce, seemed to be attacking the family as an institution and to be violating all standards of decency. The response of some critics and censors was comparable to what might be expected today if one were to propose showing an X-rated movie to children.

When *Ghosts* was produced by London's Independent Theatre, though only for members of the organization, many critics wrote scathing reviews. George Bernard Shaw, a strong supporter of Ibsen, quotes excerpts from many of these responses in his *The Quintessence of Ibsenism* (1891):

"An open drain; a loathsome sore unbandaged; a dirty act done publicly . . ." "Garbage and offal." "A piece to bring the stage into disrepute and dishonour with every right-thinking man and woman."

Ibsen's perception of women's role in society was also out of step with the time, when women were wholly subservient to fathers or husbands. In his notes on *A Doll's House,* Ibsen wrote:

A woman cannot be herself in the society of the present day, which is an exclusively masculine society, with laws framed by men and with a judicial system that judges feminine conduct from a masculine point of view.

legends, but in the 1870s he abandoned verse and turned exclusively to contemporary subjects. His plays stirred worldwide controversy because the endings of his plays did not reaffirm accepted values. These plays were denied production in many places because they were thought to be immoral and corrupting. Nevertheless, these plays were widely read and discussed, especially because they were thought to challenge moral values and social norms long considered absolute. Let us look more closely at one of Ibsen's plays.

A Doll's House

In *A Doll's House* (1879), Nora Helmer is faced with the consequences of having (several years earlier) forged her father's name to borrow the money needed to restore her husband's health (although by law she could not borrow money without her husband's consent). Now, just as happiness seems assured (her husband, Torvald,

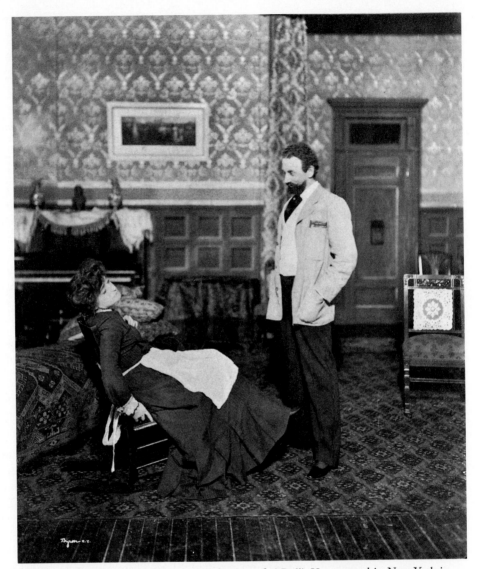

Minnie Maddern Fiske as Nora in a production of *A Doll's House* staged in New York in 1894. (Photo courtesy of the Harry Ransom Humanities Research Center, University of Texas at Austin.)

is fully recovered and has just been appointed director of a bank), the man from whom Nora borrowed the money (Krogstad) threatens to expose her as a criminal if she does not help him keep the job he is about to lose at Torvald's bank. Much of the remainder of the play is taken up with Nora's attempt to conceal the truth from her husband because she is convinced that, because of his deep love for her, he will assume responsibility for the crime and thus be ruined. When exposure comes, he reacts quite differently than she had expected, being concerned only for his own reputation; he declares her so morally corrupt that she will no longer be allowed to raise her three children. When the threat is unexpectedly withdrawn, Torvald is jubilant about his escape from ruin and, once certain of his safety, seeks to restore his previous relationship with Nora. She, however, now feels alienated not only from her husband but also from her society. She chooses to leave her husband and children because, finding herself in disagreement with both law and public opinion and not yet certain of her own convictions, she does not believe herself capable of meeting her responsibilities as wife and mother. She wishes to consider, freed from the emotional blackmail of home and children, what it means to be a woman in a society that deprives her of all rights. It is this ending that caused outrage and controversy because to many it seemed an attack on the family itself, the very basis of society. The outrage also stemmed from Ibsen's refusal to allow the audience the escape that Torvald had sought—the pretense, following a moment's anxiety, that the old social order was secure. The ending forces consideration of the status of women who, by law, are defined as inferior because a wife is required to have her husband's consent in all matters, whereas he can act wholly independently, even dispose of property that originally belonged to her, without her consent or knowledge.

Mrs. Linde (Nora's childhood friend, now a widow) and Krogstad serve as contrasts to Nora and Torvald. Mrs. Linde has considerable experience, having had to work for a living, though always in positions subordinate to men. She accepts her lot, but what she craves most is someone to look after. Nora, as she eventually realizes, has spent her life being treated like a doll, protected from harsh realities but having learned to manipulate men by feeding their fantasies about female helplessness. The mistake for which Krogstad has paid so dearly is the same one made by Nora, but because women are to be governed by men, her mistake, if revealed, will be laid to the husband's failure to control his wife. Krogstad is shunned by society as morally corrupt, in contrast with Torvald, who is considered a pillar of the community. Despite (or perhaps because of) their experiences, Mrs. Linde and Krogstad (who when young were in love but were separated by circumstances) appear at the play's end much more likely than Nora and Torvald to achieve a satisfying relationship. It is Mrs. Linde who insists that Krogstad not retrieve his letter (revealing to Torvald what Nora has done), for she believes it essential that Nora and Torvald cease their childish games so they can build a mature relationship based on truth and trust. Torvald embodies the attitudes and standards of his society. His condescension toward women, his smug conviction of his own moral superiority, his concern for public opinion and appearances, his fear of scandal are the qualities against which Nora's situation is measured.

The fifth major character, Dr. Rank, also serves as a contrast to Torvald. Nora can talk freely and share confidences with Rank about things that Torvald would find shocking. Rank probably would have made an excellent husband for Nora (a role he obviously covets) were it not for the congenital disease (probably syphilis) he has inherited from his father. He ultimately faces his unavoidable death with dignity.

Undergirding the characters and action of the play is a basic assumption that character and action are determined by hereditary and environmental forces. What

A Doll's House as produced at the Hartford Stage. Directed by Emily Mann. This scene shows Torvald (Jerry Bamman), Dr. Rank (Mark Lamos), and Nora (Mary McDonnell) having returned from the masked ball. (Photo © T. Charles Erickson.)

each character is and does is explained by information about background, upbringing, and experience. All the characters are victims of their environment, although Mrs. Linde and Krogstad, having achieved understanding of their circumstances, ultimately seem capable of rising above them. Ibsen could have made his play melodramatic by depicting Krogstad as villain and Nora as heroine. Instead, all of the characters strive for what they consider to be right; the complications arise from their differing conceptions of proper goals and means for attaining them. Thus, they appear to be complex, fallible human beings.

A Doll's House could serve as a model of cause-to-effect dramatic construction. Like most of Ibsen's plays, this one uses a late point of attack. Mrs. Linde, because of her long absence, can believably inquire about the past and thereby motivate revelation of the complex circumstances that have preceded the play's beginning. The first act, then, sets up with seeming naturalness all of the conditions out of which the subsequent action develops logically, though not necessarily predictably.

The Doll's House uses a single setting throughout. It is a *box set* (that is, one that fully encloses the acting space on three sides like the walls of a room, with one side removed). Box sets permitted far more realistic representations of indoor spaces than could be achieved with wings, drops, and borders. The realistic effect was further enhanced by the addition of those furnishings, pictures, drapes, rugs, and bric-a-brac typically found in a real room of the period. Furthermore, instead of standing throughout on a stage largely devoid of furnishings, as had been typical prior to the late nineteenth century, actors now sought to behave as they would in real rooms, rather than letting the sets serve merely as visual backgrounds. In *A Doll's House* the characters seem to live in the setting. Action, character, and environment are intertwined.

Zola and Naturalism

Naturalism, unlike realism, had little success in the theatre, probably because it was too extreme in its demands. Its chief advocate, Emile Zola (1840–1902), thought that many realists were more concerned with theatrical effectiveness (building complications, crises, and resolutions) than with truth to life. One of Zola's followers suggested that these temptations could be overcome by thinking of a play merely as a *slice of life (tranche de vie)*—a segment of reality transferred to the stage. The naturalists were far more rigorous than the realists in their demands for "truth in art" and for a drama that demonstrated the inevitable laws of heredity and environment. In practice, naturalism emphasized the influence of poverty and other deprivations on the lives of the lower classes, a subject little treated in earlier drama. (While melodrama often treated lower-class characters, it largely discounted any connection

The Earth, a play adapted from Emile Zola's novel of the same name. Directed by André Antoine at the Théâtre Antoine, Paris, 1902. Notice the many naturalistic details, including the hayloft in the background and the chickens in the foreground. (*Le Théâtre,* 1902.)

between environment and character. Often the most morally exemplary characters were among the poorest.) Zola, who often compared naturalistic art with medicine, believed that, just as the medical pathologist seeks to discover the cause of a disease so it can be treated, the dramatist should expose social ills so that their causes can be corrected. With such rigorous (and often unattainable) goals, it is not surprising that naturalism had a short life and was soon absorbed into realism. The movement produced few plays of importance. Perhaps the best known is Zola's *Thérèse Raquin,* an adaptation of his novel about a woman who, with her lover, kills her husband and then suffers with him through many years of regret.

Together, realism and naturalism struck major blows against rigid social codes and absolute values. They laid the foundations on which modernists built.

The Emergence of the Director

Throughout history, someone has assumed responsibility for staging plays. In the Greek theatre, the playwright usually staged his own works, and in later times, the heads of companies (or someone appointed by them) had that responsibility. The twentieth-century director, who assumes responsibility for interpreting the script and for approving and coordinating all the elements that make up a production, is primarily a product of the late nineteenth century.

A convergence of several complex developments led to the emergence of the modern director. One of these developments involved the growing need for someone to coordinate and unify all the elements of a production. From the Renaissance to the nineteenth century, the elements of production, though representational, had been so generalized as to require little attention. Each theatre had a stock of sets (prison, palace, street, country landscape, and so on) that was reused often. To achieve variety, prosperous theatres acquired two or more sets for each general type of scene. Costumes were typically clothing worn in contemporary life, usually chosen or supplied by the actors; some categories of characters (such as classical or Near Eastern) appeared in noncontemporary dress, but these costumes were so formalized that the same ones could be used for all characters in the same category.

Acting was also conventionalized before the late nineteenth century, in that actors were hired according to lines of business and always played the same limited range of roles. The actors usually stood near the front of the stage (in part so they would be more visible in the low-intensity lighting of the pre-gas era) and directed their lines as much to the audience as to the other characters. (The auditorium, like the stage, was lighted.) Because there was seldom any furniture on stage, the actors used a pattern of movement that gave the downstage-center position to whichever character had an important speech at that point; when the speech was over, the actor moved away from center stage so the next actor could have that position. Thus, there were frequent changes of place determined by a pattern so well understood that the actors did not need to be told when and where to move. Consequently, rehearsals were restricted largely to establishing where entrances and exits were to be made and to practicing such complex action as duels. The person in charge of staging had little to do other than to make sure that all the elements were assembled and to settle any disputes that arose. There were usually no more than seven to ten rehearsals.

As the nineteenth century progressed and the theatre became more complex, the number and specificity of sets and costumes increased, especially as elaborate spectacles and special effects multiplied. Much of the effect of melodrama depended on split-second timing and precise stage business. The introduction of box sets with furniture also served to alter the movement patterns typical of earlier times. These changes required increased supervision, coordination, and rehearsal. Nevertheless, each area of theatrical production continued for a time to work in relative isolation—scene painters did the sets, seamstresses and tailors the costumes, and so on—with little consultation. Even within an area, the work was often parceled out to several persons (for example, each set for a five-set production might be done by a different scene painter). As each element of production became more specific and complex, the need for greater unity and more control became increasingly evident in the late nineteenth century.

The acceptance of the modern director owes most to two influences: the theory of Wagner and the practice of Saxe-Meiningen. Richard Wagner (1813–1883), a German now known primarily as a composer of operas, sought to create a "master artwork" (*Gesamtkunstwerk*) through a fusion of all the arts. Opposed to realism,

Wagner's Festival Theatre, Bayreuth (Germany). The setting onstage is for Wagner's opera *Parsifal.* This "classless" auditorium, without boxes or center aisle and in which all seats were supposedly equally good for seeing and hearing, served as a model for many subsequent theatres. (*Le Théâtre,* 1902.)

Shakespeare's *Julius Caesar* as produced by Saxe-Meiningen. Shown here is Antony's oration over Caesar's corpse. (*Die Gartenlaube* [1879].)

he chose most of his stories from German myth and set his dramas to music, not only to avoid the realistic mode but also to control the way the text was performed. He argued that spoken drama is at the mercy of actors, who are free to speak the lines however they choose, whereas singers are forced to follow the tempo, pitch, and duration dictated by the musical score. He also wished through his music-dramas to create a theatrical experience so overpoweringly empathetic that the audience would be drawn out of its everyday, mundane existence into an idealized, communal, near-religious experience.

To realize his goal, Wagner erected a new kind of theatre building, opened at Bayreuth in 1876. This theatre was the first in the West to do away with the arrangement of box, pit, and gallery in favor of a "democratic" configuration, with seating laid out in a fan-shaped pattern that supposedly created equally good seeing and hearing conditions for all. This new auditorium design set the pattern for most twentieth-century theatres. It was also one of the first in which the auditorium was always darkened during performances. Wagner adopted this convention to distinguish between the everyday world (the auditorium) and the ideal realm (the stage), into which the performance sought to pull the audience. Wagner's contribution to the development of the director came from his strong demand for

Saxe-Meiningen's Crowd Scenes

The feature of Saxe-Meiningen's productions that most impressed audiences was the crowd scenes, which were quite unlike those typical of the day. After having seen the Meiningen company perform on tour in Brussels, André Antoine, founder of the Théâtre Libre, wrote in the Paris newspaper, *Le Temps:*

> Their crowds are not like ours, composed of elements picked at random, working-men not hired until dress rehearsals, badly clothed, and not used to wearing strange ... costumes.... The troupe of the Meininger is made up of about 70 actors.... All who are not cast in speaking roles ... without exception, even leading actors, appear in the crowd scenes.... In this way they achieve ensembles that are extraordinarily true to life.

The German critic Karl Frenzel, writing in the *Deutsche Rundschau*, provides an account of the crowd scenes in the Meininger production of Shakespeare's *Julius Caesar* as seen in Berlin in 1876:

> The handling of the crowd is brought to perfection here. When Casca stabs Caesar, a single, heart-rending cry runs through the crowd.... A deathly silence follows; the assassins, the senators, the people, stand for a moment as if enchanted and frozen before the body of Caesar; then a tempest erupts ... which one has to see ... to recognize how powerful ... dramatic art can be. In the following scene [Antony's funeral oration over Caesar's corpse] ... as Antony is raised on the shoulders of the mob and, in the midst of the wildest movement, reads Caesar's will; as the enraged citizens seize the bier with the corpse and others carrying torches mill about; and finally, as Cinna the poet, in the extremest turmoil, is murdered ... one could believe that one was actually present at the beginning of a revolution.

"unity of production"—that is, for productions in which everything has been filtered through a single consciousness to achieve a unified artistic effect. This theoretical position has undergirded most twentieth-century ideas of staging.

Georg II, duke of Saxe-Meiningen (1826–1914), is now usually considered the first director in the modern sense. Ruler of a small German state, Saxe-Meiningen gained international renown between 1874 and 1890 with his company's tours throughout Europe. The fame of the company did not stem from a new repertory, innovative design, or outstanding acting, but from its directorial practices. Saxe-Meiningen exerted complete control over every aspect of production. He designed the scenery, costumes, and properties himself and insisted that they be constructed to his precise specifications both in materials and appearance. Unable to afford well-known actors, he depended on long rehearsal periods (sometimes extending over several months) to achieve the effects he sought. His company was known especially for its crowd scenes, which (unlike those in other companies) were staged with great precision, variety, and emotional power. In Saxe-Meiningen's productions, the total stage picture was worked out carefully moment by moment, and the superior results were seen as convincing arguments for a strong director who can impose his authority and implement his vision. The Meiningen company validated many of Wagner's views, and the need for unified production (to be achieved primarily through the authority of the director) soon became a fundamental tenet of theatrical production.

The Independent Theatre Movement

By the 1880s, innovative plays by realists and naturalists had appeared, but censorship had kept most of them from production. Similarly, Wagner and Saxe-Meiningen had established the importance of the director, but Wagner had devoted his attention to opera, and Saxe-Meiningen's company was staging mostly poetic drama (by Shakespeare or nineteenth-century playwrights). The new drama and the new staging had remained isolated from each other. They were finally to meet in "independent" theatres.

Throughout most of Europe, plays could not be performed for public audiences until they had been approved by a censor. Some of Ibsen's prose plays were not performed in the 1880s because censors would not license them. On the other hand, "private" performances (those done by a group for its members only) were not subject to censorship. Beginning in the late 1880s, this loophole was exploited by a

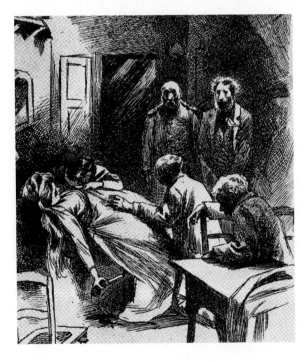

Ibsen's *The Wild Duck* as performed at the Théâtre Libre, Paris, in 1889. Directed by André Antoine.

number of small, "independent" theatres, which were open only to subscribing members and therefore were not subject to censorship. These theatres were able to accomplish what more established theatres had not: the uniting of the new drama with the new staging techniques.

The first independent theatre was the Théâtre Libre, founded in Paris in 1887 by André Antoine. An enthusiastic follower of Zola and Ibsen, Antoine produced their plays and those of similar writers in settings that reproduced every detail of an environment (in one instance, he hung carcasses of real beef in a butcher-shop set). Like Saxe-Meiningen, he exerted control over every element of production.

Antoine's was only the first of numerous independent theatres. In 1889, the Freie Bühne was founded in Berlin. It was less interested in staging than in providing a hearing for new playwrights. It is credited with launching the careers of playwrights (especially Hermann Sudermann and Gerhardt Hauptmann) who are associated with the inauguration of modern drama in Germany. In 1891, the Independent Theatre was established in London. Its inaugural production, of Ibsen's *Ghosts*, created an enormous scandal that did much to call public attention to a new type of drama. The Independent Theatre made its greatest contribution by inducing George Bernard Shaw (1856–1950) to begin writing plays. Unlike most dramatists of the new school, Shaw chose to write comedies through which he sought to puncture popular prejudices and provoke audiences into reassessing their values. In *Arms and the Man* he ridiculed romantic notions about love and war; in *Major Barbara* he suggested that a munitions manufacturer is a greater benefactor than the Salvation Army because the manufacturer provides his employees the financial means for bettering their lives, whereas the Salvation Army provides only momentary relief; in *Pygmalion* (later adapted into the musical *My Fair Lady*) he showed how the English class system is related to speech. His other plays include *Man and Superman, Heartbreak House,* and *Saint Joan.* Shaw is considered one of the major playwrights of the twentieth century.

Not only did these independent theatres meet an important need, but they also established a significant precedent, for since that time, whenever established theatres have become insufficiently responsive to innovation, small companies (variously called "art" theatres, "little" theatres, Off-Broadway, or "alternative" theatres) have been formed to meet the need.

Another organization that emerged from the independent theatre movement—the Moscow Art Theatre—was to be of special importance. Founded in 1898 by Konstantin Stanislavsky (1863–1938) and Vladimir Nemerovich-Danchenko (1859–1943), it achieved its first major success with the plays of Anton Chekhov (1860–1904), known primarily for *The Sea Gull, Uncle Vanya, The Three Sisters,* and *The Cherry Orchard,* all of which are set in rural Russia and depict the monotony and frustrations of provincial life. All the characters in these plays aspire to a better life but do not know how (or do not have the initiative) to achieve their goals. They often do not understand their own feelings, and they seek to conceal as much as to reveal their responses. In these plays, subtext is often as important as text. Chekhov does not pass judgment on his characters; rather, he treats all with tolerance and compassion. The plays intermingle the comic, serious, pathetic, and ironic so thoroughly that they do not fit comfortably into any dramatic type (tragedy,

The final act of Chekhov's *The Three Sisters* as performed at the Moscow Art Theatre. (Photo by Fred Fehl. Courtesy of the Hoblitzelle Theatre Arts Collection, Harry Ransom Humanities Research Center, University of Texas at Austin.)

comedy, tragicomedy). Chekhov's plays continue to hold a firm place in the repertory, not only in Russia but also throughout the world.

The Moscow Art Theatre eventually made its greatest impact through Stanislavsky's system of acting, which, described in his books (*My Life in Art, An Actor Prepares, Building a Character,* and *Creating a Role*), has been the most pervasive influence on acting during the twentieth century. Stanislavsky's basic premises are:

1. The actor's body and voice must be trained and flexible so they can respond to all demands.
2. To act truthfully, the actor must be a skilled observer of human behavior.
3. If actors are not merely to play themselves, they must understand a character's motivations and goals in each scene and in the play as a whole, as well as each character's relationship to all the other roles and the dramatic action.
4. Actors must project themselves into the world of the play and may learn to do so through the *magic if* (that is, through imagining how one would feel or act *if* one were this specific character in this specific situation); actors may also employ *emotion memory* (recalling one's own emotional responses in situations comparable to those in the script).
5. Onstage, the actor should concentrate moment by moment, as if the events were happening spontaneously and for the first time.

Stanislavsky

Stanislavsky, the Russian creator of the most influential acting system of the twentieth century, was born Konstantin Sergeevich Alekseev, son of a wealthy industrialist. In 1885 he adopted the stage name Stanislavsky; after extensive experience as an actor, he came to recognize that many of his shortcomings as a performer were owing to lack of a systematic approach In 1898, with Vladimir Nemerovich-Danchenko, he founded the Moscow Art Theatre, which sought to achieve the highest level of ensemble playing in productions that would make the dramatic action clear through simple, natural acting emphasizing inner truth rather than external effect. Although the company was successful in achieving most of its goals, Stanislavsky continued his search for a systematic approach to acting. He recorded the first outlines of his system in 1909, and in 1912 he established the Moscow Art Theatre's First Studio to explore the system through training and performances by young actors. Following the Russian Revolution in 1917, the Moscow Art Theatre faltered, but by the 1930s, it was considered by Soviet authorities the model that other companies should emulate. It retained this status into the 1980s.

Stanislavsky was most comfortable with realistic acting but recognized the need to master other styles. He created several studios to explore alternative approaches, but he was never fully satisfied with the results and never felt that his system was complete. He continued to work on it until his death in 1938, publishing several books describing aspects of it.

Stanislavsky sought in his system to deal with all aspects of acting. What he wrote has been interpreted variously, but it continues to be the best-known attempt to describe what is involved in effective acting.

By the late nineteenth century, realism in the theatre was well established. In some respects, it was the logical culmination of developments that began in the Renaissance, when the picture-frame stage and perspective scenery were introduced. At that time, the stage became essentially representational, and subsequent trends were toward ever-more-convincing pictures. As the nineteenth century progressed, the demand for actualistic detail reached a peak. It can be seen in melodrama first and then in realism/naturalism. Melodrama and realism differed, not so much over realistic staging, but over their views of truth and values. Melodrama was grounded in the assumption that human beings innately know the difference between right and wrong, that moral behavior has little to do with environment, class, or wealth. It taught that if one remains faithful to moral principles, everything will eventually work out satisfactorily—that good will win and evil will lose. Realism and naturalism, on the other hand, tended to view the world scientifically rather than morally, and to believe that the forces of heredity and environment are the determinants of human behavior. They did not believe that providence intervened on the part of moral goodness, but rather that it is up to human beings to analyze and discover the causes of undesirable behavior and to alter those causes to achieve the desired results. By challenging melodrama's metaphysical foundations, realism and naturalism undermined the absolutist values that had dominated art since the Middle Ages. A pathway was thereby opened for those ideas and practices that have come to be labeled "modernist."

Chapter 7

The Modernist Temperament: 1890–1940

August Strindberg's *A Dream Play* as produced at the National Theater of Norway. (Courtesy of the National Theater of Norway.)

[I]n the years following . . . 1885, all the arts changed direction as if they had been awaiting a signal. . . . In all the arts, 1885 is the point from which we must reckon the meaning of the word 'modern'.

—Roger Shattuck, *The Banquet Years*

By the time the independent theatre movement got under way in the late 1880s, another strand of performance—in rebellion against realism—was emerging. This new strand can be viewed as an alternative reaction to many of the same impulses that had led to realism and naturalism. The belief that there should be a direct relationship between human behavior and the physical world (as normatively perceived) and their artistic representation had dominated theory and practice since the Renaissance. It was a fundamental premise of realism and naturalism. Beginning in the late 1880s, however, one group of artists increasingly rejected this premise and substituted its own subjective visions and esthetic modes (usually involving some degree of abstraction and distortion) for the traditional approach that had allowed the audience to compare a subject with its artistic rendering. This rejection of the long-standing relationship between perception and representation is often considered the true beginning of the *modernist* temperament. No longer shackled to the natural world, artists could now be valued for imaginative perception and formal innovation rather than for accurate renditions of recognizable subjects.

Symbolism

The first artistic movement to reject representationalism was *symbolism*, launched in 1885. It denied the claims made by realists that ultimate truth is to be discovered through the five senses, arguing instead that truth is beyond objective examination. Because it can only be intuited, it cannot be expressed directly or through wholly rational means; truth can only be hinted at through a network of symbols that evokes feelings and states of mind corresponding imprecisely to our intuitions. Maurice Maeterlinck, author of *Pelleas and Melisande,* the best-known of all the symbolist plays, wrote that the most important element of great drama is the "idea which the poet forms of the unknown in which float about the beings and things which he evokes, the mystery which dominates them."

Unlike the realists, the symbolists chose their subjects from the past, the realm of fancy, or the mysterious present and avoided any attempt to deal with social problems or environmental forces. They aimed to suggest a universal truth that is independent of time and place and that cannot be logically defined or rationally expressed. Thus, their drama tended to be vague and mysterious.

Established theatres, finding symbolist drama incomprehensible, were even less inclined to produce it than the works of Ibsen and Zola. Consequently, the symbolists, like the realists and naturalists, established independent theatres in which to perform their plays. The most influential was the Théâtre de l'Oeuvre, founded in Paris in 1893 by Aurelien-Marie Lugné-Poë. The symbolists believed that the most important aspect of a production is mood or atmosphere. They used little scenery, and even that was vague in form and almost devoid of detail. They often placed a gauze curtain (*scrim*) just back of the proscenium so the action would appear to be taking place in a mist or timeless void. Color was chosen for its mood value rather than for representational accuracy. The actors often chanted their lines and used unnatural gestures. The goal was to remove the action from the immediate, everyday world. One can scarcely conceive of productions more unlike those of the realists and naturalists. They so differed from what audiences had become accustomed to that many spectators were baffled. As a movement in the theatre, symbolism soon lost its appeal and by 1900 had largely ceased. Nevertheless, symbolism is important as the first of the nonrealistic movements that would proliferate in the twentieth century.

Symbolism is also important because it disrupted a pattern that had persisted since the beginning of theatre. In each period, the same conventions and approaches to production had been used for all plays during that period. There had been transitions from one approach or set of conventions to another (as in England with the shifts from medieval to Elizabethan and then to the picture-frame stage), but transitions were gradual. Once established, the same conventions were used in staging all plays. This is the primary reason why no need was felt for a director in the modern sense; the conventions and working methods were so well understood that detailed supervision and control were unnecessary. The various settings for the same play could be assigned to different scene painters because the visual style, theatrical conventions, and audience expectations were so clear that detailed instructions or close supervision would have been considered a lack of trust in the artist. Common stylistic goals, and faith that each production area was capable of achieving those goals, characterized theatre until the late nineteenth century. Then, as we have seen in examining the emergence of the director, the increased complexity of production (greater number of sets, more realistic special effects, more detailed stage movement and business, and so on) had led by 1875 to recognition that greater control and better coordination from a central authority was desirable. Even then, stage conventions remained much the same; only production processes had become complex.

But when symbolism challenged realism and naturalism, two radically different sets of conventions came into conflict. The implications of this conflict are crucial to understanding modernism and its domination of twentieth-century art. Prior to the twentieth century, artistic movements occurred linearly (that is, one succeeded another chronologically); in the twentieth century, several have existed simultaneously. For example, between 1910 and 1920 movements called expressionism, futurism, dadaism, cubism, and a number of others (including realism) coexisted. Each was based on a separate set of premises about the nature of truth and the world in which we live, and consequently each required a different set of conventions to embody its vision. With such fragmentation, there was no longer a unified view based on absolute values; there were multiple views, each based on values accepted by one group but denied by others. Thus, the transition had been made from a common set of values to multiple sets of values—from the absolute to the relative—the most basic characteristic of the modernist temperament.

Modernism influenced all of the arts. From the Renaissance to the twentieth century, the visual arts (including theatrical scenery) had depicted everything in relation to a fixed eyepoint. In the early twentieth century, however, the visual arts no longer always depicted all details of the same picture as seen from one eyepoint. The best-known examples are certain of Picasso's paintings, in which various parts of the same subject are painted as though seen from different eyepoints. Attention shifted from content to the elements of art forms. In painting, recognizable subjects were sometimes abandoned altogether, resulting in wholly abstract works. Such paintings had to be judged by formal criteria (effectiveness in manipulating line, color, and composition) rather than by representational accuracy. Similar developments in music displaced melody, so that a composition could be valued not for its melodic and harmonic patterns but for its handling of time and atonal relationships.

Appia, Craig, and Reinhardt

The theatre participated in these trends. During the early twentieth century, two theorists—Appia and Craig—were especially successful in reshaping ideas about the "art of the theatre."

Born in Switzerland, Adolphe Appia (1862–1928) began with the idea that artistic unity in theatre is fundamental but difficult to achieve because of conflicting elements: the moving actor, the horizontal floor, and the vertical scenery. He sought to replace flat, painted scenery (as well as all decorative detail) with three-

Adolphe Appia's design for the entrance to the underworld in Gluck's opera *Orpheus and Eurydice.* (Courtesy of the Adolphe Appia Foundation, Schweizerische Theatersammlung, Geneva.)

A design by Gordon Craig for *Electra,* 1905. (City of Manchester Art Gallery, *Exhibition of Drawings and Models by Edward Gordon Craig,* 1912.)

dimensional structures as the only proper environment for three-dimensional actors. To overcome the limitations of the flat stage floor, he advocated the use of steps, platforms, and ramps to create transitions from horizontal to vertical planes, thereby making possible greater compositional variety in the total stage picture and the movement of actors.

Appia was also a major theoretician of stage lighting. To reveal the shape and dimensionality of the setting and actors, Appia advocated the use of light from various directions and angles. He considered light the most flexible of all theatrical elements because, like music, it can change moment by moment to reflect shifts in mood and emotion, and because it unifies all the other elements through its intensity, color, direction, and movement. Appia's views on lighting came at a crucial time—just as the technology needed to implement his theories was becoming available. The incandescent electric lamp was invented in 1879, and as the first medium that did not use an open flame, it gained acceptance rapidly because of its safety. Initially, the wattage of electric lamps was very small, and not until 1911 were lamps available with a concentrated filament of sufficiently high wattage to permit the development of spotlights. By around 1915, most of the technology (electric lamps, spotlights, color filters, and dimmers) needed to implement Appia's theories was available and in use.

Gordon Craig (1872–1966) began his career as an actor in the English theatre. Much more militant than Appia, he was always in the public eye because of his controversial views. Craig denied that the theatre is a fusion of other arts; he saw it as a wholly autonomous art whose basic elements—action, language, line, color, and rhythm—are fused by a master artist. He once suggested that actors should be replaced by large puppets (*übermarionetten*), because they, unlike actors, could not impose their own personalities on a production and undermine the master artist's intentions. Like Appia, Craig advocated simplicity in scenery, costumes, and lighting. Both sought to replace the representational approach to visual elements with one concerned with abstract structures that embodied the line, mass, color, texture, and mood appropriate to the dramatic action. Appia and Craig also promoted the concept of the director as the supreme, unifying theatre artist.

The influence of Appia and Craig was reinforced by the German director, Max Reinhardt (1872–1943), who was then amending earlier conceptions of the director. During the late nineteenth century, Wagner, Saxe-Meiningen, Antoine, Lugné-Poë, and others had won acceptance for the director, but each of these men, though they differed from the others in their approach to staging, used basically the same mode for every production they staged. As new artistic movements appeared, each movement was faced with the need to establish a theatre specializing in its distinctive style because each existing theatre was devoted to a single approach in theatrical production. A breakthrough was achieved around 1900, when Reinhardt began to treat each production as a new challenge demanding its own unique stylistic solution. Using this approach, the plays of all movements and periods could be accommodated in the same theatre. For the first time, theatre history became important to directing, for Reinhardt frequently built productions around elements significant to the theatrical context in which a play had originally appeared. Often he tried to re-create the audience-performer spatial relationship. (As examples, he remodeled a circus building to accommodate Greek plays; for a medieval play he transformed a theatre into a cathedral; and he presented many eighteenth-century plays in a hall of

Reinhardt's production of *Oedipus the King* in the Circus Schumann, Berlin, 1910. (*Le Théâtre*, 1911.)

state in an eighteenth-century palace.) He unified some productions around dominant visual motifs and others around theatrical conventions typical of the period when the plays were written. Thus, knowledge of the theatre's past was crucial in many of his productions.

Reinhardt's method further enhanced the role of the director. Because the stylistic approach to be used in any production was optional, the choice was the director's to make; as the one who chose the vision that would undergird the production, the director was also the arbiter of all choices made by those who worked to implement his vision. Although Reinhardt considered the director's the primary artistic consciousness, he did not, as many of his successors were to do, alter the time or place of a play's action. He believed that the production should serve the script (rather than the script the production, as has become common in more recent times). His productions, viewed from today's perspective, do not seem stylistically as varied as they did to his contemporaries, for most of his productions were still largely representational. Nevertheless, Reinhardt established eclecticism as the dominant directorial approach. Once accepted, eclecticism was (and continues to be) elaborated and extended by others, frequently in ways never envisioned by Reinhardt. With Reinhardt, relativism triumphed in directing (as it already had in many other areas); instead of applying the same approach to all plays (the absolutist's way), the approach was altered to suit each play (the relativist's way).

New Artistic Movements

The decade between 1910 and 1920 was one of unrest and upheaval, epitomized by World War I. Not surprisingly, this decade saw the emergence of numerous artistic movements, each championing a new perspective on human experience and new ways of expressing this perspective. Three of the most important of these movements were futurism, dada, and expressionism.

Futurism was launched in 1909 by Filippo Tommaso Marinetti (1876–1944), an Italian who glorified the speed and energy of the machine age, which he saw as the key to an enlightened future. Because he thought veneration of the past stood in the way of progress, he declared that all libraries and art museums should be destroyed. The futurists sought to replace old art forms with a number of new ones, among them collage, kinetic sculpture, and *bruitisme* ("noise music" based on the sounds of everyday life). Especially contemptuous of drama that developed leisurely and required no active involvement from its audience, the futurists issued a number of manifestos demanding change. In one of these manifestos, "The Variety Theatre," Marinetti argued that the theatre of his day was devoted almost entirely to historical drama or photographic reproductions of daily life. He considered such drama to be remnants from "the age of the oil lamp." To reform this theatre, he proposed as a model the variety theatre with its vaudeville acts, jugglers, dancers, gymnasts, and the like because of its dynamic energy and audience involvement. "The Variety Theatre is alone in seeking the audience's collaboration. It doesn't remain static like a stupid voyeur, but joins noisily in the action. . . ." Marinetti went on to suggest ways of disrupting the refined and detached behavior of theatre

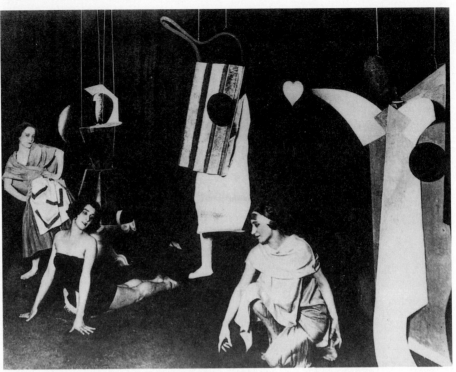

A futurist production at the Théâtre de la Pantomime Futuriste, Paris, 1927. Notice the mingling of live performers with nonhuman puppet figures. (*Le Théâtre*, 1927.)

audiences: "Spread a powerful glue on some of the seats. . . . Sell the same seat to ten persons. . . . Sprinkle the seats with dust to make people itch and sneeze."

The futurists proposed to replace existing drama with a "synthetic" drama that would compress into a moment or two the essence of a full-length play. Their desire to speed up life also led them to champion simultaneity and multiple focus. In their performances, several scenes or different kinds of events (musical, pictorial, dramatic) proceeded simultaneously in different parts of the performance-audience space. The futurists sought confrontations with audiences, whose prejudices about what art is or can be they challenged so strongly that their performances often provoked near-riots. Futurism lost much of its appeal during World War I because it praised war as the supreme expression of the aggressive life it championed.

Dada was grounded in rejection of the values that had provoked World War I. When that war broke out, many artists sought refuge in neutral Switzerland, where in 1916 dada was born. Its principal spokesman was Tristan Tzara (1896–1963). Because insanity seemed the world's state, the dadaists sought in their art to replace logic, reason, and unity with chance and illogic. They presented a number of programs in which, like the futurists, they used simultaneity and multiple focus. Among their favorite forms were "chance poems" (created by placing words in a hat, drawing them out at random, and reciting them) and "sound poems" (composed of non-

Futurist Synthetic Plays

The futurists' desire to compress dramatic action into a brief moment is illustrated in the following *sintesi*, reprinted in their entirety.

Synthesis of Syntheses
by Gugielmo Jannelli and Luciano Nicastro

Empty stage: a long dark corridor at the end of which a small red lamp flashes off and on, a long way off. Then, a streak of white light appears like a carpet along the corridor.
Five seconds.
A revolver shot. Scream. Noises. Confused cries.
Pause.
The fresh burst of a woman's laughter.
Simultaneously a door at the back is thrown open by a blow, blinding the audience with a huge, powerful light.
The curtain detaches,

and falls. [end of play]

Education
by Angelo Rognoni

A classroom.
The Professor (*thirty years old. He is reading to his students.*): Dante is a great poet. He wrote the Divine Comedy and. . . .
The Professor (*forty years old. He is reading with a bored voice*): Dante is a great poet. He wrote the Divine Comedy and. . . . (Several seconds of silence)
The Professor (*sixty years old. He is like a gramophone.*): Dante is a great poet. . . .
A Pupil (*interrupting him*): Why?
The Professor (*surprised and embarrassed*): It is printed here. Sit down and be quiet. Dante is a great poet. He wrote. . . .

[end of play]

—Translated by and reprinted with the permission of Victoria Nes Kirby

verbal sounds). They also performed short plays, dances, and music. They recognized no barriers between art forms. Dada was essentially anarchistic, thumbing its nose at a hypocritical, discredited society and the art forms it venerated.

Dada lost much of its energy when the war ended, but some of the most interesting examples occurred after the war. For example, in Cologne (Germany) in 1920 Max Ernst, Hans Arp, and Theodor Baargeld staged a dada event in a glassed-in courtyard entered through a men's toilet. The event included several unrelated features, among them a young woman, dressed as if for her first communion, reciting obscene poems, a pool of blood-red liquid from which a skull and a hand projected, and a wooden sculpture to which a hatchet was attached for the convenience of anyone wishing to attack it.

Much of what the futurists and dadaists did seems prankish, intended to provoke. It is difficult to assess their influence, but the challenges they posed aroused strong emotion and heated debate about such topics as how to define a work of art, the role of audience response, art as an instrument of change, the need for innovation in art, and the relationship of art to its culture. Their influence would resurface strongly after 1960.

Expressionism emerged around 1910 in Germany. It sought to counter materialism and industrialism, which it saw as the principal perverters of the human spirit. Unlike futurism, which glorified the machine age, expressionism charged that the industrial age had turned human beings into machines with conditioned responses and souls shriveled by materialistic values. Its proponents wished to reshape the world to make it conform to what is best in the human spirit and thereby to achieve "the regeneration of man." Unlike futurism and dada, whose theatrical programs were forerunners of today's performance art, expressionism, with its emphasis on text, was more easily assimilated and had a greater immediate impact on theatre than did futurism or dada.

Most expressionist drama focuses on how the human spirit has been distorted by false values. It usually shows the protagonist searching for identity, fulfillment, or a means to change the world. Because the protagonists have usually been warped by materialism and industrialism, the external world that they see (and that we see through their eyes) is also distorted. The walls of buildings or rooms may lean in threateningly, color may reflect emotion (for example, the protagonist's jealousy may make the sky green rather than blue), movement and speech may be robotlike, or several persons or objects may be identical in appearance (as if made by machine). Expressionism typically presents a nightmarish vision of the human situation.

Some of August Strindberg's (1849–1912) plays are often seen as forerunners of expressionism. Perhaps the most important of these is *A Dream Play* (1902), in the preface to which Strindberg wrote:

> The writer has tried to imitate the disconnected but seemingly logical form of the dream. Anything may happen; everything is possible and probable. Time and space do not exist. On an insignificant background of reality, imagination designs and embroiders novel patterns: a medley of memories, experiences, free fancies, absurdities, and improvisations.

Strindberg overcame the limitations of time, space, logical sequence, and appearance by adopting the viewpoint of the dreamer. In *A Dream Play*, one event flows into another without logical transition, characters are transformed into others, and widely separated places and times are telescoped in a story about tortured and alienated human beings. From Strindberg the expressionists borrowed many of their techniques.

Expressionism flourished in Germany, especially immediately after World War I, when optimism over the establishment of Germany's first democratic government made the realization of expressionist goals seem possible. The most important German expressionist playwrights were Georg Kaiser and Ernst Toller. By the mid-1920s disillusionment had replaced optimism, and the popularity of expressionism

Eugene O'Neill wrote in many styles. Natasha Richardson and Liam Neeson are seen here in *Anna Christie,* one of his realistic plays, a production of the Roundabout Theatre, New York. Directed by David Leveaux. (Photo © Martha Swope.)

faded rapidly. Nevertheless, expressionism had attracted a number of writers in various countries. In the United States, several noteworthy expressionist plays were written, the best known of which are Elmer Rice's *The Adding Machine* (whose accountant-protagonist is little more than an adding machine himself) and O'Neill's *"The Hairy Ape."*

Eugene O'Neill (1888–1953), son of James O'Neill and the first American dramatist to win wide and lasting international recognition, is often considered the greatest playwright America has produced. Like many American playwrights of his day, O'Neill was aided in his early career by groups modeled after Europe's independent theatres. In the United States these companies, which began to appear around 1912, were usually called "little" or "art" theatres. O'Neill was discovered by the Provincetown Players, a group that between 1915 and 1929 was concerned with promoting American playwriting. O'Neill's plays, ranging through practically every style, include *The Emperor Jones, Desire Under the Elms, Strange Interlude, Mourning Becomes Electra, The Iceman Cometh,* and *Long Day's Journey Into Night.* Let us look more closely at *"The Hairy Ape"* as an example of expressionist drama.

"The Hairy Ape"

"The Hairy Ape" derives its unity from its central theme: humanity's frustrated search for identity in a hostile environment. When the play begins, the protagonist, Yank, is confident that he and his fellow stokers on an ocean liner are the only ones who "belong" because they make the ship go (and, by extension, the factories and machines of the modern, industrialized society). Yank represents for his fellow workers "a self-expression . . . their most highly developed individual." They do not recognize that their quarters resemble "the steel framework of a cage" or that they themselves resemble Neanderthal men.

The second scene introduces Mildred Douglas, the wealthy shipowner's daughter. Seen against the natural beauty of the sea, she appears "inert and disharmonious," completely lacking in purpose. In Scene 3, she insists on visiting the stokehole to watch the men shovel the coal that makes the ship's engines run. When she sees Yank, she calls him "the hairy ape" and is so horrified that she faints and must be carried away. This is the catalytic moment for Yank because Mildred's

O'Neill's *"The Hairy Ape,"* scene 1, in its first production, 1922, at the Provincetown Playhouse, New York. Directed by James Light; designed by Robert Edmond Jones and Cleon Throckmorton. (Photo by Vandamm. The Billy Rose Collection, the New York Public Library for the Performing Arts, the Astor, Lenox and Tilden Foundations.)

O'Neill's *"The Hairy Ape"* at the Pittsburgh Public Theatre, 1987. (Photo by Mark Portland. Courtesy of the Pittsburgh Public Theatre.)

revulsion makes him begin to question all of his beliefs. According to O'Neill, from the fourth scene onward, Yank "enters into a masked world; even the familiar faces of his mates in the forecastle have become strange and alien."

In Scene 5, seeking to reestablish his sense of worth, Yank goes to New York's Fifth Avenue, where the shops catering to the rich and powerful display "magnificence cheapened and made grotesque by commercialism." The people, dressed identically, look like "gaudy marionettes." When Yank tries to get their attention, they ignore him; resorting to force, he strikes at the men, but they remain oblivious to his existence and give their full attention to a monkey-fur coat in the shop window.

In Scene 6, Yank is in jail (called "the zoo"), where the cages run on "numberless, into infinity." He decides that he will get his revenge by destroying the steel and machinery over which he originally thought he had power. Learning that the IWW (International Workers of the World) opposes the owners of factories and ships, Yank, upon being released from jail, goes to an IWW office (described as "cheap, banal and commonplace") and offers to blow up the IWW's enemies. His offer is greeted with contempt, and he is thrown into the street. In the final scene, Yank arrives at the zoo, where he finds a gorilla that seems to understand him, but

Sophie Treadwell's Machinal

Another example of American expressionism is *Machinal* (1928) by Sophie Treadwell (1885–1970), a journalist, war correspondent, novelist, and playwright who wrote four novels and more than thirty plays, of which six were presented on Broadway. Written in nine scenes, *Machinal* focuses on Miss A., a poorly educated stenographer, who is merely a cog in a mechanized society in which she cannot find for herself "any place, any peace." Treated as an object in the workplace and as a possession when she marries her boss, she eventually, in her search for liberation, murders her husband and is electrocuted. The point that nothing belongs to a woman in this society is made as Miss A.'s head is being shaved in preparation for her electrocution: "Is nothing mine? The very hair on my head—."

After its original Broadway run, *Machinal* was largely ignored until it was revived at the New York Shakespeare Festival in 1990. In 1993, it was presented to great critical acclaim at the National Theatre in a production directed by Stephen Daldry and designed by Ian MacNeil. In this London production, the action was set against a steel structure (like a skyscraper under construction) that could move to reinforce the mood—tilting, lowering, raising—and from which workers' welding torches sometimes showered the stage with sparks. In recent years, *Machinal* has come to be considered both a significant expressionist drama and a feminist play ahead of its time.

when he frees the gorilla it crushes him and throws him into its cage. Yank dies without achieving the sense of belonging that he has so desperately sought.

Yank is symbolic of modern humanity in an industrialized society—cut off from a past when human beings were an integral part of the natural environment and trapped in an existence where they are little better than cogs in the industrial machine. In a speech to the gorilla, Yank sums up his feelings of alienation: "I ain't got no past to tink in, nor nothin' dat's comin', on'y what's now—and dat don't belong."

Only a few of the characters in *"The Hairy Ape"* have names. Most are representative types or members of groups. In the stage directions, O'Neill writes that, except for slight differentiations in size and coloration, the stokers are all alike. Overall, O'Neill seems to suggest that all human beings in the modern, industrialized world have been distorted—the workers having been reduced to the level of animals, the rich having become useless puppets. These conceptions are embodied in speech and appearance. In Scene 4, almost all the speeches are described as having a "brazen metallic quality as if [the characters'] throats were phonograph horns," and much of what Yank and others say in this scene is greeted with "a chorus of hard, barking laughter." In the scene set on Fifth Avenue, the characters speak in "toneless, simpering voices," and they are masked and dressed to make them look like puppets. In comments on the appropriate performance style for the play, O'Neill suggests that, beginning with Scene 4, everyone that Yank encounters, "including the symbolic gorilla," should wear masks. Yank is set off from the other characters because he is the only one who recognizes the need to seek a coherent relationship between himself and his environment. In his search, he meets no one who understands his need, but O'Neill seems to have hoped that Yank's plight would illuminate for the audience an aspect of modern existence.

"The Hairy Ape" is representative of both the outlook and the techniques of expressionism. The episodic structure and distorted visual elements are typical, as is Yank's longing for fulfillment, with its suggestion that society be changed so the individual can achieve a sense of belonging.

By the time *"The Hairy Ape"* was written, the modernist temperament was prominent in all the arts. Yet, many persons still believed in absolute values and considered much of twentieth-century thought and art misguided or dangerous. The two points of view coexisted because standards and values (both in life and art) had become so fragmented as to be the norm rather than the exception. In this atmosphere, the varieties of theatrical experience had multiplied, several existing simultaneously.

The Postwar Era

By the 1920s, modernism dominated "high" art both in Europe and America. The mass audience, nevertheless, still preferred the types of entertainment that had been popular before modernism appeared; as film increasingly met its needs, this audience

Robert Edmond Jones' design for Act III, scene 4 (the banquet scene) in Arthur Hopkins' production of Shakespeare's *Macbeth* on Broadway in the early 1920s. Notice the three masks suspended above the stage representing the witches. (Reprinted from R. E. Jones, *Drawings for the Theatre*, by permission of the publisher, Routledge, New York.)

drifted away from the theatre. The shift was accelerated especially by the almost-simultaneous advent around 1929 of sound films and a major economic depression because not only was film's entertainment potential greatly increased by sound but

The New Stagecraft

The forces that created modernism in Europe had little impact on theatre in America until around World War I, in part because before the end of the nineteenth century the professional theatre in the United States had come to be centered in New York, from which companies were sent on tour throughout the country. Around 1896, a group of businessmen was able to gain a near-monopoly on touring. Known as the Syndicate, this organization would send out only those productions it thought capable of attracting a mass audience. It opposed the kind of innovations that had triumphed in Europe, and it effectively kept the American theatre in the pre-modern mode. The power of the Syndicate was challenged and broken in the years between 1910 and 1915 by the Shubert brothers, but the Shuberts' goals differed little from those of the Syndicate.

Significant change began around 1912, when Americans who had studied and traveled abroad began to adopt the tactics of European independent theatres. Important "little theatres," as they were called in the United States, included: the Toy Theatre (founded 1912) in Boston; the Chicago Little Theatre (1912); the Neighborhood Playhouse (1915), the Washington Square Players (1915), and the Provincetown Players (1915), all in New York. In the beginning, these were amateur groups, although some later became professional.

The first important professional work by an American in the European mode came in 1915 with the production of Anatole France's *The Man Who Married a Dumb Wife*. Designed by Robert Edmond Jones (1887–1954), who had traveled through Europe and spent a year at Reinhardt's theatre in Berlin, his set is usually called the first American expression of the "new stagecraft" (the term used in the United States for the European innovations). Jones, along with Lee Simonson (1888–1967) and Norman Bel Geddes (1893–1958), was to be the major popularizer of the new mode in America. He designed sets for many of Eugene O'Neill's plays, both on Broadway and at the Provincetown Playhouse, and he was the principal designer of Arthur Hopkins' Broadway productions.

Simplification and suggestion (rather than detailed reproduction of the real world) were the hallmarks of new stagecraft design. Jones wrote, "Stage designing should be addressed to the eye of the mind," stimulating the imagination to perceive the underlying feeling of a play rather than stifling the imagination by providing too much. Perhaps more than any other designer, Jones established the style that dominated the American theatre between the two world wars. His influence is still felt through his book, *The Dramatic Imagination* (1941).

also its ticket prices were a fraction of those for live theatre. Between 1929 and 1939 approximately two-thirds of all live-entertainment theatres in the United States closed.

In the United States, the majority of those who continued to attend live theatre still preferred some version of realism. New theatrical movements were welcomed first (and often only) by "art" or "little" theatres (the counterparts of European independent theatres). Broadway audiences were not very tolerant of innovation. The peak of post–World War I experimentation on Broadway came in the early 1920s with Arthur Hopkins' production of an "expressionistic" *Macbeth,* for which Robert Edmond Jones' set was an arrangement of Gothic arches that leaned ever more precariously as the action proceeded. Three large masks, symbols of the Witches or Fate, hung above the stage throughout. (See the illustration on page 191.) The failure of this production is sometimes said to have made Broadway producers avoid stylistic extremes thereafter and adhere closely to a modified (or simplified) realism, much less detailed than nineteenth-century realism but still basically representational. This type of simplified realism dominated the Broadway theatre from the early 1920s to the 1960s.

In addition to O'Neill, a number of other American playwrights—among them Maxwell Anderson, Elmer Rice, Paul Green, Robert Sherwood, and Lillian Hellman—gained international recognition in the years following World War I. Perhaps the best known is Thornton Wilder (1897–1975), especially for *Our Town* (1938) with its distillation of everyday human experience in small-town America, and *The Matchmaker* (1954), which was later transformed into the musical *Hello, Dolly* (1963).

The Federal Theatre Project and the Group Theatre

The economic depression of the 1930s brought a unique development in American theatre—the Federal Theatre Project, the government's first financial support of theatre in the United States. As the depression deepened and unemployment grew, Congress created the Works Progress Administration to provide jobs in many fields, including theatre. The Federal Theatre Project, which existed from 1935 to 1939, was most active in New York, although it had units in forty states. Its primary task was to provide "free, adult, uncensored theatre." It is best remembered for the Living Newspaper, a form that aimed at achieving in the theatre something comparable to the printed newspaper. In actuality, it more nearly resembled the documentary film. The most famous living newspapers are *One Third of a Nation* (on slum housing), *Triple-A Plowed Under* (on the government's farm-subsidy program), and *Power* (on rural electrification and flood control). Each of these plays explored a specific problem, along with its causes and proposed solutions. They alternated dramatic scenes (illustrating the effect of existing social conditions on human lives) with narrative sequences (which provided factual information through statistical tables, still photographs, and motion pictures, all projected onto screens). Collaborative creations of many authors, the plays advocated social reform and corrective legislation. This aggressive advocacy eventually contributed to the discontinuance of the Federal Theatre, when in 1939 Congress refused to appropriate funds for it.

Power, a "living newspaper" presented by the Federal Theatre Project. The scene shows an argument before the Supreme Court over the constitutionality of the Tennessee Valley Authority. (The Billy Rose Collection, the New York Public Library for the Performing Arts, the Astor, Lenox and Tilden Foundations.)

During the years between the two world wars, Konstantin Stanislavsky became a major influence on American acting after the Moscow Art Theatre toured the United States in the early 1920s. Following that visit, two of Stanislavsky's former students, Richard Boleslavsky and Maria Ouspenskaya, founded the American Laboratory Theatre in New York, where from 1923 to 1930 they taught his approach to acting. But the upsurge in Stanislavsky's influence owed most to the Group Theatre, founded in 1931 by former students of the American Laboratory Theatre and modeled on the Moscow Art Theatre. For the next ten years, it was the most respected theatre in the United States. Among its members were Lee Strasberg, Harold Clurman, Stella Adler, Elia Kazan, Cheryl Crawford, Robert Lewis, Lee J. Cobb, and Morris Carnovsky—the directors, actors, teachers, and producers who most actively promoted Stanislavsky's system in the United States. During the de-

The Group Theatre's production of Clifford Odets' *Awake and Sing,* 1935. (The Billy Rose Collection, the New York Public Library for the Performing Arts, the Astor, Lenox and Tilden Foundations.)

pression years, the Group Theatre presented many of the best productions on Broadway, most dealing with the pressing economic and social issues of that time. Largely because of internal dissension in the company, the Group Theatre was disbanded in 1941.

Epic Theatre

While simplified realism and musicals dominated the theatre in the United States, innovations were common in Europe after World War I. Many made little impact, but a few eventually exerted significant influence. One of the most important was *epic theatre.*

Epic theatre developed in Germany during the 1920s in the wake of expressionism. It is associated above all with Bertolt Brecht (1898–1956), who shared the expressionists' desire to transform society but thought their methods vague and impractical. Brecht's ideas lacked focus at first, but around 1926 he embraced Marxism and its belief that values are determined by the prevailing economic mode of production. Brecht came to view many of the world's problems as the result of capitalism and to believe that they could be resolved by the adoption of socialism or communism. Thereafter, he sought to make audiences evaluate the socioeconomic

Bertolt Brecht's *Threepenny Opera* (with music by Kurt Weill) as performed at the Berliner Ensemble. This scene shows the marriage of Mack the Knife and Polly Peachum. Notice the onstage musicians (at top). Directed by Manfred Wekwerth and Jürgen Kern; setting by Matthais Stern; costumes by Christine Stromberg. (Photo by Vera Tenschert. Courtesy Bertolt-Brecht-Archiv, Berlin.)

implications of what they saw in the theatre; he was convinced that, if this was done effectively, audiences would perceive the need to alter the economic system and would work to bring about appropriate changes. He was also convinced that his goals could not be attained in the kind of theatre then dominant—one that sought to evoke an empathetic response so overwhelming that the spectators suspended their critical judgment, letting themselves be carried along passively by the performance. In such a theatre, according to Brecht, all the problems raised are resolved at the end of the play, and there is no demand that the audience relate what they have seen to the real world. Brecht wished to alter the audience's relationship to the production by encouraging spectators to watch actively and critically.

As a means to his goal, Brecht arrived at the concept of "alienation" (*Verfremdung*)—distancing the audience from the stage events so it can view them critically. To achieve alienation, Brecht adopted many conventions not previously used but which, through his influence, have since become common. First, he reminded the audience that it was in a theatre by calling attention to the theatre's means (which had been concealed in the belief that to allow the audience to see them would destroy theatrical illusion). He insisted that lighting instruments be left unmasked, that scenery be fragmentary (merely sufficient to indicate place), that musicians be visible (sometimes on stage), that captions, maps, or other images be projected onto screens, that when objects were suspended the ropes supporting them be clearly visible. Actors often sang directly to the audience or commented on the action. Brecht sometimes advised his actors to *present* their characters rather than *become* the characters (as Stanislavsky wished). To help actors achieve distance from their roles, Brecht advised them to speak of their characters in the third person. For example, an actor might verbalize a character's action in "He crosses the stage and says. . . ." Such conventions marked a conscious break with practices that had long dominated the stage, the goal having been to make the audience suspend its consciousness of watching a theatrical performance. Brecht saw the theatre not as a place to escape one's problems but as a place to recognize problems, which are then to be solved outside the theatre.

Brecht sought to achieve alienation by distancing the story either through time or place. According to Brecht, most historical drama treats its subjects from a present-day point of view, thereby creating the impression that conditions, having always been the same, are unchangeable. Brecht, contrarily, sought to make the differences between past and present readily apparent so the audience would recognize that, because the world has changed, it can still be changed if we do not like conditions as they now exist.

Brecht further sought alienation through his handling of the various theatrical elements. He opposed the notion (championed by Wagner and embraced by most of Brecht's contemporaries) that the most effective theatrical production is a synthesis of all the arts, each part reinforcing the others in a fully unified work. Brecht called this practice redundant and wasteful because each element is seeking to duplicate in its own way what is being done by all the others. He advocated instead that each element make its own comment. The disparity among elements would then arouse alienation by making the audience assess the varying comments. For example, Brecht's songs often set ironic or disillusioned lyrics to lighthearted tunes; the disparity between melody and words was intended to make the listener more critically aware of the song's implications.

Brecht adopted a number of structural devices to create alienation. Rather than have one scene flow smoothly into another, he wished, as he put it, to call attention to the knots tying the scenes together. Therefore, he used captions (projected on screens), songs, or other devices to emphasize breaks in the action. Captions also were used at the beginning of scenes to summarize the content of the scene to follow to divert attention from story or suspense and direct it to the social implications of the events.

These conventions may suggest that Brecht was heavy-handedly didactic, but he was also intent on entertaining. His stories have many complications and reversals and are leavened with songs and other devices intended to capture and hold attention. In fact, Brecht the storyteller so often subverts Brecht the propagandist that many theatregoers remain oblivious of his desire to provoke social change. Brecht's concept of alienation is often misinterpreted as a demand that spectators be continuously distanced from the events. In actuality, Brecht engages the audience empathetically and then, through some device (such as a song), creates the distance that the audience needs to evaluate what has been experienced during the empathetic moments. Thus, there is a continuing alternation of empathy and distance (much like that created through the alternation of episodes and choral odes in Greek drama). One might also get the impression from reading Brecht that settings and costumes played little role in his productions. But, though scenery was restricted in quantity, in his own theatre it was always designed and executed with great care; each piece was meticulously crafted and sometimes intricately detailed. The costumes often looked used and worn, in accordance with the character and situation, but many were elegant. The overall effect was one of considerable richness.

Brecht called his theatre *epic* because he thought it had more in common with epic poetry (in which dialogue and narration alternate and in which time and place are quickly transformed) than with the dramatic traditions that had dominated the theatre since the Renaissance. Of Brecht's many plays, perhaps the best known are *The Threepenny Opera*, *Mother Courage and Her Children*, *The Caucasian Chalk Circle*, and *The Good Woman of Setzuan*. Let us look at the last of these as an example of Brecht's epic drama.

The Good Woman of Setzuan

The Good Woman of Setzuan, written between 1938 and 1940 and first performed in 1943, is a parable distanced by setting it in China. The epic nature of the play is established by the prologue, in which narration and dialogue are mingled and in which time and place are telescoped. The prologue demonstrates the irony that permeates the piece: The waterseller, Wong—having assured the gods, who have come to Earth looking for a good person, that everyone is waiting to receive them—can find no one who will give them lodging except the prostitute, Shen Te. In addition, the prologue establishes the situation: The gods find the good person for whom they have been searching—Shen Te—and enjoin her to remain good. When she objects that she cannot be good unless she has the financial security that will permit her to refuse evil, the gods are unmoved, declaring that they "never meddle with economics." Herein lies the conflict, for to Brecht economic need is the root of evil because it forces people to do things that are wrong merely to survive. Brecht implies that the solution to human problems is not to be found in divine injunctions.

The scenes following the prologue show Shen Te buying a small shop to support herself, only to have greedy relatives and hangers-on descend on her and take advantage of her goodness. When she falls in love with the penniless Yang Sun, who wishes to become a pilot, Shen Te gives him money she needs to pay her bills.

Brecht's *The Good Woman of Setzuan* as produced at the American Repertory Theatre. Seen here is Shen Te (Priscilla Smith) and her lover Yang Sun (James Andreassi). Directed by Andrei Serban; settings by Jeff Muskovin; costumes by Catherine Zuber. (Photo by Richard Feldman.)

On the verge of ruin, she disguises herself as a male cousin, Shui Ta, who suppresses humanitarian feelings and demands that those who want assistance must work—on his capitalistic terms. Thereafter the action is devoted to the conflict between good and evil as seen in the protagonist's two personae. Shui Ta appears for short intervals at first, but eventually takes over as the capitalist boss who exploits his workers and does whatever is needed to survive. The other characters suspect that Shui Ta has killed Shen Te. When the gods return disguised as judges before whom Shui Ta is brought, he reveals to them privately not only that he is Shen Te but also that she is pregnant and must provide for her child. But the gods can only admonish Shen Te to be good and to disguise herself less often as Shui Ta. The play ends with Shen Te's dilemma unresolved. An epilogue suggests that it is up to the audience to find a way out, presumably by changing the economic system.

The Good Woman of Setzuan alternates short and long scenes. The short scenes serve two purposes: to break up the action, and to comment on the long scenes used to develop the action. Brecht makes no attempt to create the illusion of everyday reality. For example, when Wong says he will find a place for the gods to spend the

The Good Woman of Setzuan as produced at the Arena Stage, Washington. Shen Te's tobacco shop has been invaded by relatives who want her to support them. (Photo by Joan Marcus. Courtesy of the Arena Stage.)

night, he merely suggests the attempt by circling the stage and pantomiming knocking on imaginary doors that are slammed in his face. This approach allows Brecht to telescope events and to eliminate transitions, as can be seen clearly in the scene during which Shen Te rescues and falls in love with the would-be pilot Yang Sun. There has been no preparation for this complication; it is as if a storyteller had said, "One day, when Shen Te was walking in the park, she saw a young man trying to hang himself."

Brecht's structural techniques are explained in part by his belief that scenes should be clearly separated as one means of creating alienation. He also insisted that it should be possible to express the social content of each scene in one sentence (a *gestus*), and that all parts of the scene should be clearly related to this statement, which in performance may be projected onto a screen prior to the beginning of the scene.

Brecht oversimplifies characters, for he is principally concerned with social relationships. He is not interested in total personalities or the inner lives of his characters. Instead of names, most characters in *The Good Woman of Setzuan* are designated by their social functions, such as Wife, Grandfather, or Policeman. Their desires are stated in terms of social action: Shen Te wishes to treat all persons hon-

The Berliner Ensemble

Brecht left his native Germany in 1933 when the Nazis came to power and remained in exile, much of it in the United States, until after World War II. Upon returning to Europe, he took up residence in East Berlin, where in 1949 he and his wife, the actress Helene Weigel, established the Berliner Ensemble, where he worked to develop the style of production he thought best suited to his plays.

Brecht perfected his productions in rehearsal periods that sometimes continued for six months or longer. Thorough records of the production process were kept and published in books that contained six hundred to eight hundred photographs of each production. These records influenced many who had never seen performances by the Berliner Ensemble. The Berliner Ensemble rapidly gained international recognition, especially after it won the prize for best production two years in a row (1954 and 1955) at the Théâtre des Nations, which under the auspices of the United Nations brought together in Paris each year major companies from throughout the world. By 1956, when Brecht died, the Berliner Ensemble was considered one of the great theatres of the world. After Brecht's death, the theatre continued but many critics charged that it had become a showcase for out-of-date productions. With the collapse of communism and the reunion of Germany, it was privatized (though it continued to receive a large government subsidy) and came under a five-person management. Having lost its primary focus, the Berliner Ensemble has been left to seek a new artistic vision.

orably, to make it possible for Yang Sun to become a pilot, to provide proper food for children, and so on. Brecht did not intend to portray well-rounded individuals but instead to interpret social forces. The action does not exist to display character; rather, character demonstrates social attitude. The only character who seems concerned about morality is Shen Te; the plot progresses in large part through the series of choices she makes about dilemmas created by economic conditions. The other characters are primarily concerned with selfish goals or (in the case of the gods) sustaining a dogmatic view.

Today, many of our most familiar theatrical conventions (no front curtain to hide the stage, the use of fragmentary scenery and visible lighting instruments, and other practices that call attention to the theatrical medium) derive in large part from Brecht, although Brecht's intention of provoking social change is often ignored.

Artaud and the Theatre of Cruelty

Another strain of theatre in the 1920s and 1930s focused on forces quite different from those Brecht emphasized; it was concerned with those impulses buried within the unconscious mind. The most influential representative of this strain was

Antonin Artaud (1896–1948), whose views, like those of Brecht, were not immediately accepted but, like Brecht's, became influential after his death. Whereas Brecht thought the key to improving the human lot lay in transforming external circumstances, Artaud thought the key lay in confronting internal divisions.

Artaud for a time was a member of the surrealist movement, which flourished during the 1920s. *Surrealism* emphasized one aspect of Freud's teachings: the importance of the unconscious. According to the surrealists, significant truths are those deeply buried in the psyche, suppressed by the conscious mind. In order to expose these "truths," the conscious mind must be subverted. The surrealists promoted dreams, automatic writing, and stream of consciousness as paths through which images, ideas, and experiences buried in the subconscious could escape the conscious mind's control and rise to the surface, where the insights they offered could be utilized. Surrealism made its greatest impact in painting, especially in the work of Salvador Dali, in which familiar objects are used in unfamiliar ways, juxtaposed with unrelated objects, or placed in "dream landscapes" creating visual metaphors that stimulate the imagination and lead to new perceptions. Artaud eventually broke with the surrealists, but his experience with them was crucial to his work both in theatre and in film.

Artaud expressed his major ideas about theatre in a series of essays collected in *The Theatre and Its Double* (1938). According to Artaud, the theatre in the Western world has been restricted to a narrow range of human experience, primarily the psychological problems of individuals or the social problems of groups. Artaud considered such theatre insignificant because it failed to touch the most important influences on human behavior—those buried in the unconscious. But if these influences remain buried and unconfronted, they lead to divisions within the person (and between people) and ultimately to hatred, violence, and disaster. Artaud believed that if theatre were used properly, it would free people from destructive impulses. As he put it, "The theatre has been created to drain abscesses collectively."

Artaud was certain that his goals could not be reached through appeals to the rational mind (Brecht's approach) because the conscious mind has been conditioned to sublimate and ignore the very things that need to be examined. Thus, he argued, it is necessary to subvert the audience's defenses. Artaud sometimes referred to his as a "theatre of cruelty," not because it was physically cruel but because it forced the audience, against its wishes, to confront itself. Because he considered the conventions of the established theatre to be directed to the conscious mind, he proposed to replace them with a "new language of the theatre." Believing that the proscenium-arch theatre created a barrier between performers and spectators, he proposed replacing it with large, undivided spaces such as barns, factories, airplane hangars, and warehouses. Within these spaces he wanted to locate acting areas in corners, overhead on catwalks, and around the walls so as to place the audience in the midst of the action.

Artaud wanted to do away with scenery altogether and replace it with symbolic costumes and properties. In discussing lighting, he wrote of a "vibrating, shredded" effect with pulsating changes (comparable to present-day strobe lighting). He favored great variety in sound, ranging in volume from a whisper to a factory at peak production; he advocated using the human voice not primarily for speech but for

Marat/Sade as produced by the Williamstown Theatre Festival. Directed by Paul Weidner; set by Robert Darling; costumes by Kenneth Mooney; lighting by Thomas R. Skelton. (Photo by Richard Feldman.)

yelps, cries, and varied emotional and atmospheric effects. He considered these innovative means capable of bypassing the conscious mind. As he put it, "Whereas most people remain impervious to a subtle discourse . . . they cannot resist effects of physical surprise, the dynamism of cries and violent movements, visual explosions, the aggregate of tetanizing effects called up on cue and used to act in a direct manner on the physical sensitivity of the spectators." These conventions were to be coupled with stories of mythical proportions and implications. The ultimate purpose was to break down the audience's defenses, drag suppressed impulses to the surface, and force the audience to face and deal with those influences that, if unacknowledged, create hatred and violence.

As this broad survey of theatrical developments suggests, during the years between 1885 and 1940 the modernist temperament achieved dominance. For the first time in history, multiple artistic movements existed simultaneously and challenged each other for supremacy. Some of these movements flourished for a time and then faded, but all left residues that were assimilated into the theatre's mainstream. Together they gained acceptance of the view that there is no single correct approach to theatrical production and that each artist is free to offer his or her own vision of truth and human experience no matter how eccentric. Absolutist notions

Peter Brook and the Theatre of Cruelty

Although Artaud's theories had already influenced some directors and critics, they did not attract wide attention in England and America until Peter Brook began to experiment with them in the early 1960s.

In 1963, Brook, assisted by Charles Marowitz and with support from the Royal Shakespeare Company, selected a group of twelve actors with whom he worked throughout the 1963–64 theatre season. Through exercises they experimented with sound (made with their voices, on their bodies, and with objects), movement, rhythm, and pantomime; they sought to replace clichéd solutions with innovative, nonrealistic means of expression. They also sought to replace the typical pattern of beginning-middle-end development with discontinuous or simultaneous scenes. They performed a "Collage Hamlet" with sequences from Shakespeare's text rearranged, lines from different scenes juxtaposed, characters dropped or blended, and discontinuous fragments inserted. A five-week public showing of the group's work was presented under the title "Theatre of Cruelty." Though what the group did deviated in many ways from Artaud's ideas, critics began to equate Artaud with Brook's experiments, especially after his production of Peter Weiss' *Marat/Sade* (which offered almost endless opportunities for actors—playing inmates of an insane asylum—to make use of Artaudian techniques), which was one of the most successful and influential productions of the 1960s. In both England and America (where it achieved both long runs and high critical praise), this production was hailed as a practical application of Artaud's theories. With the success of this production, Artaud became widely known for the first time.

were largely denied, but not wholly abandoned. Similarly, though the avant-garde was favored by elitist critics, a modified realism remained the most popular mode in mainstream theatre.

Chapter 8

Reevaluation, Decentralization, and Subsidization

Shakespeare's *As You Like It* as produced at the Alley Theatre (Houston), one of the country's oldest regional not-for-profit theatres (founded in 1947). Oliver (Peter Webster, at right) practices his wooing of Rosalind on Ganymede (Lolita Lesheim, Rosalind in disguise). Directed by Gregory Boyd. (Photo by Jim Caldwell. Courtesy of the Alley Theatre.)

> [Because of decentralization and subsidization] Good theatre is available throughout the country—some of it truly exceptional in quality—and without question, it is providing forums to communities that were not available four decades ago. . . . this is an extraordinary achievement in a very short time.
>
> —Peter Zeisler, "Seize the Moment," *American Theatre* (September 1994)

World War II disrupted theatrical activity in many countries of Europe, and almost everywhere it motivated reassessment of values and theatrical practices. In many countries reassessment led to decentralization of the theatre, which often was accomplished only through financial assistance in the form of subsidization.

Postwar American Theatre

The United States (perhaps because it was geographically removed from the fighting, and gained, rather than lost, in optimism) saw little change in theatre during and immediately following the war years. Modified realism continued to be the major approach in theatrical production, and psychological realism, derived from Stanislavsky, strengthened its hold on acting. In 1947, Robert Lewis, Elia Kazan, and Cheryl Crawford, all former members of the Group Theatre, founded The Actors Studio in New York to provide its members an ongoing opportunity to develop their craft. The Actors Studio was not a school and there were no fees. The premise was that an actor's training never ends, and that experienced performers need a place where they can continue to develop their skills within a group of nurturing peers; once accepted into The Actors Studio (after rigorous auditions), one remained a member for life. Lee Strasberg soon became the Studio's director and major teacher and continued as such until his death in 1982. Awareness of the Studio's work grew quickly after Marlon Brando, a Studio actor, captured the public's imagination with his portrayal of the inarticulate, uneducated, and assertive Stanley Kowalski in Tennessee Williams' *A Streetcar Named Desire* (1947), directed by Kazan. Brando's impact was enormous, not only affecting acting style but also contributing greatly to the influence of The Actors Studio and its version of the Stanislavsky system, usually referred to as "the method." This approach, which concentrated on the actor's belief in the truth of the dramatic moment, could give scenes considerable psychological intensity. A frequent criticism of the method, however, was that actors using it often seemed so self-absorbed that they neglected the technical skills needed to externalize internal feelings and that they mumbled rather than speaking audibly and intelligibly. Members of The Actors Studio included James Dean, Paul Newman, Al Pacino, Robert de Niro, Dustin Hoffman, Shelley Winters, Geraldine Page, and many others who became widely known, especially through their film roles.

Psychological realism also dominated the plays of the postwar period. The two major dramatists were Arthur Miller (1916–   ) with *All My Sons, Death of a Salesman,* and *The Crucible;* and Tennessee Williams (1911–1983) with *The Glass Menagerie, A Streetcar Named Desire,* and *Cat on a Hot Tin Roof.* The Actors Studio's

Arthur Miller's *Death of a Salesman*, 1949. Lower level, Lee J. Cobb as Willy and Mildred Dunnock as Linda; upper level, Arthur Kennedy as Biff and Cameron Mitchell as Happy. Directed by Elia Kazan; designed by Jo Mielziner. (Photo by Eileen Darby.)

reputation was enhanced by Kazan's direction of several of these plays, on which he collaborated with designer Jo Mielziner. Kazan and Mielziner established the production style that dominated the American theatre from the late 1940s until the 1960s. This style combined psychological realism in acting and directing with simplified, skeletal settings that permitted fluid shifts in time and place. Let us look more closely at a play that is both representative of the period and of the Kazan-Mielziner approach to staging.

Cat on a Hot Tin Roof

Tennessee Williams' *Cat on a Hot Tin Roof* (1955) is a play about mendacity—deception and lying, both to oneself and others. Although divided into three acts, the action is continuous; each act takes up precisely where the preceding one left off; no more time elapses in the play than it takes to perform it. The play, then, has a late point of attack and the amount of exposition about past events is considerable, although skillfully worked into the action.

Ben Gazzara as Brick and Barbara Bel Geddes as Maggie in the original production of Tennessee Williams' *Cat on a Hot Tin Roof.* Directed by Elia Kazan; setting by Jo Mielziner. (Photo by Bob Golby. Courtesy of the Harry Ransom Humanities Research Center, University of Texas at Austin.)

The occasion that ostensibly has brought all the characters together is Big Daddy's sixty-fifth birthday, which coincides with receipt of results of Big Daddy's clinical tests for cancer. Big Daddy and Big Mama are told that he has merely a spastic colon, news that puts them in a highly celebratory mood, though based on a lie. The others know that Big Daddy is dying, and because he is extremely wealthy—he owns twenty-eight thousand acres of the "richest land this side of the valley Nile" and at least ten million dollars in cash—and because he has not made a will, they are concerned with who will inherit his wealth. The obvious candidates are Big Daddy's two sons. The elder, Gooper, a corporation lawyer, is married to Mae and has five children. They covet Big Daddy's wealth and spend most of their time in transparent attempts to ingratiate themselves or to discredit Gooper's younger brother, Brick. A former football star and sports announcer, Brick now concentrates on alcohol. He and his wife, Maggie, have no children; he is as indifferent to his father's wealth (and everything else) as Gooper is fixated on it. Throughout the play Brick walks with the aid of a crutch, having broken his ankle the night before while attempting to jump hurdles. Both the crutch and the constant resort to alcohol are symbolic of what Williams calls Brick's "spiritual disrepair," born out of his disgust with mendacity.

But if Brick has no interest in Big Daddy's wealth, his wife does. Having escaped a background of genteel poverty, Maggie is determined not to return to it; she sees having a child by Brick as her only hope of avoiding that fate. Unfortunately for her, Brick refuses to touch her, believing that she is to blame for the death of his best friend, Skipper, who destroyed himself after Maggie accused him of being in love with Brick. According to Brick, Maggie turned the purest thing in his life into something ugly. His drinking and disgust with the world apparently are related to Skipper's death.

The play concentrates primarily on three characters: Maggie, Brick, and Big Daddy. Big Daddy's situation is the primary motivator of the action, and it is he who forces Brick to acknowledge his own responsibility in Skipper's death. Brick's withdrawal and inaction are a primary spur for others who throughout the play seek to provoke him into action. Maggie, judging by the play's title the principal character, wants to act but is thwarted by Brick until the final scene.

The first act is devoted almost entirely to Maggie and Brick as she tries to make him understand their precarious position in relation to Big Daddy's wealth. Because Brick has abdicated any concern for life and because they have no children, they are in danger of being disinherited altogether or having to accept whatever Gooper may choose to dole out to them. It is during this scene that Maggie likens herself to a cat trying to hold on to a hot tin roof. Brick refuses to cooperate in her desire to be pregnant. The only time he shows anything more than indifference comes when she (or Big Daddy) insists they talk about Skipper.

The second act is devoted primarily to Brick and Big Daddy. Much of this act is taken up with Big Daddy trying to work up to a serious talk with Brick. During these preliminaries we find out much about Big Daddy who, beginning in poverty, has made himself rich through his own efforts. He makes it clear that he dislikes Gooper but that he does not want what he has accumulated to be wasted. He sets out, therefore, to find out why Brick drinks, and he ultimately forces Brick to acknowledge that when, in a phone conversation, Skipper admitted his love, Brick had hung up on him. Big Daddy says that it was Brick's unwillingness to face this situation with his friend, rather than Maggie's accusations, that caused Skipper's death. Hurt, Brick in retaliation reveals the truth about the cancer tests. The act ends with both men denouncing liars.

The final act is taken up with a gathering of all the characters except Big Daddy during which they reveal the truth to Big Mama. Gooper and Mae try to coax Big Mama into approving papers that Gooper has had drawn up about authority over the property. She refuses, and Maggie takes control by announcing that she is pregnant. Gooper and Mae accuse her of lying, but later Maggie attempts to make it true by depriving Brick of access to alcohol until he makes love to her. Although what he will do is unclear, he seems to acquiesce.

There is an alternative third act to *Cat on a Hot Tin Roof,* written at the insistence of Elia Kazan, the original director of the play on Broadway. Kazan thought that Big Daddy was too powerful a character not to reappear in the third act (in Williams' original script Big Daddy appears only in the second act), and that Brick should undergo significant change as a result of his confrontation with Big Daddy in the second act. In the Broadway version, Big Daddy does appear in the third act, although primarily to show that he favors Brick and to ask that a lawyer be sent for so he can make a will. In both versions, Big Daddy is later heard off stage howling in pain as the cancer ravages him. In the alternative version, Brick does show change. Early in the act he suggests that Maggie arrange for him to go to a treatment clinic, and later, when Gooper and Mae accuse Maggie of lying about being pregnant, he defends her and subsequently appears to acquiesce to her demands.

Cat on a Hot Tin Roof at the McCarter Theatre Center for the Performing Arts (Princeton, NJ). James Morrison as Brick, Jo Beth Williams as Maggie. Directed by Emily Mann; setting by Derek McLane; lighting by Peter Kaczorowski; costumes by Martin Pakledinaz. (Photo by T. Charles Erickson.)

The overall effect of the Broadway version is to make the play far more positive than Williams wished. He argues that no conversation, "however relevatory, ever effects so immediate a change in the heart or even the conduct of a person in Brick's state of spiritual disrepair." The disagreement between Williams and Kazan illustrates the power that directors may have over a script and how they can persuade playwrights to make changes, even ones they do not approve of.

Kazan collaborated on the Broadway production with Jo Mielziner, the best-known American stage designer of that time. Mielziner's set was basically a platform, one corner of which jutted out over the orchestra pit toward the audience; above the platform a ceiling was suspended to outline the room, and a few shutters and curtains suggested the walls. The furnishings were minimal, the most important features being the bed and a combined radio-TV console and liquor cabinet. Williams clearly saw this console as a symbol: "a very complete and compact little shrine to virtually all the comforts and illusions behind which we hide from such things as the characters in this play are faced with." The skeletal setting and psychologically realistic acting were the hallmarks of the Kazan-Mielziner production style.

Despite its great power, *Cat on a Hot Tin Roof* can, from today's perspective, be faulted on two scores—gender and race—though both were treated in ways typical of their time. The play seems almost misogynistic in its representation of women. Both Big Daddy and Brick treat their wives with near-contempt, and Mae is shown to be avaricious and calculating. Williams has expressed his admiration and affection for Maggie, but she, as well as the other female characters, apparently believes she has no identity except through her husband. And though Williams himself was homosexual, he treats the very notion of homosexuality as so unacceptable to Brick as to paralyze him psychologically. The play also includes several African-American characters. Although how they are treated was not unusual in plays of the time, in *Cat on a Hot Tin Roof* the white characters are by today's standards unthinking or callous in their dealings with the black characters and in their references to blacks in general. Williams seemingly adopts unquestioningly the stereotype (often used for enslaved people in the nineteenth century) that servants are happy to be used and patronized by their masters.

The Musical in Postwar America

Along with the modified realism of spoken drama, the musical was the most popular form of theatre in postwar America. In fact, although spoken drama has received more serious study, the musical has been the most popular theatrical form in the United States during the twentieth century. Musical drama is not of recent origin. The choral passages of Greek drama were sung and danced; the majority of the lines in Roman comedy were accompanied by music; the Italians developed wholly sung opera; and Shakespeare introduced many songs into his plays. The eighteenth century introduced a number of popular musical forms, including ballad opera and comic opera, and the nineteenth century used music to underscore melodrama's action. When the plays did not require music, some type of musical entertainment was usually included on the bill.

Even so, musical comedy did not begin to emerge as a distinct type until the late nineteenth century. Early examples of musical comedy usually emphasized the romantic appeal of faraway places or exotic situations; the stories were primarily excuses for songs and ensemble choral numbers, often sung and danced by beautiful young women. Around World War I, a change occurred when ballroom dancing and ragtime music, both then in vogue, were introduced into musicals; with them came more familiar characters and surroundings. Nevertheless, story line remained relatively unimportant, and the emphasis continued to be on spectacular settings, songs, dances, and chorus girls. Not until the late 1920s—most notably in *Show Boat* by Jerome Kern and Oscar Hammerstein II—did story and psychological motivation begin to be important. The new status of the form was recognized in 1931 when for the first time a musical (*Of Thee I Sing* with text by George S. Kaufman and Morrie Ryskind and music by George Gershwin) won the Pulitzer Prize for the best drama of the year.

By 1940, the musical, according to many critics, had become distinctively American and America's most significant contribution to world theatre. It was then

The "rumble" scene between the rival gangs, the Jets and the Sharks, in *West Side Story* by Leonard Bernstein, Arthur Laurents, and Stephen Sondheim. Directed by Jerome Robbins; sets by Oliver Smith; lighting by Jean Rosenthal. (The Billy Rose Collection, the New York Public Library for the Performing Arts, the Astor, Lenox and Tilden Foundations.)

on the threshold of its greatest period. *Oklahoma* (1943), by Richard Rodgers and Oscar Hammerstein II, is often cited as the first work in which music, story, dance (choreographed by Agnes DeMille), and visual elements were fully integrated so that all contributed significantly to the dramatic action. Rodgers and Hammerstein solidified this approach in such pieces as *Carousel* (1945), *South Pacific* (1949), and *The King and I* (1951). Several other composers and authors in the post–World War II period followed the lead of Rodgers and Hammerstein, among them Alan Jay Lerner and Frederick Loewe with *Brigadoon* (1947) and *My Fair Lady* (1956); Frank Loesser with *Guys and Dolls* (1950); and Leonard Bernstein and Arthur Laurents with *West Side Story* (1957).

The popularity of the musical is probably attributable to its multiple appeals. The musical and choreographic elements, sources of pleasure in their own right, can also facilitate storytelling. For example, the lyrics of songs contribute to clarity by expressing emotional response and intention directly, much as soliloquies and asides did in earlier drama. Music, through such conventions as the reprise (the repetition of musical phrases or fragments of lyrics), can connect or recall moments separated in time. Furthermore, music assists in condensing time, as when a song or musical passage is used to show quickly a progression of events that in actuality occurs over a long period. For example, in *My Fair Lady*, the speech lessons that alter the flower seller Eliza's accent so she can pass as a duchess are condensed primarily into one

Plate 1: The theatre at Epidaurus, the best-preserved of all ancient Greek theatres, is still used today as a site for performances during festivals. The stage house seen here is temporary, erected on the ruins of the original. (Photo by Constantine Manos/Magnum.)

Plate 2: Euripides' *The Bacchae* at the Guthrie Theatre, Minneapolis. Agave (second from the right) has just discovered that while possessed she has killed her son. Directed and designed by Liviu Culei; costumes by Patricia Zipprodt; masks by Mary Walker; lighting by Marcus Dillard. (Courtesy of the Guthrie Theatre.)

Plate 3: A double page from the manuscript of the medieval outdoor drama staged at Valenciennes (France) in 1547. At bottom, the text of the play; above, simultaneous drawings of several scenes. At left, Christ being nailed to the cross; center, the crucifixion; right center, Christ being taken off the cross; right, the entombment. (Courtesy of the Bibliothèque Nationale, Paris.)

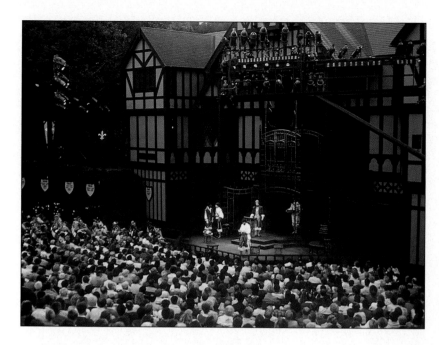

Plate 4: Performance in the outdoor theatre of the Oregon Shakespeare Festival. The theatre structure is meant to simulate an Elizabethan public stage. (Photo by Christopher Briscoe. Courtesy of the Oregon Shakespeare Festival.)

Plate 5: A painting entitled *Les Delices du Genre Humaine*, showing major French actors and popular stage characters of the seventeenth century. Molière is seen at extreme left; Harlequin is at center front; Dottore, Pantalone, and Brighella are at right. (Courtesy of the Comédie Francaise, Paris.)

Plate 6: Interior of the Theatre Royal, Turin (Italy) in 1740. Notice that the proscenium arch is so thick that it is able to contain a box for spectators on each of five levels. The male actors at left and center are wearing the *habit à la romaine*, while the actress between them is dressed in the fashion of the eighteenth century. In the auditorium a vendor is selling fruit and drink, and a soldier is posted to keep order. The setting is by Giuseppe Bibiena, noted for his monumental painted scenery. Despite the setting's apparent realism, all of the details are painted on wings, drops, and borders. Painting by Pietro Domenico. (Courtesy of the Civic Museum, Turin.)

Plate 8: Scene from Carlo Gozzi's *The Serpent Woman*, an eighteenth-century commedia dell'arte script, as performed at the American Repertory Theatre. Directed by Andrei Serban; costumes, masks, and puppets by Setsu Asakura; lighting by Victor En Yu Tan. (Photo by Richard Feldman.)

Plate 9: Anton Chekhov's *The Cherry Orchard* as performed at the Arena Stage, Washington. At front, Shirley Knight as Madame Ranevskaya. Directed by Lucian Pintilie. (Photo by Joan Marcus. Courtesy of the Arena Stage.)

Plate 10: Shakespeare's *A Midsummer Night's Dream* as performed by the Royal Shakespeare Company under the direction of Peter Brook. At center, Oberon is applying a potion that will release Titania from the spell that caused her to fall in love with Bottom, seen here asleep in the bower of feathers. Bottom, instead of being transformed into an ass, has been given a clown's nose. Notice the trapeze used for flying in this production, which used many conventions of circus and magic. The set, by Sally Jacobs, was a square box composed of white, unadorned walls. (Photo by Max Waldman/Magnum.)

Plate 11: Shakespeare's *A Midsummer Night's Dream* as performed at the Hartford Stage under the direction of Mark Lamos. In this production, the magic was so powerful that even buildings floated about. Settings by Michael H. Yeargan; costumes by Jeff Goldstein; lighting by Pat Collins. (Photo by Jennifer Lester. Courtesy of the Hartford Stage.)

Plate 12: Peter Brook's production
of Peter Weiss's *Marat/Sade* at the
Royal Shakespeare Company. The
setting is an insane asylum where
inmates act a play about the French
Revolution for visitors who come
from nearby Paris. (Photo by Dennis
Stock/Magnum.)

Plate 13: Bertolt Brecht's *The Good Woman of Setzuan* as produced at the American Repertory Theatre. The costumes in the background reflect the influence of Beijing Opera, China's major theatrical form. Directed by Andrei Serban; costumes by Catherine Zuber. (Photo by Richard Feldman.)

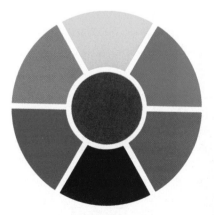

Color Wheel

Plate 14: Color wheel, showing six hues arranged in a circle. The primary colors are yellow, blue, and red. Opposite hues are located directly across from each other on the wheel. If all the colors were mixed, they would produce the gray shown at center.

Plate 15: Shakespeare's *Henry IV, Part I* as performed by the Théâtre du Soliel (Paris) under the direction of Ariane Mnouchkine. This production intermingled Asian and Western theatrical conventions. Notice the Noh-like mask on Henry IV, lying on the ground; notice also the layered costume worn by Prince Hal (at left) and the Elizabethan doublet sleeve of Hotspur's costume (center). Red strings are used to simulate blood. (Photo by Martine Franck/Magnum.)

Plate 16: Jean Genet's *The Screens* as performed at the Guthrie Theatre, Minneapolis. Directed by JoAnne Akalaitis; sets and props by George Tsypin; costumes by Eiko Ishioka; lighting by Jennifer Tipton. (Photo by Michal Daniel. Courtesy of the Guthrie Theatre.)

Plate 17: Robert Wilson's *CIVIL warS* as presented at the American Repertory Theatre. Set design by Robert Wilson and Thomas Kamm; costumes by Yoshio Yabara; lighting by Jennifer Tipton and Robert Wilson. (Photo by Richard Feldman.)

Plate 18: Ming Cho Lee's setting for John Osborne's *The Entertainer* at the Guthrie Theatre, Minneapolis. The play draws parallels between the decline in the vitality and fortunes of a family of music-hall entertainers and the British Empire. As written, the text indicates a number of separate locations, but the design seen here uses a single setting to suggest all the places, while providing a commentary through the figures of the lion (symbol of the Empire) and the female figure (a music-hall showgirl dressed in the colors of the British flag, representing Britannia.) (Courtesy of the Guthrie Theatre.)

Plate 19: *The Phantom of the Opera* by Andrew Lloyd Webber and Charles Hart. The performers are Michael Crawford and Sarah Brightman. Directed by Harold Prince; designed by Maria Bjornson; lighting by Andrew Bridge. (Photo by Bob Marshak.)

Plate 20: Peter Brook's production of Jean-Claude Carriere's adaptation of the Sanskrit epic, *Mahabharata*. Designed by Chloe Oblensky. (Photo by Martha Swope.)

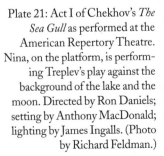

Plate 21: Act I of Chekhov's *The Sea Gull* as performed at the American Repertory Theatre. Nina, on the platform, is performing Treplev's play against the background of the lake and the moon. Directed by Ron Daniels; setting by Anthony MacDonald; lighting by James Ingalls. (Photo by Richard Feldman.)

Plate 22: For *42nd Street*, based on a Busby Berkeley film musical, Gower Champion, who also directed, devised spectacular dances such as the one seen here. Settings by Robin Wagner. (Photo by Martha Swope.)

Plate 23: Glenn Close as Norma Desmond in Andrew Lloyd Webber's musical, *Sunset Boulevard*, adapted by Don Black and Christopher Hampton from Billy Wilder's movie. Directed by Trevor Nunn; designed by John Napier. (Photo by Joan Marcus.)

Plate 24: The pinball machine in the rock musical *Tommy* by Pete Townshend. Directed by Des McAnuff; sets by John Arnone; costumes by David C. Woolard; lighting by Chris Parry; projections by Wendall K. Harrington. (Photo by Joan Marcus.)

Plate 25: Scene from the revival of the 1955 musical *Damn Yankees*, with book by George Abbott and Douglass Wallop and score by Richard Adler and Jerry Ross. For the 1994 revival, the book was revised by George Abbott and Jack O'Brien, who also directed the production. Settings by Douglas Schmidt; costume by David C. Woolard. (Photo by Carol Rosegg.)

Plate 26: J. B. Priestley's 1946 play *The Inspector Calls* had long been considered hopelessly dated until it was revived in 1993 in a production directed by Stephen Daldry. Much of the play's success was owing to its setting by Ian McNeill. The house shown here opened to reveal a dining room inside and eventually the entire house collapsed spilling its contents onto the pavement only to reerect itself. (Photo by Joan Marcus.)

Plate 27: Makeup and costume by Irene Corey for Prospero in Shakespeare's *The Tempest*, directed by Orlin Corey. The production concept set the action on an island where everything had been affected by underwater forms. The cloak seems encrusted with coral, and Prospero's magic is suggested by the glowing headdress. (Courtesy of Irene Corey. From her *The Face is a Canvas: The Design and Technique of Theatrical Makeup*. New Orleans: Anchorage Press, 1990.)

Play into Musical

Many of America's most popular musicals have been adapted from existing plays or novels. *Oklahoma!* was adapted from Lynn Riggs' *Green Grow the Lilacs, Carousel* from Ferenc Molnar's *Liliom, South Pacific* from James Michener's *Tales of the South Pacific*, and *West Side Story* from Shakespeare's *Romeo and Juliet*. Musical adaptation requires many script changes, often to provide more opportunities for chorus and dance numbers and increased variety in settings, costumes, and spectacular elements.

Alan Jay Lerner and Frederick Loewe's *My Fair Lady* (1956), adapted from George Bernard Shaw's *Pygmalion* (1912), provides a good example. Shaw's comedy about a flower girl transformed by a speech professor into a lady who can pass as a duchess is divided into five acts, never changes place within an act, and is restricted to three locales, only one of which permits the use of a crowd. *My Fair Lady* is divided into two acts composed of eighteen scenes that provide greatly expanded opportunities for dances, crowd scenes, and spectacle. Some of the new scenes are set in the crowded slums from which Eliza, the protagonist, comes, thereby creating excuses for songs and dances; the flower market there (Eliza sells flowers on the street) offers rich opportunities for spectacular color. In Shaw's play, Professor Higgins takes Eliza to his mother's house for tea as a trial outing to see how much she has progressed in her training, but in the musical this confined setting and small group are replaced by a pavilion and crowd at the Ascot racetrack. In Shaw's play, we only hear of Eliza's triumph at the ball, but in the musical we see the ball. Scenes in the play are curtailed in the musical to create space for the songs and dances. On the other hand, the added songs, dances, and spectacle condense much that is talked about at length in Shaw's play. Adapting a play into a musical is analogous to the process of "opening up" a play when it is made into a film.

song, "The Rain in Spain." In addition, music establishes mood and builds expectation. Even before the action begins, an overture establishes the general mood of the work to follow, and thereafter music helps to establish the appropriate emotional tone and, through modulations in tempo, key, and volume, to build individual scenes and the work as a whole.

A musical usually provides considerable visual stimulation. Scenic, costume, and lighting designers typically are offered wide scope for their talents in musical productions. There are usually several changes in time and place and a large cast (often with much doubling), which require multiple sets and costumes. Dance usually plays a large role, commenting on the action and forwarding the story much as the songs do. Considering all of these appeals, it is not surprising that the musical has long been among the most popular of theatrical experiences. It is also not surprising that audiences have found in the musical an antidote to the dark vision of humanity offered by much twentieth-century drama.

Rex Harrison and Julie Andrews in the opening scene of the original production of *My Fair Lady* by Alan Jay Lerner and Fred Loewe. (Courtesy of the Theatre and Music Collection, Museum of the City of New York.)

Postwar Europe

These American musicals and plays were quite unlike the theatrical fare typical of postwar Europe. Perhaps because Europe had suffered so much devastation and been subjected to so many atrocities, its postwar mood was much darker than that of America. Many questioned the very foundations of truth and values. This questioning was not entirely new but it was more pervasive than in the past. Among those who earlier had questioned the concept of absolute (or verifiable) truth was the Italian Luigi Pirandello (1867–1936), one of the most important dramatists of the twentieth century. In his plays, among them *Right You Are (If You Think You Are); Six Characters in Search of an Author;* and *Henry IV,* the dramatic action turns on a question of fact that cannot be resolved because each character is convinced that his or her own version of it is the true version. Pirandello raises doubt about the possibility of determining truth through direct observation. He concludes that "truth" is personal, subjective, relative, and ever-changing.

During and following World War II, a group of philosophers and dramatists, the existentialists, adopted a more radical version of Pirandello's views. Jean-Paul Sartre (1905–1980), the best-known existentialist, denied the existence of God, the validity of fixed standards of conduct, and the possibility of verifiable moral codes. He concluded that because none of the institutions (church, state, society) from which we have taken our standards can prove the correctness or necessity of those standards, human beings are "condemned to be free" (that is, people deprived of absolute standards are condemned to choose individually the values by which they will live). He insisted that unquestioning conformity to values established by others is immoral, whereas choosing (and living by) one's own values is to define oneself as a moral being. Sartre's views were persuasive because they came at a time when many Nazis were seeking to escape punishment for war crimes by arguing that they had merely obeyed German laws or carried out their government's policies. The crucial question was: Which takes precedence—law and policy (no matter how perverted) or individual moral values? Many Nazis were convicted on the premise that the individual should refuse to obey unjust or inhuman demands, even legal ones. This conclusion, which reflects Sartre's, has since undergirded the civil disobedience used as a weapon in the civil rights movement, demonstrations against the Vietnam War, anti-abortion campaigns, and other protests.

Sartre was echoed by Albert Camus (1913–1960), whose description of the human condition as "absurd" supplied the label ("absurdist") by which a subsequent group of dramatists came to be known. Camus concluded that our situation is

Pirandello's *Six Characters in Search of an Author* as produced at the American Repertory Theatre. Directed by Robert Brustein; setting and costumes by Michael H. Yeargan; lighting by Jennifer Tipton. (Photo by Richard Feldman.)

absurd because our longing for clarity and certainty is met with, and forever thwarted by, the irrationality of the universe into which we have been thrown; it is absurd also because we can neither rid ourselves of the desire for order nor overcome the irrationality that stands in the way of order. The only recourse is to choose one's own standards and live by them. Both Sartre and Camus were convinced that we can examine our situation and make decisions that permit us to act meaningfully in accordance with those decisions. Both wrote plays that are traditional in structure, showing a protagonist facing a problem, pursuing it through a set of complications to a point of crisis, and making choices that permit a clear resolution. Among Sartre's plays, the best-known are *The Flies* and *No Exit;* Camus' best-known plays are *Caligula* and *The Just Assassins.*

Absurdism

The absurdists, who emerged in France around 1950, accepted the views of Sartre and Camus about the human condition, but unlike those two writers they saw no way out because rational and meaningful choices seemed impossible in such a universe. Thus, to the absurdists truth consisted of chaos and lack of order, logic, or certainty, and their plays embodied this vision in a structure that abandoned cause-and-effect relationships for associational patterns reflecting illogic and chance.

Among the absurdist playwrights, who included Eugene Ionesco and Jean Genet, the most influential was Samuel Beckett (1906–1989), whose *Waiting for Godot* (1952) first gained international recognition for absurdism. This play, in which two tramps improvise diversions while they wait for Godot (who never arrives), is now one of the best-known plays of the twentieth century. As a group, Beckett's plays suggest the impossibility of certainty about anything but the need to accept and endure. Let us examine one of his plays, both as representative of his work and of absurdist drama.

Happy Days

The story line of *Happy Days* (1961) is very simple. In the first act, Winnie, a middle-aged woman embedded up to her waist in a mound of earth, passes time by following a daily routine, recalling the past, and attempting to communicate occasionally with her husband, Willie, who for the most part remains silent and unseen, hidden behind the mound. The second act follows the same pattern. But now Winnie is embedded up to her neck, unable to turn her head; she is uncertain whether Willie is still alive. She has been forced to adapt herself to an altered routine, but she remains cheerful and brave. At the end of the play, Willie crawls up the mound to Winnie, and in joy she sings a song from *The Merry Widow.* There are no complications, crises, or resolutions in the traditional sense. Rather, themes are introduced and developed.

One major theme is the isolation and loneliness of human beings. It is embodied visually in the setting: a mound of earth beyond which one sees an "unbroken

Samuel Beckett's *Waiting for Godot* as produced at the Long Wharf Theatre, New Haven, with the South African actors John Kani and Winston Ntshona. (Photo © Gerry Goodstein.)

plain and sky receding to meet in far distance." It is even more fully embodied in Winnie's entrapment, which throws her back on her own resources, for she can never be certain whether she is communicating with the only other human being within earshot. The setting and Winnie's entrapment create a metaphor of the human predicament. As in other of his plays, in *Happy Days* Beckett shows human beings isolated in a symbolic wasteland, cut off from all but the most minimal

Irene Worth as Winnie in Beckett's *Happy Days* at the New York Shakespeare Festival's Public Theatre. Directed by Andrei Serban. (Photo © George E. Joseph.)

human contact, passing the time as best they can while waiting doggedly or hoping desperately for something that will give meaning to the moment or to life itself.

The play suggests that human beings organize their days around routines to convince themselves that they are in control of their lives. That human beings are conditioned to live by routine is reinforced by the bell that awakens Winnie to start her day or whenever she dozes off.

Another theme is the ability of human beings to endure and to consider their lives normal and happy despite all evidence to the contrary. Winnie never questions why she is buried in the mound, nor does she wonder at her isolation. She apparently accepts her lot as something to be challenged no more than existence itself. Throughout the play, she remains determinedly cheerful, finding something to wonder at in the smallest occurrence and speaking often of her blessings and of the things that will make this another "happy day." Only occasionally does she show a momentary flash of sadness.

The role of Winnie makes great demands on an actress because she alone must hold the interest of the audience. Unable to move about the stage, the actress must rely on voice, small gestures, and stage business; the skillful handling of pauses, volume, tempo, and rhythm; and other means to achieve the variety and intensity normally sought through a much larger range of possibilities. Willie, though essential to the action, has very little to do in sight of the audience. Nevertheless, he reinforces Winnie's situation.

In his plays, Beckett increasingly reduced the scope of action and means to those absolutely essential for projecting his vision. Many of his late plays have only one character. Because of his methods, audiences and critics have often puzzled over Beckett's intentions. He has said that his plays formulate what he is trying to convey as clearly as he can. Their form, structure, and mood cannot be separated from their meaning. They explore a state of being rather than develop an action. Perhaps more than those of any other dramatist, Beckett's plays embody the absurdist vision and methods.

In many ways, absurdism extended the relativist view as far as it could go because it implied that we have no way of proving or disproving the validity of any position. Whereas Brecht suggested that, by examining and weighing arguments, we can arrive at rational conclusions about the changes needed to make the world more just, Beckett suggested that the very notion of rational choice is a delusion. That works embodying such polar visions were often presented in the same theatre for the same audience indicates how varied theatrical experiences had become in the postwar era. Although it did not die out, after the 1960s the appeal of absurdism declined.

Decentralization and Subsidization

The postwar period also brought interest in making the theatre more readily available beyond established theatre centers. By the end of World War II, live theatre in the United States was confined primarily to New York or to touring productions that originated there. Similarly, in England, the theatre was largely restricted to

Jean Genet's *The Blacks,* staged in a film studio in West Berlin by the heavily subsidized Schaubühne am Halleschen Ufer, Berlin. Directed by Peter Stein, one of Germany's most admired directors. (Photo by Ruth Walz. Courtesy German Information Center.)

London, and in France, to Paris. Each of these countries wished to decentralize its theatre by having companies scattered geographically rather than concentrated in one large city. Implementing this goal required money, much of which came from subsidies.

Subsidization is as old as the theatre. It began with the Greeks and remained the primary means of supporting performances until the Renaissance, when the theatre became a commercial venture. Even thereafter, many rulers subsidized the theatre. For example, the king of France provided at least some financial support to all the companies in Paris during the seventeenth century; and it was by his decree that the Comédie Française was created in 1680. The world's first national theatre, the Comédie Française has continued to the present day and has received governmental subsidies throughout its three-hundred-year history. Seeking to emulate France, the Scandinavian countries, Russia, and most of the small German states (Germany was not united until 1870) founded state-subsidized theatres in the eighteenth century. Most of those theatres still survive and are so geographically dispersed throughout northern and eastern Europe that the countries in those areas were not faced, as France, England, and America were following World War II, with the need to decentralize their theatres.

The Germanic and Scandinavian countries consider state or municipal funding for the arts a cultural responsibility like that for education. (Each of these countries also has privately owned and operated theatres run much like Broadway theatres are in America.) While these governments do not underwrite all of a theatre's expenses, they own the theatre building and subsidize as much as eighty percent of the theatre's operating expenses, making it possible to keep ticket prices relatively low. The companies usually offer seasons of representative plays from the past in combination with new or recent plays. The theatre staffs (including directors, designers, and actors) are employed on renewable contracts, complete with pension plans and other benefits comparable to those for workers in industry and government. These are the companies and practices that theatre workers in England and America looked to as models.

At the end of World War II, France had four state theatres like those in Germany, but all were located in Paris. In 1947, in an effort to decentralize French theatre, the government began to establish dramatic centers in cities throughout France. It later financed several "cultural centers" devoted to various arts activities. There are now eighteen dramatic centers and fifteen cultural centers, all receiving financial subsidies from the central government.

The Postwar British Theatre

England, unlike most European countries, had never awarded government subsidies, on the premise that theatre is a business that must be self-supporting. But during World War II, the government began to allocate funds to underwrite performances intended to build the morale of military troops and factory workers. When the war ended, financial support for the arts was continued through an Arts Council created to decide which organizations should receive funds. State funding increased after 1948, when Parliament authorized local governments to devote a percentage of their revenues to the arts. More than fifty cities and towns in Great Britain now subsidize theatres.

Equally important, Parliament authorized the formation of a National Theatre, which, after numerous delays, was inaugurated in 1963 under the direction of Sir Laurence Olivier, perhaps England's foremost actor. In 1976, the National Theatre moved into its newly completed facilities, the most elaborate in England, with three performance spaces (a thrust-stage theatre, a proscenium-arch theatre, and a flexible theatre). Its varied repertory and overall excellence have made it a major force in world theatre.

Although it does not have the title, the Royal Shakespeare Company is often looked upon as England's second national theatre. Its origins can be traced to 1879, when the Shakespeare Memorial Theatre in Stratford became the home of an annual summer festival of Shakespeare's plays. Over the years, this festival grew, until by the 1950s it was presenting plays for about seven months each year. After Peter Hall became its director in 1960, it was given a new charter and name: the Royal Shakespeare Company (RSC). Hall leased a theatre in London as a second base,

Scene on the barricades in *Les Miserables,* the musical by Alain Boublil and Claude-Michel Schönberg based on Victor Hugo's novel. Directed by Trevor Nunn and John Caird. Settings by John Napier; costumes by Andreane Neofitou; lighting by David Hersey. (Photo by Bob Marshak.)

and thereafter the company performed year-round in a diversified repertory that featured both Shakespeare and some of the most innovative non-Shakespearean productions of the time. Peter Brook, one of the world's finest directors, was associated with the RSC during the 1960s and staged a number of its best-known and most-influential productions, among them *Marat/Sade* (which critics labeled an example of Artaud's "theatre of cruelty" and which called wide attention to Artaud's ideas for the first time in England and America) and *A Midsummer Night's Dream* (which utilized circus and acrobatic techniques). From 1968, when Hall left, until 1987 the RSC was headed by Trevor Nunn, who, in addition to directing Shakespeare's plays, came to be known for his staging of musicals (among them *Cats* and *Les Miserables*). In 1982, the RSC moved into elaborate new facilities in London, the Barbican Theatre, while retaining its headquarters in Stratford. The RSC ranks among the world's best companies and is the recognized leader in Shakespearean performance. After 1987, it was headed by Terry Hands, who was succeeded in 1991 by Howard Davies. Like the National Theatre, it owes much to government subsidy.

A third English group, the English Stage Company (ESC), founded in 1956, made its mark by assisting new playwrights. Its work motivated a reevaluation of the British theatre following its production of John Osborne's *Look Back in Anger* (1956). Prior to this production, the postwar English theatre had been devoted primarily to revivals or innocuous, "proper" dramas. Osborne's play—an attack on the English class system and traditional values—was a slap in the face of "respectability." It brought a new audience into the theatre and inaugurated a new school of writers (the "angry young men"). Within a brief time, the tone of English theatre shifted as the speech and attitudes of disaffected groups brought new vigor to the stage. The ESC, with its willingness to give unknown dramatists a hearing, must be given much of the credit for creating conditions that have continued to favor an unusual number of outstanding English playwrights since the 1950s.

Among the playwrights who reshaped the English theatre, some of the most important are Edward Bond, Harold Pinter, Tom Stoppard, and Peter Shaffer. Edward Bond has long been one of England's most controversial playwrights because of such plays as *Saved* (1965), in which a baby is stoned to death onstage. Attempts to ban Bond's plays aroused such controversy that, following Parliamentary hearings, the censorship of plays, which had been in effect in England since 1737, was abolished in 1968, thereby further decentralizing its focus. All of Bond's plays, which include *Lear, Bingo,* and *War Plays,* depict a world in which the absence of love and compassion has bred a callousness so complete that violence is considered normal.

Harold Pinter, often considered England's greatest living dramatist, opened up still another path. His plays, which include *The Birthday Party, The Homecoming, Old Times,* and *Moonlight,* share common characteristics: The action usually involves a small group of people and takes place in a single room; all the events could occur in real life (sometimes the situations and dialogue suggest naturalism); nevertheless, they create a sense of ambiguity and menace, primarily because the motivations of the characters are never clarified. Because Pinter believes that people use speech to conceal more than to reveal their attitudes and feelings, we often have to guess why they act as they do. It is during the pauses and silences that we often glimpse the unspoken subtext.

Tom Stoppard won recognition first with *Rosencrantz and Guildenstern Are Dead* (1967), a play reminiscent of Beckett's, focusing on two minor characters from *Hamlet* who sense that important events are going on around them but who die without ever understanding the action of which they have been an insignificant part. In subsequent plays, among them *Jumpers, Travesties, The Real Thing,* and *Arcadia,* Stoppard has continued his highly theatricalized comments on contemporary perceptions of reality.

Peter Shaffer has been writing plays since the 1950s. He is best known for the stage and film versions of *Equus* and *Amadeus,* in both of which a competent professional is faced with a character whose strength comes from sources beyond the reach of rationality; both envious and repelled, the professional is forced to reassess his own being but with no satisfying results. Shaffer seems to bemoan the loss of faith, even as he acknowledges that faith cannot be willed.

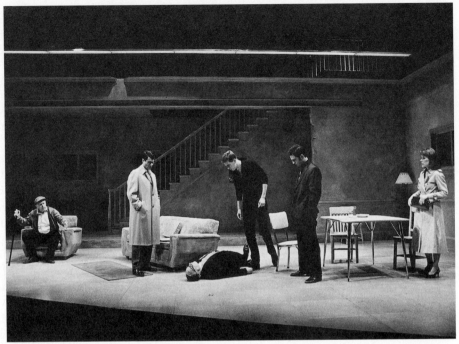

Harold Pinter's *The Homecoming* as produced at the American Repertory Theatre. Directed by David Wheeler; setting by Derek McLane; costumes by Catherine Zuber; lighting by Frances Aronson. (Photo by Richard Feldman.)

Among Britain's more recent dramatists, several began their careers either in the provincial theatre or in the fringe theatres (comparable to Off-Broadway and Off-Off-Broadway) that mushroomed in number once censorship was removed. The plays and experimentation there did much to diversify Britain's theatre. Among the best known of these playwrights are Hare, Ayckbourn, and Churchill.

David Hare began his career in fringe theatres with plays, such as *Slag,* that focus on the deprivations and emptiness of working-class life. In his later plays, among them *Plenty, A Map of the World,* and *Secret Rapture,* he extends his concern to include ineffectual intellectuals or bureaucrats on whom he blames the malaise of English society. In recent years, his plays have critiqued major social institutions: the church (*Racing Demon*), the judiciary and legal system (*Murmuring Judges*), and government (*The Absence of War*). Hare's literate, often witty plays depict a severely flawed world seemingly beyond repair. Hare often directs his own plays and is now an associate director of the National Theatre.

Alan Ayckbourn, England's most popular playwright, is often compared to America's Neil Simon. His plays are tested first in his theatre in Scarborough (Yorkshire) before bringing them to London. His plays deal with contemporary middle-class manners and morals seen from a satirical, jaundiced point of view. He is especially admired for his sharp dialogue, intricate situations, and telling observations of human behavior. As time has gone by his plays have become increasingly less benign. Among his best-known plays are *How the Other Half Loves, The Norman Conquests, A Small Family Business,* and *The Wildest Dreams.*

Most of Caryl Churchill's plays have originated in fringe theatres. She has written primarily about the effect of socioeconomic forces on human relationships, especially those of women. *Top Girls* contrasts famous women of the past (who recall the price they paid for asserting themselves in a male-dominated world) with a group of present-day women (still trapped in a male world that devalues the work of women). *Fen* shows female farmworkers trying to cope with low wages and unsatisfying personal lives. Her most popular play has been *Cloud 9*, which explores how social forces determine the stereotyped sexual roles people adopt. This play attracted special attention because, to make her point, Churchill used cross-gender

Caryl Churchill

Caryl Churchill (1938–   ) is among the most successful of today's playwrights. Born in England, she grew up in Montreal but returned to England to attend Oxford University. After graduation, she married a lawyer and became the mother of three sons. Because the restrictions of home life left her little time to write or to attend rehearsals, she began her professional career by writing short radio plays. In the late 1960s, Churchill and her husband reoriented their lives: He joined a legal aid center, and she turned to writing plays with feminist and socialist themes. Her first play to be performed in London, *Owners* (1972), concerned housing conditions. She then began to create plays in collaboration with small ensemble groups—mainly the Joint Stock Company and Monstrous Regiment (a feminist theatre). A subject would be chosen, everyone would become involved in doing research and improvising scenes, and the playwright would bring it all together in a script. The first of these plays, *Light Shining in Buckinghamshire* (1976), concerned the disintegration of an attempt to reform society in the seventeenth century. Churchill's most successful collaboration (as well as her greatest commercial success) came with *Cloud 9* (1979), which draws parallels between British imperialism and sexual stereotyping, a relationship underlined by cross-gender and cross-racial casting. Other collaborative projects included: *Vinegar Tom* (1976), which argues that preoccupation with witchcraft in the seventeenth century was grounded in the fear of women who did not conform to social norms; *Serious Money* (1987), about the greed that dominates the lives of a group of stockbrokers; and *Mad Forest* (1990), about the lives of Romanians before and after the fall of Ceaucescu. Others of Churchill's plays include *Top Girls* (1982) and *Skryker* (1994). Although Churchill has a strong social conscience, she is not a propagandist. She has stated that her primary concerns are issues of "power, powerlessness and exploitation." By exploring these issues, her plays have forced audiences to confront what she considers the corruptive forces of a materialistic, success-oriented society.

Carol Churchill's *Top Girls* as produced by the Virginia Stage Company, Norfolk. Scene from Act I, in which women from the past who have defied convention assemble at a banquet. Directed by Christopher Hanna. (Courtesy of the Virginia Stage Company.)

casting for several of the roles. More recent works include *Lives of the Great Poisoners* and *Skryker*.

Off-Broadway and Off-Off-Broadway

The conviction that theatre must be entirely self-supporting persisted longer in the United States than anywhere else. The government had financed the Federal Theatre during the 1930s, not because it valued theatre but to reduce unemployment. After the Federal Theatre came to an end in 1939, no further government assistance was given until the mid-1960s. Following World War II, however, a number of nongovernmental groups sought means to decentralize the theatre.

The first important development began in New York City around 1950. Believing that financial conditions forced Broadway producers to cater almost exclusively to mass audiences, theatrical groups found out-of-the-way buildings where low production costs permitted them to offer short runs of plays not likely to appeal to Broadway audiences. These ventures marked the beginning of Off-Broadway. Most groups, working in buildings never intended for theatrical purposes, were forced to experiment with spatial arrangements unlike those in Broadway's proscenium houses. Thus, they contributed to the retreat from the picture-frame stage. Many Off-Broadway companies played to small audiences because theatres seating more than two hundred persons had to adhere to fire and safety provisions more stringent than the companies would have been able to meet. Off-Broadway thus also contributed to the preference for intimate theatres, which steadily increased after World War II (partly because of television, a medium that became available nationwide around 1950).

Off-Broadway proved so attractive that about fifty groups performed there during the 1950s. Of these, the most important was the Circle in the Square, which won critical acceptance both for itself and for Off-Broadway when in 1952 it achieved resounding success with Tennessee Williams' *Summer and Smoke*, a failure on Broadway.

By the 1960s, Off-Broadway had become so successful that theatrical unions insisted on stricter working conditions and higher wages. As a result, production costs rose until the advantages originally offered by Off-Broadway largely disappeared. This prompted the development of Off-Off-Broadway—in still more out-of-the-way spaces where unions were largely ignored (though most unions eventually approved a special Off-Off-Broadway contract with conditions less restrictive than those in Off-Broadway contracts). Off-Off-Broadway has continued to be the most flexible and diverse venue for productions in New York. As many as 150 groups often are active at the same time.

Of the early Off-Off-Broadway groups, the most important was the LaMama organization, founded in 1961 by Ellen Stewart. LaMama provided a place free from restrictions (except those imposed by limited funds) where dramatists could

Tom O'Horgan's staging of Julian Barry's *Lenny*, based on the life of the comedian Lenny Bruce. The 15-foot puppets represent such popular-culture figures as Little Orphan Annie, Boris Karloff, and the Lone Ranger. The musicians are dressed as bandaged accident victims. Scenery by Robin Wagner; costumes by Randy Barcello. (Photo by Martha Swope.)

Joe Papp's production of Chekhov's *The Cherry Orchard.* Usually staged realistically, here the wall of the house is indicated only by the chest at center. The entire stage is covered with a white carpet; the cherry trees, usually only glimpsed, serve as the dominant visual motif throughout the action. Directed by Andrei Serban; setting by Santo Loquasto. (Photo © George E. Joseph.)

see their plays performed. By 1970, LaMama was presenting more plays each season than all the Broadway theatres combined. Although these plays varied enormously, many were determinedly innovative, defying and altering accepted notions of dramatic effectiveness. This free-ranging experimentation in playwriting also extended to directorial techniques. Tom O'Horgan was the most successful of LaMama's directors. He subsequently directed *Hair, Lenny,* and *Jesus Christ, Superstar* on Broadway, using the approach he had perfected at LaMama, which seemingly owed much to Artaud: extensive use of nonverbal vocal sound, extensive overamplification of sound, highly varied lighting (including strobe), oversized effigies or symbolic stage properties, and the "physicalization" of almost every moment. His productions were colorful and uninhibited. When LaMama toured abroad, it seemed so innovative that it was asked to establish branches in various countries. Its influence was not merely American but international.

By 1970, the distinctions between Off-Broadway and Off-Off-Broadway were so eroded that they were often indistinguishable. (They are differentiated primarily by the type of union contracts under which they operate.) A few of their organizations have been especially important. The Circle Repertory Company has produced most of Lanford Wilson's plays as well as new works by many other playwrights. The Manhattan Theatre Club and Playwrights Horizons have also been especially helpful to playwrights. But the most influential of these organizations is the New York Shakespeare Festival Theatre, headed by Joseph Papp until his death in 1991.

After a modest beginning in the 1950s, Papp persuaded municipal authorities to let him stage plays free of charge in Central Park. This program became so popular that in 1962 the city built the Delacorte Theatre there. In 1967, Papp acquired the former Astor Library on the edge of Greenwich Village and transformed it into the Public Theatre with five performance spaces. Not only does this organization maintain a heavy production schedule, composed of Shakespeare's plays, revivals, and new plays, but it also provides performance space for many other companies. Several of its productions, most notably *A Chorus Line* (the longest-running production in Broadway's history), moved to Broadway. After Papp's death, the New York Shakespeare Festival was headed briefly by JoAnne Akalaitis and then by George C. Wolfe. It remains one of the greatest influences on theatre in New York.

Regional Theatres

While Off-Broadway and Off-Off-Broadway were diversifying New York's theatre, decentralization was under way elsewhere. During the 1950s, a few companies—in Washington, Houston, San Francisco, and elsewhere—struggled to survive and

The Guthrie Theatre, Minneapolis. Designed by Tyrone Guthrie and Tanya Moiseiwitch, the theatre seats 1,441, with no spectator more than 52 feet from the center of the thrust stage. (Photo by Robert Ashley Wilson. Courtesy of the Guthrie Theatre.)

Subsidization and the NEA

With the establishment of the National Endowment for the Arts (NEA) in 1965, the United States joined the majority of other countries that had long believed that an enlightened government should provide financial support for the arts. In its first year of operation, the NEA had only $2.5 million (slightly more than one cent for each person living in the United States) to distribute among all the arts. In 1993-94, the NEA's budget was $170.2 million (about sixty-eight cents per capita), a sum smaller than that appropriated to support the armed forces' marching bands, and considerably less than the approximately $375 million allotted the arts by Britain and $2.3 billion by France.

Although it had faced some opposition from time to time, the NEA seemed secure until 1989, when some members of Congress introduced legislation to place strictures on the type of art that could be subsidized; others campaigned to abolish the NEA altogether. In the ensuing furor, defenders of the NEA argued that the new proposals would impose censorship on the arts, endanger the freedom of expression guaranteed by the Constitution's First Amendment, discourage innovative and challenging art, and advocate officially approved standards for art not unlike those of Communist Eastern Europe, which were then being rejected. Supporters of the proposed strictures responded that "this is not a question of censorship. This is a question of whether the American people should continue to subsidize this art with their hard-earned money."

The issues involved in this controversy have not been resolved. On one side, many oppose subsidies for the arts, believing that art is a commodity that must compete in a free market and that if it deserves support it will find it. Others believe that the government has a duty to protect them (and all others) against works they perceive either as obscene or as attacks on long-established values. Others declare that they don't care what artists do so long as tax money is not used to support them.

On the other side, many are convinced that an enlightened government has a duty to support the arts. They believe that the best art often challenges existing values and artistic conventions and that publicly sanctioned restrictions only make artists timid and lead to mediocre art. They argue that most great art did not win popular acceptance immediately and that to support only art favored by the majority, who tend to be conservative in their tastes, is shortsighted.

As in most controversies over such issues, the differences involve attitudes about the nature and function of art: whether it should reaffirm values and remain within familiar conventions, or whether art should be free to raise questions and open new possibilities even if in doing so it offends some persons. The controversy reminds us that either awarding or withholding subsidies is a political act, because it involves public policy about goals and how they are to be pursued.

ultimately received a major boost from the Ford Foundation, which in 1959 made large grants to several companies that had succeeded in winning local support. Thus, the major impetus for decentralization in America came from private rather than governmental subsidy. Decentralization received another boost in 1963 with the opening of the Guthrie Theatre in Minneapolis. Tyrone Guthrie, then one of the world's foremost directors, selected Minneapolis over established theatre centers as the site for his company, and funds were raised locally to construct a new building for it. The publicity surrounding this theatre aroused considerable interest (or envy) in other cities. Something approaching a boom in the construction of new arts centers followed. Today, almost every major city in the United States has such a complex.

Subsidization of the Arts in the United States

Such changed treatment of the arts, however, probably owes most to the legislation that in 1965 established the National Endowment for the Arts (NEA). Like Britain's Arts Council, the NEA dispenses federally appropriated funds to arts groups throughout the United States. The federal government encouraged states to establish their own arts councils, and in turn the states encouraged cities and communities to form such councils. Today, federal, state, and local governments appropriate funds to subsidize the arts. The sums are not large, but that they exist at all marks a major change in American attitudes toward the arts, one that has not gone unchallenged by those who believe that the government should have no role in the arts.

Tax laws also encouraged corporations and foundations to make grants to arts organizations by making all or part of the gifts tax-deductible. Such grants and subsidies made it feasible for resident theatres to be established throughout the country. These companies are linked through the Theatre Communications Group (TCG), which was created in 1961 with funds supplied by the Ford Foundation. TCG serves as a centralized source of information for more than three hundred not-for-profit, professional theatres and provides a forum where common problems can be discussed and solutions sought.

The existence of so many theatres may make theatrical conditions appear more stable than they are. Few of these theatres could exist without financial support from governments, corporations, foundations, or private donors. Unlike European theatres, for which ongoing support is assured, American theatres receive grants for periods ranging from one to five years. They cannot be sure that grants will be renewed, and they must devote much of their time to developing grant proposals and soliciting support. Unable to make firm, long-range plans, they must be prepared to alter their programs if support is not forthcoming. Continued existence cannot be taken for granted. Nevertheless, it is subsidization that has made possible the decentralization of the American theatre.

Most regional theatres offer a season of plays that intermingles revivals of classics with new works. They do not seek long runs and can afford to take greater chances than Broadway does. They have become attractive to playwrights who wish

The Actors Theatre of Louisville is among the most active of not-for-profit regional theatres. It is noted especially for its new play festival in the spring and its "Classics in Context" symposia and productions in the fall of each year. Seen here is *The Three Cuckolds,* an adaptation by Bill Irwin and Michael Greif of Leon Katz' version of a commedia dell'arte script. Directed by Jon Jory; scenery by John Conklin; costumes by Marcia Dixcy. (Photo by David S. Talbott. Courtesy Actors Theatre of Louisville.)

to avoid reshaping their plays to fit the demands of Broadway producers. Several (among them the Actors Theatre of Louisville) now offer festivals of new plays each year.

Broadway and Musicals After Subsidization

Decentralization and subsidization altered the character of Broadway. Formerly the primary producer of new plays in America, Broadway after the establishment of the NEA and regional theatres came to present new works less and less frequently, choosing instead to present plays that had been successful in regional, Off-Broadway, Off-Off-Broadway, or British theatres and thought to have the potential for drawing large audiences over an extended period of time. This lessened somewhat the uncertainty of success but did not eliminate it, in part because audiences were not always eager to attend productions of plays for which ticket prices came to exceed fifty dollars.

The situation was somewhat different for musicals, which remained Broadway's favorite fare; most of the productions that originated on Broadway were mu-

Into the Woods by Stephen Sondheim and James Lapine. Directed by James Lapine; settings by Tony Straiges; costumes by Patricia Zipprodt and Ann Hould-Ward; lighting by Richard Nelson. (Photo by Martha Swope.)

sicals. Until around 1968, the type of musical that achieved dominance during and following World War II continued. Some of the best were *Funny Girl* (1964) by Jule Styne, *Hello, Dolly* (1964) and *Mame* (1966) by Jerry Herman, *Cabaret* (1966) by John Kander, and *Sweet Charity* (1966) by Sy Coleman. But beginning in 1968, the musical underwent significant change. The crucial production was *Hair* (1968) with its rock music, barely discernible story, single setting, "hippie" dress, strobe lighting, highly amplified sound, and nonconfrontational promotion of alternative life-styles. *Hair* was also the first Broadway production to include nudity and obscene language. Several musicals using the rock idiom followed; perhaps the most successful was *Godspell* (1974) by Stephen Schwartz. Although the older type of musical continued sporadically in such works as *Annie* (1977) by Charles Strouse and *La Cage aux Folles* (1983) by Jerry Herman, after 1970 the musical seemed to lack direction, and the number of new musicals on Broadway declined. The most successful writer/composer was Stephen Sondheim, who experimented with various approaches: *Company* (1970) had no chorus and used the principal performers in the song-and-dance sequences; *Pacific Overtures* (1976) borrowed conventions from Japanese theatre; *Sweeney Todd* (1979), based on a nineteenth-century melodrama,

Andrew Lloyd Webber's *Jesus Christ, Superstar.*
(Photo by Richard Feldman.)

was operatic in its use of music throughout; *Sunday in the Park With George* (1983) took its inspiration from a painting by Georges Seurat; *Into the Woods* (1987) deconstructed fairy tales; *Assassins* (1991) interwove vignettes of those who have sought to assassinate presidents of the United States; and *Passion* (1994) focused on compulsive love. Almost all of these depart from previous American musicals, with their upbeat optimism, in offering ironic and melancholic views of human behavior and social values and in avoiding happy endings. While Sondheim is much admired, he is also frequently accused of setting the musical on a path that audiences find difficult to follow.

Michael Bennett's *A Chorus Line* (1975) was innovative in its use of the chorus as the principal character and in its presentational style in which dancers auditioning for a chorus job tell their personal stories. It became the longest-running show in Broadway's history, continuing until 1990.

Despite several successful productions, the American musical after 1970 was often said to have lost its vitality. The most popular musicals on the Broadway stage were those imported from England. Andrew Lloyd Webber, with *Jesus Christ, Superstar* (1971), *Evita* (1976), *Cats* (1981), *Phantom of the Opera* (1986), and *Sunset Boulevard* (1993), became the most successful composer of musicals. His work was joined by other imports by way of the London stage, among them *Les Miserables*

Stephen Sondheim

Stephen Sondheim (1930–   ) is usually considered the most influential writer of musicals for the contemporary theatre. As a child, he was befriended by Oscar Hammerstein, then perhaps the best-known lyricist of American musicals. Sondheim says that it was Hammerstein who taught him to use character and story to structure a song like a one-act play, a practice he still follows. Sondheim began his career on Broadway as a lyricist, first for *West Side Story* (1957) and then for *Gypsy* (1959). The first show for which he wrote both music and lyrics was *A Funny Thing Happened on the Way to the Forum* (1962). Among his subsequent works are *Company* (1970), *A Little Night Music* (1973), *Sweeney Todd* (1979), *Sunday in the Park With George* (1984), *Into the Woods* (1987), *Assassins* (1990), and *Passion* (1994).

Sondheim changed musicals in part by making the songs and music much more complex. Rather than writing songs that express an unambiguous emotion or point of view, as was typical in earlier musicals, Sondheim filled his lyrics and music with inner tensions that suggest unacknowledged conflicts or hidden desires and reveal multiple possibilities of meaning. Subtext is a significant element in his lyrics and music, contributing to the sense of ironic acceptance characteristic of much of Sondheim's work. Sondheim likes to complete his music as late as possible, preferably after knowing who will be in the cast. He uses audience reactions to help sharpen his writing. If the audience does not respond as he anticipated, he analyzes the reasons and revises accordingly. "That's my idea of a collaboration with the audience."

(1985) and *Miss Saigon* (1989) by the Frenchmen Alain Boublil and Claude-Michel Schonberg. In the 1990s, the strength of the American musical was reasserted primarily through revivals—among them *Gypsy, Guys and Dolls, Damn Yankees, Crazy for You,* and *Carousel.*

American Playwrights After 1960

Although after 1960 Miller and Williams continued to write, they were overshadowed by a new generation of playwrights, among them Edward Albee, Lanford Wilson, David Rabe, David Mamet, and Sam Shepard. During the 1960s, Edward Albee was the most honored American playwright, especially after the production of *Who's Afraid of Virginia Woolf?* in 1962. He followed that success with *Tiny Alice, A Delicate Balance, Seascape,* and others, but, like Williams and Miller, his reputation gradually faded until 1994 when his receipt of the Pulitzer Prize for *Three Tall Women* brought a reappraisal of his work.

Lanford Wilson began his career in the Off-Off-Broadway theatre. He has written a large number of plays, among them *Balm in Gilead, Hot L Baltimore, Talley's*

David Rabe's *Streamers* as produced at Lincoln Center, New York. Directed by Mike Nichols. (Photo by Martha Swope.)

Folly (Pulitzer Prize, 1980), *The Fifth of July, Burn This,* and *Redwood Curtain.* The story line in these plays is minimal; the focus is on character relationships and the eventual revelation of hidden feelings, disappointments, and hopes. Wilson's compassionate treatment of the misfits and rejects of society marks him as one of the most humane of contemporary playwrights.

David Rabe wrote most of his early plays in response to the Vietnam War. *The Basic Training of Pavlo Hummel, Sticks and Bones,* and *Streamers* all show the price exacted by violence and war, which leads to the rejection of other more humanizing impulses. His more recent *Hurlyburly,* set in Hollywood, treats characters who apparently are indifferent to the casual cruelties they inflict on each other. *Those the River Keeps* develops further one of the characters from *Hurlyburly.* The moral void suggested by these plays reflects Rabe's perception of contemporary American society.

David Mamet, who began his career in Chicago, has written many plays, among them *American Buffalo, Glengarry Glen Ross* (Pulitzer Prize, 1984), and *Speed-the-Plow,* about the debasement and distortion of human beings by the materialistic goals of American society as epitomized in its business dealings. Other plays, among them *Sexual Perversity in Chicago,* explore the inability to make personal commitments and establish satisfying relationships. *Oleanna* treats contemporary issues of "political correctness," and *The Cryptogram* traces the disintegration of trust within a family.

Sam Shepard has been among the most prolific and provocative of contemporary American playwrights. He began his writing career in 1964 in the Off-Off-Broadway theatre, and for many years thereafter turned out a large number of plays, among them *Chicago, Mad Dog Blues,* and *The Tooth of Crime,* without revising the scripts because he considered it dishonest to change what he had originally written. In the mid-1970s, he altered this view and wrote his most successful plays, including *Curse of the Starving Class, Buried Child* (Pulitzer Prize, 1979), *True West,* and *A Lie of the Mind.* Although there is much variety in Shepard's work, a number of motifs recur: attempts to escape or deny the past; the cowboy and the West as basic American myths; the family as a battleground; and characters caught between empty dreams and an insubstantial reality.

During the years between the end of World War II and the 1970s, the theatre underwent many changes. Perhaps the most significant development was the decentralization of theatre (which saw the establishment of permanent companies where previously there was none) and the increase in subsidization (both by public and private sources). But this period also saw increased questioning of individual values and social conventions. The absurdists extended the challenge to truth and certainty about as far as it could go, but ultimately more far-reaching was the challenge to legal and governmental sanctions of inequities in society. These challenges came to affect almost every aspect of theatre beginning in the 1960s and accelerating thereafter.

Chapter 9

Contemporary Diversity

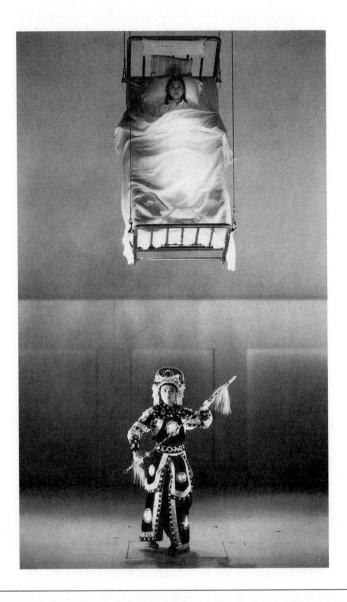

Scene from *The Woman Warrior*, adapted by Deborah Rogin from the works of Maxine Hong Kingston, in its world premiere at the Berkeley Repertory Theatre. Lydia Look above and Yunjin Kim below. Directed by Sharon Ott. (Photo by Ken Friedman. Courtesy the Berkeley Repertory Theatre.)

America . . . , more than any other country in modern times, is again reconstituting the idea of the 'New Man': *homo multiculturans.* America has always been a culture of more ethnic diversity than any in the West, and singularly, it has been for centuries the land where people have come to escape their own histories and cultures, even as they cling fiercely to those values and symbols left behind.

—Bonnie Marranca, "Preface," *Interculturalism and Performance*

The years since the late 1960s have been noteworthy for challenging dominant (primarily white middle-class) cultural standards and demanding that the diversity of American society not only be acknowledged but also accepted and celebrated. Efforts have been made to open mainstream theatres to plays about groups (African Americans, Asian Americans, Latinos or Hispanic Americans, Native Americans, women, gays and lesbians, and others) previously ignored or marginalized, and also to establish theatres to give these groups their own voice. Still other companies and directors have championed radical change both in ideas about the nature and purpose of theatre and in theatrical conventions. All of these efforts have done much to alter attitudes and practices. Their collective influence has created significant diversity.

Alternative Theatre Groups

In the 1960s, the Living Theatre, more than any other organization, epitomized rebellion against established authority in all its aspects: values, behavior, language, dress, theatrical conventions. Founded in New York in 1946 by Judith Malina and Julian Beck, it was originally devoted to poetic drama but during the 1950s was influenced increasingly by Brecht, Artaud, and anarchist theory. In 1964, its theatre having been closed for failure to pay taxes, it left the United States and until 1968 toured Europe, where it gained a large and enthusiastic following, especially among disaffected young people. In 1968, it returned to the United States with the repertory it had created during its exile. The most extreme of the Living Theatre's pieces was *Paradise Now.* It began with actors circulating among the spectators denouncing strictures on freedom (to smoke marijuana, travel without a passport, to go nude in public, and the like). Thereafter, both spectators and actors roamed the auditorium and stage indiscriminately; many removed their clothing and some smoked marijuana—in other words, many of the strictures they denounced were defied. The performance continued for four or five hours with scenes proceeding simultaneously throughout the theatre. Actors provoked some spectators into voicing opposition and then overrode them, often by shouting obscenities or even spitting on them; at the end, the company sought to move the audience into the streets to continue the revolution begun in the theatre. Its aggressive behavior, combined with its anarchistic politics, won the Living Theatre enormous notoriety and called attention to several challenges to long-accepted theatrical conventions, especially those that distinguished the fictional from the real: They treated space and time as real; actors played themselves rather than characters; actors wore their own clothing instead of costumes; the subject matter—political and social issues of the day—was pursued in improvised confrontations rather than through predetermined text.

The Living Theatre's production of *Paradise Now* during which actors mingled with the audience, urged them to remove their clothes (which many did), attacked (even spat on) those who seemed to oppose them, and in general urged the need for revolutionary change. (Photo by Ken McLaren. Courtesy of the World of Culture, Ltd.)

Two important changes made by theatre groups during the late 1960s were the introduction of obscene language and nudity. While obscene language and simulated nudity were common features of early Greek comedy and late Roman mimes, neither had been considered acceptable in legitimate theatrical performances since the fall of Rome. But during the 1960s, the rebellion against accepted attitudes and assumptions that had begun with the civil rights movement gradually passed over into other areas, until almost every standard was challenged. Demonstrations, then common, usually involved the deliberate public violation of some convention or law considered unwarranted or unjust. Continued assaults on the conventions of polite behavior, and the inability of authorities to prevent violations, gained tolerance of behavior previously considered unacceptable.

Nudity and obscenity first came to Broadway in 1968 in *Hair*, a good-natured plea for tolerance of alternative life-styles. In contrast, the Living Theatre abused (and made clear its intention of destroying the society represented by) middle-class spectators who had paid to see its performances. Rather than being entertained, many spectators were subjected to physical and political intimidation. Why, then, did audiences attend? Novelty and notoriety probably attracted many, while others probably came out of sympathy for the group's political goals and defiance of authority; still others probably applauded the group for using the theatre for purposes

A Critique of the Living Theatre's Work

In "An Open Letter to the Becks," Charles Marowitz offered a critique of the strengths and weaknesses of the Living Theatre's *Paradise Now:*

> Of all your works, I think *Paradise Now* has gone furtherest in obliterating that impregnable line that separates life and art. By asserting that whatever happens on the evening is part of the event, you have created a marvellously open-ended structure which, quite clearly, defies critical analysis. As with all happenings, the judgment of the evening is a judgment on oneself. One gets from it what one is prepared to bring. The free-floating event in which members of the company . . . swandive from a rostrum into the arms of the actors is a staggering metaphor for your whole philosophy of life: a man takes a risk; a group undertakes a responsibility. . . . But when the more psychopathic members of your company antagonise the audience then complain about 'bad vibrations,' or ruffle superior sensibilities with fatuous reasoning . . . , how can you expect not to alienate the more discerning members of that audience? . . . your preaching and your practice collide badly. An anarchistic revolution based on the tenets of non-violence is not achieved through organised bouts of aggression which inevitably muster intellectual resistance.

other than diversionary entertainment and for insisting on the responsibility of theatre to play an active role in social change. By the early 1970s, however, the group, probably because of its excesses, had lost most of its following. Still, its influence continued. By the 1970s, though the limits of permissibility were vague, almost any subject, behavior, or manner of speaking was potentially acceptable in the theatre.

Although the most radical, the Living Theatre was not the only group seeking to change society through theatre. Among these, two of the most effective were the Bread and Puppet Theatre (founded in 1961), which used both actors and giant puppets to enact parables (often based on the Bible) to denounce war and the futility of materialism, and the San Francisco Mime Theatre (founded in 1966), which performed satirical pieces promoting civil rights, equality for women, and various other causes. The Bread and Puppet Theatre and the San Francisco Mime Theatre were also two among many theatres that sought to attract audiences by breaking down the distinctions between high art and popular culture. They borrowed freely from commedia dell'arte, festivals, parades, circuses, and variety theatre.

Poor and Environmental Theatres

All of these groups had limited resources. Most never controlled a theatre and had to perform wherever they could. They were what Jerzy Grotowski, director of the Polish Laboratory Theatre in Wroclaw, Poland, called "poor" theatres. Grotowski also made his own a poor theatre, not from necessity but out of conviction. He believed that most contemporary theatres had gone astray by depending on the technological devices of other media, especially movies and television. Rather than a technologically rich theatre, then, he sought to create one in which everything not absolutely necessary would be eliminated. He hoped in this way to rediscover the essence of theatre. Eventually, he concluded that only two elements are essential: the actor and the audience.

Because of the actor's central role in performance, Grotowski devoted much of his attention to actor training. He coupled intensive physical exercises with training designed to remove the performer's psychological inhibitions and sought to develop the actor's voice as an instrument capable of exceeding all normal demands. Ultimately, he wished actors to surpass so completely the spectators' own capabilities as to arouse a sense of magic. In performance, actors were permitted to use only those costumes and makeup essential to the action; they were not allowed to change costumes merely to indicate a change in role or psychological condition; properties were minimal; there was no scenery in the usual sense; any music had to be produced by the actors themselves. The performers, deprived of all nonessential and technological aids, had to depend entirely on their own resources.

Grotowski worked in a space that was reconfigured for each production. At first he tried to involve the audience directly in the action, but he concluded that this attempt only made spectators self-conscious. He then concentrated on creating spatial relationships among spectators and actors that would permit the audience to interact unself-consciously. For example, *Kordian,* which takes place in an insane asylum, was staged in a large room throughout which double-decker beds were spaced irregularly; audience members sat on some of the beds, while other beds were used by actor-patients, and the action, which took place in and around the beds, placed the spectators in its midst, allowing them to function as passive inmates or observers. For *The Constant Prince,* in which the title character patiently accepts mistreatment and suffering, the theatre was arranged so that all the spectators looked down into a space that resembled a hospital teaching theatre where, as Grotowski put it, psychic surgery takes place. (See the illustration below.)

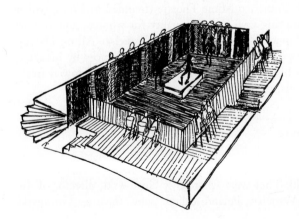

Arrangement of the performance space for Grotowski's *The Constant Prince.* (© 1968 Jerzy Grotowski and Odin Teatrets Forlag. Courtesy H. Martin Berg.)

Grotowski viewed the theatre as the modern equivalent of a tribal ceremony. He searched scripts for archetypal patterns of human behavior independent of time and place and developed them (often severely changing the original script) to make both actors and audience confront themselves spiritually. His goals resembled Artaud's, though his means differed markedly. In the 1970s, Grotowski moved away from theatre into other explorations only partially related to theatre.

During the late 1960s, Grotowski became a major influence on theatre in Europe and America. His company performed widely, and he conducted workshops for various other theatres and for some of the world's best directors. His influence was further disseminated through his book *Towards a Poor Theatre* (1968). Although few others attempted to restrict resources as severely as he did, many groups adapted his approach to staging and actor-training.

The Open Theatre (1963–1974), based in New York and headed by Joseph Chaikin (previously a member of the Living Theatre), was also a "poor" theatre. Like Grotowski, Chaikin concentrated on what he considered essential to theatre. But his work was grounded in contemporary theories of role-playing and theatre games. Above all, he was concerned with "transformation"—a constantly shifting reality in which the same performer assumes and discards roles or identities as the context changes. Reality was treated not as fixed but as ever-changing, implying that, because reality is not fixed, we can reshape ourselves and our society into what we would like them to be. The Open Theatre's scripts, which sought to reveal fundamental moral and social patterns buried beneath troubling contemporary events or preoccupations, usually evolved in its workshops in close collaboration with its playwrights. Through improvisations, the actors explored the potentials of situations and characters; the playwright then chose and shaped the discoveries that seemed most effective into a written script. One of the Open Theatre's most successful collaborations was with Jean-Claude van Itallie on *The Serpent*, in which the assassinations of Martin Luther King and John F. Kennedy are interwoven with the story of Adam and Eve and other biblical events to suggest that God is a force that sets limits on our behavior and that the Serpent is a force that tempts us to breach those limits. Another successful collaboration resulted in Megan Terry's *Viet Rock*, which (with scenes that moved quickly between battlefields, congressional hearings, and family life) ridiculed bureaucratic justifications of the war in Vietnam and praised the simple pleasures of the life that war disrupts and destroys. Such collective creation was a distinctive contribution of the theatre in the 1960s and 1970s.

In 1968, Richard Schechner, having examined various contemporary practices, including those of the "poor" theatres, sought to describe the conventions of an approach to performance that he labeled "environmental theatre." Some of these conventions concern the performance space. "The event can take place either in a totally transformed space or in a 'found' space," Schechner wrote. In other words, space may be adapted to make it appropriate to the action, or a suitable space not requiring alteration may be found (for example, a production depicting war as a game might be performed in a gymnasium or on a playground). "All the space is used for performance; all the space is used for the audience." That is, the way in which the total space can be used is entirely flexible; any part of the space may be used by performers or spectators, or performers and spectators may be intermingled.

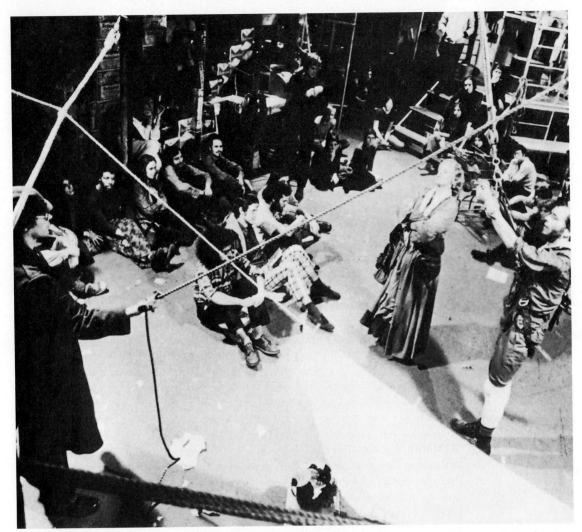

The Performance Group's production of Brecht's *Mother Courage.* Notice the author-performance relationship in the flexible theatre space. (Courtesy Richard Schechner.)

Other conventions relate to what is performed: "A text need be neither the starting point nor the goal of a production. There may be no text at all." Unlike traditional performances (which seek to embody a preexisting dramatic text), in environmental theatre, performance takes precedence over text and may be entirely improvisational, leaving no text behind once the performance ends. During a performance, "focus is flexible and variable"—that is, a production need not be shaped by the assumption (typical of traditional theatre) that all spectators must be able to see the same thing at the same time. Instead, several scenes may be going on simultaneously in various parts of the space; spectators are free to choose which they will watch.

Environmental theatre blends categories long treated as distinct during performance: acting space and nonacting space (stage and auditorium); performer and spectator; text and performance; sequentiality and simultaneity. It challenges conventions previously considered necessary for effective theatrical production and enjoyable audience experience, suggesting how easy it is to confuse the theatre's essence with its prevailing conventions.

Multimedia, Happenings, and Performance Art

Even as the "poor" theatres were restricting their means, other theatres were emphasizing the very elements (electronic and spectacular) that the poor theatres were seeking to eliminate. Living as we do in the "electronic age," it seems inevitable that the theatre would exploit electronic devices. Marshall McLuhan, mass-communication critic, argued that, as electronic media have replaced the printed page as our primary mode of communication, we have become increasingly adept at processing multiple and concurrent stimuli (we watch on television events going on halfway round the world as we simultaneously carry on conversations in our living rooms). McLuhan concludes that we no longer require that messages be received in orderly sequence or one at a time.

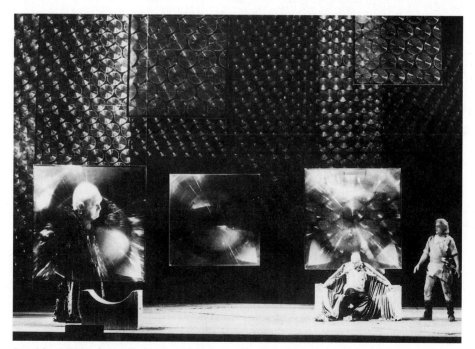

Josef Svoboda's setting for Richard Wagner's *Die Götterdammerung* at the Royal Opera, Covent Garden, London. The large lenses are used to magnify features as in a film closeup (see figure at stage left). The background is composed of similar lenslike surfaces. (Jarka Burian, *Svoboda: Wagner.* © 1983 by Jarka Burian. Reprinted by permission of University Press of New England.)

Electronic media affected the theatre by creating the desire to make the representation of place as transformable in the theatre as it is in film and television. One result was to reduce the amount and specificity of built scenic elements (because of the time required to shift full-stage sets). Another was to encourage experimentation with "multimedia"—combinations of elements from several media. The best-known multimedia experimentation was done by the Czech designer Josef Svoboda. Around 1958, Svoboda began work on two projects—*Polyekran* (multiple screen) and *Laterna Magika*. Polyekran used filmed images entirely but sought to overcome the "visual paralysis" of a single screen by hanging screens of differing sizes at various distances from the audience, projecting different images on each, and changing the images at varying time intervals—thus creating a dynamic visual field and giving the audience a choice of images to watch. Laterna Magika used motion pictures in combination with live actors. Often the performers in the film and on the stage were the same, and at times a live performer seemed to emerge from the screen.

In 1959, Svoboda began to incorporate elements from these experiments into stagings of drama. He also experimented with devices for moving scenic units and platforms in ways intended to make the stage instantly transformable both in configuration and visual appearance. Some of his productions used closed-circuit television, with some scenes performed in a studio miles from the theatre and projected onto screens hung above a stage on which other live scenes were being acted. Closed-circuit television was also used to project close-up images of the actors' faces on screens during moments of crisis. Such experiments by Svoboda and others popularized several practices: using projected still pictures on multiple screens as a scenic background, interjecting filmed sequences into the dramatic action, manipulating the volume, direction, or quality of stereophonic sound, and using closed-circuit television in multiple ways.

These developments are related to others then occurring in the visual arts. Painters, stimulated by dissatisfaction with restrictions imposed by the media in which they worked (for example, two-dimensionality), sought to overcome the restrictions by such devices as gluing three-dimensional objects to paintings. Sculptors, to overcome the static nature of their medium, attached motors to sculptures to make them move or used light to vary the appearance. Out of such experiments eventually came *happenings*, pioneered by the painter Allan Kaprow, who argued that not only the art objects on display but also the space and all those who attend must be considered essential parts of the total artistic experience. For his first happening in 1959, Kaprow divided a gallery into three compartments, in each of which were several types of visual art and a number of individuals who performed assigned tasks repetitively while images were projected onto various surfaces, including human beings, as taped music and sound effects were played. All those who attended were expected to carry out instructions handed them as they entered. Subsequent happenings varied, but most had common characteristics with implications for theatrical performance: (1) Happenings were multimedia events that broke down the barriers between the arts and mingled elements from several; (2) happenings shifted emphasis away from creating a product to participating in a process; (3) because there was no single focus, emphasis shifted from the artist's intention to the participants' awareness; each participant, as partial creator of the event, was free

Performance Art

Matthew Goulish, a performance artist and teacher of performance art, writes: "The performance event at its best may serve as what I call 'transgressive ritual,' that is, an enactment that distorts or subverts the limits and rules of our everyday lives to reveal hidden truths. . . . Through that subversion of reality, the rules that we take for granted reveal themselves, giving us the opportunity to question them and consider alternatives. . . . The shocking qualities, so offensive to some, are not an end in themselves, but merely a means of propelling us beyond the accepted forms of public demeanor. . . ."

The transgressive nature of much performance art has been a source of considerable controversy in recent years. In 1990 the grants that four performance artists had received from the National Endowment for the Arts were rescinded because their work was considered offensive for its sexuality, nontraditional views of religion, obscene language, or attacks on political and religious opponents. The furor that followed threatened the very existence of the NEA. One of the artists, Karen Finley, was denounced especially for a piece entitled *We Keep Our Victims Ready,* in one part of which, wishing to show the degradation of women, she stripped nude, covered her body with chocolate, and decorated it with candy and tinsel while reciting a text that compared herself to a penned veal calf. The work of Tim Miller, another of those whose grants were rescinded, deals with his experiences as a gay man, using his work to explore what being gay in America means and to comment on the homophobia it incites.

Not all performance art is transgressive in the manner of Finley and Miller, but much of it transgresses in other ways by calling into question traditional behavior, values, and art, or by crossing the boundaries of art forms to create innovative works. Among the latter, Martha Clarke has been one of the most successful. Originally a dancer, she was at one time a member of Pilobolus (perhaps the most successful dance company in America) and later head of her own company before creating intermedia pieces. She first won widespread critical acclaim with *The Garden of Earthly Delights,* based on Hieronymus Bosch's fifteenth-century paintings of Heaven, Hell, the Garden of Eden, and the Seven Deadly Sins. Using seven dancers and three musicians (who also performed in the piece), it was composed of a collection of imagistic events, many of them involving flying. Using the paintings as inspiration, Clarke created a scenario in which the images, always inventive and beautiful, moved from innocence to corruption to despair, ending in Hell. The setting, by Robert Israel, was minimal—a white-walled room. Effects were created primarily through smoke and lighting (by Paul Gallo) that sculpted the bodies, many of them nude, as they moved on the floor or floated in space. The music by Richard Peaslee, played on a variety of instruments, was lyrical except in the Hell scenes. Performed by the musicians as they themselves moved through the space, the music seemed created by the action. The effect was of images released from the subconscious.

Martha Clarke's *The Garden of Earthly Delights* as seen at the Seattle Repertory Theatre. Lighting by Paul Gallo. (Photo by Chris Bennion.)

to derive from it whatever he or she could; no single "correct" interpretation of the artwork was sought; and (4) happenings did much to undermine professionalism and disciplined technique because anyone could participate, and there was no right or wrong way of doing anything. Many aspects of happenings and environmental theatre recall futurism and dada.

Perhaps because they were anarchistic, happenings soon passed out of vogue. But the artistic impulse that had prompted them remained and resurfaced in the 1970s as *performance art*. Performance art may intermingle borrowings from (any or all of) visual arts, dance, music, video, and theatre. It may be scripted or improvised. It may or may not make use of props and costumes. Often a solo performance, it also may use multiple performers. It may be highly personal or confrontational, and it often explores issues of sexuality, violence, and power in ways that challenge marketplace values, governmental authority, and the way the media manipulate perceptions (especially of the body as object and commodity). Perhaps the essence of performance art is that there are no rules about what is allowed. Because some artists have used nudity, obscenity, unfamiliar conventions, and attacks on authority, performance art has been at the center of several attempts in recent years to censor art or to curb (or end altogether) government support of the arts.

The major creators of performance art originally came from the visual arts, dance, or music; they were attracted to performance art in part because it disregarded boundaries among the arts, thereby greatly expanding the means of expression. Theatre artists originally found performance art less attractive, perhaps because theatre has always combined elements from various other arts and because performance art tended to deemphasize story/text and to use performers not as actors but as narrators or as objects to be manipulated spatially. For several years now, however, the label "performance art" has been extended to include solo theatre pieces by such performers as Spalding Gray, Eric Bogosian, and John Leguizamo. Several persons have also blended theatre and performance art, among them Martha Clarke, Meredith Monk, Ping Chong, and Laurie Anderson. Aspects of performance art have also been appropriated by music videos and other media adaptations. Because of these alterations and expansions, some critics insist that performance art in the 1990s has been swallowed up by theatre and entertainment media on the one hand and by the commodity-driven art world on the other. Certainly the performance art of the 1990s differs significantly from that of the 1970s, and the term is now applied to so many diverse activities that it has lost specificity. Nevertheless, "performance art" continues to be useful as an indication of the contemporary tendency to break down barriers between the arts and as an acknowledgement that "performance" can take many forms.

Postmodernism

The ideas and practices of environmental theatre and performance art are related to *postmodernism,* an imprecise label but one that suggests major changes in modernism. Most of these changes involve the breakdown of clear-cut categories. With modernism, the crucial battles had involved absolute versus relative standards and values. The triumph of relativism meant that artists did not all have to work in the same style; each could choose the one that seemed most appropriate. In the theatre, directors came to consider each production a problem requiring its own stylistic solution. In addition, many new styles (symbolism, expressionism, surrealism, and the like) enlarged the available choices. After a stylistic choice was made, however, the director sought to shape every aspect of a production to fit that mode. For modernists, then, though there were many stylistic categories, each was clearly differentiated.

Postmodernism melded categories by ignoring or deliberately violating differentiations by breaching the boundaries between the arts, as in performance art and multimedia; by breaking down the barriers between spectator and performance space, as in environmental theatre; and by removing distinctions between audience and performers, as in happenings. Postmodernists also ignored previous distinctions between popular and high culture and often intermingled them, as in the production of *The Comedy of Errors* (at New York's Lincoln Center), in which the Flying Karamazov Brothers (a comic juggling team) not only played key roles but also incorporated juggling and acrobatics into Shakespeare's play. Another sign of postmodernism is the blurring of distinctions between dramatic forms, as in absurdist and much other contemporary drama. Postmodernism also mingles elements from disparate styles, periods, or cultures. Postmodernist architecture is recognizable in large part by the combination within single buildings of various stylistic motifs and forms from the past. Similarly, directors have utilized conventions borrowed from several cultures. Since the early 1970s, Peter Brook has been exploring the theatrical conventions of various cultures in an attempt to bridge cultural and language barriers. Perhaps the best known of the productions growing out of these explorations is his nine-hour adaptation of the Indian epic, *Mahabharata*. In a somewhat similar vein, the French director Ariane Mnouchkine, working with her company, the Théâtre du Soleil, has drawn on Asian performance conventions in productions of several of Shakespeare's plays and in a tetralogy of Greek plays (Euripides' *Iphigeneia at Aulis* and Aeschylus' *Agamemnon, The Libation Bearers,* and *The Eumenides*) presented under the title, *Les Atrides*. These productions by Brook and Mnouchkine have been performed in major cities throughout Europe and America.

Many aspects of postmodernism came together in the theatre pieces of Robert Wilson, among them *A Letter to Queen Victoria, Einstein on the Beach, CIVIL warS,* and *The Forest*. In these pieces, Wilson borrowed from several media, cultures, and historical periods. They were essentially visual pieces (though there was much music and sound) in which juxtaposed visual images appeared, disappeared, grew, diminished, and metamorphosed. The connections among these images were not

Robert Wilson's *CIVIL warS* at the American Repertory Theatre. The tall figure at right is Abraham Lincoln; at left, an owl; at center back, King Lear carrying Cordelia. Design and lighting by Robert Wilson with Tom Kamm and Jennifer Tipton. (Photo by Richard Feldman.)

always apparent. Time was an important element; typically, it was slowed until movement became almost imperceptible, permitting every detail to be experienced; different elements within a scene progressed at different tempos. While some of Wilson's pieces included spoken portions, they did not have scripts in the traditional sense. Text and performance could not be separated (as they can be with a traditional playscript). Most of the pieces were very long, from four to twelve hours; one lasted seven continuous days and nights. *CIVIL warS,* intended for the Olympic Arts Festival in Los Angeles in 1984, was created in segments, one each in West Germany, the Netherlands, Italy, France, Japan, and the United States. It included such disparate historical figures as Abraham Lincoln, Karl Marx, Frederick the Great, Voltaire, and a Hopi Indian tribe, as well as wholly invented present-day and fictional characters. It was intended to reflect all types of conflicts (public and private) that interfere with human relationships. Utilizing twelve languages, it was not meant for an audience from a single culture.

According to Wilson, in his pieces there is nothing to understand, only things to experience, out of which spectators construct their own individual associations and meanings. Many spectators have been infuriated or bored by the length and lack of clear-cut intention in Wilson's pieces, but many critics consider him the most innovative and significant force in today's theatre. In recent years, Wilson has begun staging plays and operas, among them Shakespeare's *King Lear,* Euripides' *Alcestis,* Wagner's *Parsifal,* Büchner's *Danton's Death,* and Ibsen's *When We Dead Awaken,* as well as collaborating with others in creating new pieces (among them *The Black Rider,* on which he collaborated with Tom Waits). Even when he stages classical texts, however, he avoids visual elements that merely illustrate what is in the text; rather, he seeks to suggest other dimensions through imagery that is not literally (although perhaps thematically) related to the text.

Trends in Directing

Postmodernism has influenced directing in several ways, perhaps most significantly by altering attitudes about the director's relationship to the playwright and the script. Modernists assumed that the director's task was to translate the playwright's script faithfully from page to stage. This assumption incorporated another: that the director can determine a playwright's intentions through a meticulous analysis of the script. Postmodernists, on the other hand, argue that there can be no single "correct" interpretation of a text because words do not convey precisely the same meanings to everyone. Furthermore, once a work is finished, its creator's statements about its meanings have no more authority than anyone else's because the text, and not the author, elicits the responses and interpretations. Such arguments free a director to interpret a script as he or she thinks appropriate even if this interpretation is at odds with the playwright's. These views also encourage directors to propose new interpretations of well-known plays. In fact, in recent times, directors have often been judged by the novelty (sometimes more than by the aptness) of their interpretations. Some directors have argued that many classics have come to be so revered that we can see them with a fresh eye only in radical reinterpretations.

Beckett's *Endgame* as directed by JoAnne Akalaitis. Setting the play in an abandoned subway station and using a black actor made Beckett threaten to withdraw permission to produce the play. Setting by Douglas Stein; costumes by Kurt Wilhelm; lighting by Jennifer Tipton. (Photo by Richard Feldman.)

Most radical reinterpretations have involved plays by authors long dead. But since the 1980s, some directorial decisions have elicited strong objections from living authors. Samuel Beckett threatened to withdraw his *Endgame* from production at the American Repertory Theatre in Cambridge, Massachusetts, because the director, JoAnne Akalaitis, had relocated the action in a derelict subway station and made one of the leading characters black. In 1994, Beckett's estate forced the closure of an English production of his *Footfalls* because it did not adhere to Beckett's stage directions. In another instance, Arthur Miller threatened to sue the Wooster Group, a New York company directed by Elizabeth LeCompte, to prevent it from using, in a piece called *L.S.D.*, portions of *The Crucible* to illuminate contemporary attitudes about hallucinogenic drugs by juxtaposing them against attitudes about witchcraft in colonial New England as shown in Miller's play. The Wooster Group had previously incorporated portions of Thornton Wilder's *Our Town* into a piece called *Route 1 & 9*, where they were juxtaposed with a black vaudeville routine and a pornographic film. The group's idea was to comment on Wilder's idyllic view of America in which ethnic groups and sex are ignored, as are the industrial wastelands through which run the two highways that give the piece its title.

These productions raise important questions. Can playwrights protect their work from distortions? Are directors justified in reshaping (even radically altering) a script to suit their own vision even if it distorts the playwright's intentions? What are the implications of demanding that directors adhere to playwrights' notions about how their works should be staged? Should the playwrights' preferences be honored even after audience tastes and staging conventions have changed? What is the place of the script in performance (does it guide everything else, or is it as malleable as acting, scenery, lighting, and the like?)? What is the role of the director (principal creative artist, as in film, or servant of the script)? None of these questions can be answered definitively, but recent trends have created heated debate about them.

Cultural Diversity

Broadway, because it is a sign of professional acceptance, continues to represent for many people the test for theatre in America. Nevertheless, the number of new productions presented there each season is relatively small, from thirty to forty (as compared to more than 200 each season in the 1920s). In the 1993–94 season, thirty-seven new productions opened. Usually no more than twenty-five are running at the same time. In 1993–94 thirty-five theatres were classified as Broadway houses. They had a total attendance of 8.1 million, and their gross receipts were $356 million. Ticket prices had reached fifty dollars for most productions and seventy-five dollars for some. The majority of productions were musicals, and most had originated elsewhere.

During 1993, 177 (out of the more than 300) not-for-profit theatres in the United States had a total attendance of 16.5 million at 2,319 productions; their income amounted to $342.5 million, of which about one-third came from grants and contributions. Earned income reflected ticket prices considerably lower than those of Broadway theatres. Although these statistics establish that much more theatrical activity occurs away from than on Broadway, they fail to reflect the diversity that has occurred in American theatre since the 1960s. Broadway and regional theatres see themselves as serving the needs of all segments of society. They see the theatre as having universal appeal independent of race, class, or gender.

Much of what has happened in theatre since the 1960s calls these assumptions into question. Americans have long accepted the notion that the United States is a "melting pot" without always acknowledging that many groups, because of skin color or ethnicity (African, Asian, Native American, and some Latino/Hispanic), have been denied full absorption into the mainstream where "whiteness" and European cultural values have been accepted as the norm. Still others—women, gays and lesbians, the economically deprived, and the physically disadvantaged—have been denied equity for other reasons. Since the 1960s, most of these groups have rebelled against marginalization and have asserted their determination to have their worth

The Berkeley (California) Repertory Theatre is representative of the more than 300 not-for-profit theatres in the United States. Its wide-ranging repertory includes plays from many times and places. Shown here is Lope de Vega's seventeenth-century Spanish play, *Fuente Ovejuna*. Directed by Sharon Ott. (Photo by Ken Friedman. Courtesy Berkeley Repertory Theatre.)

acknowledged and their needs met in the theatre. Some of these groups have come to question the desirability of absorption into the "melting pot" if that means denying or abandoning their own cultures, traditions, and esthetic sensibilities. They have argued that, instead of trying to achieve homogenization, America would be better if it acknowledged, accepted, and valued differences. Efforts to implement these ideas have done much to diversify the American theatre both through plays by and about various groups and through theatres devoted to or sensitive to their needs.

African-American Theatre

Theatres and plays concerned with African Americans have probably made the greatest impact. One of the first African-American playwrights to win wide critical acclaim in the postwar period was Lorraine Hansberry (1930–1965) with *A Raisin in the Sun* (1959), a drama about a black family in Chicago. It explored most of the themes that would be significant in subsequent African-American drama: integration versus separation of the races, inequities and injustices inflicted on African Americans, aspirations for the good life and the obstacles to achieving one's potential, maintaining dignity in the face of overwhelming circumstances. *A Raisin in the Sun* was the first play by an African-American woman to be presented on Broadway, where it won the New York Drama Critics Circle Award. Although no longer as provocative as it once was, it raises issues about American society that remain to be answered satisfactorily.

African-American playwrights and production organizations have greatly increased since *A Raisin in the Sun* was first produced. Among the early playwrights, one of the most important was Amiri Baraka (LeRoi Jones), who set out to develop a black esthetic. In 1966 he founded Spirit House in Newark, where he promoted a separatist black society and a theatre devoted to the credo "By us, about us, for us." Among his best-known plays are *Dutchman* and *Slave Ship*.

Another important African-American theatre was the New Lafayette Theatre, founded in Harlem in 1967, which sought to provide leadership for black theatres in America through an information service and *Black Theatre Magazine*. Owing to dissension within the company, it came to an end in 1973. The most durable of the companies was the Negro Ensemble Company (NEC), founded in New York in 1968 by Douglas Turner Ward. It produced a wide range of plays meaningful to African Americans but not necessarily written by African Americans. In recent years it has fallen on hard times and has been barely able to survive. Other African-American companies have been established throughout the United States. Among these, some of the best are the Lorraine Hansberry in San Francisco, the Crossroads Theatre Company in New Brunswick, New Jersey, the North Carolina Black Repertory Company, Penumbra Theatre Company in St. Paul, the Oakland (California) Ensemble Theatre, Jomandi Productions in Atlanta, and the New Federal Theatre in New York. In 1989, when the first National Black Theatre Festival was held, representatives of almost 200 African-American theatre companies attended. This festival, held every two years, includes performances and discussions of common issues.

Developing a Black Consciousness

During the 1960s many African Americans felt the need to establish a sense of identity different from that associated with the older terms "Negro" and "colored." The key concept became "blackness." As Larry Neal, an African-American critic, explains in "Into Nationalism, Out of Parochialism,"

> The ideology of blackness sprang out of American blacks' legitimate need to develop a philosophical orientation which would let them find some space within themselves to move, a private space that set them apart from whites, from the European value system. It was also a reaction to a racist language and imagery that had made blackness a thing of evil. . . . It's a frame which finally provided operational identity to black artists.

August Wilson's *Two Trains Running* as produced at the Huntington Theatre Company (Boston). The actors are Chuck Patterson, Al White, Ella Joyce, and Jonathan Earl Peck. Directed by Lloyd Richards; setting by Tony Fanning; costumes by Christi Karvonides; lighting by Geoff Korf. (Photo by Richard Feldman.)

The upsurge in African-American theatrical activity provoked a corresponding increase in opportunities for actors, directors, and playwrights. Among recent playwrights, perhaps the most successful has been August Wilson, who has declared his intention of writing a play about black experience in each decade of the twentieth century. His first success came in 1984 with *Ma Rainey's Black Bottom*, concerning the humiliations, small victories, and defeats of African-American musicians working for exploitative whites in Chicago in the 1920s. *Fences*, set in the 1950s, treats a man who might have been a great baseball player had it not been for discrimination in the sport and the effect on him and his family of his sense of waste. It won the Pulitzer Prize in 1985. Wilson's other plays include *Joe Turner's Come and Gone*, *The Piano Lesson* (winner of the Pulitzer Prize in 1990), and *Two Trains Running*. Wilson's plays, unlike those of several earlier African-American dramatists, do not exploit themes of rage about whites so much as concentrate on African-American identity and quests for fulfillment and dignity.

Another important African-American playwright is George C. Wolfe, who first gained wide recognition in 1986 with *The Colored Museum*. More recently his musical, *Jelly's Last Jam*, which traces the career of Jelly Roll Morton, had a long run on Broadway. As head of the New York Shakespeare Festival Theatre since 1993, Wolfe is now one of the most influential figures in the American theatre. He is also considered to be one of America's leading directors, a status confirmed by his staging of Tony Kushner's *Angels in America* for the Broadway stage. Let us examine *The Colored Museum* as an example of African-American theatre.

The Colored Museum

The Colored Museum, originally staged by the Crossroads Theatre Company in New Brunswick, New Jersey, and subsequently at the New York Shakespeare Festival Theatre and elsewhere, is conceived as a series of eleven exhibits of African-American history and life. As the title suggests, various aspects of past and present black experience are exhibited so they can be examined. The use of "colored" is deliberately provocative because this label had been abandoned as demeaning, it serves as a reminder of the past that one would like to forget but that cannot be so easily discarded. In displaying his exhibits, Wolfe confronts audiences with behavior and attitudes reflecting both the oppressions of the past and the compromises and hopes of the present. In doing so, he alternates between (and sometimes combines) comic exposure and fierce defense. Some audiences have been offended by the play because they have failed to recognize the serious purpose of the humor. Wolfe satirizes black stereotypes to force African Americans to recognize that, even as they seek to escape stereotyping, they are living according to labels forced on them not only by others but also by themselves. Wolfe says that he wrote *The Colored Museum* "in order to undefine myself in relation to all these labels." He does not ask African Americans to forget their past; rather, he suggests, they should face it and move beyond it. As one of the characters in the final exhibit says, "I can't live inside yesterday's pain, but I can't live without it." A major concern of the play, then, is how African Americans can acknowledge and make productive use of the past.

The double tone of the play is established in the opening exhibit when the stewardess Miss Pat cheerfully instructs passengers on how to fasten their shackles for this trip aboard the Celebrity Slaveship. During this time-warp journey through 200 years of black experience, her bland advice to passengers to abandon their African gods, music, and customs for those of their white oppressors is accompanied by projected images showing scenes of degradation and suffering under slavery. When the ship arrives in Savannah, passengers are warned (significantly in light of the play's major themes), "any baggage you don't claim, we trash."

The "Cooking with Aunt Ethel" exhibit uses the stereotypical "black mammy" of theatre, film, and white popular culture to show that beneath the veneer of cheerful acceptance lies resistance expressed through the "attitude" she imparts to her creations. "The Photo Session" exhibits a male and a female model who, unable to resolve "the contradictions of our existence," have given "away our life" to "live inside *Ebony Magazine.*" In "A Soldier with a Secret" a shell-shocked figure from the Vietnam War decides to kill his comrades in order to save them from the disappointments and pain they will have to undergo when the war ends. In "The Gospel According to Miss Roj," a "snap queen" dressed "in striped patio pants, white go-go boots, a halter, and cat-shaped sunglasses" delivers a simultaneously

The Colored Museum as produced at the Yale Repertory Theatre. This scene shows the end of the first exhibit as passengers embark from the slave ship; Miss Pat in the background. Directed by Donald Douglass; settings by Monica Raya; lighting by Trui Malten; costumes by Elizabeth Michal Fried. (Photo © T. Charles Erickson.)

funny and scathing (and ultimately chilling) monologue about how "a whole race of people gets trashed and debased." But despite, or because of, the treatment he has received, he demands respect: "We don't ask for acceptance. We don't ask for approval. We know who we are and we move on it!" "The Hairpiece" is primarily a dialogue between two wigs, one Afro, the other long and flowing (making its wearer look like a "Barbie doll dipped in chocolate"). Bickering over which wig their owner should wear, they describe her as being entirely bald from having "fried, dyed, de-chemicalized" her hair because each time her male friend "changed his ideology, she went and changed her hair to fit the occasion."

The heart of the play, especially for those interested in theatre, is "The Last Mama-on-the-Couch Play." It is a satirical look at the stereotypes that had come to dominate black family plays in the wake of Lorraine Hansberry's *A Raisin in the Sun,* especially the strong, religious matriarch who valiantly holds her family together while seeking to instill strong traditional values, and the son who complains continuously about his treatment by "the man." There is also satire of Ntozake Shange's *For Colored Girls Who Have Considered Suicide When the Rainbow is Enuf* in the woman who sees herself as a primal African princess and whose vengeful husband drops her children from the window of a tenement and is then himself killed by police fire. The daughter of the family seeks to escape her roots by becoming an actress playing Medea in classical tones learned in drama school at Juilliard. A master of ceremonies enthuses about all these performances and gives them awards for their (over)acting. After her son is killed, Mama bursts into song lamenting that her son was not born into an all-black musical, for in these popular Broadway productions no one ever gets killed. The scene climaxes in a production number using "a myriad of black-Broadwayesque dancing styles" undercut by projected images "of coon performers," who in earlier times had presented song-and-dance shows demeaning to blacks but popular with whites.

The exhibit entitled "Symbiosis" shows The Man dressed in a business suit trying to discard all the cultural symbols that stand in the way of his success in the corporate world. His younger self, The Kid, tries to thwart this attempt, but The Man eventually throws The Kid into a Dumpster along with the artifacts of his past. He declares: "Being black is too emotionally taxing; therefore I will be black only on weekends and holidays." As The Man discards the last item, The Kid's hand emerges from the trash and gets a "death grip on The Man's arm."

"Lala's Opening" concerns a female performer who to become internationally famous has denied her past and created a fictional persona who sings in French and continually refers to her famous friends. As the scene progresses, she is gradually

"The Last Mama-on-the-Couch Play" exhibit in *The Colored Museum* as produced at the New York Shakespeare Festival. Danitra Vance as "Medea" and Vickilyn Reynolds as "Mama." (Photo © Martha Swope.)

provoked into dropping her mask and in a near-mad state comes face to face with the little black girl inside whom she had tried to destroy.

"Permutations" is an imaginative look at teenage pregnancy, and the final exhibit, "The Party," acknowledges the great variety, even contradictions, of black experience, past and present, "being lynched, rioting, partying, surviving." The characters from previous exhibits join in as they proclaim, "My power is in my madness and my colored contradictions." Miss Pat from the opening scene ends the play: "Before exiting, check the overhead as any baggage you don't claim, we trash." Taken all together, these eleven exhibits ask us to look at attitudes and stereotypes that have shaped aspects of African-American sensibilities. It does so in a form that is both imaginative and entertaining.

Other African-American playwrights include Ntozake Shange, Alice Childress, Adrienne Kennedy, Ed Bullins, Charles Fuller, Leslie Lee, and Susan Lori Parks, among many others.

Latino Theatre

After African-American theatre, Latino (or Hispanic-American or Chicano—the acceptable term is a matter of considerable contention) is the most extensively developed alternative theatre in the United States. The first play known to have been

Luis Valdez' *I Don't Have to Show You No Stinking Badges* as performed by El Teatro Campesino. The actors are (left to right) Alma Martinez, Kinan Valdez, Mike Moroff, and Marion Yue. (Photo by Alan McEwen. Courtesy of Luis Valdez/El Teatro Campesino.)

Maria Irene Fornes' *And What of the Night* as produced at the Milwaukee Repertory Theatre. The actors are Daniel Mooney, Marie Mathay, and Kenneth Albers. Directed by Maria Irene Fornes. (Photo by Mark Avery. Courtesy Milwaukee Repertory Theatre.)

staged in what is now the United States was performed by Spanish soldiers near El Paso in 1598. But it was not until the nineteenth century that Spanish-language theatre became common, first in California, then in Texas, and, by the early twentieth century, in all the territories bordering Mexico. From 1918 into the 1930s, Los Angeles supported five professional Spanish-language theatres, and professional companies toured widely throughout the country. During the 1930s, economic depression and the inroads of film ended most of this activity, although amateur theatres continued to fill the need. All of these developments made little impact on the dominant white culture, which remained largely oblivious to them.

Not until the 1960s did Latino theatre begin to make an impression on the wider American consciousness, first through the work of El Teatro Campesino, a bilingual Chicano company founded by Luis Valdez in 1965. Valdez was very successful in calling attention to the plight of migrant workers in California and winning public support for them during a strike by grape pickers. Valdez later turned to writing plays about the heritage and lives of contemporary Mexican Americans. Valdez achieved his greatest popular success with *Zoot Suit* (1976), which mingled traditional Mexican musical forms with Living Newspaper techniques in a play based on an actual case of injustice against a group of young Mexican Americans during World War II. *Zoot Suit,* which enjoyed a long run in the theatre before being made into a film, influenced many other Hispanic-American writers to treat similar themes. A prolific playwright, Valdez also wrote *Los Vendidos, Corridos,*

I Don't Have to Show You No Stinking Badges, and *Bandito.* Valdez is probably best known to the general public for his film work, especially *La Bamba.*

One of the most notable Hispanic-American playwrights is Maria Irene Fornes, a Cuban American who began writing plays in 1965. Although she has never achieved wide popular recognition, she has won six awards for Off-Broadway productions. Among her plays are *Fefu and Her Friends,* in which eight women hold a reunion and look back over their lives in a male-dominated world, and *The Conduct of Life,* which draws parallels between political subjugation and the subjugation of women in Latin America. Another notable Latina dramatist is Milcha Sanchez-Scott, daughter of a Colombian father and an Indonesian mother. She was educated partially in England and since the age of fourteen has lived in California. Her first play, *Latina* (1980), concerning women she met while working in an employment agency in Los Angeles, won several awards. Later plays include *Dog Lady, Cuban Swimmer,* and *Evening Star.* Her best-known work is *Roosters.* Let us examine it as an example of Latina drama.

Roosters

Roosters, which takes place in the present-day Southwest, uses cockfighting as its basic metaphor. The father of the family is named Gallo ("rooster," a word also signifying "macho," the male animal focused on his own needs). The primary action of the play is concerned with the struggle for dominance between the forty-year-old Gallo (who returns home after several years spent in prison for killing a man) and his twenty-year-old son, Hector (who rejects his father's braggadocio in favor of a determinedly unromantic view of himself and his family). Gallo considers it a betrayal that Hector has taken a job working in the fields because none of the family's male members had ever stooped so low (although such menial work seems the accepted fate of the females, who apparently provide financial support while Gallo plays his macho games). Gallo prefers a life focused on cockfighting, winning at which in his eyes justifies any behavior, including cheating, con games, and even murder (it was a fight over a rooster that led to his imprisonment). Hector, on the other hand, dreams of going beyond the mountains (visible in the background) to escape his family and the kind of life Gallo envisions for him. The struggle between the two men is brought to a head in their attempts to assert ownership of Zapata, a fighting cock that Gallo considers the culmination of his efforts to breed a champion but that has been given to Hector by his grandfather, who died while Gallo was in prison. Hector's determination to take Zapata into the cockfighting ring himself, and to dispose of him after the fight is over, conflicts with Gallo's belief that he is the rightful owner of Zapata and that, as a legendary figure in cockfighting, he should be the one to take Zapata into the ring. The life-and-death nature of their struggle is made clear in a fight between two roosters (represented by actor-dancers), one of whom is viciously killed during a fight for which razors have been attached to the roosters' feet; it is further implied in several references to Zapata destroying his own offspring. The ultimate parallel between Zapata and Gallo comes when Gallo challenges Hector to a fight with knives, Gallo apparently being

Roosters as produced at the New Mexico Repertory Theatre. As the family gathers around the table, Angela (in the background) makes off with the fighting cock Zapata. Directed by Roxane Rogers; setting by Rosario Provenza; costumes by Tina Cantu Navarro; lighting by Robert Wierzel. (Photo by Murrae Haynes, New Mexico Repertory Theatre.)

willing to kill his son in order to gain possession of Zapata, a goal that also makes him callously betray his daughter Angela's trust. The struggle is ultimately resolved when Hector overpowers Gallo and reveals that, despite his denunciations of his father, he has been motivated by resentment that his father has ignored his family and failed to offer Hector the love and approval he needed. It is also revealed that Hector has insisted on keeping and disposing of Zapata in order to save his father's life, which is in clear danger from the family whose son Gallo killed and from whose stock Zapata is descended (illegally, through another example of Gallo's chicanery). Once overpowered by Hector, Gallo seems reconciled to his son, finding in him the potential to carry on the macho tradition, although Hector repeats his intention of leaving this kind of life behind.

Set against this struggle between males are the three women of the family: Juana, Gallo's worn-down, thirty-five-year-old wife; Chata, Gallo's fleshy, forty-year-old sister, who "gives new meaning to the word blowsy"; and Angela, Gallo's fifteen-year-old daughter who wears angel wings, plays with dolls dressed as saints, creates a cemetery with headstones bearing the names of those who have offended her, and spends much of her time under the house. Unlike Gallo and Hector, both of whom are described as being unusually handsome, the women are all homely. The men are set off by the women, like colorful roosters surrounded by drab hens, and the women apparently are expected to feel grateful to be associated with these handsome creatures. Juana, who bore her first child at the age of fifteen, has spent her life supporting her family and waiting patiently for the return of Gallo (who apparently in the past has come and gone on whim), adoring him, making possible his macho existence. Chata once aspired to home and family but, seduced and betrayed early, has since followed the migrant farm workers, living a life of sexual promiscuity; she is the proverbial "fallen woman with a heart of gold," providing earthy wisdom, sharp commentary, and momentary comfort. Angela, on the verge of womanhood, clings to childhood and religion as a buffer against hurt. Torn between Gallo and Hector, she, on the one hand, accepts Hector's view of Gallo as a con man, but, on the other hand, clearly desires to be loved and accepted by her father. Hers is the most touching betrayal when Gallo, by promising to take her on a trip to the ocean, cajoles her into telling where Zapata is hidden, even though she has given her oath to Hector that she will not do so. After Gallo has Zapata, he has no more use for Angela. Her disillusionment is intense and her attempt to retrieve her faith culminates in her levitation, wings spread, a manifestation of the "magic realism" that is characteristic of much Latino literature. The play ends in a suspended moment during which all the characters seemingly accept themselves and each other.

Roosters is divided into two acts and eight scenes. The elapsed time is unclear but apparently not more than a day or two. The setting is simple: A house, set against a desert landscape with mountains visible in the distance, is raised sufficiently to allow space for Angela to slip under it easily. The porch and yard are the principal playing areas. There is also a chicken-wire enclosure for Zapata and a tree that provides some shade. The atmosphere, shifting easily between realism and fantasy, is characteristic of Latino "magic realism." Overall, *Roosters* is a powerful play that has much to say about machismo, women, love, and psychological need in a male-dominated Latino culture.

Roosters was developed in INTAR's (International Arts Relations, Inc.) Hispanic Playwrights-in-Residence Laboratory and was then co-produced by INTAR and the New York Shakespeare Festival in 1987. Subsequently it has been seen at Latino (and other) theatres throughout the country. It has also been filmed for PBS television.

A survey made in the 1980s identified approximately 100 Hispanic-American theatre groups—Chicano, Puerto Rican, Cuban, or other categories. Some of the best known of these are INTAR, Repertorio Español, and the Puerto Rican Traveling Theatre, all in New York; and Latino Theatre Lab, El Teatro de la Esperanza, and the Bilingual Foundation of the Arts in California. An international festival of Chicano and Latino theatre was established in 1970. At first held annually, it is now held biannually under the auspices of TENAZ (Teatros Nacionales de Atzlan). It is the oldest artistic organization of the Chicano and Latino theatre community.

Asian-American Theatre

Asian Americans also have made their mark. Asians first came to America in large numbers when Chinese workers were imported in the mid-nineteenth century to help build railroads. Those who remained clustered together, usually within such cities as San Francisco, New York, Chicago, Los Angeles, and Seattle. In some of these cities, theatres were established to cater to Asian audiences. San Francisco, for example, maintained a Beijing Opera company until the 1940s. World War II, the Korean War, and the Vietnam War tended to make Americans more aware of Asian cultures and to increase the immigration of Asians to the United States.

When Asian Americans were depicted in drama, they were usually reduced to a few stereotypes: dutiful houseboy, inscrutable detective, wise Confucian patriarch, treacherous dragon lady, or submissive Asian doll-bride. Asian Americans began to rebel against these stereotypes around 1965, writing their own plays and founding their own theatres. Some of the most important of the companies were: the East-West Players, founded in Los Angeles in 1965; the Asian Exclusion Act, founded in Seattle in 1973 and later renamed the Northwest Asian American Theatre Company; the Asian American Theatre Workshop, founded in San Francisco in 1973; and the Pan Asian Repertory Theatre, founded in New York in 1977.

Frank Chin was the first Asian-American playwright to win wide recognition; his *Chickencoop Chinaman* satirized both self-stereotyping and media stereotyping, and his *The Year of the Dragon* was said in 1977 to be the first Asian-American play ever produced in New York. Philip Kan Gotanda's *The Wash* concerns the disintegration of a Japanese-American family as the father clings to Japanese ideas while his wife and children accept American customs. In Gotanda's *Yankee Dawg You Die* a young Asian-American actor is contemptuous of an older one for accepting the stereotypical roles implied in the play's title only to find as time passes that he must

The Pan Asian Repertory Theatre's production of *Letters to a Student Revolutionary* by Elizabeth Wong. Directed by Ernest Abuba. (Photo by Corky Lee. Courtesy of the Pan Asian Repertory Theatre.)

Should We Write Only About Our Own Culture?

In debates over multiculturalism, an ongoing issue concerns whether playwrights should (or can effectively) write about cultures other than their own.
Writers from minority cultures are especially subject to pressure, often being
accused of betraying their own heritage when they choose to write about
other topics.

August Wilson, among the best known of African-American playwrights, feels strongly that he must write about his own culture: "I am more
and more concerned with pointing out the differences between blacks and
whites as opposed to pointing out similarities. We're different people. We do
things differently.... We have different ideas of justice and morality....
blacks have been all too willing and anxious to say that we are the same as
whites." A proposed movie to be based on his 1987 Pulitzer Prize–winning
play *Fences* has been held up for several years because Wilson insists that no
one other than an African American can direct it effectively, and so far no
one whom he considers satisfactory has been found.

On the other hand, Ping Chong, a major Asian-American perfor-
mance/video artist, playwright, and director, argues: "I'm not going to let myself be ghettoized as an Asian-American artist. I'm an *American* artist. . . . we
cannot lose sight of the fact that we all live in a society where we have to coexist. It doesn't mean that I have to like your culture. But we have to be *sensitive* to each other's cultures. I think it extremely naive to think that no one
but Asians can write about Asians. It would simply be another point of view.
I do make shows about white characters even though I didn't grow up Anglo.
Does that mean I shouldn't write about them? . . . I believe it is important to
be inclusive; a free society should allow for a multiplicity of views."

Daryl Chin, an Asian-American critic, writes: "These debates [over mul-
ticulturalism] are about feelings of disenfranchisement and exclusion. . . . The
reason the debates are so painful is that they strike at the very heart of who
people think they are." Some members of specific cultures believe that their
experience is so complex that no outsider can understand or represent it adequately. Similarly, they may resent having aspects of their cultural heritage
"appropriated" by outsiders who incorporate it into their own works without
acknowledging its origins or who distort it through lack of understanding.

do the same if he is to survive as a performer. *Day Standing on Its Head* concerns
the midlife crisis of an Asian-American law professor.

The best-known Asian-American dramatist is David Henry Hwang (1957–),
who first came to prominence in 1980 with *F.O.B.* His subsequent plays include
The Dance and the Railroad, Family Devotions, Face Value, and several works written
in collaboration with Philip Glass. Hwang's best-known work is *M. Butterfly* (1988).
Let us look at this play as an example of Asian-American drama.

Ping Chong's *Nosferatu* which, like most of his works, is concerned with the interactions of "race, culture, history, art and technology in the modern era." Directed and choreographed by Ping Chong; setting by Ping Chong and Matthew Yolobosky; lighting by Thomas C. Hase; costumes by Matthew Yolobosky. (Photo © Carol Rosegg.)

M. Butterfly

The title *M. Butterfly* immediately associates Hwang's play with *Madame Butterfly*, Giacomo Puccini's well-known opera (based on a play by David Belasco). Hwang uses this association to focus attention on race, gender, and politics. Overall he suggests that Westerners have viewed "Orientals" (both individuals and nations) as submissively "feminine," willing to be dominated by the aggressive, "masculine" West. Hwang fuses this perception with a real-life story in which a French diplomat carried on a twenty-year relationship with a Beijing Opera performer of female roles (and a spy for the Chinese government) without recognizing that the performer was male. Hwang's play is focused on the diplomat's (Gallimard) attempt to understand and to explain to the audience his relationship with the performer (Song Liling).

The play is divided into three acts and twenty-seven scenes, although these formal divisions often seem irrelevant because the action moves freely between the

In *M. Butterfly* Gallimard applauds a scene from a Beijing opera. Directed by John Dexter; scenery and costumes by Eiko Ishioka; lighting by Andy Phillips. (Photo by Joan Marcus.)

present (in Gallimard's prison cell) and the past (ranging through various locales from 1947 to 1987), often intermingling different times and places within a single scene. Nevertheless, the action is divided into phases roughly marked by the act divisions. Act One is devoted primarily to establishing *Madame Butterfly* as a frame for the action. It establishes Gallimard's fantasized notion of the ideal woman as one who accepts and loves a man unquestioningly no matter how badly he may treat her. After seeing Song Liling performing as Madame Butterfly, Gallimard has by the end of the first act convinced himself that "she" embodies the ideal woman and has begun a sexual relationship with "her," although always in the dark. Song's unwillingness to fully disrobe only feeds Gallimard's fantasy of his modest Butterfly.

Act Two shows the development of this relationship, with Gallimard alternately testing Song (by staying away for several weeks at a time and entering into an affair with another woman) and affirming that she is the creature he has envisioned in his fantasies. But we also see Song's manipulation of Gallimard, who has become head of French intelligence services in China, in order to learn from him the United States' plans in Vietnam. Song's hold on Gallimard is clinched by the announcement that "she" is pregnant by him. From this point major changes begin in their lives. Gallimard is discredited as an analyst of political events in the Far East and sent back to Paris in a low-level assignment, while Song is humiliated during the Cultural Revolution. Nevertheless, by the end of Act Two, Song has been sent to Paris to reestablish a relationship with Gallimard.

Act Three is devoted to making Gallimard face the truth. The espionage in which the two have been involved for twenty years is revealed in court, Song is deported to China, and Gallimard is sentenced to prison. To make Gallimard acknowledge that "she" is a man, Song insists on stripping completely nude before him. Gallimard finds this new Song a shallow man who dresses like a pimp. "I'm a man who loved a woman created by a man. Everything else—simply falls short." In the final scene, Gallimard, realizing that the Butterfly he has cherished is a fantasy now threatened by the revelations of a mere, petty man, puts on makeup and robes that convert him into an image of Butterfly and, like the character in Puccini's opera, he commits suicide.

M. Butterfly makes explicit what in contemporary criticism is called the "male gaze": the representation of reality as it concerns women through the male sensibility; drama, depicting women as objects of male desire and domination, makes female spectators, if they enter empathetically into the action, collude in their own diminishment by acquiescing to the male vision of what it means to be female. As Song says in explaining why men traditionally played female roles in Beijing Opera: "Only a man knows how a woman is supposed to act." That view ultimately undergirds Gallimard's creation of his ideal woman, based in part on *Madame Butterfly* and projected onto Song. He maintains that vision in the face of all contrary evidence and reaffirms it with his death.

Whereas Gallimard's view of the feminine is primarily personal and romantic, Song's is political and pragmatic: "The West thinks of itself as masculine—big guns, big industry, big money—so the East is feminine—weak, delicate, poor . . . but good at art, and full of inscrutable wisdom—the feminine mystique. . . . The West believes the East, deep down, *wants* to be dominated—because a woman can't think for herself." He adds: "You expect Oriental countries to submit to your guns, and you expect Oriental women to be submissive to your men. That's why you say they make the best wives."

Gallimard and Song, with their relationship and contrasting views, are the heart of the play. The other characters are minor but utilitarian. Marc, with his sexual experience, provides a contrast and serves as a mentor to Gallimard. Toulon makes French bureaucracy concrete by serving first as the head of the French embassy in China and later as the judge at Song's trial. Comrade Chin is the representative of Chinese bureaucracy, and doubles as Suzuki in the *Madame Butterfly* excerpts. Helga, Gallimard's wife, and Renee, his mistress, serve as contrasts and foils for Song. None is characterized in any depth.

Perhaps the most distinguishing feature of *M. Butterfly* is its theatricality—its acknowledgement that the place of the action is the stage where ideas and events are examined rather than re-created in detail. Gallimard, and sometimes other characters, addresses the audience directly. In some scenes, multiple places and times blend; at no time is there an attempt to represent a scene illusionistically. This fluidity allows the action to move freely through space and time. The most striking visual feature is the use in several scenes of performance conventions borrowed from Beijing Opera, a device that reinforces the differences between East and West.

Taken all together, *M. Butterfly* is a complex play, both in its personal and ideational dimensions. It reminds Asian Americans of the theatrical heritage they

Song Liling and Gallimard after Song's gender has been made clear in the production of *M. Butterfly* at Wisdom Bridge Theatre (Chicago). The actors are Ahmed Elkassabany and Robert Scogin. Directed by Jeffrey Ortmann. (Photo Roger Lewin/Jennifer Girard Studio. Courtesy Wisdom Bridge Theatre.)

have left behind and suggests as well that the Western attitudes toward Asians seen in the play are still prevalent in American attitudes toward Asian Americans. It also offers provocative commentary on male/female (and, secondarily, homosexual) relationships.

Other Asian-American playwrights include Ric Shiomi, Hans Ong, James Yoshimura, Elizabeth Wong, Rosanna Yamagiwa Alfaro, Winston Tong, Daryl Chin, and Ping Chong.

Native-American Theatre

There have been a few Native-American theatre groups. The first all–Native-American company, the Native American Theatre Ensemble, was founded by Hanay Geiogamah in 1972. With support from the LaMama company in New York, it presented plays based on myths and contemporary life with the aim of building pride in the Native-American heritage. Geiogamah's plays include *Body Indian* and *49*. The American Indian Community House in New York has long served as a community center for Native Americans living in New York and has maintained a

The Denver Theatre Center's 1994 production of *Black Elk Speaks,* based on the book by John G. Neihardt, dramatized by Christopher Sergel. Seen here are Lakota warriors at the Battle of Little Big Horn. Directed by Donovan Marley. (Photo by Terry Shapiro. Courtesy Denver Theatre Center.)

performing arts program that has sought to revive authentic Native-American rituals and performance traditions. Spiderwoman Theatre, founded by three Native-American sisters, is the oldest female group still performing in the United States. Another successful Native-American company is Naa Kahidi (Clan House) Theater in Alaska, which has performed its adaptations of Tlingit myths at numerous theatre festivals in the United States and Europe. Other Native-American performers include Vira and Hortensia Colorado, whose *Walks of Indian Women—Aztlan to Anahuac* traces the history of Native-American women since pre-Columbian times; and Rudy Martin, whose one-man *My Place* explores the life of a Native-American man in a large city.

Still other theatres and playwrights reflect the concerns of such groups as the deaf, the blind, and the elderly. The National Theatre of the Deaf, founded in 1967, has toured widely to great critical acclaim both nationally and internationally. About 100 groups now serve the elderly and have established a National Adult Theatre Festival.

Spiderwoman Theatre

One of the most important Native-American theatre groups is Spiderwoman, founded in 1976 by Muriel Miguel, Gloria Miguel, and Lisa Mayo, three Cuna-Rappahannock sisters. (Although the company has at time included as many as seven members, these three have always been the core.) Their first piece was *Women in Violence,* the success of which led to an invitation to perform at the World Festival of Theatre in Nancy, France, as the first feminist theatre group to perform there. Their enthusiastic reception led to appearances in several other European cities. Subsequent productions include *Lysistrata Numbah* (which borrows from Aristophanes to comment satirically on such topics as sexuality and violence against women), *The Three Sisters from Here to There* (a reworking of Chekhov's *Three Sisters*), *3 Up, 3 Down* (a spoof of works by the Brontë sisters used to comment on Native-American politics), *Winnetou's Snake Oil Show from Wigwam City* (which intermingles themes of racism with a medicine show that sells Indian spirituality to white people), and *Power Pipes* (an exploration of the performers' own spiritual heritage).

Although Spiderwoman's concerns are ultimately serious (and some of its works remain serious throughout), the group typically uses broad comic devices, ranging from Three Stooges slapstick to tongue-in-cheek satire, along with music and videos, to make its points. For example, in *Winnetou's Snake Oil Show from Wigwam City,* it offers a workshop (satirizing what it calls "New Age plastic shamanism") for audience members who want to become Indian. All of its works blend Native-American and feminist concerns.

Women's Theatre

Among the most active of alternative groups have been women's theatres. Women, representing as they do one-half of the world's population, cannot on one level be considered a minority. Nevertheless, throughout the theatre's history they have been relegated to a minor position. Although written about in ancient Greece, for example, they did not themselves either write plays or act in them. In England they were not permitted to appear on the stage until 1661, and though prominent as actresses thereafter, seldom did they write plays or attain positions of power in the theatre until recently. In the twentieth century, women began to write plays more frequently, although even those sufficiently successful to have won Pulitzer Prizes (among them Susan Glaspell, Zoe Akins, and Mary Chase) have largely disappeared from memory. Only gradually since World War II have women come to be accepted as directors and heads of theatre companies, and even now the number in such positions is relatively small.

Changes have come about primarily through concern for women's rights, which dates back to at least the nineteenth century but was given new energy by the civil rights movement that accelerated in the 1960s. Many women have been concerned primarily with gaining equal rights within the existing system; others have perceived such a clear difference between men (characterized as competitive, aggressive, and violent) and women (seen as cooperative, nurturing, and pacifistic) that they have advocated replacing male with female values. Still others have seen themselves as members of an oppressed group within a white, male, Eurocentric society and have sought alliances with other groups who have been comparably marginalized because of such factors as ethnicity, economic class, or sexual preference. These differences have influenced plays written by women.

A number of theatre groups have been founded to present the work of feminist writers. Some of the most important of these have been Women's Experimental Theatre, WOW Cafe, Spiderwoman Theatre, the Women's Project of the American Place Theatre, and Split Britches, all in New York; Double Edge in Cambridge, Massachusetts; the Rhode Island Feminist Theatre; At the Foot of the Mountain in Minneapolis; Lilith Theatre in San Francisco; and the Omaha Magic Theatre. More than ten national festivals of women's theatre have been held in the United States.

Many female playwrights have written almost exclusively for feminist theatres and have not sought a larger audience. Others have won recognition in mainstream theatres. Among the best known of the latter group are Marsha Norman, Beth

Wendy Wasserstein's *The Sisters Rosensweig*. The actors are Madeline Kahn, Jane Alexander, and Frances McDormand. Directed by Daniel Sullivan; sets by John Lee Beatty; costumes by Jane Greenwood; lighting by Pat Collins. (Photo © Martha Swope.)

Henley, and Wendy Wasserstein. Norman is best known for *'night, Mother*—winner of the Pulitzer Prize in 1983—in which a woman, having lost all desire to live, matter-of-factly announces and carries out her plan to commit suicide. Beth Henley has written primarily about colorful characters in small Southern towns. She was most successful with *Crimes of the Heart*—winner of the Pulitzer Prize in 1981—a play about three sisters who, faced with charges of murder and the death of their grandfather, eventually recognize how they have shortchanged themselves through the choices they have made about their lives. Wendy Wasserstein is best known for *The Heidi Chronicles,* winner of the 1989 Pulitzer Prize. The action, which begins in the mid-1960s and ends in the late 1980s, traces changes in the political and personal life of the protagonist as she develops a feminist consciousness and eventually comes to feel that the feminist movement has failed to fulfill its promises.

Among contemporary female playwrights, Paula Vogel has become prominent. Head of the Playwriting Workshop at Brown University and winner of numerous awards, she has written, among others, *Desdemona, The Oldest Profession, Meg, And Baby Makes Seven,* and *Hot 'n' Throbbing.* Let us look more closely at one of her plays, *The Baltimore Waltz.*

The Baltimore Waltz

The Baltimore Waltz is a play that deals with AIDS and impending death through various strategies that create distance from the reality. The play begins with Anna, a first-grade teacher, talking both about foreign travel and foreign languages—things that are threatening because strange and unknown. The scene shifts quickly to Anna's brother, Carl, who is being fired from his position as a librarian because he is gay. Though not mentioned directly, he also has AIDS. Before this information can be fully absorbed, the scene shifts to a meeting of Anna and Carl with a doctor whose language is more impenetrable than the foreign phrases Anna has sought to decipher. AIDS, still unmentioned, is distanced further by being transmuted into a fictional disease—ATD, Acquired Toilet Disease, which is transmitted to unmarried teachers by small children with whom they share toilet facilities. The remainder of the play proceeds on the premise that it is the heterosexual Anna who has the deadly disease rather than Carl (probably because the playwright wished to suggest that AIDS should be looked at medically rather than through the lens of homophobia, which often blames the victim). ATD, however, is not sexually transmittable, and Anna decides that she will spend the rest of her doomed existence having sex as often as possible during the European tour she and Carl embark on (at least in her imagination; in actuality the entire play transpires in the Baltimore hospital where Carl is dying).

In the scenes that follow, several types of occurrences overlap. Carl and Anna make their way through several cities of Europe, a progression suggested through differences in foreign languages, through descriptions of food and sights, and the rather comic couplings of Anna with various partners. Anna's encounters are paralleled by Carl's somewhat furtive meetings with men, all with stuffed rabbits hidden beneath their coats. Anna, who witnesses some of these encounters, never compre-

The Baltimore Waltz as produced at the Goodman Theatre (Chicago). In this scene Anna and Carl, taking a stroll through the streets of Paris, are shadowed by the mysterious Third Man. The actors are Jenny Bacon, Jerry Saslow, and Christopher Donahue. Directed by Mary Zimmerman. (Photo by Liz Lauren. Courtesy of the Goodman Theatre.)

hends their significance, nor are they explained. They apparently represent that secret aspect of Carl's life that is beyond Anna's knowledge. Both Carl and Anna accept each other's behavior without judgment. They share the same bed and rebond as they recall their childhood. As they travel through Europe, they also travel through the six stages that terminally ill patients pass through according to Elizabeth Kubler-Ross: denial and isolation, anger, bargaining with some higher power, depression, acceptance, and hope—to which they add a seventh, lust.

Throughout, a sinister note links Carl and Anna with their final destination, Vienna, and the vague promise of a cure through drugs not available elsewhere and treatment by a doctor using unorthodox means. Much of this recalls both the desperate willingness of those who are terminally ill to try any treatment, no matter how farfetched, the secrecy in the pharmaceutical industry over drugs, the indecisiveness in the medical profession over treatment, and the slowness of governments to fund research about AIDS. A sense of intrigue and mystery is furthered through references to Carol Reid's film, *The Third Man,* set in Vienna during the Cold War. The connection is established through the use of the zither-music theme from the film and the appropriation of one of its characters, Harry Lime, as Carl's connection in Vienna.

The Vienna scenes are divided between Anna's encounter with Dr. Todesrocheln ("Deathrattle"), whose treatment is based on drinking one's own

The Baltimore Waltz as produced at the Yale Repertory Theatre. Carl and Anna share a bed on their tour of Europe. Directed by Stan Wojewodski, Jr.; setting by David Maxine; lighting by Lynne Chase; costumes by Dennis Hudson. (Photo © T. Charles Erickson.)

urine (if the doctor doesn't drink it first), and Carl's meeting with Harry Lime, his closest friend in college and now a drug dealer who has just staged his own death so he can go underground. When Carl and Harry meet secretly on the Ferris wheel in the Prater (Vienna's entertainment park), Harry confesses that his drugs will do nothing for Anna. When Carl chides him for his criminal behavior, Harry responds, "if you want to be a millionaire, you go into real estate. If you want to be a billionaire, you sell hope." After Carl threatens to expose him, Harry pushes Carl from the Ferris wheel to his death during a waltz that is also a struggle for the rabbit. In this scene there is a strong suggestion that Harry is the source of Carl's AIDS and that Carl's journey in the play has been back to that time in his life.

When Anna sees Carl's corpse, she refuses at first to accept that he is dead, lifts him up, and performs a grotesque dance with him set to a Viennese waltz. There is a swift change to "harsh, stark and white" lighting as the preceding scenes of fantasy are replaced by the reality of the hospital room and Carl's actual death. But as the play ends, fantasy returns as Anna waltzes with Carl as a healthy young man dressed in a Viennese military uniform.

The Baltimore Waltz is divided into thirty scenes and is meant to be performed without intermission. One scene flows into another smoothly; often within the same scene events happening in different places are intercut. Narration and action also flow together. The rapid shifts in time and place are reminiscent of film but without the use of realistic scenic backgrounds or clothing. The setting is essentially a neutral space; within it there are only a platform that can be used as a (hospital or hotel) bed or a bench, and perhaps a table and two chairs, although suitcases can substitute for chairs. Costume is also simple, blending hospital and street dress. Carl wears a blazer over pajamas, Anna a trench coat over a slip or negligee. All of the characters other than Anna and Carl (more than a dozen) are played by a single actor, usually referred to as The Third Man, further connecting the play with Reid's film. Although he changes some items of clothing, this third character always wears latex gloves, relating him back to the hospital. Lighting, the script suggests, should be "highly stylized, lush, dark, and imaginative" except in the final hospital scene. The playwright also requests the use of a musical score made up of "every cliché of the European experience as imagined by Hollywood."

The Baltimore Waltz, relatively simple on the surface, is complex in its layering of reality and fantasy and in the implications of its intertwined references. It won an Obie Award for Best Play in 1992, as well as an AT&T New Play Award.

Gay and Lesbian Theatre

Although homosexuality has been an occasional topic in drama since the Greeks, it was the primary focus in few plays until recently. Matt Crowley's *The Boys in the Band* (1968), the first play on Broadway specifically about gay men, is often said to have marked a turning point in the acceptability of plays about homosexuality, although all of its characters were still treated as doomed or irrevocably unhappy. Following the Stonewall riots in 1969 (when a group of homosexuals, reacting to years of intimidation, attacked police who were raiding a gay bar), advocates of "gay pride" encouraged greater openness in plays and productions about gay life.

One of the best-known exponents of gay theatre was Charles Ludlam (1943–1987), the head of the Ridiculous Theatrical Company from 1967 until his death and the author of several plays, among them *Bluebeard, Camille,* and *The Mystery of Irma Vep,* which parodied familiar literary genres and the absurdities of art and life. Ludlam acted in his own plays, often playing several roles, most of them female. After Ludlam's death the company was continued by Everett Quinton. Harvey Fierstein won mainstream acceptance for his *Torchsong Trilogy* on Broadway in 1981 and for the book of the musical *La Cage aux Folles.*

Beginning in the 1980s, the AIDS crisis generated numerous gay plays, among the first of which were Larry Kramer's *The Normal Heart* and William Hoffman's *As Is,* both in 1985. Later AIDS plays include Cheryl West's *Before It Hits Home,* Terrence McNally's *Lips Together, Teeth Apart,* and Paul Rudnick's *Jeffrey.* Tony Kushner became the most praised American playwright of the 1990s for his *Angels in America: A Gay Fantasia on National Themes,* which consists of two parts: *Millennium Approaches* and *Perestroika.* This epic play, which requires seven hours to perform, treats not only AIDS but also the crisis that faces America as concern for self overwhelms the needs of others, even loved ones. It nevertheless holds out the possibility of change (as suggested in the titles of the two parts). Few lesbian plays have made

The final scene in Tony Kushner's *Angels in America: Millennium Approaches.* The Angel is played by Ellen McLaughlin; Prior Walter by Stephen Spinella. Directed by George C. Wolfe; scenery by Robin Wagner; costumes by Toni-Leslie James; lighting by Jules Fisher. (Photo by Joan Marcus.)

their way into the mainstream. Jane Chambers' *Last Summer at Bluefish Cove* and Holly Hughes' *The Well of Horniness* are among the best known of lesbian plays.

Gay theatre companies in the United States have included TOSOS (The Other Side of the Stage), the Stonewall Theatre, The Glines, and the Meridian Gay Theatre, all in New York; Theatre Rhinoceros in San Francisco; Diversity in Houston; Lionheart in Chicago; Triangle in Boston; and Alice B. in Seattle. In 1978 a Gay Theatre Alliance was formed to link gay theatre companies. Lesbian theatres have included Lavender Cellar in Minneapolis; the Red Dyke Theatre in Atlanta; the Lesbian-Feminist Theatre Collective in Pittsburgh; and the WOW Café in New York.

As this survey indicates, the theatre has become quite diverse. Although productions seem increasingly unable to achieve universal appeal, each still may capture the attention and fill the needs of a specific group. Broadway's attempt to encompass all tastes often leaves no one satisfied. The strength of the theatre may have come to be its ability to focus and represent the interests of specific communities. Once each community has the opportunity to satisfy its own needs, it may discover the desirability of understanding others and come to recognize that major problems often stem not from the failure to understand one's own culture but the failure to understand other cultures. Ultimately, the need for intercultural may exceed the need for unicultural theatres.

Diversity and Community

In June 1994, the Theatre Communications Group, the organization created to serve not-for-profit theatres in America, held a conference titled "Theatre and Community." Much of the discussion was about the difficulty of defining "community," of discovering which community one belongs to, and whether large white-dominated theatres damage small minority-based theatres by raising funds to produce plays about African Americans, Asian Americans, Latinos, or Native Americans. One participant charged that, because they now have adopted multicultural goals, "the same flagship theatres get funded rather than the theatres really connected to the community, serving the community." Contrarily, a representative of a Latino company stated: "As far as I am concerned, when a big theatre does a Latino play, that's great, because their audiences are exposed to my culture when they otherwise might not be. I think that is a victory for us and we should celebrate it rather than saying, 'Hey, that's mine and you can't have it.'" Overall, the conference seemed to indicate that in 1994 there was more diversity than community among theatres in the United States, and that no one was sure how to harmonize the goals of disparate theatre groups. But as Peter Zeisler, executive director of Theatre Communications Group, stated: "the 'unity' at the end of the word *community* does not connote uni*formity.*" Joyce Carol Oates perhaps best summed up the hope implied by the conference title: "Where there isn't a community, we try to create one with our art. Theatres don't represent community so much as they create communities."

Epilogue

In the chapters that make up Part Two of this book, we have looked at several varieties of theatrical experience. While those we have examined are important, they do not exhaust the possibilities. Several others from the theatre's long past might justifiably have been selected for study, as might those of Asian or African societies or other aspects of today's theatre. The theatre is always in flux. Thus, the versions with which we are now familiar will change as conditions alter. We can only speculate about what these changes will be, although we can be sure they will come. Although changes are not always welcome, they are necessary, for theatre can remain vital only by reflecting the dynamics of the cultures within which it exists.

PART THREE

Theatrical Production

As we have seen, theatrical conventions and practices vary widely from one period to another and from one culture to another. So far, we have been looking at the theatre from the theoretical or historical point of view in an attempt to understand the nature of theatre and some varieties of theatrical experience. We need now to examine how the theatre functions today.

What follows is an overview of the purposes, principles, materials, and working methods of each of the theatre arts—the varied processes involved in the creation of a production. The primary focus is on typical procedures, although important variations are noted. Topics explored include types of theatrical spaces and how they influence production; the elements and principles of design used in all the theatre arts; and the work of playwrights, dramaturgs, producers, directors, actors, and designers (scenery, costume, lighting, and sound). Taken together, these topics provide an overview of theatrical production today.

The Hartford Stage production of Shakespeare's *Pericles,* an episodic play in which characters seek to find lost relatives and to mend relationships in a fragmented, unpredictable world. The narrator, center left, is dressed in Elizabethan garments, while the others are in periodless or modern dress to suggest the timelessness of the tale and its relevance to our own times. The elements of the setting and the groupings of the characters embody the fragmentation of the story. Directed by Mark Lamos. Designed by John Conklin. (Photo by T. Charles Erickson. Courtesy of the Hartford Stage.)

Chapter 10

Theatrical Space
and Production Design

Josef Svoboda's setting for Shakespeare's *Romeo and Juliet* at the Prague National Theatre. The structure at upper left seems to float in space and to disappear into a void. (Photo by Jaromir Svoboda.)

The elimination of stage-auditorium dichotomy is not the important thing—that simply creates a bare laboratory situation, an appropriate area for investigation. The essential concern is finding the proper spectator-actor relationship for each type of performance and embodying the decision in physical arrangements.

—Jerzy Grotowski, *Towards a Poor Theatre*

Because the essence of theatre lies in the interaction of performers and audience assembled in the same place at the same time, the physical space in which a performance occurs is a crucial element in the theatrical experience. Like other elements, the theatrical space can be organized in several ways, each with its own potentialities and limitations.

The Influence of Theatrical Space

The characteristics of the theatrical space influence both how the audience responds and how production elements are used. First, the degree of formality acts as an influence. An elaborate theatre building with carpeted lobbies and auditorium, fixed comfortable seating, and complex equipment creates a different set of expectations than does a theatrical space improvised in a warehouse, where the audience sits on the floor, wooden platforms, or folding chairs, and in which the equipment is minimal. The former suggests refinement, permanence (including continuity with the past), and extensive resources; it may arouse expectations of elaborate design, skilled acting, and polished productions. The latter suggests roughness, temporariness (perhaps a deliberate break with tradition), and limited resources; it may arouse expectations of experimentation and the need for imagination to supply what can only be suggested. An indoor theatre usually seems less festive than an outdoor theatre.

Second, the size of the theatrical space exerts an influence. Very large spaces make it difficult for all members of the audience to see and hear all that the performers are doing or saying; small details are likely to be lost; stage business may be simplified or enlarged; spectacle may be given increased emphasis; and sound may need to be amplified. More intimate spaces permit greater subtlety in the use of voice, gesture, and facial expression; more detail in dress and properties can also be used effectively. Intimate spaces are now generally preferred over large ones, in part because close-ups and sound tracks in television and film have conditioned audiences to expect to see and hear everything clearly. The influence of size (overall scale) on the total theatrical experience accounts for many of the differences among theatres of the past and present. A Greek theatre holding fifteen thousand demanded conventions quite different from those used in today's theatres intended for a few hundred.

Third, the arrangement (or configuration) of theatrical space is an important influence. Not only does it define the physical relationship between the performer and the audience, but it also determines how production elements can be used. There are four basic physical arrangements: (1) The acting area is placed at one end of the space, with all the spectators facing it—long the most common arrangement,

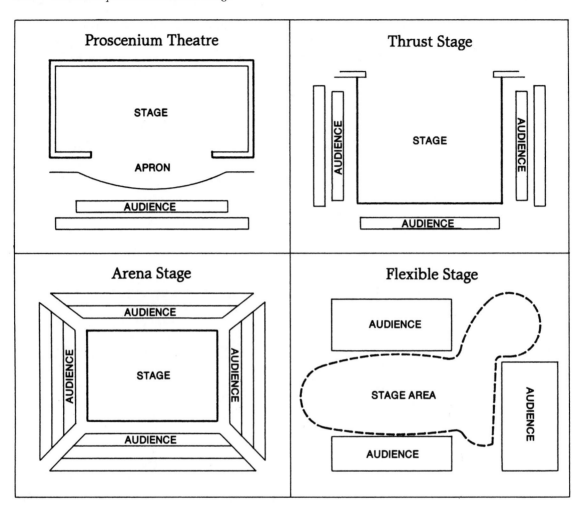

Four organizations of theatrical space: proscenium, thrust, arena, and flexible. Flexible space, as the name implies, can take many forms: the audience and performers can remain separated or be intermingled; the configuration can change during the course of a performance. (Drawings by David Betts.)

the one used for the picture-frame or proscenium arch stage; (2) the acting area is surrounded on two or three sides by the audience—the arrangement used with a thrust stage; (3) the acting area is completely surrounded by the audience—the configuration used with the arena stage (or theatre-in-the-round); and (4) the relationship of performer to audience is flexible and variable—an arrangement that may change from one production to another or even during the same performance; in such an arrangement, spectators and actors may be intermingled in multiple playing and seating areas, or the place of performance may shift, as when scenes are played at various sites along a procession route (as in medieval theatre or in some contemporary street theatre), or there may even be a different audience for each scene or at each site, although the configuration of the theatrical space may not have changed.

Overall, then, theatrical space creates an environment that influences the theatrical experience. Let us look more closely at the typical configurations and their influences.

The Proscenium Arch Theatre

Probably the most familiar type of theatre is still that with a raised stage framed by a proscenium arch, although other types have become increasingly common. In the proscenium theatre the division between stage and auditorium is clearly marked by the proscenium arch, although some part of the acting platform may extend forward of the proscenium. (This extension is called the *apron* or *forestage.*) In the auditorium, all the seats may be on the same level (though usually with the floor raked upward toward the rear to improve the view of the stage), or there may be one or more balconies. In the proscenium theatre, the stage is designed to be seen from the front only. This affects the director's use of actors in creating stage pictures, the uses of movement, gesture, and business, and the means used to achieve emphasis and subordination. It also affects the actors' bodily positions, their use of voice and speech, and all other aspects of their performance. Because the stage action is oriented in one direction, the designer may utilize three sides of the stage for the scenery, entrances, and exits. The scenery may be as tall as the designer wishes, and may consist of few or many units. There is only one fundamental restriction: The view of the audience must not be blocked. The lighting designer needs to be concerned with giving three-dimensionality to actors and objects only as dimension is perceived from the auditorium.

The proscenium stage is usually equipped with a curtain that may be used to conceal or reveal the playing space (although today the front curtain is infrequently used). The stage ordinarily has an overhead system of ropes, pulleys, and battens that permit drapes or scenic pieces to be hoisted into the space above the stage or lowered to stage level; there is usually offstage space on either side to permit the shifting and storage of scenery. There also may be other machinery for shifting scenery, such as hydraulic lifts (elevators, on which portions of the stage are mounted, thus permitting them to be lowered or raised), or turntables (revolving stages, which permit portions of the stage to be revolved). Such complex machinery is not common because of its cost.

In the proscenium theatre, the action and scenery are usually farther from the audience than in other types of theatres. There may be an orchestra pit or forestage between the first row of seats and the acting area. Because scenery and costumes typically are not viewed at close range, they may be less precisely detailed than in other types of theatres.

The Thrust Stage

In a theatre with a thrust stage, the seats are usually arranged around three (or occasionally two) sides of a raised platform. The thrust stage brings the audience and performers into a more intimate relationship than in the proscenium theatre because

The thrust stage at the Stratford (Canada) Shakespearean Festival Theatre. Designed specifically to accommodate Shakespeare's plays, it incorporates features of the Elizabethan public stage. (Courtesy of the Stratford Shakespearean Festival Foundation of Canada.)

more of the audience is closer to the action than is possible in a proscenium theatre of the same size. Because it is usually seen from three sides, the acting area is a more three-dimensional space than the proscenium stage; the director, actors, and designers must seek to project in three directions simultaneously rather than, as in the proscenium theatre, only one.

The thrust stage discourages realistic spectacle of the type made possible by the picture-frame stage. Its use of scenery must be restricted. Tall units must be kept to the rear of the platform so as not to interfere with sightlines. Although some thrust stages are backed by an area equipped with flying facilities like those of a proscenium stage, extensive use of scenic effects there divides audience attention between the action on the main stage and scenic or lighting effects on a rear stage. Most thrust theatres make no provision for flying scenery, drops, or curtains above the main platform, although lighting instruments are usually mounted in recesses in the ceiling above the stage. As a rule, furniture, properties, and scenic units are shifted by hand. Some furniture or properties may be mounted on wheeled platforms and moved on and off the stage from the rear of the platform. A few thrust stages have some portions mounted on hydraulic lifts, and there may be several traps in the stage floor. But all onstage units must remain simple to avoid interfering with audience sightlines.

The Arena Stage

The typical arena theatre has no stage as such (that is, there is no raised platform). Rather, an open space is left at floor level in the middle of the auditorium. In some arena theatres, the floor of the performance area can be raised or lowered in segments to provide variety in levels or to differentiate locales. The seating is usually a stepped arrangement on four sides of the acting area. In some theatres of this type, the seats are not permanently installed, and the configuration may be varied at will, but in others comfortable armchair seating of the kind typical of proscenium theatres is used.

Because the arena theatre provides a three-dimensional playing area, the director, actors, and designers must be concerned with expressiveness from every angle. The costumed actors, lighting, furniture, and properties are much more important than scenery. The scene designer may use a few open structures—such as trellises and pavilions, through which the audience can see—but ordinarily depends on furniture and properties. Provision is seldom made for flying scenery, although a few architectural fragments may be suspended overhead. Occasionally, multileveled settings are used, but they must be constructed so that the audience can clearly see the action on all levels. Screens for projections are sometimes hung at various spots over the acting area, over the audience, or around the walls (the same image may be projected on different screens simultaneously so that all members of the audience can

Setting on an arena stage for Miller's *Death of a Salesman*. Notice how the demand to keep sightlines open from all sides has influenced the design. The Lomans' house is suggested by the suspended roof overhead and a sense of period is created by the detailing on the upright posts. Design by Karl Eigsti. (Courtesy of the Arena Stage, Washington.)

see it), but usually the set designer must suggest locale, period, mood, and style with a few touches.

Because there is no curtain, all changes are made either in full view of the audience or in semidarkness. All shifting is usually done by hand. Many arena theatres have passageways (vomitoria) running under the seating and opening onto the acting area. These serve as exits and entrances for actors and as means of getting scenic units or properties on and off the stage. Most arena stages are relatively small and intimate but make special demands on staging because all elements are viewed and must communicate from every angle.

Flexible Space

In modern times, the intermingling of performers and audiences has occurred primarily since the 1960s. This arrangement usually requires an open space without fixed seating or stage. Many regional and university theatres have such a space, usually in addition to a proscenium or thrust stage. Often referred to as a "black box" (because it is basically a bare room with black walls), it is most frequently used for productions with limited or special appeal—nontraditional works or performance modes, new or untested plays, low-budget or student productions.

A flexible space may be indoor or outdoor, small or large. The areas used by the performers or by the audience may be varied from one production to the next

Flexible space as created by the Bread and Puppet's *Domestic Resurrection Circus*. The audience in the foreground moves to follow the puppet figures from one place to another. (Photo by Craig Hamilton.)

Theatre Architecture

In *The Shapes of Our Theatres*, Jo Mielziner writes: "All theatre interiors consist of two essential areas: one is 'the auditorium,' which is designed specifically for the audience; the other, designed for the production, we know as 'the stage.' . . . Independently they have no life; together they produce a living theatre. It is therefore the sensitive interrelationship of the two that makes a theatre design either a success or a failure."

In the twentieth century, however, many persons have objected to the dichotomy between auditorium and stage and have sought means to bridge them. Laszlo Moholy-Nagy writes: "Stage and spectator are too much separated, too obviously divided into active and passive, to be able to produce creative relationships and reciprocal tensions. It is time to produce a kind of stage activity that will no longer permit the audience to be silent spectators." He suggested building auditoriums with "suspended bridges and drawbridges running horizontally, diagonally, and vertically." He also suggested segments of the stage capable of moving toward the spectators to create effects similar to those of close-ups in film; runways that extend completely around the seating area; and other devices that place the spectator in a dynamic relationship with the action.

Marvin Carlson concludes in his *Places of Performance* that, as a result of twentieth-century experiments with theatrical space, "Never before in history has a public had available for its consideration" so many diverse "physical spaces in which theatre today may be presented. . . . In addition to this huge selection of historical spaces, the twentieth century has produced experimental directors who have explored the possibilities of an almost infinite variety of nontraditional spaces": streets, parks, woodlands, factories, warehouses, and "all manner of public and private buildings."

or even during the course of a single performance. In this type of arrangement, different scenes are sometimes performed at various places within the space simultaneously. Unlike most theatrical performances, which seek to have all members of the audience see and hear the same things at the same time, the intermingled arrangement may use multiple focus. Some spectators may be watching one scene while others are watching another, or spectators may be able to choose which scenes they will watch, moving about in the space in order to see the scene that has attracted their attention. Sometimes spectators participate in the action and are asked by the performers to move or to assist with some task. In other instances, the distinctions between performers and spectators remain clear and the space each group occupies remains distinct; in still others, the entire space becomes both acting area and spectator space. Flexibility also encompasses processional staging, with the performers moving from one location to another (usually outdoors). The key is flexibility in the use of all theatrical elements.

Beginning in the 1960s, there was a movement to reject theatre buildings altogether. Some argued that, like museums and concert halls, theatres discourage all except a cultural elite. These innovators sought instead to take performances into parks, streets, and other places where theatrically unsophisticated spectators might discover the theatre. Instead of a building, they advocated the use of "found" space, either adapting a production to fit existing areas or altering existing areas to fit the needs of the productions. The variety of audience-performer configurations was great, but all could be reduced to one or some combination of the four basic types of theatrical space. Experimentation with performance spaces reminds us that theatre does not require a permanent structure built especially for it, and that all spatial arrangements are merely ways of facilitating the interaction of performers and audiences.

Auxiliary Spaces

In addition to the performance space, theatre buildings usually have a number of auxiliary spaces. Several of these are intended to serve the audience—lobby, rest rooms, corridors, exits, and refreshment stands. Others are spaces for theatrical personnel, such as box office and other work space.

The amount of work space provided in theatres varies widely. A well-designed, self-contained theatre (one with facilities for preparing productions as well as performing them) will include all or most of the following: a scene construction shop (with space to store equipment and materials), painting facilities, an area for assembling scenery, sufficient offstage space for storing and shifting scenery during performances, and permanent storage space for scenery not in use; a property room near the stage and another area for the permanent storage of furniture and bulky props; a costume construction shop, with laundry, dyeing, cleaning, and pressing facilities, and an area for permanent storage of costumes; a work space for lighting personnel, a storage area for lighting equipment, and a lighting booth for the controlboard operator during performances (ideally with full view of the stage); multiple large rehearsal rooms; several dressing rooms, each with makeup facilities (unless a separate makeup room is provided); adequate showers and rest rooms for the actors and crews, and an area (the *green room*) where all the actors and crew members can assemble to receive instructions or relax; space to house sound equipment and from which to operate it; and adequate office and work space for such personnel as dramaturgs, artistic directors, and business managers.

Many theatres, especially those on Broadway, as well as many of those used by low-budget companies, do not include the full range of work facilities listed above. On Broadway, theatres provide performance space only; productions are rehearsed elsewhere, costumes and scenery are built in studios far removed from the theatre, and backstage space is often minimally equipped. Broadway theatres host productions rather than serve as the permanent home of a company. Many small companies, such as Off-Off-Broadway groups, even if they are permanent, often function in very limited facilities. Regional and university theatres usually have the best facilities.

Using the Theatrical Space

Normally, in planning a production little is done to shape the audience and its space. Most directors assume that the audience space of the theatre in which they will be working is fixed—as is the case in the majority of theatres. While directors must take into account the auditorium's size, shape, sightlines, acoustical properties, and the physical relationship it creates between audience and performers, most tend to view these factors as given and unchangeable circumstances. Directors may try to predict what the makeup of the audience will be and how it is likely to respond, but for the most part they conceive of the audience members as reactors who come to see a production created for them. Some theatrical spaces are designed so that their overall configuration and audience-actor relationship can be easily altered. In these instances, directors may shape the audience space to suit their production.

Jerzy Grotowski made audiences an integral part of his production design. For each production, he had a specific number of spectators in mind (never more than one hundred), and he would permit no more than that number to attend. He also sought to induce the audience to participate in the action unself-consciously. In his production of *Doctor Faustus*, Grotowski organized the space like a banqueting hall. The audience, treated as friends invited to share Faustus' last meal before his soul is claimed by the Devil (to whom he has sold it many years earlier), sat at the tables while the action took place on, under, and around the tables. The German director Peter Stein staged several productions in film studios or gutted and rearranged theatrical spaces. In his production of *Peer Gynt*, all of the seats in a conventional proscenium arch theatre were removed to clear the floor space for the dramatic action. New bleacher-style seating was erected along the sides, leaving an area approximately seventy feet long on which scenic units, representing the various locales of the action, were erected. The actors moved from one locale to another as in a medieval outdoor theatre. This production required two full evenings to perform.

Grotowski's arrangement of the space for *Doctor Faustus*. The dark figures are performers, the lighter figures spectators. Faustus is seated at the smaller table at top. (Copyright 1968 by Jerzy Grotowski and Odin Teatrets Forlag. Courtesy of H. Martin Berg.)

Peter Stein's production of Ibsen's *Peer Gynt*. This scene shows the insane asylum at the foot of the Sphinx in Egypt. The audience seating is beyond the board wall at left. (Courtesy of the German Information Center.)

(One scene is shown in the photo above.) The Living Theatre often encouraged the audience and actors to use the same space indiscriminately, thereby forcing some spectators to become unwilling participants in the action.

But these are atypical approaches. Normally, the director lets others (through publicity, news releases, and other means) attract as large an audience as possible to the space being used for the production.

Production Design

A production is a composite of messages composed by combining visual and aural signs. The director, actors, and designers shape the signs to arouse a set of desired audience responses. But the possibilities are so numerous (in terms of the ways the signs can be shaped, how skillfully they are shaped and coordinated, and how spectators respond to the shaping) that the results can seldom be fully controlled. Nevertheless, each production has an overall design, an assemblage of many parts.

The total theatrical design usually addresses only two of the spectators' five senses: hearing and sight. Hearing is addressed primarily through the sound of the actors' voices but also through music or sound effects. A large proportion of the director's and actors' work is devoted to conveying relationships, motivations, emotions, ideas, and meaning through the skillful handling of dialogue, intonation, stress, rhythm, volume, and rate. Other (or many of the same) messages may depend on elements directed to sight. Although we normally think of visual design in terms of scenery, costumes, and lighting, directors and actors also make use of visual design. How the actors are grouped and move on stage, how much space they use, and how they relate to each other and to the setting, costumes, and properties communicate messages quite apart from or in conjunction with the spoken dialogue.

Preparing a theatrical production involves encoding messages that the audience decodes. Among the means that the various theatre artists use in creating messages are the elements and principles of design. How audiences respond depends on how these aspects of design have been shaped. Although in discussion elements and principles may sound abstract, they are manifested concretely during every moment of a theatrical performance. One of the challenges of production arises from the need to coordinate individually conceived parts (in acting, scenery, costumes, lighting) to create a whole capable of eliciting desired responses and interpretations.

The Elements of Visual Design

All visual aspects of a production are composed from the same basic elements—*line, shape, space, color, texture,* and *ornament.*

Line defines boundaries and permits us to perceive shape and form. There are two kinds of line—straight and curved—but these may be combined to form zigzags, scallops, and many other variations. The dominant lines of the performance space (with the scenery in place but without performers) are horizontal (the floor and any overhead masking) and vertical (the upright scenic units). This basic pattern is varied by the addition of furniture, ramps, steps, and platforms. In performance, other lines are created through movement and by the placement of the actors in relation to each other and to the scenic elements. The costumes worn by the actors have their own lines created by the silhouette of garments and by darts, seams, ornamentation, and other features that result in visible lines.

Line is often said to evoke identifiable responses: straight lines, stability; curved lines, grace; zigzags, confusion. Therefore, line may be manipulated to achieve desired effects. In scenery, two lines that move farther apart as they rise vertically may generate a feeling of openness, whereas lines that lean in as they rise may create a sense of oppression. Line is important in creating mood and atmosphere as well as in defining shape.

Shape and *space* are closely related and are frequently treated together as a single element: *mass.* While line has only direction or length, mass involves three dimensions. It identifies shape (square, round, oblong, and so on) and space (height, width, and thickness). The stage may be thought of as a hollow cube that can be organized or altered in a variety of ways. Scenery may outline or limit the space. So may light, the actors' movement, or the seating around a thrust or arena stage. Like line, shape and space may be used to affect audience response. An effect of compression may be achieved through the use of thick, horizontal forms overhead (such as a low ceiling

Line plays a major role in this setting by Douglas Stein for Ostrovsky's *Too Clever by Half* at the Guthrie Theatre. The setting seemed to be constructed of lined yellow legal paper, giving a house-of-cards effect. Notice also how the costumes distort shape. The actors are Monica E. Scott, Jennifer Jordan Campbell, Cheryl Moore Brinkley, Julie Briskman Hall, and Brenda Wehle. Directed by Garland Wright. (Courtesy of the Guthrie Theatre.)

with thick beams), while a sense of openness and grace may be achieved with narrow, vertical, and pointed forms (such as thin, tall columns and high gothic arches). Mass is also reflected in the overall shape of costumes and furniture, the space they occupy, and in the way a director groups or isolates actors. Perhaps the most effective means of revealing, concealing, or altering apparent mass is lighting, which through its direction and intensity can create or eliminate those contrasts of light and shadow that let us perceive shape and dimension.

Color may be described in terms of three basic properties: hue, saturation or intensity, and value. *Hue* is the attribute that allows us to identify a color (red, green, blue, and so on). *Saturation* or *intensity* refers to the relative purity of a color (its freedom from its complementary or opposite hue). *Value* is the lightness or darkness of a color—its relation to white or black. A color that is light in value is usually called a *tint,* one dark in value is called a *shade.* Hues are classified as primary, secondary, or intermediate. The *primary* hues are those that cannot be created by mixing other hues, but from which all other hues are derived. The primary hues in pigment are yellow, red, and blue. The *secondary* hues—orange, violet, and green—are created from equal mixtures of two primary hues. The *intermediate* hues are mixtures of a primary with a secondary hue. Hues may be arranged around a wheel to indicate their relationships. (See the color wheel, plate 14.) Those opposite each other on the wheel are called complementary, those next to each other,

Texture is one of the most important elements in these costumes by Desmond Heeley for *Oedipus the King*. Notice the difference between the textures of the costumes worn by Oedipus (standing center), the Shepherd (kneeling), and the Guards (in the background). (Courtesy of the Guthrie Theatre.)

analogous. The primary hues are equidistant from each other on the wheel. Hues may further be described as warm or cool. Red, orange, and yellow are warm; green, blue, and violet are cool. Almost any combination of hues may be used together if saturation, proportion, and value are properly controlled.

Mood and atmosphere depend much on color. Many people believe that light, warm colors are more suitable to comedy than are dark, cool colors. Some color combinations are considered garish, others sophisticated. Designers may manipulate color to create the appropriate mood and atmosphere and to establish the tastes of the characters who inhabit the settings or wear the costumes. Color can suggest the relationship among characters (either sympathetic or antipathetic) through the colors of their garments. Color can be used to make some characters stand out and others fade into the background (for example, Hamlet wears mourning black in the midst of others dressed in colors of rejoicing). As with mass, lighting is one of the most important means of controlling color because it can enhance, distort, or reduce apparent color in scenery, costumes, makeup, and all the other elements.

Texture may help to elicit the desired response through such qualities as smoothness, roughness, shininess, softness, or graininess. Some plays seem to demand rough textures, others smooth. Such qualities as sleaziness, fragility, or richness depend much on the texture (actual or simulated) of settings, costumes, and (by analogy) acting.

Ornament includes the paintings, decorative motifs, wallpaper patterns, moldings, and similar details of settings. It is one of the chief means of achieving distinctiveness. In costume, ornament includes ruffles, buttons, fringe, and lace. Ornament can be used to indicate taste or the lack of it. Too much ornamentation or too many kinds of ornamentation may indicate lack of restraint or impart a sense of clutter. Accessories, such as canes, swords, purses, and jewelry, may also be considered ornaments. In acting, gesture and stage business (the amount and complexity, and its relative simplicity or fussiness) serve much the same function as ornament in visual design.

The Principles of Design

In applying the elements of design, certain principles must be used if the results are to be effective. The principles of design are harmony, variety, balance, proportion, emphasis, and rhythm.

Harmony creates the impression of unity. Typically directors and designers seek to harmonize the parts of each setting or costume and to relate the various settings and costumes in such a way that all are clearly parts of a whole. If monotony is to be avoided, however, *variety* is needed. Similarly, directors seek both harmony and variety through their choice of actors and through each actor's use of movement and gesture.

Balance is the sense of stability that results from the distribution of the parts that make up the total picture. There are three types of balance. The most common is *axial*, achieved by the apparent equal distribution of weight on either side of a central axis. This type is especially pertinent to the proscenium stage, which may be

Proportion, or scale, is manipulated in these costume designs to comment on character stereotypes. The figure at left, one actor on the shoulders of another, is a psychiatrist, while the figure at right is physically and psychologically subordinated by making him appear small and dressing him in child's clothing. Scene from *The Managed Mind* as performed at the Hamburg Schauspielhaus. (Courtesy of the German Information Center.)

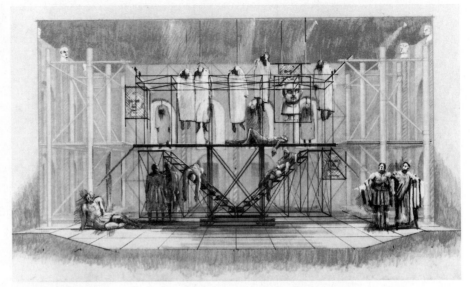

In Richard Isackes' sketch of a setting for Shakespeare's *Julius Caesar* at the Utah Shakespearean Festival considerable variety is achieved through contrasting line (vertical, horizontal, diagonal, curved) and rhythmic progressions (seen in the upright scaffolding and the stairways); balance is achieved through contrasting mass; overall harmony is maintained through stylistic unity. (Courtesy Richard Isackes.)

thought of as a fulcrum (or seesaw) with the point of balance at the center. Axial balance is achieved if the elements placed on each side of the central line appear equal in weight. Apparent visual weight is not the same as actual weight because a large light-colored object may appear to weigh no more than a small dark-colored object, and a small object near the outer edge may balance a large object near the center. A second type of balance, *radial,* is organization that radiates in every direction from a central point. It is especially important on arena and thrust stages because these stages are viewed from several angles. A third kind of balance is usually called *occult.* It is especially pertinent to flexible and variable staging, in which there may be no readily discernible axis or center. Occult balance results from the relationship of mass to space and among unlike objects.

Balance, especially axial, may also be thought of as symmetrical or asymmetrical. *Symmetrical* balance means that if an object or space is divided down the middle, each side mirrors the other. Most costumes (especially before ornaments or accessories are added) are symmetrical. Complete symmetry in a stage setting creates a sense of formality and order; *asymmetry,* which depends on irregularity, may create a sense of informality or casualness. In performance, when the stage picture is constantly shifting because of the movement of the actors, directors must be especially aware of balance and how it is affected by what the actors do. During rehearsals, a director may adjust the position of actors in order to achieve balance.

Proportion involves the relationship between the parts of individual elements as well as the relationship among all the parts that make up the total picture: the scale of each part in relation to all the others; the relationship among shapes; and the division of the space (for example, the length of a dress bodice in relation to the skirt). Proportion can create the impression of stability or instability, of grace or awkwardness. Furniture disproportionate to the size of a room may create either a cramped or meager feeling. Our perception of beauty or ugliness depends largely on the proportion of parts. In costume, the manipulation of proportion can do much to change an actor's appearance and enhance or disguise attributes.

All designs need a focal point, or center of *emphasis*. Directors are constantly seeking to focus attention on what they consider most important and to subordinate the things of lesser concern. A well-composed scene or design directs attention to the most important point immediately and then to the subordinate parts. Emphasis may be achieved in several ways, among them line, mass, color, texture, ornamentation, contrast, and movement. The setting may make one area of the stage more emphatic than others; a costume may use emphasis to draw attention to an actor's good points and away from defects; movement within an otherwise-still picture will always attract the eye.

Rhythm is the principle that leads the eye easily and smoothly from one part of a design to another. All the elements of design may be used for rhythmic purposes. Lines and shapes may be repeated; the size of objects or the amount of movement may be changed gradually to give a sense of progression; gradations in hue, saturation, and value may lead the eye from one point to another; changes or repetitions in texture and ornament may give a sense of flow and change; and the movement of the actors may increase or diminish in tempo.

Appia on Hierarchy in Production Design

Many persons have commented on the relative importance of the elements that make up a production. Adolphe Appia, one of the twentieth century's major theoreticians of the theatre, had strong convictions about hierarchy in production design:

> The first factor in staging is the interpreter, the actor. The actor carries the action. Without him there is no action, hence no drama. Everything must be subordinated . . . to this element—which takes first rank hierarchically. . . . the body is alive, moving and plastic; it has three dimensions. Space . . . must conform to his plastic form, his three dimensions. What else is there: Light! . . . Like the actor, light must become active; . . . it must be put to the service of . . . the actor's dramatic and plastic expression. . . . Here is our normally established hierarchy: the actor presenting the drama, three-dimensional space at the service of the actor's plastic form, light, giving life to both.

—*Adolphe Appia, "Actor, Space, Light, Painting"*

Sound in Design

Sound is also an essential part of the total production design. Sound in the theatre may be divided into three categories: vocal, musical, and sound effects. Of these, the sound of the actors' voices is usually the most important, for it is through what the characters say and how they say it that we typically assess situations, motivations, and responses. Voice may also be used to sing or to create a variety of sounds that do not involve words. Music may be a necessary feature in a theatrical production, as in musicals, or it may be incidental, an optional addition to establish mood or to enliven an occasion. Sound effects may be realistic (doorbells, alarm clocks, breaking glass, thunder, and the like) or wholly abstract (sounds with no recognizable origin used to punctuate the action, to underscore a theme, or establish a mood).

Robert Wilson's production of Büchner's *Danton's Death* at the Alley Theatre (Houston). Notice the bold contrast between the rear and forward stage spaces and how the pointed arm and stretched cloth draw focus to the figure at rear despite the strong frontal position of Danton (Richard Thomas). (Photo © T. Charles Erickson.)

Sound has several controllable properties: pitch (or frequency), volume (or amplitude), quality (or timbre), direction, and duration. Sound is created by pressure waves that move outward from the source of the sound. Each sound has its own wavelength or frequency, usually referred to as *pitch,* the primary way by which we distinguish one sound from another. In the theatre, pitch is probably most important as it relates to the speaking or singing voice, but even a doorbell and other sound effects have pitch. It is possible to choose voices and other sounds in terms of pitches that will create the desired effects.

Amplitude is the height of a sound wave, most frequently referred to as *volume* or *intensity.* As sound waves move, they diminish in height and thus in volume. Volume is measured in decibels. Any pitch (or frequency) can be produced at any decibel level, which may be controlled either through the natural capacity of the instrument (the human voice, trumpet, and so on) or through electronic means. In the theatre, it is often necessary to lower the volume of some sounds and increase the volume of others to achieve the desired balance. For example, the audience may need to understand what characters are saying, even though they are speaking against the noise of a passing train. In large theatres, it is often difficult for actors to make themselves heard clearly even when they are not competing with other sounds; in such instances, amplification may be used.

Sound has *quality* (or *timbre*). Most sounds are combinations of frequencies and amplitudes; this complexity creates distinctive qualities. Timbre permits us to distinguish between two human voices even if the same sounds are spoken at the same pitch and volume. It also permits us to distinguish between types of musical instruments and natural sounds. Thunder is recognized in part by its rumbling, echoing quality, just as an alarm clock may be by its shrillness or a gunshot by its explosiveness. In the speaking or singing voice, quality is especially important. Shrill, harsh vocal qualities seem inappropriate in admirable characters because the unpleasantness of the voice contradicts the pleasant traits. The selection of appropriate sound qualities, whether in the actors' voices or in sound effects, is an important part of production design.

Sound also has *direction.* With well-designed and skillfully operated equipment, it is possible to make sound appear to begin at any place in the theatre and move from one point to another. For example, the sound of a car may become barely audible from one side of the stage, seem to approach, pass behind the set, and then pass out of hearing on the other side. Or directional sound may make an airplane seemingly pass directly over the audience.

Sound has *duration;* it can be prolonged or shortened. Many decisions about duration also involve timing. In a storm scene, for example, someone must decide when thunder is to begin, how long it is to continue, when it is to reach its peak, and when it is to die away.

All of the controllable properties of sound may be varied in relation to each other and in accordance with the demands of a production. Like the visual elements, they need to be shaped in terms of unity, variety, proportion, balance, emphasis, and rhythm.

The Integrated Production Design

Although each visual and aural element, considered in isolation, is capable of projecting a message and evoking a response, in actuality elements are seldom wholly separated from each other. In theatrical production, most are present simultaneously, and their relationships change continually as the action develops. The messages of individual elements are modified by those of all the other elements and combine to make up the total impact. How each is shaped also depends in part on the theatrical space in which the performance occurs. The ways in which theatre artists in each area of theatrical production seek to shape the elements at their disposal are explored in the chapters that follow.

Chapter 11

Playwriting and Dramaturgy

A read-through of a play at the National Playwrights Conference in the Barn Theatre at the Eugene O'Neill Theatre Center, Waterford, CT. (Photo by A. Vincent Scarano. Courtesy of the Eugene O'Neill Theatre Center.)

[A] play in a book is only the shadow of a play and not even a clear shadow of it. . . . The printed script of a play is hardly more than an architect's blueprint of a house not built or built and destroyed.

—Tennessee Williams, "Afterword," *Camino Real*

In the contemporary theatre, although a script is typically the beginning point of a production, its creator, the playwright, is usually the theatre artist most removed from the process of play production. It has not always been so. Greek playwrights usually staged their own works. Shakespeare wrote his plays for the company in which he acted, apparently knew in advance who would play each role, and was undoubtedly involved in staging his own plays. Molière was head of his own company as well as its principal playwright and actor. But since the nineteenth century, playwrights have usually worked in isolation—not knowing, while writing, who would act in their plays or if they would be able to find someone willing to produce their scripts. Only a few playwrights today have close ties to theatre organizations. Even those writers fortunate enough to have directors or theatres to collaborate with them on developing scripts usually work alone until the script has reached a point where input from others can be helpful. Thus, the initial stage of writing is typically a personal and isolated process.

The Playwright

The source of inspiration for a play cannot be foreseen. It may be a newspaper article, a personal experience, a criminal act (for example, a mother killing her children) for which the motives are unclear, or from almost any other source because the possibilities of drama are ever-present and because almost anything has the potential to stimulate a dramatist's imagination. Each writer has a view of the world or a range of interests that make some subjects more attractive than others. Samuel Beckett was preoccupied with the human predicament in an unknowable universe, whereas Henrik Ibsen was concerned with personal and social morality in an explainable universe. While both sought to write truthfully, their interests drew them to widely differing subjects, just as their perceptions about human beings and the human condition caused them to treat their subjects distinctively.

Playwrights' working methods vary widely. Bertolt Brecht began with an outline and then elaborated on it. Victorien Sardou (the most successful French dramatist of the nineteenth century) wrote the climactic scene first and then worked backward from it. Henrik Ibsen made numerous notes about situations and characters, often over a period of years, before actually beginning a play. Sam Shepard has said that he begins with a visual image and starts writing without knowing where it will lead. Since the 1960s, several plays have been written with the aid of group improvisations. The playwright presents an outline, situation, or idea to a group of actors who then improvises on this material; as story, movement, and dialogue develop, the dramatist selects and shapes what seems most effective until a script has emerged. As these variations suggest, writers discover those procedures that work best for themselves without regard for what works for others.

The mechanics of playwriting also vary widely from one writer to another. (Basic structural patterns, form, and style are discussed in Chapter 3, to which the reader is referred for those aspects of playwriting.) Beckett did most of his writing by hand in bound notebooks. Some writers compose at a typewriter or word processor; others talk into tape recorders. However they proceed, writers seldom arrive at the final version of a script in the first draft. It is sometimes said that plays are not written but rewritten. Some writers spend years refining a script. On the other hand, Sam Shepard long refused to revise at all on the grounds that to do so would be like lying because it would deny what he had originally set down.

Because plays are intended for the stage, most writers need to see their work performed before they can be sure they have accomplished what they intended. Lines that look effective on paper may sound contrived when spoken. A writer needs to be certain that the dialogue places the emphasis of a speech at just the right point, that the rhythms are effective when spoken aloud, that speeches make their intended points, that the vocal patterns are appropriate to each character, and that the interaction among characters seems believable. The writer usually also seeks to make sure

Playwrights Horizons

In developing a script, most playwrights feel the need to see their work performed, to be allowed time to revise it in light of what has been learned, and then to see it performed again. One group dedicated to working with writers in this fashion is Playwrights Horizons. Founded in 1971 by Robert Moss to "support and develop the work of contemporary American playwrights, composers, and lyricists," it was under the direction of André Bishop from 1978 to 1991 and subsequently Don Scardino. To accommodate its productions, the company has carved two spaces out of a former pornographic film house on West 42nd Street in New York City. The larger space seats 147, the smaller 74. A number of notable plays have originated there, including Wendy Wasserstein's *The Heidi Chronicles,* Alfred Uhry's *Driving Miss Daisy,* Stephen Sondheim and James Lapine's *Sunday in the Park with George,* Christopher Durang's *Sister Mary Ignatius Explains It All For You,* and William Finn's *Falsettoland.* Plays are revised and rehearsed, given a limited number of performances, reworked (sometimes over several years), and performed again. In the 1993–94 season it read, evaluated, and responded to almost two thousand plays, produced more than thirty readings of new plays, staged four productions on its main stage and three in its smaller theatre; it also began development on four new musicals, continued three musical projects from the preceding season, awarded three new playwriting commissions, and started a film-development program with Steven Spielberg's Amblin Entertainment. Few organizations maintain such an ambitious program, but several others seek to assist writers in developing their scripts until they are ready for public performance.

Falsettoland, a musical by William Finn and James Lapine, was developed at Playwrights Horizons before moving first to an Off-Broadway and then to a Broadway theatre. In the foreground are Stephen Bogardus (left) and Danny Gerard. Directed by James Lapine. (Photo © Gerry Goodstein.)

that the dramatic action is clear, that revelations create the intended effect, that tension mounts, relaxes, and builds to a climax. In summary, the dramatist must create a play that is effective in performance and not merely on the page.

The types of assistance the playwright needs and can get in developing a script vary widely. An initial step may involve a reading of the play aloud by one or more persons (preferably a different person for each character) so the playwright can hear his work. Others who are present may voice their reactions so the writer can get some sense of how an audience responds to the script. This type of reading usually provides the playwright a basis for revisions, but it also creates a problem that every playwright must ultimately deal with: assessing the validity of the responses. Many listeners may volunteer advice, but advice from one source often contradicts advice from another; the writer must decide which responses are valid or helpful. After revisions have been made, the next step may be a staged reading, in which actors, usually with scripts in hand and after some rehearsal, not only speak the dialogue but also sketch out the stage action. After assessing the script as presented and the audience's responses, the playwright usually makes further revisions.

Some playwrights are fortunate enough to be members of a playwrights' workshop where scripts can be worked on over a period of time in a process that in-

Among the plays first developed in workshop productions and then produced at regional not-for-profit theatres before coming to Broadway is Wendy Wasserstein's *The Heidi Chronicles*. This play also won the Pulitzer Prize, Tony Award, and the New York Drama Critics' Circle Award. Shown here is a scene from the production at the Trinity Repertory Company (Providence, RI). The actors are Fred Sullivan, Jr., Cynthia Strickland, Andrew Mutnick, and Nanette Van Wright. Directed by Leonard Foglia. (Photo by Mark Morelli. Courtesy of the Trinity Repertory Company.)

cludes multiple opportunities for rehearsed readings or performances. The Eugene O'Neill Theatre Center in Waterford, Connecticut, is one organization providing this kind of help. Each summer it selects a few playwrights to be in residence and develop their scripts with the help of a director, actors, critics, and audience.

Ultimately, full production is the goal. The Actors Theatre of Louisville has been especially helpful to playwrights in realizing this goal. Each fall it mounts a festival of new short plays, and in the spring a festival of new full-length plays. Critics and producers from the United States and abroad attend this major showcase of playwriting talent. In New York, several organizations, including the LaMama Experimental Theatre Club and the Manhattan Theatre Club, assist dramatists in developing scripts through fully mounted productions. In recent years, a few playwrights have had their plays given fully mounted productions at multiple regional professional theatres, the intervals between the productions usually being used to revise the script. Among the scripts that have gone through this process are Wendy Wasserstein's *The Heidi Chronicles*, August Wilson's *The Piano Lesson*, and Tony Kushner's *Angels in America*, all of which won Pulitzer Prizes. Most of the plays now seen on Broadway have profited from some comparable developmental process before being presented there.

Unfortunately, the number of writers who obtain assistance in developing their scripts is relatively small. Many writers complete their scripts without the benefit of readings or performance. However it has come into being, a script will probably seem only partially complete to its author unless it is translated from the page to the stage; this requires finding a producer. Playwrights frequently send copies of their plays to various resident theatres, but because these theatres often receive several hundred unsolicited plays each year, they may not read all of them. Some read no unsolicited scripts. Thus, despite playwrights' efforts, some plays are never produced. In fact, relatively few plays receive productions in professional theatres.

The difficulties of finding a producer and making contractual arrangements are so complex that most writers prefer to work through an agent. Securing an agent is not easy because agents make their living from a percentage (usually ten percent) of each client's earnings and therefore choose to represent only those they consider potentially successful. Agents can be of great help, nevertheless, because they understand the legal and financial aspects of producing and can help to place plays and negotiate contracts.

A producer who is interested in a script may take an option on it, which gives the producer the exclusive right to the play for a specified period of time. If the producer decides to stage the play, a contract is drawn up. The typical provisions of contracts are set forth by the Dramatists Guild, an organization to which most playwrights belong and which seeks to protect the rights of playwrights by establishing professional and contractual standards for its members. The writer seldom relinquishes television, film, amateur, or foreign rights to the producer because these may eventually be far more financially rewarding than the initial production. The contract usually specifies that the writer must be available for consultation and revisions throughout the rehearsal period—conditions that most playwrights are eager to meet.

During rehearsals, many changes may be made in a script. Some of these may result from work with a new-play dramaturg (a process discussed later in this chapter). The director, as the artist (next to the writer) most fully involved in the script, often makes suggestions for revisions. The playwright-director relationship can be productive when it is based on mutual respect. But sometimes directors make demands that writers think unjustified. When *Cat on a Hot Tin Roof* was first presented on Broadway, Tennessee Williams was cajoled by the director, Elia Kazan, into rewriting the final act. Williams was so unhappy with the results that when he published the play he included both his preferred version and the one he had written to please Kazan. Producers may also suggest or demand revisions thought to increase the play's box-office appeal or to keep down costs. Although playwrights' contracts state that they need not make changes they consider undesirable, they often accede to changes rather than risk cancellation of the production or denial of future productions. Most playwrights now prefer to work in regional or Off-Off-Broadway theatres because such organizations are much more sensitive to the writer's wishes than is Broadway, where the sums of money invested make producers less willing to take chances.

Most new scripts are revised right up to opening night. Many theatres now have a series of preview performances to which tickets are sold but from which critics are excluded. Previews supposedly permit audience response to be assessed and used in fine-tuning the script and production before the official opening takes place and reviews are written for publication. Further rewriting may be done following the initial production, but most playwrights feel the need to put this experience behind them and go on to new projects. Nevertheless, a playwright may continue to rework a script over many years and through several productions. Tennessee Williams, late in his career, wrote new versions of many of his earlier plays.

The Dramaturg

Many theatres now have a dramaturg (sometimes with assistants) on their staff. Because this position is relatively recent in the United States (primarily only in the past twenty years or less), it is still not widely understood, in part because the duties and working procedures of the dramaturg differ markedly from one theatre organization to another.

The dramaturg is not a recent innovation. In Europe the position is usually traced back to Gotthold Ephraim Lessing, an eighteenth-century German playwright and critic. In 1767, upon being asked by the newly created Hamburg National Theater to serve as its resident playwright, Lessing declined but suggested instead that he become its in-house critic, offering advice on the selection of plays, critiquing the company's productions, and publishing a journal through which he sought to influence public taste by setting forth his theories about the nature and purposes of drama. His offer was accepted and, although the Hamburg National Theater lasted only two years, Lessing's work there established a precedent for later companies. The function he fulfilled later became standard in the many government-owned and -subsidized theatres of Germany and elsewhere in Europe. Only gradually did it find favor in English-speaking theatres, in which it has gained ground gradually only since the 1970s.

Dramaturgy and Literary Management

In the United States, the scope of dramaturgy varies widely from one company to another. It can be divided roughly into two parts: (1) literary management—finding, developing, or shaping scripts, and (2) production dramaturgy—working with directors on specific productions of plays (new or old). In some theatres, the role of the dramaturg is confined to the first of these functions, and the person who fulfills this function is often called a literary manager.

The literary manager's duties may vary considerably from one company to another, but as a minimum includes reading new scripts. Almost every not-for-profit professional theatre is inundated with new scripts each year. Literary managers read, or arrange for others to read, scripts. They choose those few that appear to have sufficient potential to warrant further consideration by the company. Because the volume is usually great, many companies will read only those plays submitted by agents or recommended by persons whose judgments they trust.

Milcha Sanchez-Scott's *Roosters* originated in INTAR's Hispanic Playwrights-in-Residence Laboratory (New York) with the encouragement of Maria Irene Fornes. It was developed further at the Sundance (Utah) Institute Playwrights Laboratory before being co-produced by INTAR and the New York Shakespeare Festival. Seen here in a studio production at INTAR are Angela (Sara Erde) and Hector (Jonathan del Arco). (Photo © Carol Rosegg.)

Literary management may also include new play development. This involves working with playwrights to help them realize the full potential of their scripts. (This process is sometimes taken over by the director or producer but, because it is a dramaturgical function, it is discussed here.) New play development is a delicate process, for it is not so much a matter of advising writers what they should do or demanding that they make certain changes as it is helping them clarify for themselves what they are seeking to do and finding means to do it. Dramaturgs sometimes describe to the writer what they find in the script and ask if that is what was intended. If it is not, then discussions may help the writer clarify what he or she is seeking to do and why it is not coming through. This, or some variation on it, may go on over a long period—before a play has received a reading, following readings of a script before an audience, during and following workshops in which a director and actors work on the play, and during and following partially or fully mounted productions of the play. The goal is to help authors realize as fully as possible the vision they set out to embody. Although some type of new play development has probably existed since the beginning of theatre, current practices vary considerably from those typically used earlier in this century, when producers often demanded changes intended primarily to increase the play's box-office appeal, or when directors requested changes based on their ideas about theatrical effectiveness, or when starring actors demanded changes that would enhance or make their roles more attractive. Such practices have not disappeared, but it is now more common, especially in not-for-profit theatres, for those working with playwrights to be most concerned with helping the writer achieve the full potential of a script. For this reason, most playwrights prefer to work with one or a series of not-for-profit theatres.

Literary managers are also usually involved in helping to select a company's season of plays. This usually involves keeping informed about and reading new plays that have been presented elsewhere, especially in the United States and Europe, as well as finding plays from the past that seem particularly relevant to current interests and issues. In considering plays for production, one of the dramaturg's primary duties is to ask of any script proposed for production this three-part question: Why this play for this audience at this time? Unless compelling answers can be offered, there seems little reason to produce a play.

The literary manager may also be involved in the preparation of production scripts. (This task might also fall to the production dramaturg.) If a script was originally written in another language, the problem of effective translation arises. The dramaturg usually examines all the available translations and (in consultation with the director) assesses their relative effectiveness. If none is satisfactory, a new translation may need to be made. If the literary manager is qualified, he or she may make a new translation. More often, someone thought to be particularly appropriate is commissioned to make the translation. Plays from the past, even if in English, often pose comparable problems because they may include obsolete phrases, outmoded social customs, or unfamiliar ideas. Sometimes the dramatic or theatrical

---

Playwriting as Collaborative Process

Concern with "new play dramaturgy" has in recent years served to remind us that the theatre, including playwriting, is a collaborative process, although all those involved may not be equal partners. In the "Afterword" to the published version of his *Angels in America, Part Two: Perestroika*, Tony Kushner writes:

> The fiction that artistic labor happens in isolation, and that individual talents are the sole provenance of artistic accomplishment, is politically, ideologically charged and, in my case at least, repudiated by the facts. While the primary labor on *Angels* has been mine (defensively, nervously, I hasten to shore up my claim to authorship), over two dozen people have contributed words, ideas, structures to these plays.... Had I written these plays without the direct and indirect participation of my collaborators, the results would be entirely different and much the poorer for the deprivation—would, in fact, never have come to be.

Frank Galati adapted John Steinbeck's novel, *The Grapes of Wrath,* for the stage and then directed it himself. Thus, he served as adapter, dramaturg, and director. Shown here is a scene from the original production by Steppenwolf Theatre Company (Chicago) as performed at La Jolla (CA) Playhouse. It was subsequently seen on Broadway and on PBS television. (Courtesy of the La Jolla Playhouse.)

conventions that shaped a play are barriers to present-day production. The chorus in Greek tragedy almost always creates difficulties for modern productions, as do plays from other cultures (for example, African or Asian). Decisions must be made about how these difficulties can be overcome in a production intended for the theatre's present-day audience. Sometimes the answer is to adapt the script, a task that may fall to the literary manager or to someone selected by the literary manager and director.

Production Dramaturgy

Production dramaturgy is concerned with specific productions. The production dramaturg works most closely with the director, but may also work with designers and other members of a production team, as well as those concerned with publicity, programs, and outreach. The production dramaturg's work used to be (and often still is) considered the responsibility of the director. Some directors refuse to work with dramaturgs, preferring to do this work themselves or (in some instances) viewing the dramaturg as usurping functions that should be theirs. The director-dramaturg relationship works best when it is grounded in mutual respect and a desire to explore fully how to make the script come to life on stage. If disagreements arise, the dramaturg usually retreats to performing only those functions specifically requested by the director.

The production dramaturg usually works with the director on various tasks. The dramaturg does not make decisions but helps the director make them by asking questions or supplying information crucial for clarifying the goals of the production and the interpretation of the script. The dramaturg assists in creating a

Heinar Müller's plays challenge dramaturgs since they often avoid punctuation, stage directions, or even indications of who speaks the lines. Seen here is Robert Wilson's staging of Müller's *Quartet* at the American Repertory Theatre. Wilson also designed the set and the lighting (with Howard Binkley). (Photo by Richard Feldman.)

production script—the version of the play that is to be used as a basis for the production. This may involve merely participation in selecting the play to be performed. It may involve making (or securing) a translation or adaptation; or it may involve cutting and rearranging the text. The dramaturg may also work with the director on script analysis and interpretation and do much of the research that provides an informational base. Dramaturgs usually seek information about the author's life and writings in an effort to understand more fully the concerns that have shaped the play. They may also explore the period or cultural environment depicted in the play or in which the author lived. They may read what critics have written about the play or what reviewers have said about previous productions. They may examine still other sources to increase their understanding of the script and the context out of which it came. Dramaturgs usually attend rehearsal often. They may discuss with the director what he or she was trying to achieve, the disparities between the director's intentions and what the dramaturg saw on the stage, and possible reasons for the differences. These and other types of feedback can assist directors in clarifying and realizing their interpretation of the script.

Dramaturgs often have some responsibility for educating the audience. They may supply information about the play, its past, this production, or other matters that will help those who do publicity to make the play more attractive and accessible to an audience. They may also have some responsibility for the printed program (especially if it includes materials that support and elaborate on the interpretation given the script). If the theatre has an outreach program that takes productions into schools or brings audiences to the theatre, the dramaturg may have responsibility for preparing the materials to be used. The dramaturg may also be responsible for "talk back" sessions following performances.

Overall, then, the dramaturg serves a critical and advisory function, assists in articulating the production team's vision of the production, seeks to help clarify and refine that vision during rehearsals, seeks to prepare audiences for experiencing the production most fully, and helps in evaluating the results after the production ends. Because dramaturgs are involved in the work of every member of the production team, it is often difficult to separate the dramaturgical from other functions, especially those of the director.

Although the playwright and the dramaturg serve different functions in the theatre, their work often converges. The playwright is concerned with creating a script, whereas the dramaturg is concerned with ensuring that the final version of the script realizes the playwright's intentions and that those intentions are embodied on the stage.

Chapter 12

Directing and Producing

JoAnne Akalaitis' production of Jean Genet's *The Balcony* at the American Repertory Theatre. The characters on the pedestals represent authority figures: mayor, judge, queen, bishop, and police chief. Sets by George Tsypin; costumes by Christi Zea; lighting by Jennifer Tipton. (Photo by Richard Feldman.)

> Directing is psychology. It's about how to work with other human beings. It's also the art of inducing a psychological effect on a group of people who have come into a theatre to experience that effect. In your mind you're saying to yourself: 'What do I want the audience to feel?' From there it's a process of moving toward that feeling with actors, designers, etc., yet allowing yourself to discover the unexpected along the way.
>
> —Mark Lamos in *The Director's Voice,* ed. by Arthur Bartow

Although directors have ultimate responsibility for the artistic aspects of productions, they depend on playwrights to provide the scripts and on producers to provide the necessary resources. The director, working with the actors and designers, translates the playwright's script into concrete stage reality using the resources (money, space, and personnel) provided by the producer. Thus, though the functions of playwright, producer, and director are distinct, they are intertwined on the practical level. The way they come together varies from one situation to another: A producer may discover a script and then employ a director to stage it; a director may like a script and convince a producer to finance a production of it; a director may like a particular playwright's work and approach that writer about directing one of his or her scripts; or, playwrights may search for directors or producers to stage their scripts. There are other possibilities but, whatever the starting point, the three functions—writing, producing, directing—ultimately meet in production.

The Producer

The financial and managerial tasks of making productions available to the public fall to producers who, though they may not make artistic decisions directly, nevertheless influence artistic decisions through their willingness or unwillingness (or ability or inability) to meet the requests of the playwright, director, and other artists. Producers in the Broadway theatre are often accused of placing financial considerations above artistic integrity, but it is their job to stay within a budget and, if possible, to recover the investment made in the production. Someone must carry out the producer's functions, for otherwise productions would never reach the stage.

Although almost all producers have the same basic responsibilities, the specific conditions governing their work vary from one type of organization to another. The producer's responsibilities are most clearly defined in the Broadway theatre. Today, producers of Broadway shows usually are organizations, a groups of individuals, or consortia who raise the necessary capital and carry out the other functions of a producer in return for payment for these services plus a large percentage of any profit. Because production costs on Broadway are so great, usually running into millions of dollars, and success is so unpredictable, producers usually have to seek financial backing from many people or groups because few individuals are willing to assume all the risk. They usually approach prospective investors with a proposed budget (covering expenses up to opening night) and a statement about how profits will be divided. Sometimes it takes months, even years, to raise the money needed for a production. Each production is usually capitalized as a corporation or partnership to limit the financial liability of investors.

After the necessary capital has been raised, producers negotiate contracts with all the persons who will be involved. This process can be difficult because eleven different unions may be involved—those representing dramatists; directors and choreographers; actors; musicians; stagehands; wardrobe attendants; press agents and managers; treasurers; ushers and doorkeepers; porters and cleaners; and engineers. Producers also rent space for auditions and rehearsals, lease a theatre for performances, and make sure the production is publicized and tickets sold. They are responsible for the payroll, keeping financial records, and making reports to investors at specified intervals. Occasionally, productions return very large profits, but a production can run for two or three years and never recover its original investment because the weekly running costs on a large show may consume most of the income from ticket sales, leaving little to repay the money spent before the production opened. The producers are also responsible for closing a show at the end of its run.

The producer's responsibilities are not so clearly defined in other situations. Most professional resident companies are ongoing not-for-profit organizations that present a number of plays each year. They often own a theatre, or perform in one owned by a municipality or arts organization or in a space leased for an extended period; they are more concerned with financing an ongoing organization than with a single production (although each production has its own budget within the theatre's total budget). In most companies of this type, responsibility is divided between an artistic director, who is concerned primarily with staging, and a managing director (or producing director), who is concerned with finances and marketing. Both are usually involved in raising money, establishing policy, and choosing the repertory. There is also a board of directors, which must be consulted about many issues that concern the organization's well-being and which may assist in raising funds. Because resident professional companies cannot support their activities entirely from box-office receipts, much time is spent pursuing grants or soliciting contributions. As not-for-profit organizations, they are eligible for grants from foundations, the National Endowment for the Arts, state and local arts councils, and private donors. Although this form of organization distributes the producer's responsibilities somewhat differently than is the norm on Broadway, a large portion of those responsibilities is usually delegated to the managing director.

In community theatre, the organization itself is usually the producer, although many of the responsibilities are carried out by volunteers under the supervision of the organization's officers and board of directors. Some of the duties may be delegated to an individual (president or treasurer) or to a production committee. Many community theatres hire only a director and a designer-technician because the purpose of such organizations is to provide an outlet for the talents of persons for whom theatre is an avocation.

In educational theatre, the producer's functions may be divided among several persons. Usually, the performance space is owned by the school, and most of the supervisory work is done by persons who are on the payroll in other capacities. The chair of the department or the director of theatre may have responsibilities that combine those of the artistic and managing directors of a resident company. Some theatre programs have a paid business manager who is responsible for keeping accounts, making purchases, running the box office, and handling publicity. In many

The Arena Stage

The Arena Stage in Washington, D.C., is one of the oldest and most successful not-for-profit producing organizations in the United States. Founded in 1950 by Edward Mangum, Zelda Fichandler and Thomas Fichandler, it originally performed in a 247-seat movie house in a slum area on a budget of $800 per week. Today it owns its own theatre complex in southwestern Washington and has an annual budget of more than $9 million. The complex includes three theatres—the Arena (a theatre-in-the-round seating 827), the Kreeger (a thrust stage theatre seating 514), and the Old Vat Room (a flexible space theatre seating about 180). It was the first theatre outside of New York to receive a Tony Award for excellence, and was one of the first regional theatres to transfer a play to Broadway. It has also taken a number of productions abroad. The theatre has made a special effort to meet the needs of Washington's population, which is 70 percent African American. Its Allen Lee Hughes Fellowship Program supports apprenticeship training for ethnic minorities in all aspects of theatre. The Arena Stage has also commissioned new plays with ethnic themes. In 1993 (in collaboration with the Cornerstone Theatre Company), it developed and presented an adaptation of Charles Dickens' *A Christmas Carol* set in contemporary Washington using primarily African-American characters. Nevertheless, the Arena's overall repertory of approximately ten productions each season is diverse, ranging from classics to musicals and experimental pieces. Since 1991, when Zelda Fichandler (artistic director since 1947) resigned, Douglas Wager has served as artistic director of the Arena Stage.

small schools, the director of each play may have to assume many of the producer's functions.

Regardless of the type of organization, then, tasks are much the same, though who performs them and the procedures may vary. In all cases, financial support must be provided, contractual arrangements made, space and personnel provided, publicity for productions disseminated, tickets sold, and bills paid. The producer is concerned with the business of show business.

The producer is also often involved in choosing the scripts to be produced. On Broadway, it is the producer who selects the play. Often the director and designers are not even contacted until after this basic decision has been made, although increasingly producers bring to Broadway productions that have been successful in regional theatres, Off-Broadway, or abroad (principally London).

Most permanent organizations present a season composed of several plays covering a range of periods. In choosing a season of plays, the group may take into consideration: (1) the desire to present varied types of plays; (2) the production requirements of each play (including size of cast, and the scenic, costume, and lighting demands); (3) total cost in relation to the organization's budget and projected income;

Exterior of the Arena Stage, Washington, DC. (Courtesy of the Arena Stage.)

and (4) tastes of local audiences and probable box-office appeal. During the play-selection process, advice may be sought from a number of sources. Much of this work may involve a literary manager or dramaturg, as discussed in Chapter 11.

Professional organizations deal directly with living authors or their agents in negotiating arrangements to produce plays. Amateur production rights are usually handled by play agencies, such as Samuel French or Dramatists Play Service. A play under copyright (which continues for the lifetime of the author plus fifty years) may not be performed without written permission (usually in the form of a contract) from the copyright owners or their authorized agent. Such contracts require that royalties be paid for each performance. Older plays may not require payment if their copyrights have expired, but recent translations or adaptations of older plays may be copyrighted even if the original copyright has expired.

After the script is selected and production contracts are negotiated, the process of mounting the play begins.

The Director

Just as the producer is concerned with the financial aspects, the director is responsible for the artistic aspects of production. Ordinarily, the director: (1) decides upon the interpretation to be given the script and the production concept that will shape the staging, (2) casts the actors, (3) works with the designers, (4) rehearses the actors, and (5) integrates all the elements into a finished production. In the first of these functions, the director may work closely with a dramaturg, if one is available, or may choose to work alone. (Much of this process is discussed in Chapter 11.)

Analyzing and Studying the Script

Regardless of working procedures or personnel, the starting point for most productions is a script. Although the printed script may be adequate as it is, it may require alterations of various kinds before it is acceptable for this production. Creating a production script may involve choosing or making a translation, cutting or adapting the text, transposing scenes, or changing the time or place of the action. To arrive at a production script, the director needs first to understand the play as thoroughly as possible.

Understanding usually demands a thorough analysis of the script. There is no standard way to analyze a script (one way is described in Chapter 3). Most directors (whether working alone or with a dramaturg) begin by reading the play several times to become familiar with its overall qualities. They may note its structural pattern of preparation, complication, climax, and resolution. Some directors divide a script into short segments (units) and examine each in terms of the characters' motivations within that segment and the function of the segment in relation to those that precede and follow it and to the play as a whole. They may define the "through line" (or "spine") of the action that holds the play together and determines its overall thrust—its themes, point of view, and implications. The director studies all the characters to understand their individual functions in the play and the demands they will make on the actors who play the roles. The director may note scenic, costume, and lighting demands in order to work intelligently with the designers. Through such study, the director becomes aware of the script's potentials and pitfalls and of the opportunities and difficulties they pose for the production.

Directors (either alone or in cooperation with a dramaturg) also typically consult sources beyond the script so as to understand better the author's life and other works and the concerns that have shaped the script. They may also explore the cultural environment depicted in the play. They may read what critics have written about the play or what reviewers have said about previous productions. They may examine still other sources to increase their understanding of the script and the context out of which it came. All of this may be crucial in shaping the production text and in the formation of the director's concept of the production that he or she will seek to realize on the stage.

If the script is new, the director may work directly with the playwright. This can simplify the director's task because many questions about the script can be answered by its author, but it may also complicate the director's work if what the playwright says he or she intended is not, in the director's opinion, clearly embodied in the script. In the latter case, the director may suggest revisions, although most contracts specify that the playwright cannot be required to alter the script. Fortunately, most dramatists welcome the insights offered by the director and the rehearsal process, and they frequently revise the script up to opening night.

Approaches to Directing

The next step involves decisions about staging the script. Several approaches to directing have become common. One stems from the belief that the director is an interpretive artist who serves the playwright by transferring the script as faithfully as

For his production of Mozart's eighteenth-century opera *Don Giovanni,* Peter Sellars set the action in New York's present-day South Bronx peopled by drug dealers and pimps. In the final scene of the Mozart opera, Don Giovanni is swallowed up by Hell amidst smoke and flames; in Sellars' production, figures rise from the sewers to pronounce judgment on the protagonist. Settings by George Tsypin; lighting by James Ingalls. (Photo by Beatriz Schiller.)

possible from page to stage. Directors who accept this notion of their function usually retain the time and place specified in the script and follow (though not necessarily slavishly) the playwright's prescriptions about staging. A second approach stems from a view of directors as translators whose goal is to capture the spirit of the playwright's script, although to do this they may depart from the playwright's specifications. Just as a literal translation of a literary piece from one language to another may distort the spirit of the original, an overzealously faithful production may fail to project a play's essential qualities, especially if the play is from the past or another culture and the conventions for which the play was written differ markedly from those familiar in our theatre.

This second approach is probably now the most common, although the way it is applied varies widely from one director to another and even from one production to another. Directors using this approach usually search for a metaphor, dominant theme, or set of conventions that will define the focus—the *directorial* (or *production*) *concept*—that will give shape to the production. A Soviet director, Nikolai Okhlopkov, shaped a production of *Hamlet* around the metaphor of the world as a prison, using a setting composed of cell-like cubicles in which various scenes were played. Perhaps a more common practice is to base a production on a simile rather than a metaphor, suggesting that the action in a play is like that in another time and place. For example, Orson Welles set *Macbeth* in Haiti, replacing the witches with voodoo priests. Other directors have relocated the action of *Troilus and Cressida* (which is set during the Trojan War) to the American Civil War.

Peter Brook shaped his widely admired production of *A Midsummer Night's Dream* around a central motif: the potentials and dangers of love. The fantasy scenes in the woods became dreamlike demonstrations to Theseus and Hippolyta, who are about to be married, of the effects of misunderstandings between lovers and about love. To underscore these connections, Brook used the actors cast as Theseus and Hippolyta to play Oberon and Titania (their parallels in the fantasy world). Most earlier productions of the play had exploited the opportunities for visual spectacle offered by Theseus' court and the enchanted wood. Brook used the same set throughout—a white box (with front and top removed), totally devoid of decoration. Thus, the stage was treated not as a place to re-create the locales indicated in Shakespeare's script, but as a space where its fundamental human relationships could be isolated and examined. Most earlier productions had emphasized the magical aspects of the fairy world and had sought to make Puck's flying convincingly real. For the fairy magic, Brook substituted stage and circus magic: Trapezes were used for the flying scenes, and characters on the trapezes performed tricks of stage magic such as keeping plates spinning on sticks. Bottom, rather than being transformed into an ass, became a clown with a red rubber ball for a nose. Thus, the magic was translated from fairyland into a context more familiar, though no less magical, to a modern audience. Despite his visual substitutions, Brook altered none of the lines. His goal was to make audiences consider the implications of certain human relationships rather than concentrate on the spectacle and fantasy. (See color plate 10.)

Ariane Mnouchkine, working with the Théâtre du Soleil in Paris, has used conventions borrowed from Asian (especially Indian and Japanese) theatre in several productions of Shakespeare's history plays and Greek tragedies. She believes that the conventions are so strange that they call attention to themselves; she then uses them to distance the dramatic actions from the audience so as to illuminate the repetitive, ritualized power struggles in these plays. (See color plate 15 for an example of Mnouchkine's work.)

Other variations on this second approach could be cited, but all are based on the assumption that, though the script's dialogue should be respected and retained, its significance can best be conveyed to a present-day audience through devices that, though they depart from the playwright's instructions, convey the script's intentions by calling attention to the fundamental patterns hidden beneath the surface detail. While this approach can be effective, if ineptly applied it can distort the script by calling attention to bizarre staging rather than the play's themes and implications. Directors may appear to be more concerned about innovative than illuminating staging.

A third approach to directing places less emphasis on the script. Using this approach, directors may begin with the script but feel free to reshape it as they see fit. Although this approach is less common, it has been increasingly accepted since the 1960s. The Polish director Jerzy Grotowski often began with well-known scripts, uncovered what he considered to be basic (archetypal) patterns of human behavior in them and then reshaped the scripts (through cutting, rearranging, and relocating scenes), with the intention of provoking audiences into self-examination and self-recognition. One of his best-known and most radical reshapings of a play involved Wyspianski's *Akropolis* (1904), one of Poland's most revered classics, set in the royal palace at Cracow (the Polish equivalent of the Athenian Acropolis) on the Feast of the Resurrection. During the action, the walls' tapestries come to life and enact what amounts to a history of Western civilization, at the end of which the resurrected Christ leads all the figures in a procession to liberate Europe from its past errors. Grotowski saw the play as treating hopes and fantasies that had been destroyed by World War II and the Nazi concentration camps. He reshaped the play so that rather than stressing the possibility of redemption it depicted "the cemetery of our civilization." Reset in the extermination camp at Auschwitz, its characters are prisoners who, during the course of the play, build cremation ovens and occasionally in their nightmares perform scenes based, in a distorted way, on those in Wyspianski's play. At the end they march into the ovens they have built, following a lifeless figure representing Christ. In such an approach the director's vision overrides the playwright's, and the original script becomes material to be shaped (just as acting, lighting, scenery, and costumes are). This approach to directing reflects that of film, where the director is usually considered the principal creative force (the *auteur*).

Still another approach to directing virtually eliminates the playwright (or at least the distinctions between writer and director). In Robert Wilson's early theatre pieces, the written scripts are so short and convey so little information that they are

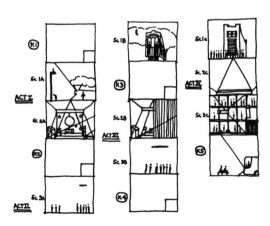

Robert Wilson's storyboard outline of the four acts of his opera *Einstein on the Beach*. (Courtesy of the Byrd Hoffman Foundation.)

Wilson elaborates his storyboard outline with a number of sketches (in this instance eight to ten) for each scene. The sketch shown here is for Act I, scene 2A of *Einstein on the Beach*. (Photo by Geoffrey Clements. Reprinted by permission of the Byrd Hoffman Foundation.)

Act I, scene 2A of *Einstein on the Beach* in performance as staged by Robert Wilson. Notice the costume (pants, shirt, suspenders) worn by most characters throughout the opera, becoming one unifying motif. (Photo by Babette Mangolte. Reprinted by permission of the Byrd Hoffman Foundation.)

inadequate as bases for productions by others. He usually lays out each piece as a storyboard. A master board shows at a glance the development of the entire piece; then each segment is elaborated in detailed storyboards and finally is translated to the stage. (This process can be seen in the illustrations on pages 323–324.) Some of Wilson's pieces can properly be said to exist only in the performances. Similarly, performance artists usually conceive their pieces as performances rather than as scripts; consequently only they can stage their works.

Regardless of the approach, directors have to work with others in transforming their vision into reality because at least some production tasks must be delegated to others. The discussion that follows will undoubtedly make directing seem far more rational and precise than it is. In actuality, though most directors begin with a reasonably clear idea of what they wish to accomplish, they also make discoveries (through interactions with designers and actors as well as through new insights into the script) that alter their initial plans. Where directors ultimately arrive may be different from (and more rewarding than) their original destination. But such discoveries are unpredictable, and we must be content with a look at some typical working procedures used by directors.

Harold Prince

Harold Prince (1928–   ) is perhaps the most successful contemporary American director of musicals. He had gained considerable managerial experience and had produced a series of hits (*The Pajama Game, Damn Yankees, West Side Story,* and *Fiorello!*) before he turned to directing, first with *She Loves Me* in 1961. This was followed by *Cabaret* and *Zorba* before he began, in 1970, his long association with Stephen Sondheim, with whom he worked on such productions as *Company, Follies, A Little Night Music, Pacific Overtures,* and *Sweeney Todd.* Around 1980, Prince gave up producing and increased his involvement in directing, especially opera. Among his most successful productions in recent years have been *Evita, Phantom of the Opera, Kiss of the Spider Woman,* and *Show Boat.*

Prince prepares carefully for productions, sometimes over as long as five years, often stopping to complete another project and then coming back to the one put on hold. He does extensive background research and exhaustive character analyses. Feeling that he cannot proceed until he has place clearly in mind, he has models of the settings made and studies them carefully, sometimes for months. Because of this intense preparation, he knows what he wants to achieve when rehearsals begin. Consequently, his rehearsal periods are short. Prince prefers productions that go beyond entertainment and stir up thought: "Entertainment is simply an experience that takes you out of your own life. When you come out of the theatre you should know that something has been said that was arguable. You should have something to take away with you."

The Director and the Designers

Some directors (among them Robert Wilson) serve as their own designers, but that is not usual. Because designing and constructing the visual elements are a lengthy process, the director meets as early as possible with the designers to discuss the play and the production concept. The concept may evolve out of such discussions. However it is arrived at, the production's focus should be clear to the designers if they are not to work at cross-purposes with the director and each other and if they are to contribute significantly to the production. The director needs to be clear about any specific demands he or she may have, such as the shape of the set, the need for multiple levels, the placement of entrances, specific mood lighting, garments with specific features, and so on.

After the initial meetings, designers must be allowed time to conceive designs and make sketches. At subsequent meetings, designs are considered and revisions requested until director and designers are mutually satisfied. Before designs are approved, a number of questions are usually asked. Do designs adequately project the production concept? Do they fit the play's action, mood, theme, and style? Are they functional? Do the designs for each aspect (scenery, costumes, lighting) complement and support those for the other aspects? If changes must occur during performance, will the proposed costumes, scenery, and lighting permit changes without undue

Harold Prince's production of *The Phantom of the Opera* by Andrew Lloyd Webber, Charles Hart, and Richard Stilgoe. Michael Crawford as the Phantom; Sarah Brightman as Christine Daaé. Designed by Maria Bjornson, lighting by Andrew Bridge. (Photo by Bob Marshak.)

delays? Can they be achieved within the limits of the budget? Consideration of such questions during the planning stages can prevent costly last-minute changes.

After the designs are approved, there may be regular conferences, but each artist works more or less independently until the final rehearsals. Meantime, the director's prime task becomes casting and rehearsing the actors.

Casting

Various methods of casting are used. One is the open tryout, which permits all those interested to apply. But even though tryouts may be called "open," access is usually restricted in some way. For example, in many educational theatres, "open" tryouts are open only to theatre majors, and in some community theatres only to its members. In professional theatres, Actors Equity may demand that a certain amount of time be devoted to open tryouts, but these are open only to its members. If there are many applicants, some may never be auditioned, having been eliminated on the basis of resumés or preliminary interviews. Even those granted auditions usually have only a short time initially (two minutes is typical) in which to demonstrate their suitability. Under such circumstances, choices may be made on the basis of personal or physical attributes rather than proven ability.

Because the number of would-be auditionees is so great, many professional producing organizations (theatre, television, and film) have come increasingly to depend on casting directors to save them time by creating a small pool of likely candidates. These casting directors sift through resumés, confer with agents, conduct initial auditions, and call on their own memories or videotapes of the performers' previous work. This pool of prescreened candidates is then usually auditioned thoroughly by the director, often in consultation with the casting director, producer, or playwright. The tryout process usually progresses from open to closed (or invitational) auditions. During the latter type, candidates are given considerably more time to demonstrate their suitability for the roles and may be called back several times.

Procedures used during tryouts vary. Sometimes actors are asked to prepare two short, contrasting audition scenes unrelated to the play being cast. Sometimes actors are able to study the script being cast and read a passage from it as an audition piece. The director may ask actors to read material they have not previously seen, then give explanations and ask the actor to read the same material again with these instructions in mind. In this way, directors seek to judge the actor's flexibility and quickness in assimilating direction. Some directors use improvisations or other methods to test imagination, inventiveness, and physical agility.

Many factors determine final casting. Some roles demand specific physical characteristics (such as being fatter or taller than others), accent, or vocal quality. The director must consider the emotional range of each role and the potential of actors to achieve this range. Characters often need to be paired or contrasted (in romantic situations, for example), and casting must answer this need. The director must also look at the cast as a whole and the way the actors will look and work together. After weighing all these factors, the director eventually chooses the actors who seem most capable of embodying the qualities he or she is seeking.

Nontraditional casting in Shakespeare's *The Taming of the Shrew* as produced by the New York Shakespeare Festival. The place of the action has been moved to the American West in the nineteenth century. Tracy Ullman as Katharine and Morgan Freeman as Petruchio. Directed by A. J. Antoon. (Photo © Martha Swope.)

Nontraditional Casting

A controversial issue today is nontraditional casting—which, as the term implies, involves casting actors in roles for which in the past they might not have been considered. There are many approaches to this kind of casting. One involves "color-blind" casting—ignoring race or ethnicity and casting solely on the basis of talent and suitability to a role. Such casting has become relatively common in many professional companies, perhaps most noticeably in the New York Shakespeare Festival and in several regional companies. It is also common in many colleges and universities. But such casting is widely opposed, especially when it leads to mixed-race family groups or when it denies social realities. Commenting on the revival of *Carousel* that opened in New York in 1994 (with thirteen actors of color in a cast of forty-four), one critic declared it ludicrous that blacks would coexist happily with whites in nineteenth-century coastal Maine and too much to ask audiences to accept.

Some observers argue that color-blind casting shifts the question of minority underrepresentation to casting and away from the failure of plays to include minority characters. Others charge that color-blind casting allows cultural differences to be ignored by absorbing representatives of other cultures into the dominant white, Eurocentric culture. Another approach is "conceptual" casting, which often involves changing the race or ethnicity of some or all characters to bring a new perspective to a play. Arthur Miller's *After the Fall*, for example, includes a leading character usually interpreted as based on Marilyn Monroe (to whom Miller was married), and in most productions this real-life relationship has been emphasized. But by casting a black actress in this role, one recent production diverted attention from Monroe to the character as presented in the play.

Another issue associated with nontraditional casting involves injustices to minority actors. Until recently, nonwhite characters were usually played by white actors, making it virtually impossible for nonwhite actors to be cast in significant roles. Although this practice has diminished, it has not wholly disappeared. The issue of nontraditional casting received wide public attention when Actors Equity objected to a white British actor being cast as a Eurasian in *Miss Saigon*, an extraordinarily successful London musical being imported to New York. Equity charged that the producer, Cameron Macintosh, had refused to employ minority actors for his hit show *Les Miserables* on the grounds that it did not contain ethnic roles but was now insisting on casting a white actor in a role that called for ethnicity. Although Equity eventually softened its position, the issue of opportunities for minority actors is not likely to go away.

Issues of nontraditional casting are not restricted to race and ethnicity. They also extend to actors who are impaired in hearing, seeing, or movement and to failures to cast them, even in roles of characters with those impairments. Because the controversy over casting reflects divisions within American society, it is not likely to be resolved until those divisions are healed and diversity is embraced.

Working with the Actors

After casting is completed, the director works to mesh actors with roles and dramatic action to bring the script to life on the stage. The director supervises rehearsals, reacts to characterizations and stage business, and makes suggestions for improvements. But a director is not a dictator. Actors bring their own insights, many of which may be novel or provocative. Most (though not all) directors are willing to discuss the actors' responses and needs and are sufficiently flexible to adopt those that improve the initial plans.

Most directors attempt to create an atmosphere free from unnecessary tensions in which the actors may explore and develop their roles. The director needs to be tactful and understanding because each actor has unique problems and favorite working methods. Some actors take criticism gracefully in the presence of others, but some become argumentative or are so embarrassed they find it difficult to continue.

Because actors cannot see their own performances from the point of view of the audience, the director must perform this service for them, assess the probable effects, and work with them to perfect characterizations. Effective directors are usually sensitive listeners and observers, critics, disciplinarians, teachers, and friends. Ultimately, they are the audience's surrogate because they try to shape the performance in ways that will be most effective for those who will see it.

The Director's Means

The director's means include the entire resources of the theatre: the script; the voice, speech, physical appearance, movement, and psychological and mental capacities of the actors; the stage space, scenery, and properties; costumes and makeup; electronic equipment, lighting, and sound. Because each of these elements is discussed elsewhere in this book, the focus here is on the director's work with the actors: the stage picture, movement, gesture, and stage business; voice and speech.

The Stage Picture

Each moment of a performance may be thought of as a picture that transmits messages to the audience quite apart from speech and movement. The director needs to be aware of the visual design of scenes moment by moment, not as beautiful pictures but as visualizations of situation, emotions, and character relationships. (In actuality, these pictures operate in conjunction with the actors' lines and movements, but left to chance, they can contradict what is said by sending the wrong messages.) In composing visual messages, the director uses various devices to emphasize what is most important and to subordinate other parts of the visible whole. These devices will be described first as they relate to the picture-frame stage and later as they are modified for other types of stages.

One of the most important controls over emphasis and subordination is that regarding the *bodily positions* of the actors because (all other factors being equal) the actor facing the audience most fully will be the most emphatic. (Bodily positions are

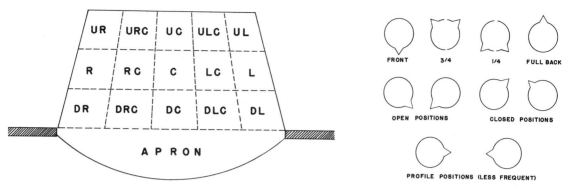

Stage areas (at left) and bodily positions (at right).

explained more fully in Chapter 13.) A second source of emphasis is *height* because, if other factors are equal, the most elevated character will be the most emphatic. To vary and control height, the director may have characters stand, sit, kneel, lie down, or mount steps or platforms. A third means of controlling emphasis is through the use of *stage areas*. Because center stage and downstage are the most emphatic areas in the proscenium theatre, the director may control emphasis by the placement of actors within the stage space. (One way of dividing the proscenium stage into areas is illustrated in the diagram above.) The use of stage areas is closely related to a fourth means of controlling emphasis: *spatial relationships* among the characters, as, for example, when a single character on one side of the stage is given emphasis by massing a group of actors on the other side. This example also illustrates a fifth means: *contrast*. Emphasis may also be created through *visual focus*—as when all those on the stage look at the same person or object, thereby creating the equivalent of a pointing finger. Other ways of gaining emphasis include *costume* (one example of which would be placing a brilliantly colored garment amid drab clothing), *lighting* (using, for example, a spotlighted area while other areas are relatively dark), and *scenery* (by placing a character in a doorway or against a piece of furniture, for example, to strengthen the visual line). Directors seldom depend on a single source of emphasis; several are often used simultaneously, especially when emphasis needs to be divided among several characters, each requiring differing degrees of emphasis.

When one moves from the proscenium to the thrust stage (which is viewed from three sides) or the arena stage (which is viewed from four sides), some of the devices most effective on the proscenium stage are no longer useful. For example, bodily position becomes relatively meaningless because actors facing one part of the audience may have their backs turned to another. For much the same reason, stage area loses much of its effectiveness because nearness to one part of the audience may be distance from another part. But most of the other devices apply. Nevertheless, in thrust and arena theatres it is difficult to compose visual messages that are expressive from every angle, and they need to be recomposed frequently from different angles so that no part of the audience is neglected.

The way the devices for achieving emphasis are used depends greatly on the stage setting. The placement of doors and furniture encourages some compositional patterns and impedes others. The absence of furniture in settings for many period plays (for example, *Oedipus the King* and most of the scenes in *Hamlet*) rules out the detailed routine of daily life that is typical in such modern plays as *A Doll's House*. Picturization is also affected by the type of play (many of the visual devices appropriate to a farcical *commedia dell'arte* script would be out of keeping with an expressionistic play such as *"The Hairy Ape"*).

Some directors consider picturization and composition to be legacies of a time when the picture-frame stage was the only type in use, and they argue that its conventions have been invalidated by more recent stage forms. Others believe that concern for picturization leads to a self-conscious or unnatural positioning of actors on stage. Still others argue that if the actors understand the dramatic situation, they will instinctively group themselves properly. The most serious challenge to the concept of picturization has been posed by flexible (or variable) stages because several scenes may proceed simultaneously in various parts of a space shared by both spectators and performers. This use of theatrical space rejects the traditional view that each moment of a performance should have a major focal point to which every spectator's attention is directed and which should be visible and audible to every member of the audience. But the flexible theatre's primary break with past practice is in its use of multiple focal points. The individual simultaneous scenes still create visual messages, planned or not.

Many objections to deliberate picturization concern the possibility that compositions will draw attention to themselves and distract attention from more important elements. No doubt poorly conceived or inappropriate composition may have this effect. But one cannot deny that the visual pictures that continually form, dissolve, and transform as the audience watches are a major component of any production and that they convey messages. Therefore, although there may be controversy over the way this element is to be approached, its importance cannot be denied.

Movement, Gesture, and Business

So far, the stage picture has been treated as static, but in performance the dominant impression is one of movement—flow, change, and development. Consequently, movement is among the director's most powerful means of expression.

Movement can be divided into three main types: *from place to place, gesture,* and *business.* Each type may be dictated by the script or invented by the director or the actors. Many movements (such as entering, exiting, dancing, or lighting lamps) may be specified in stage directions or dialogue. On the other hand, many older plays include no stage directions, and all movement must be deduced. Because a completely static stage picture becomes boring, the director usually introduces much physical action. In doing so, the director takes cues from the script, so that movement seems motivated rather than aimless. Character relationships and emotional connotations are among the most common motivators of movement—love, anger, and eagerness normally move characters toward each other, whereas disgust, fear, and reluctance separate them.

In "The Last Mama-on-the-Couch Play" exhibit in *The Colored Museum,* exaggerated gesture and movement are integral parts of style. Not only does the gesture place focus on the "Medea" character, so does the attention of all the other characters. The exaggeratedly enlarged picture of Jesus in the background also helps to establish the overblown style. Directed by Donald Douglas at the Yale Repertory Theatre. (Photo © T. Charles Erickson.)

Movement serves many functions. First, it *gives emphasis* because it catches the eye and directs attention to the strongest movement. Second, it *characterizes.* An elderly person normally uses fewer and slower movements than a young person, just as a nervous or angry person moves differently from a casual or relaxed person. Third, movement *clarifies situation.* Highly emotional scenes normally incite more movement (and more rapid and sharply defined movement) than do quiet moments. Fourth, movement may be used to *build scenes to a climax,* for *contrast,* and for *tempo.* Gradually increasing the amount and size of movement can create a sense of growing confusion, conflict, or development and change. Contrast in movement from one scene to another can point up differences in mood, tempo, and situation, as well as provide variety. Fifth, movement may be *indicative of dramatic type.* The movement of *Oedipus the King* is more stately and formal than that of *The Colored Museum.* Plays that depart from realism, such as *"The Hairy Ape,"* deliberately distort or stylize movement.

Much stage movement does not involve movement from place to place. *Gesture, facial expression,* and *bodily attitude,* which together create what is usually called *body language,* are of special importance for achieving subtlety and clarity. Gesture normally involves only the hands and arms, but at times the torso, head, feet, or legs may be used gesturally. Gesture is especially important as a subtle means of gaining emphasis because a gesture by an actor who is about to speak is usually sufficient to shift attention to that actor at the right moment. Gesture is indicative of basic psychological traits: A great many spontaneous gestures suggest an uninhibited, outgoing personality, whereas few and awkward gestures suggest the opposite. Bodily attitude—stiffly upright, slumping, relaxed, and so on—is an especially useful means for displaying emotional states and for indicating immediate reactions. So is facial expression, which, though it is not always visible in a large auditorium, is a supplementary aid in projecting response.

Another kind of movement, *stage business,* involves detailed actions such as filling and smoking a pipe, arranging flowers, wrapping packages, eating and drinking, dueling, and so on. Such business is frequently prescribed by the script, but it may also be invented by the director or actors to clarify action or enrich characterization. Stage business needs to be carefully timed to make appropriate points and to be coordinated with dialogue to avoid diverting attention from important lines or action.

In recent years, several nontraditional uses of movement, gesture, and business have become common. Actors may writhe on the floor in tangled masses, crawl about the set, and perch on various structures. Movement in general has become more uninhibited, and the range of acceptable movement has been considerably extended.

Voice and Speech

The director's means also include the voice and speech of the actors. Just as innovative movement has become important, so, too, has nonverbal vocal sound. In nonrealistic plays, directors may use voice to create dissonances, modulations ranging from the loudest to the softest, cries, yelps, and so on. Nevertheless, the director is still most commonly concerned with voice as a medium for language or song. (Because voice and speech are more fully the actor's concern, they are discussed at greater length in Chapter 13.) The director needs to understand voice and speech thoroughly in order to use them effectively and to coach actors intelligently.

In using voice and speech, the director must make sure the dialogue is both audible and understandable, that there is variety, and (most important) that voice and speech enhance characterization, situation, and meaning. As with movement, voice and speech may be used to build scenes (or the entire play) to a climax.

Thus, the director's means are varied. Although they have been discussed separately here, they are applied simultaneously in the theatre, first one and then an-

Anne Bogart

One of the most controversial directors in America today is Anne Bogart (1951–), who insists that her work, rather than being avant-garde, as is often charged, is rooted in history. "Our role as artists is about remembering vital issues and vital questions that have been passed down for centuries." To call attention to these issues and questions, she often surrounds a script with a "play within a play" framework that grows out of her query: "What metaphor can we find that relates to the play and also relates to the audience?" Her staging usually forces her audience to see the play in a new light. She set the musical *South Pacific* in a clinic for emotionally disturbed war veterans. Her production of *A Streetcar Named Desire* was set in a German club whose members take turns playing scenes from the play; there were ten Stanleys and twelve Blanches (one of them a man). She has said of this approach, "The more cultural baggage a play carries, the more I have to go through the back door." In recent years she has created plays that examine (both the form and significance) of early twentieth-century entertainment; *American Vaudeville* (1993) and *Marathon Dancing* (1994) have been performed, and a third on early film is in preparation. She has won two Obie Awards (for Off-Broadway productions), the first for *No Plays No Poetry*, a playful walk-through of Brecht's theories and criticism, and the second for her staging of Paula Vogel's *Baltimore Waltz*. She has directed for many companies, perhaps most compatibly at the American Repertory Theatre. She served as artistic director of the Trinity Repertory Theatre for one season, but her approach proved too radical for that company. In 1992, she co-founded with Tadashi Suzuki, the Japanese director and acting theorist, the Saratoga International Theatre Institute, the goal of which is to "revitalize the theatre from the inside out"; it has conducted acting workshops and symposia (on such topics as "A Theatre Towards the 21st Century") and has presented plays directed by Bogart and Suzuki. Bogart directed there Charles L. Mee Jr.'s version of *Orestes,* which Bogart set on the White House lawn following the Persian Gulf War to explore "our society's malfunction." She has also conceived and directed at Saratoga *The Medium*, a collage of the theories of Marshall McLuhan that concern "how technology is changing our relationships." About her work, which has a feminist base, she has said: "Feminine aesthetics are inherently subversive."

other being given primacy. Through such continuous adjustments, the director seeks to achieve clarity in motivation, action, and meaning, in addition to creating that underlying and indefinable sense of excitement that characterizes theatrical performance at its best.

Anne Bogart's production of Paula Vogel's *Hot 'n' Throbbing,* concerning pornography and domestic violence, as produced at the American Repertory Theatre. The bed, mirrors, bright lights, and transparent screen all contribute to a voyeuristic tone. Setting by Christine Jones; lighting by John Ambrosone; costumes by Jenny Fulton. (Photo by Richard Feldman.)

Rehearsing the Play

Rehearsals can seldom be held under conditions approximating those of performance. As a rule, the scenery, costumes, lighting, and properties are not available until the final days, and the rehearsal space is seldom the stage on which the play will be presented. Therefore, the director and actors must rely heavily on imagination during rehearsals.

The typical rehearsal space is a large room (at least as large as the stage) on the floor of which the ground plan of the set is outlined with tape or paint (as shown in the photo on page 337). If there is more than one set, each is indicated with different colors. Chairs, tables, and improvised doors and levels help the actors become familiar with the setting. Temporary properties that approximate those to be used in performance are necessary if there is complex stage business, such as serving a meal or fighting a duel. Similarly, rehearsal garments may be needed for plays in which unusual headdresses, hooped skirts or trains, and other unfamiliar features or accessories will appear.

In order to plan rehearsals adequately, the director needs to know how much time will be available. In the nonprofessional theatre, actors are usually available only in the evenings for three or four hours and for a period of four to eight weeks. In the professional theatre, a rehearsal period of about four weeks is typical, with actors available for approximately eight hours each day. A group that evolves its own scripts may require months to prepare a performance. Whatever the situation, the director ascertains the approximate number of hours available for rehearsals and plans a schedule to utilize the time to maximum advantage. Because all problems cannot be worked on simultaneously, the director breaks down the schedule into phases and objectives.

Before beginning rehearsals on the script, some directors devote time to group activities (such as improvisations and theatre games) intended to familiarize the actors with each other, break down inhibitions and encourage trust, and prepare the actors for the work ahead.

The first phase of rehearsals is usually devoted to reading and discussing the script. The amount of time devoted to textual study varies with the director, with the complexity of the script, and with the experience of the cast. During this period, the director tries to see that all the actors have a basic understanding of their roles and how they function within the action. The director may explain the production concept and clarify the main objectives toward which everyone should be working.

The next phase is usually devoted to *blocking* (establishing each actor's movements from place to place and position at each moment). For example, an actor might be asked to enter up center, cross slowly to the sofa down left, and stand facing front. At this time, the director is concerned only with the gross patterns of movement; subtleties and refinements come later. When the blocking for one unit is clear, the director moves on to the next, repeating the process until the entire play

A rehearsal room with the set marked out on the floor with tape. A rehearsal of Arthur Miller's *After the Fall*. (Photo by Inge Morath/Magnum.)

is blocked. The process as described here is far more orderly than in most actual blocking rehearsals. Many directors consider all blocking to be tentative, and they adjust it often as rehearsals proceed. Others believe that blocking should evolve out of character relationships and the actors' sense of their roles—a collaborative process among actors and director, often a slow one. Regardless of how blocking is achieved, eventually it should be set so that it will not be a source of distraction and misunderstanding among the actors; or, if it is not to be set, the actors should be made aware that they must be prepared to adjust to changes as they occur.

The next phase is usually devoted to lines. For each act, the director normally specifies the date by which the actors should know their lines. As with blocking, there is disagreement about the best time to learn lines (early, or after the actor is thoroughly familiar with the role), although it is generally acknowledged that it is difficult for performers to achieve subtlety or to build scenes properly if they must continually consult their scripts.

After the actors have mastered their basic movement patterns and lines, the director can proceed to the next phase: detailed work on characterization, line readings, business, transitions, progression and intensification, variety, and ensemble playing. Much of this phase may be spent exploring motivations or clarifying relationships. If the actors have difficulties, the director may ask them to do improvisations that are designed to stimulate those responses he or she is seeking and that can then be adapted to the scripted situation. During this phase, directors may go over the same scene repeatedly to achieve proper timing or intensity, just as they may adjust the pacing of scenes for the sake of variety.

With musicals, the director's task becomes especially complex during this and later phases of rehearsals. For musicals, a choreographer normally creates and rehearses the dances separately, just as the musical director rehearses the singers and chorus separately (normally with only piano accompaniment). The director must eventually integrate songs and dances into the whole and devise the transitions that lead smoothly from spoken lines into song and from stage movement into dance.

The final phase of rehearsals is devoted to integrating all of the elements of production. For the first time, the actors are able to rehearse in their costumes and makeup, and with the scenery, lighting, and sound (including, in musicals, the full orchestra) that will be used in performance. Frequently, this is also the first time the actors have rehearsed in the actual performance space. Many adjustments generally have to be made during these final rehearsals. It is usual to have at least one technical rehearsal to work out problems with lighting levels and cues, costume and scene changes, sound, music, and properties. Typically, there are then two or three dress rehearsals intended to approximate as nearly as possible the conditions of performance. During these rehearsals, difficulties are noted and attempts are made to correct them before the next rehearsal. Some directors invite several people to dress rehearsals to get indications of probable audience response and to prepare the performers for a larger audience. In the professional theatre, preview performances function as a series of additional dress rehearsals, after each of which changes may be made. The alterations are then tried out on other audiences until the play opens.

When the play opens, the director's job is considered to be complete, although many directors come back at intervals to revitalize performances. By opening night

Jonathan Miller, right, directing actors in a production of Richard Sheridan's eighteenth-century comedy, *The School for Scandal,* at the American Repertory Theatre. (Photo by Richard Feldman.)

a *production promptbook* has been compiled; it records the blocking, stage business, lighting cues, sound cues, and everything that is required to run the show as the director intended.

The Director's Assistants

In fulfilling these functions, the director usually has several assistants, the most important of which are the rehearsal secretary, assistant director, and stage manager.

The *rehearsal secretary* takes notes from the director during rehearsals about points to discuss with the actors, designers, or technicians. The secretary may also post notices and keep everyone informed of things they need to know. The *assistant director* performs whatever tasks are assigned by the director: attending conferences, serving as liaison with designers, coaching actors, or rehearsing scenes. The *stage manager* is responsible for running the show at each performance and, during the rehearsal period, for compiling the promptbook, which becomes the blueprint for performances. In the professional theatre, the stage manager may organize and run auditions and, after the show opens, may rehearse the actors if necessary. The stage manager is the director's surrogate during performances, charged with seeing that everything functions as the director intended.

Thinking About . . .

The Director's Work

Today, not only are approaches to directing varied, but so, too, are the scripts (ranging from the Greeks to the present, and from tragedy to comedy to indeterminate forms) and the theatrical conventions (ranging through the whole history of Western theatre and borrowing liberally from other cultures). When we attend the theatre, our experiences may also be varied: We may find ourselves confronted with the commonplace and boring, the exotic and puzzling, the novel and exciting, or some combination of these. Such variety often makes it difficult to respond intelligently. Here is a list of questions that may help the theatregoer assess the director's contributions.

1. *Was there an identifiable production concept, unifying metaphor, or interpretational approach? If so, what was it and how was it manifested in the production? To what effect?*
2. *How closely did the production adhere to the playwright's script? (In the script, where and when does the action take place? Did the production alter time, place, or other aspects of the script? If so, how? To what effect? If not, how did this production make—or fail to make—the script's action understandable or relevant to its audience?)*
3. *Did the production make use of any unusual conventions? If so, which? With what effect?*
4. *In what type of performance space was the production staged? How was the production affected by the space? With what gain or loss?*
5. *How did the visual elements (scenery, costumes, lighting) support (or fail to support) the production concept? Were they coordinated? Did the director make specific use of any of them? With what effect?*
6. *How did sounds (the actors' voices, special effects, music) support (or fail to support) the production concept? Were they audible, understandable, properly balanced?*
7. *How did casting influence the production?*
8. *Was the action clear? Did it build climactically? Was there appropriate variety in mood and tempo?*

9. *Were all the elements of the production compatible and coordinated? If not, what seemed out of place or inadequately integrated with the rest? With what effect?*
10. *Overall, did the production achieve its apparent goals? If not, where did it fall short? With what overall results?*

Other questions could be posed, but many of them will arise as other areas of production are examined in the chapters that follow.

Chapter 13

Acting

Pat Carroll as Mother Courage and Floyd King as the Chaplain in Bertolt Brecht's *Mother Courage and Her Children* as performed at The Shakespeare Theatre (Washington, DC). Directed by Michael Kahn. (Photo by Joan Marcus.)

Of all the arts, I think acting must be the least concrete, and the most solitary. . . . [A]udiences . . . are the only means by which an actor may gauge the effect of his acting. . . . [But] I have often wished that I were able to . . . examine some performance of mine calmly and dispassionately as I looked at it standing on the mantelpiece.

—John Gielgud, *Early Stages*

Of all theatre workers, the actor most nearly personifies the stage for the general public, perhaps because the actor is the only theatre artist the audience normally sees. The actor's function is to give concrete embodiment to characters that otherwise exist only in the written word and the imagination. A play's action is created out of what the actors say and do and the way they interact with each other and their surroundings. Though the script may provide the blueprint, the designers the visual context, and the director the overall focus, it is the living presence of the actor that is most essential to the audience's theatrical experience.

Actors are among the few artists (along with dancers and singers) whose basic means of expression cannot be separated from themselves; they must create roles by using their own bodies and voices. The director, designers, and playwright can sit in

Christopher Walken as Astrov and Lindsay Crouse as Yelena in David Mamet's adaptation of Chekhov's *Uncle Vanya* at the American Repertory Theatre. Directed by David Wheeler; costumes by Catherine Zuber. (Photo by Richard Feldman.)

the auditorium and watch what they have created, but stage actors can never completely separate themselves from what they are creating. Even a filmed stage performance violates the essence of stage acting: the interaction moment by moment of the live performer and the live audience. In films, scenes are almost always shot out of sequence and over a span of several months; the actors usually have only a general notion of how the scenes will fit together; typically film actors do not see the scenes in sequence until the film is ready for release months later. Even then, the performance they (and the public) see has been given much of its shape by the film's editor. Audience response cannot alter or influence what happens during a screening. All of these factors do not make the screen actor's job less difficult than the stage actor's, but they do make it different. Stage actors play scenes in the order specified by the script and complete the entire play at each performance. They must be fully aware of how the action develops, and they must shape their performances to increase and relax tension, vary tempo, create appropriate emphases, and build the action to a climax. They have been prepared for these tasks by many rehearsals with a director whose critical advice and editing have shaped the total production, but it is the actors who must re-create the performance each time—and for a new audience, whose immediate feedback continuously influences that performance.

In many ways, acting is an extension of everyday human behavior. Almost everyone speaks, moves, and interacts with others. We also play many "roles," during the course of a day adjusting to changing contexts: home, business, school, recreation, and so on. Perhaps it is not surprising, then, that it is not always easy to distinguish acting talent from certain personality traits or to convince would-be actors that rigorous training is necessary. Nevertheless, acting requires carefully honed skills, for the ability to use behavior expressively in the theatre differs from the ability to function adequately in daily life.

Acting skill is a mixture of three basic ingredients: innate ability (a special talent for acting), training, and practice (or experience). Talent is perhaps most essential, but usually it is not enough in itself; it needs to be nurtured and developed through extensive training and repeated application in performance.

The Actor's Training and Means

In acting training, though the process of acting as a whole is the ultimate concern, not all the parts can be addressed simultaneously. Therefore, different aspects of acting (voice, movement, scene study, etc.) are singled out for specialized attention even as attention is being paid to the interrelationship of the various parts. Ultimately the goal is to integrate all the parts into a seamless whole.

Body, Voice, and Inner Impulse

As the actor's primary means of communicating, the body and voice need to be flexible, disciplined, and expressive. Flexibility is needed so the actor can express physically or vocally a wide range of attitudes, traits, emotions, responses, and situations. But flexibility alone is not sufficient; actors must also be able to control body

Actors' Thoughts About Acting

Many well-known actors have been quite articulate about their profession. Here are a few excerpts.

John Barrymore (one of America's legendary classical actors, known best for his performance as Hamlet): "Acting is the art of saying a thing on the stage as if you believed every word you utter to be as true as the eternal verities of life; it is the art of doing a thing on the stage as if the logic of the event demanded that precise act and no other; and of doing and saying the thing as spontaneously as if you were confronted with the situation in which you were acting for the first time."

Joseph Chaikin (leading actor of the Open Theatre): "Only when [the actor] is awake to the whole event of the piece, rather than just his part, and his interest in what is told in the piece is immediate . . . can his work be organized to each performing situation. What he learns is how to live through the situation each time, instead of just repeating the results. [Otherwise] his performance is without the most essential acting dimension—that of being there and inhabiting the play as it's performed."

Fiona Shaw (leading contemporary British actress, speaking of her performance as Electra): "Literature, I think, is humanity's dialogue with itself and an actor is the interpreter of the text of the *writer*, who is tapping the soul of who we all are. The best one does is to give it expression—the key being one's own grief that reveals a very dark pool of basic grief that everybody has. In the end, I suspect, that dark pool is a very similar pool to everybody else's pool."

Judi Dench (one of England's major actresses, twice honored by Queen Elizabeth II, most recently in 1988 with the title Dame of the British Empire): "What I like is doing as many different things as possible in the theatre at the same time. I like being in a repertoire of four or five plays. . . . You're kept very much on your toes. . . . It's like a permanent first night and that keeps it very alive; doing a play eight times a week is a killer."

and voice at will, and such control comes only through understanding, practice, and discipline.

One of the actor's primary challenges is to understand how the body and voice function. Actors typically begin by learning how the body and voice operate in a general, physiological sense, and then proceed to explore how one's own body and voice actually are functioning. If one can discover what one's normal body alignment is, how one's center of balance functions, how one is breathing, what one's sources of tension are, and so on, one is then in a position to work toward gaining control over one's physical and vocal instrument. The initial goal is to eliminate inhibiting tensions so one can move freely and effortlessly and achieve a resonant, flexible voice; the ultimate goal is control over both body and voice for expressive use in performance.

Bill Irwin and David Shiner in *Fool Moon*, a mostly silent comedy of their own devising, relying primarily on pantomime. (Photo by Joan Marcus.)

Because the body and voice are integral parts of a total system that includes psychological forces, it is difficult to achieve physical and vocal freedom and expressiveness without some concern for the psychological processes that create tensions and blocks. Perhaps the most popular means of dealing with these has been through improvisational theatre games designed to break down inhibitions, build self-confidence, and foster trust in fellow actors. Other exercises have been borrowed from a variety of sources, both Western and Asian, most of which treat inner impulse, body, and voice as interrelated processes. Therefore, to work on any one of these is to help the others. The goal is to produce sensitive, skilled, and expressive actors.

In addition to mastery of body and voice, actors usually seek more specialized training in dancing, fencing, singing, and other skills that increase their ability to play a wide range of roles in a variety of theatrical forms.

Lee Strasberg on the Role of Imagination

Lee Strasberg exerted enormous influence on acting in America through his work at the Actors Studio, where he taught his version of the Stanislavsky "method" to many of those who would become leading performers in theatre and film. Here are some of his thoughts on the necessity for actors to project themselves into the fictional situation:

> Essentially the actor acts a fiction, a dream; in life the stimuli to which we respond are always real. The actor must constantly respond to stimuli which are imaginary. And yet this must happen not only just as it happens in life, but actually more fully and expressively. Although the actor can do things in life quite easily, when he has to do the same things on the stage under fictitious conditions he has difficulty because he is not equipped as a human being merely to playact at imitating life. He must somehow believe. He must somehow be able to convince himself of the rightness of what he is doing in order to do things fully on the stage.

—*Strasberg at the Actors Studio,* ed. by Robert Hethmon

Observation and Imagination

Actors must also be concerned with developing their powers of observation and imagination. Because human beings learn about each other in large part through observation, actors need to develop the habit of watching other people (for example, the dominant behavioral patterns of various personality types or age groups). While observed behavior may not always be directly transferable to the stage, it can be drawn on in creating convincing characterizations.

Actors must also develop imagination in order to "feel their way" into the lives of others and into fictional situations. They are sometimes counseled to develop "emotion memory"—recalling how they felt in certain types of situations—as a resource for building psychologically convincing characterizations.

Control and Discipline

No matter how well actors have mastered the basic skills, they are unlikely to use these skills effectively onstage unless they have also learned to control, shape, and integrate them as demanded by the script and the director. Control is usually achieved only through daily practice and disciplined effort over a long period.

One mark of control and discipline is *concentration*—the ability to immerse oneself in the situation and to shut out all distractions. In performance, some actors, having played the same scenes many times, may seem to be responding mechanically to cues, whereas effective actors create the illusion that this is the first time

Peter Brook includes actors in his company from many countries and trained in various traditions. He believes they learn much from each other in ways that help to transcend any one language or style of performance. In this scene from *Mahabharata*, the actors are English, Kenyan, and Polish. Ryszard Cieslak, formerly Grotowski's leading actor, is seen at right. (Photo © Martha Swope.)

they have experienced these situations, no matter how often they have performed the roles. To create such an illusion, actors must concentrate on what is developing around them—not in a general way but on the specific speeches, gestures, and movements of others in the scene—and must respond with the appropriate level of intensity at the appropriate moment. This requires actors to immerse themselves in the "here and now" of the stage action.

Stage Conventions

Over the centuries actors have developed certain ways of doing things onstage because they have proven more effective than others. Many routine tasks have been reduced to a set of conventions that actors are expected to know. Directors take for granted that actors are familiar with these conventions and give many instructions in a kind of stage shorthand.

Among the basic conventions is the division of the stage into areas, which facilitates giving directions. *Upstage* (a term dating from the time when the stage actually did slope upward toward the back) means toward the rear of the stage, just as *downstage* means toward the front; *right* and *left* refer to the actor's right or left when facing the auditorium. The stage floor may also be spoken of as though it were divided into squares, each with its own designation: *up right, up center, up left, down right, down center, down left.* (See the diagram on page 331.) The actor is expected to be familiar with body positions. *Full front* means facing the audience; *one-quarter* indicates a quarter-turn away from the audience; *one-half* or *profile* means turned ninety degrees away from the audience; *three-quarter* designates a 135-degree turn away from the audience; and *full back* means turned completely away from the audience. (See the chart on page 331.)

Other terminology may supplement designations of area and bodily position. *Open up* means to turn slightly more toward the audience; *turn in* means to turn toward the center of the stage; *turn out* means to turn toward the side of the stage. Two actors are sometimes told to *share a scene,* meaning that both should play in the one-quarter or profile position so they are equally visible to the audience. To *give stage* means that one actor gives the dominant stage position to another by facing away from the audience more than the other actor. In most scenes, emphasis shifts frequently from one character to another, and the actors may constantly be giving and taking the stage according to who needs to be most emphatic at a specific moment. To *focus* means to look at or turn toward a person or object so as to direct attention there. Actors may also be told to *dress the stage* (that is, move to balance the stage picture). Experienced actors make such movements unobtrusively and almost automatically.

Some devices are commonly used to emphasize or subordinate stage business. An object (such as a letter) that is to be important later may need to be *planted* in an earlier scene. To make sure it is noticed, the actor may hesitate, start to put it one place, then select the final spot. Conversely, some actions need to be masked from the audience. Eating, for example, must be faked to a large degree because actors can seldom eat the actual food or the amount indicated in the script. Scenes of violence (such as stabbings, shootings, and fistfights) must also be faked. To be convincing, they require careful planning and timing. Sometimes a special fight director is employed to work out fight scenes to make them convincing and safe.

In whatever they do, actors normally strive to be graceful because gracefulness is usually unobtrusive, whereas awkwardness is distracting. Movement should be precise and clear because imprecision suggests vagueness and indefiniteness. (Awkwardness and imprecision can, of course, be used to dramatic effect if they are deliberate.) Actors are better prepared if they are familiar with all aspects of theatrical production because the more they know about scenery, costumes, and lighting, the better they will be able to utilize these elements in their acting.

Scene Study

While actors are involved in gaining control over themselves as instruments, they are simultaneously involved in scene study, based either on scripts as a whole or scenes from scripts. This involves close attention to dramatic action and how it develops; learning to break scenes into beats or units (based on alterations in motivation or a change in tactics by a character, or some other change such as the entrance or exit of a character); noting changes in tempo and mood, and so on. This study is usually preliminary to enacting the scene with other actors. Scene study and its embodiment in performance (both in the classroom and in fully mounted productions) ultimately brings together all the elements of actor training.

From Training to Performing

Prior to the twentieth century, would-be actors usually learned on the job. First, they had to be accepted into a company as "utility" actors, roughly equivalent to being apprentices. They then played small roles in a variety of plays and observed the established actors closely. Training was essentially a mixture of observation and trial-and-error. After a few years, young actors discovered the types of roles to which they seemed best suited and settled into that "line of business," usually for the rest of their careers. But in the late nineteenth century, when resident companies were driven out of existence by touring productions (usually cast in New York with experienced actors), would-be actors were deprived of their traditional training ground. Although some acting schools had existed before this time, the demise of the resident companies was the principal spur to the founding of actor-training programs in the United States. In the twentieth century, actor training gradually gained a foothold in colleges and universities, which have now become the principal trainers of actors, although there are still many actor-training studios, especially in large cities. Although resident theatre companies have become prominent in the United States again, most of them employ actors who are graduates of university or other training programs. A few resident companies have their own training programs.

Most training programs stage productions to provide students opportunities to apply what they are taught. Today's training programs retain some features of the earlier apprentice system, although in today's schools learners often play major roles that in professional companies would be cast with experienced professionals. All training schemes, old or new, attempt (though often in quite different ways) to stimulate and integrate the three foundations of artistic skill—talent, training, and practice.

Although would-be actors may complete training programs and receive degrees or certificates, there are no exams or boards as there are for lawyers or doctors to certify an actor's readiness to practice the profession. Certification, such as it is, comes from being cast in professional productions. The decision to become a professional actor takes courage, for the number of aspirants greatly exceeds the available jobs. Although there are now more acting jobs in the nation's resident companies than in New York's theatres, the majority of theatre companies still hold auditions and do much of their casting in New York. Though it is possible to be an actor and live in one of the many cities that support professional companies, aspiring stage actors still gravitate to New York, just as aspiring film and television actors gravitate to Los Angeles. Chicago and a few other cities have managed to remain largely independent of both New York and Los Angeles.

Natasha Richardson and Liam Neeson in Eugene O'Neill's *Anna Christie* produced at the Roundabout Theatre, New York, under the direction of David Leveaux. (Photo © Martha Swope.)

Wherever actors live or wish to work, they all face the problem of being cast. To work in the professional theatre, an actor must be a member of Actors Equity Association, the actors' union. But less than one-quarter of Equity's members are ever employed at the same time, and only a small percentage make a living from acting. For most actors, the chances of being cast are improved if they have an agent, whose job it is to help them get employment and whose own income depends on their clients' success because the agent usually receives at least ten percent of a client's earnings. Despite the odds against success, many people persist, and enough are sufficiently successful to encourage others to try. Nevertheless, any aspiring actor must be prepared to accept rejection as part of the actor's life. Many, perhaps most, aspiring actors spend more time working as waiters or in temporary office jobs while they make the rounds of auditions than they do performing for pay on the stage. Patience and persistence are necessary attributes of would-be actors.

Most of the procedures involved in casting have already been discussed in Chapter 12. Let us assume that the actor is one of those lucky enough to have been cast and is now ready to create a role.

Creating a Role

Each time actors undertake a new role, they are faced with a number of tasks. Perhaps the most basic is to understand the role. (One approach to analyzing script and role is described in Chapter 3.) It is usually helpful to look at the role in relation to levels of characterization:

1. Biological (what does the script reveal about the character's gender, age, physical appearance, and condition of health?).
2. Sociological (what does the script reveal about the character's profession, social class, economic status, family background, and standing in the community?).
3. Psychological (what does the script reveal about the character's attitudes, likes, dislikes, general emotional makeup, motivations, and goals?).
4. Ethical (what does the script reveal about the character's system of values and choices when faced with crises and conflicts?).

Because a character may have been given many traits, it is also helpful to determine which among these traits are necessary within the dramatic action. Such inquiries form a broad base for further explorations.

The most essential aspects of a role are what the character wants and what the character is willing to do to get it. But though these define the "spine" of a role, the actor needs to examine how they are manifested in each scene or unit and how they change and evolve. This investigation helps the actor find the focus of each unit, just as examining individual units in relation to the play as a whole shows how the role builds, grows, or changes.

The actor also needs to examine how the role relates to all the others in the play. What does the character think of each of the others? How does the character present himself or herself to each of the other characters? What does each of the others think of the character? What is the function of each of these variations within the dramatic action?

The actor needs to understand the script's themes, implied meanings, and overall significance, which demands not only attention to observable relationships among characters and ideas but also sensitivity to subtext—the emotional undercurrents and unexpressed motivations and attitudes. Many plays, notably those by Anton Chekhov and Harold Pinter, depend heavily on subtext because the characters cannot or will not deal directly with problems or feelings that lie just beneath the surface. In such scripts, the actor must make the audience sense these unstated elements or the action will lose much of its power.

The actors also need to examine their roles in relation to the director's interpretation of the script (the production concept). They may wish to talk with the director about their reactions to the interpretation and how it affects their roles; some may even try to persuade the director to alter the production concept. Ultimately, however, the actors must make their roles fit whatever interpretation is used to shape the production.

Psychological and Emotional Preparation

In addition to understanding the script and the way a role fits into the total concept, the actors must be able to project themselves imaginatively into the world of the play, the specific situations, and their individual characters' feelings and motivations. An actor who has difficulty doing this may need to experiment with ways of inducing empathetic involvement. One method, borrowed from Stanislavsky, is to employ emotion memory (searching in one's own past for a parallel situation,

The emotionally climactic scene between Biff and Big Daddy in *Cat on a Hot Tin Roof*. The actors are Ray Chambers and Wayne Ballantine. (Courtesy of the Alabama Shakespeare Festival.)

recalling the emotion felt at that time, and using that emotion in acting the present scene). Another is to search out persons similar to the character and find out more about their situation and feelings. For example, an actor playing a hospital worker may come to understand the character's attitudes and frustrations more fully by spending time in a hospital participating in or observing what goes on there. The most typical method is the use of improvisations and theatre games to explore, in collaboration with other actors, multiple feelings about, and responses to, situations similar to those in the script. Such explorations may be necessary in many different scenes during the preparation or rehearsal process.

Movement, Gesture, and Business

As a rule, blocking is done in an early phase of rehearsals. The director may indicate where each character is to be at each moment or may, at least initially, let the actors position themselves and move about as their responses impel them. Actors need to feel comfortable with their blocking and movement; if they do not, they should tell the director. Most discrepancies can be settled if the actor and director discuss the character's motivations, relationship to other characters in the scene, and the function of the text unit. If they can agree on these points, they can also usually agree on how the role is to be enacted.

Even if the director specifies much of the movement, the actor still must fill in many details—the character's walk, posture, bodily attitudes, and gestures. (For a discussion of movement and its purposes, see Chapter 12.) Actors may find it helpful to approach physical characterization in three steps. First, they need to take into consideration the physical traits required by the action and any changes that occur during the play. Second, they may wish to assess which of a character's physical traits need to be dominant in any given unit. It is sometimes helpful to think of a play as though it had no dialogue; actors would then have to convey through visual means the situation, motivations, and emotional responses. This approach, if followed fully, would probably lead to an overabundance of movement (and overacting), but using it in the preparatory stages can stimulate the imagination and provide the actors with a number of possibilities from among which they can choose. It may also require actors to execute each movement precisely, helping them avoid vague, indefinite, and confusing movement. Third, without violating the limits established by the script, role, and production concept, the actors may work for distinctiveness and avoid clichés. A physical characterization can be judged by its appropriateness, clarity, expressiveness, and distinctiveness.

Vocal Characterization

Although actors cannot radically change their dominant vocal traits during a rehearsal period, they may, if they have well-trained voices, modify their vocal patterns considerably for purposes of characterization. The variable factors in voice are *pitch*, *volume*, and *quality*, each of which may be used to achieve many different effects. (For a discussion of these aspects of sound, see Chapter 10.) Typically, the voice is used to speak lines in a manner that evokes or defines emotions, ideas, or situations.

Actors in a twentieth-century commedia dell'arte play, *The Strolling Players* by Darwin Reid Payne and Christian Moe, as performed by Theatre London's Young Company (Canada). (Photo by Carolyn A. McKeone/FPG.)

The voice is also sometimes used as a type of sound gesture or to create mood through nonverbal dissonances, harmonies, or rhythmical effects.

The variable factors of speech are articulation, duration, inflection, and projection (or audibility). *Articulation* involves the production of sounds, while *pronunciation* involves the selection and combination of sounds. A person may articulate sounds clearly but mispronounce words, just as a person may know how to pronounce a word but articulate sounds so imprecisely as to be unintelligible. The well-trained actor should be able to speak clearly or to alter articulation and pronunciation as needed to suit character and situation. One of the most memorable features of Marlon Brando's roles is his vocal characterizations, achieved through control over articulation, pronunciation, and quality.

Duration refers to the length of time assigned to any sound, *inflection* to rising and falling pitch. Both duration and inflection are used to stress some syllables and subordinate others. Without proper stress, words may be unrecognizable. (Try, for example, shifting stress from the first to the second syllable of *probably*.) Duration also refers to the number of words spoken per minute. Slowness can create the impression of laziness, old age, or weakness, whereas a rapid rate may suggest tension

Directors' Thoughts About Acting

Directors frequently comment on acting because the actor is the primary material they use to embody their interpretations of scripts. Here are some statements about acting by major directors.

Peter Brook (perhaps the best-known director of the English-speaking world): "Acting is in many ways unique in its difficulties because the artist has to use the treacherous, changeable and mysterious material of himself as his medium. He is called upon to be completely involved while distanced—detached without detachment. He must be sincere, he must be insincere; he must practice how to be insincere with sincerity and how to lie truthfully."

Bertolt Brecht (one of the twentieth century's major playwrights and directors, explaining the kind of acting he sought for his epic theatre): "The actor does not let himself be transformed into the man he presents so that nothing of himself is left. He is not Lear, Harpagon, or the good soldier Schweik—he is 'showing' them to an audience. . . . Giving up the idea of complete transformation, the actor brings forward his text, not as an improvisation, but as a *quotation*. . . . In this sort of acting, where the transformation of the actor is incomplete, three devices can contribute to the alienation of the words and actions of the person presenting them: 1. The adoption of a third person. 2. The adoption of a past tense. 3. The speaking of stage directions and comments. . . . Through this threefold process the text is alienated in rehearsal and in general will remain so in performance."

Jerzy Grotowski (Polish director who exerted great influence on the training of actors beginning in the 1960s): "One must not think of the spectator while acting. . . . If the actor has the spectator as his point of orientation, he . . . will be offering himself for sale. . . . A sort of prostitution. . . . at the same time, he must not neglect the fact of the public. . . . he must act *vis-à-vis* with the spectators . . . he must . . . do an act of extreme yet disciplined sincerity and authenticity. He must give himself and not hold himself back, open up and not close in on himself in a narcissistic way. . . . The most important thing for me . . . is to rediscover the elements of the actor's art."

or vivacity. Inflection (change in pitch) is one of the principal indicators of meaning. Surprise, disgust, indifference, and other reactions may be indicated by tone of voice, and the alteration of inflection can often completely change the meaning of a line or transform a statement of fact into a question. Duration and inflection play key roles in dialects (regional "accents"). Acting coaches often counsel those working on a Southern accent, for example, to end sentences on a rising inflection and to prolong the final sounds.

In performance, actors should be both audible (which depends on *projection* or volume) and intelligible (which depends primarily on articulation and pronunciation) because the audience needs both to hear and to understand what the characters are saying. Actors must also be concerned with *variety* (which may be achieved through alterations in any of the variable aspects of voice and speech). Nothing is more deadening than hearing all lines delivered at the same pace and intensity. Variety is more easily achieved if the actor clearly understands situation and motivations because any change in thought or feeling triggers changes in volume, pitch, or quality, as well as in the variable factors of speech.

Memorization and Line Readings

A task that every actor faces is memorization. It is usually helpful to memorize speeches and movements simultaneously because they reinforce each other. Furthermore, because blocking is done in relation to specific speeches, this conjunction ultimately becomes fused in the memory.

Memorization is aided by a few simple procedures. Because it is impossible to memorize everything at once, the script may be broken into units and mastered one unit at a time. In each, the actors must ultimately not only learn their own lines but also be familiar with the lines of others in the scene. In addition, actors must memorize *cues* (the words or actions of others that immediately precede and trigger their lines) as thoroughly as they memorize their own lines. Before trying to memorize specific lines, it is helpful to study the sequence of ideas or shifts in emotion and tone—the overall development of the unit. Familiarity with sequence and a thorough understanding of the meaning and purpose of each line in a unit are the greatest aids to memorization. (The actual process of memorization requires going over the lines many times, usually while someone else keeps an eye on the script as a check on accuracy as well as to provide the appropriate cues.)

After the actors know their lines well enough not to need the script as a crutch, they usually need to do some fine-tuning to mesh their understanding of the lines with their use of the controllable factors of voice and speech. They must be concerned with timing, pacing, and pauses. They must make sure that speeches, especially long ones, build properly, that their line readings create a sense of spontaneity and conviction, and that the readings are appropriate to character, emotion, and situation.

Refining the Role

The foundation work (understanding the role; psychological and emotional preparation; movement, gesture, and business; vocal characterization; memorization) proceeds simultaneously with rehearsals, some of it in isolation, much of it with the director and other actors. In the early phases, different approaches to a scene or aspects of character may be tried and abandoned. Eventually, the major decisions are made, the movement and vocal patterns become clear, and the lines are committed to memory. There follows a period of refining and perfecting the role and integrating it into the whole performance.

This phase is difficult to describe because it varies with the actor, the role, and the production. Typically, much of the time is spent on deepening one's understanding of motivations and relationships. Other concerns during this phase are

Laurence Olivier (right front) as the tormented Captain in Strindberg's *Dance of Death* at the National Theatre, London. The other actors are Geraldine McEwen and Robert Stephens. (Photo by Zoe Dominic.)

complex business, precise timing, pacing, and variety. Actors must make sure their roles progress and build appropriately.

No single role (except in those rare plays with one character) is complete in itself. It is sometimes said that performing in a play is not acting so much as reacting. The director usually works to achieve the sense of give-and-take, cooperation, and mutual support that characterizes *ensemble playing*. The goal is a seamless whole rather than a series of separate performances; it can be reached only if all actors are willing to subordinate themselves to the demands of the production. Ensemble playing depends on the actors' awareness of each other's strengths and weaknesses, where they will get support, and where they need to compensate for another's weakness.

Dress Rehearsals and Performance

Not until dress rehearsals are actors usually able to work with all properties, settings, costumes, makeup, and stage lighting. Frequently, this is also the first time

Laurence Olivier (1907–1989)

Many consider Laurence Olivier to have been among the greatest male actors of the twentieth century. After attending the Central School of Speech in London, he achieved his first London and New York successes in Noel Coward's *Private Lives* in 1929. During the 1930s, he became an accomplished Shakespearean actor, gaining recognition for alternating the roles of Mercutio and Romeo with John Gielgud in a 1935 production. He also played such roles as Hamlet, Macbeth, and Henry V at the Old Vic. After an unpromising start, he achieved stardom in films in the 1930s, first in *Wuthering Heights* and subsequently during the 1940s in *Rebecca* and a series of Shakespearean films that he both directed and starred in: *Henry V, Hamlet* (for which he won an Academy Award), and *Richard III.* After World War II, he headed the Old Vic with Ralph Richardson and made that theatre the best in the English-speaking world. At the Old Vic, he achieved one of his greatest triumphs in playing on a single bill the title character in Sophocles' *Oedipus Rex* and the foppish Mr. Puff in Sheridan's *The Critic.* Olivier's scream when Oedipus learns that he has killed his father and married his mother became legendary. Until 1957, Olivier was noted primarily as a classical actor, but in that year he revitalized his career when he triumphed in the role of Archie Rice, a decaying music-hall performer in John Osborne's *The Entertainer.* His success did much to stimulate other classical actors to undertake a new repertory. In 1963, when England created the National Theatre, Olivier was named artistic director. He served in that capacity, and was one of the company's stars, until 1974. During those years, the National Theatre became one of the world's most respected companies. In 1970, Olivier's status in his profession was acknowledged when he became the first actor in English history to be raised to the peerage. In 1974 Olivier gave up stage acting but continued to perform in films and television until 1988. He died in 1989.

Olivier was noted for the wide range of roles he played, from Greek and Shakespearean tragedy to contemporary domestic drama and from classical to modern comedy. He was also noted for the originality and power of his characterizations, his attention to detail, and his complete assurance. He devoted long hours to perfecting accents and experimenting with makeup. One of his most daring stage feats came in a production of Shakespeare's *Coriolanus* in 1959, when at a climactic moment he flung himself headfirst from the upper level of a set, depending on two actors to catch him by the ankles.

In his autobiography, Olivier declared that to be a successful actor one needs "an equal trinity of contributing qualities: talent, luck, and stamina." In his book *On Acting* (1986), he commented: "If somebody asked me to put in one sentence what acting was, I should say that acting was the art of persuasion. He persuades himself, first, and through himself, the audience. In order to achieve that . . . you need . . . observation and intuition. . . . you've got to find, in the actor, a man who will not be too proud to scavenge the tiniest bit of human circumstance; observe it, find it, use it. . . ."

they have been able to work on the stage that will be used for performances. Thus, dress rehearsals may be occasions of considerable stress.

Of special importance to actors are their costumes because they affect not only appearance but also movement and gesture. Actors should find out everything they can about their costumes in advance of dress rehearsals—which movements a garment enhances or restricts, its possibilities for use in stage business, and so on. If stage garments will be significantly different from clothing they normally wear, actors should have been provided suitable rehearsal garments from the beginning. Actors should also give thought to their makeup before the dress-rehearsal period begins. They should know what effects they wish to create and how to achieve them. They should also have rehearsed with reasonable facsimiles of the properties they will use in performances.

Performance is the ultimate goal. The better prepared the actors are, the more confident they will feel on opening night, although it is a rare actor who does not experience some stage fright—which, because it increases alertness, may be turned to advantage. Some actors feel a letdown after opening night and must guard

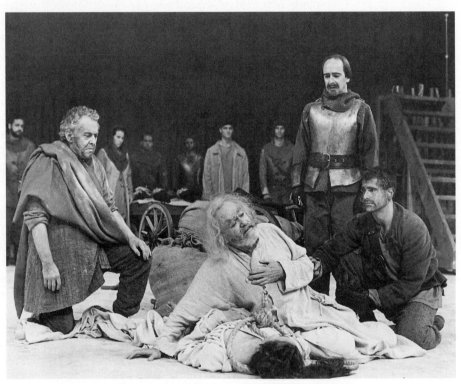

One of the great acting roles is that of King Lear in Shakespeare's play of the same name. Shown here is the final scene of the play with Kent (Jeremy Geidt), Lear (Jerome Kilty), Cordelia (Stephanie Roth), Albany (Martin Rayner), and Edgar (Stephen Skybell). Directed by Adrian Hall; setting by Eugene Lee; costumes by Catherine Zuber; lighting by Natasha Katz. (Photo by Richard Feldman.)

against diminished effectiveness during the following performances. Long runs create special dangers because the actors may begin to perform mechanically because of overfamiliarity with their roles. The best guards against such letdowns are concentration and reminders that each performance is the first for this particular audience. Ultimately, performance offers the actor one of the best opportunities for learning because the ability to affect or control an audience's responses is a major test of acting skill.

Thinking About . . .

The Actor's Work

When we attend the theatre, our attention is focused primarily on the characters, for it is through them that the action develops. But what the actors who play the characters do and say is based on the dramatist's script, just as the interpretation and overall production concept are decided by the director. What the actors wear is provided by the costume designer; the stage environment is created by the scenic designer; and much of the mood and visual emphasis is created by the lighting designer. In such a cooperative venture, it is not easy to isolate the actors' contributions. Perhaps that is as it should be because usually the director's goal is to create a unified whole rather than a collection of easily distinguishable parts. Nevertheless, even if we cannot determine precisely what is to be attributed to each production element, we often are impelled to make the attempt. Here are some questions that may help us assess the actors' performances and estimate their contributions to the production:

1. *Were the roles appropriately cast? Were actors and roles adequately meshed? Were some actors inadequate to their roles? In what ways? How did this affect the other roles and the action of the play? Were some actors especially effective? If so, how and with what effect?*

2. *In what type of space did the performance take place? How did this affect the actors' tasks? With what results?*

3. *Were the actors audible? Understandable? Were the vocal characterizations suited to the roles? Were there actors whose voices noticeably enhanced or detracted from their performances? In what ways?*

4. *Were the physical characterizations suited to the roles? Were there actors whose movements or gestures noticeably enhanced or detracted from their performances? In what ways? How extensively were movement and stage business used? Did they have distinctive qualities? If so, what was the result?*

5. *Were the characters' psychological attributes and motivations clear? Were some actors especially effective or ineffective in projecting these aspects of characterization? If so, how and with what effect?*

6. *Were the relationships among the characters clear? Were some actors especially effective or ineffective in clarifying relationships? If so, how and with what effect?*

7. *Were any special skills (such as dancing, singing, fencing, playing a musical instrument) required of any of the actors? If so, how effectively were the demands met? With what effect on the production?*

8. *Did the actors make any special use of costume, scenery, properties, or lighting? If so, in what ways and with what effect?*

9. *Did the actors achieve a sense of "the first time"? Did they work together effectively as an ensemble? If so, with what effect? If not, what interfered? With what result?*

10. *Overall, were the themes and implications of the play clear? Was the clarity or lack of it attributable to the acting? Script? Directing? Visual design? Total production?*

Most of these questions cannot be answered precisely, not only because some of the needed information may not be available but also because, even if the information were available, responses would be at least partially subjective. Answers to each question are likely to vary widely from one audience member to another. Nevertheless, trying to answer these questions as they relate to specific productions or performances will focus attention on the processes and results of acting and will encourage detailed attention to actors' performances.

Chapter 14

Scenic Design

Setting by Rudi Barch for Goethe's *Iphigeneia in Tauris*. This abstract design does not attempt to represent place but rather to symbolize the interlocking ethical positions of the play. (Courtesy of the German Information Center.)

A stage setting has no independent life of its own. Its emphasis is directed toward the performance. In the absence of the actor it does not exist. . . . The actor adds the one element that releases the hidden energy of the whole. Meanwhile, wanting the actor, the various elements which go to make up the setting remain suspended . . . in an indefinable tension. To create this suspense, this tension, is the essence of the problem of stage designing.

—Robert Edmond Jones, *The Dramatic Imagination*

The scene designer is concerned with the organization and appearance of the performance space. The designer defines and characterizes the space, arranges it to facilitate the movement of the actors, and uses it to reinforce the production concept.

The Designer's Skills

Scene designers need a variety of skills, many of them pertinent to other arts, especially architecture, painting, interior design, and acting. Like architects, scene designers conceive and build structures for human beings to use. Although scene designers do not design entire buildings, as an architect does, they sculpt space and, like the architect, must be concerned with its function, size, organization, construction, and visual appearance. Also like the architect, they must be able to communicate their ideas to others through sketches, scale models, and construction drawings that indicate how each element is built and how it will look when completed.

Scene designers, in some aspects of their work, use skills similar to the painter's. For example, one of the designer's primary ways of communicating with the director and other designers is through sketches and drawings. During preliminary discussions of a production, designers usually make numerous sketches to demonstrate possible solutions to design problems; before these designs are given final approval, they usually are rendered in perspective and in color. For final designs, watercolors are the scene designer's most common medium, but pastels and other color media are sometimes used. In addition to making sketches showing entire settings, designers also make painters' elevations—scale drawings of each piece of scenery showing how it is to be painted and the painting techniques to be used. Designers sometimes must paint (or supervise others who paint) the scenery they have designed.

In other aspects of their work, scene designers use the skills of an interior decorator because many sets are incomplete without furniture, rugs, drapes, pictures, and decorative details. In creating appropriate interiors, designers also need some of the actor's skills because they must understand the characters who inhabit the spaces and whose tastes have dictated the choice of furnishings and decorative features.

Additionally, scene designers need to be grounded in art history (including architecture, crafts, and decorative arts) because in creating settings designers must be familiar with architectural styles and the history of decorative motifs, furniture, and accessories. In stage settings, such details not only reflect a specific period or place but also indicate the economic status and tastes of the characters. Similarly, designers need to know stage history so they may (when appropriate) draw on the theatrical conventions of other times, places, or cultures to connect the play with its original context or to enhance the production concept.

Scene designers must understand scenic construction techniques (because they must specify how each part of their settings is to be built) and scenic painting (because they must specify the color of each visible surface and the painting techniques to be used). Designers should also be familiar with new materials and technologies and their potential for design purposes. Plastics, Styrofoam, and laser projections, for example, have opened up new possibilities and stimulated innovative designs. Many designers now use computers in creating their designs.

The Functions of Stage Design

Scenic design serves many functions. It *defines the performance space* by establishing distinctions between onstage and offstage. Through the use of flats, drapes, platforms, or other means, designers delineate the areas that will be used for the dramatic action. Designers may employ a great deal of masking so that persons or objects outside a clearly marked area cannot be seen by the audience; or they may use virtually no masking and thereby acknowledge that the place of the action is a stage that continues into the wings as far as the audience can see. In arena and thrust theatres, the layout of audience seating may outline the acting space. In a variable space, acting space and audience space may be intermingled.

Scene design *creates a floor plan* that provides multiple opportunities for movement, composition, character interaction, and stage business. The location of exits and entrances, the placement (or absence) of furniture, the presence or absence of steps, levels, and platforms—all the elements of the setting and their arrangement—are among the greatest influences on blocking, picturization, and movement. A setting can be organized in many different ways; arranging it to maximum advantage for a specific production requires careful and cooperative planning by designer and director.

Scene design visually *characterizes the acting space.* Just how it does so depends on the production concept. If the concept demands that locales be represented realistically, the designer will probably select architectural details, furniture, and decorations that clearly indicate a specific period and locale. For example, the designer might create a setting for *A Doll's House* that suggests a room in a Norwegian house around 1880. Another production concept might demand fragmentary settings with only enough pieces to establish the general character of the locale. Another might rely largely on visual motifs and theatrical conventions from the era when the play was written. A setting for *Tartuffe,* for example, might use decorative motifs and a wing-and-drop setting reflecting the age of Louis XIV. Or, as has become increasingly common, the concept might demand that the time and place of the action be altered (such as *Hamlet* being translated to an American Mafia context).

Another way of characterizing the space is to treat it as flexible and nonspecific, a common practice for plays with actions divided into many scenes and set in many places, as is typical in most of Shakespeare's plays. To represent each place realistically would require a large number of sets as well as a great deal of time to

Realistic restaurant setting for August Wilson's *Two Trains Running* as produced by the Huntington Theatre Company, Boston. Directed by Lloyd Richards; setting by Tony Fanning. (Photo by Richard Feldman.)

change them, thereby interrupting the continuity, rhythm, and flow of the action. On the other hand, to play all the scenes on the flat floor of an undecorated stage might become monotonous. A common solution is an arrangement of platforms, steps, and ramps that breaks up the stage space, provides several acting areas that can be used all together or isolated singly through lighting, and that can be localized as needed through the addition of a few well-chosen properties, pieces of furniture, banners, images projected on screens, or through other means.

Scene design may *make a strong interpretational statement*. The setting for Beckett's *Happy Days* visually sums up the human condition as depicted in the play: an individual isolated, trapped, forced to make the best of her lot. For a play about war, the game of chess has been used as a metaphor, with the stage floor laid out in black and white squares, and the characters costumed to suggest chess pieces. The settings for *"The Hairy Ape"* incorporate images of human beings caged and dehumanized.

Scene design *creates mood and atmosphere*. Robert Edmond Jones' setting for *Macbeth* creates a powerful mood of foreboding as the masks of the witches brood

Ezio Frigerio's setting for Goldoni's *The Servant of Two Masters* at the Piccolo Teatro, Milan. The theatricality and playfulness of the commedia script are captured in the setting, which simulates a makeshift stage erected within the ruins of a building. (Courtesy of the Piccolo Teatro, Milan.)

over the stage and the Gothic arches lean ever more precariously. (See the illustration on page 191.) On the other hand, Ezio Frigerio's settings for *The Servant of Two Masters* (above) create a sense of carefree improvisation through details painted on cloths (with slits for entrances) suspended like shower curtains on visible rods.

Scene design is only one *part of a total design,* which includes costumes, lighting, acting, and all the other elements of a production. It should evolve in consultation with those responsible for the other parts of the whole. It is not, as a painting is, complete in itself; it cannot be judged entirely by appearance, for it should not only look appropriate but also function appropriately.

Working Plans and Procedures

Scene designers, like other theatre artists, usually begin their preparations by familiarizing themselves with the play. Initially, they try to understand the script as a total structure—its action, characters, themes, language, meaning—because what they design may be affected by all of these and because the scenery needs to reflect or enhance all of these elements. As designers continue their study of the script, they focus increasingly on clues about scenic demands and visual style. During this process, they accumulate information of various sorts: the number of locales; the types of locales (prison, living room, park, and so on); the amount of space required by the action in each scene; the arrangement (location of entrances and exits, placement of furniture, need for steps and levels, and the like) required by the action in each scene; the period, geographical place, and socioeconomic conditions; and any other factors that influence the scenery.

Designers may also utilize information from sources other than the script. They may wish to know about the manners and customs, decorative motifs, architectural styles, furnishings, and favorite color schemes in use during the period of the play's action. They may wish to understand the political and social context out of which the play came. They may explore the staging conventions for which the play was originally written. Or they may undertake various other explorations. Although they may not incorporate all they learn into their designs, their imaginations may be stimulated by the fuller understanding they have gained of the script and its context.

Before they make sketches and plans (and perhaps before they have begun to study the script and its context), scene designers meet with the director and other designers to discuss the play and the production concept. The director may use an initial meeting to elicit ideas from the designers and ask them to participate in formulating a production concept. Many directors explain the production concept they have already formulated, although they may still be open to suggestions and willing to make alterations in the concept. However it evolves, a concept (or interpretational focus) is needed as a guide for the designer's work. In addition to the concept, other information should be made available to the designers before they begin work. They need to know if the director has any special demands (location of entrances and exits; specific floor plan; space for dances or fight scenes, and the like).

Designer's sketch by Richard Isackes for a production of Ibsen's *Ghosts* for the Court Theatre, Chicago. (Courtesy of Richard Isackes.)

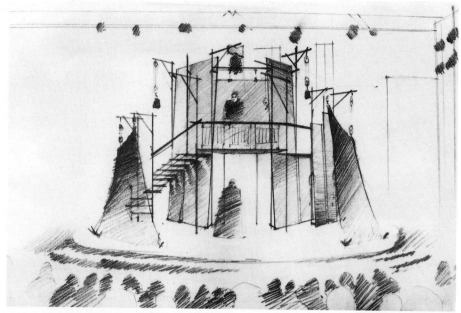

Robert Schmidt's preliminary sketch for Shakespeare's *Richard III* for a production at the Colorado Shakespeare Festival. (Courtesy of Robert Schmidt.)

They need to know the budget for scenery, the space to be used for performances, what equipment and personnel are available. After they understand the limits within which they must work—the script, the production concept, the performance space, the budget, and the personnel—the designers are ready to proceed.

There is no standard way of moving through the design process. Most designers make many tentative, preliminary sketches as a means of thinking through possibilities. Much of this preliminary work can now be done using computer-assisted design programs. Some designers make a scale model of the empty performance space and try different arrangements of scenic pieces on this model. Some think in terms of design elements—the line, mass, color, or texture needed to capture the dominant qualities of the dramatic action or the production concept. However they work, designers eventually arrive at preliminary designs to present at a conference with the director and the other designers. (Design decisions involve not only how the settings function as acting spaces, but also how they relate to costume and lighting designs and the total "look" of the production.) Through a process of reaction and revision, tentative agreement is reached, but before the designs are given final approval, they must usually be rendered as perspective color sketches that indicate how the sets will look on stage when lighted. Scene designers must also supply floor plans (drawn to scale) that show the layout of each set on the stage. Designers may also be asked to construct three-dimensional scale models that show in miniature how each set will look when completed. (It is not unusual for directors to ask for either a color sketch or a scale model, although in many situations both are expected.)

Model of the setting for *Richard III*. (Courtesy of Robert Schmidt.)

After the designs have been approved, the next step is to make working drawings. The number and type of drawings needed vary from one type of organization to another. For example, in a permanent company that maintains a stock of scenic units, it may be unnecessary to make working drawings of every flat and platform because many will be pulled from stock. In the Broadway theatre, every piece is usually built new by union workers who insist on precise drawings for every detail. The designer may have to provide some or all of the following, in addition to perspective sketches, floor plans, and scale models: (1) rear elevations, which indicate the type of construction, materials, and methods to be used in assembling each unit as seen from the rear; (2) front elevations, which show each unit in two dimensions from the front, with indications of such features as molding, baseboards, and platforms; (3) side elevations, which show units in profile, indicating the thickness and shape of each unit; (4) detailed individual drawings, which show the methods by which such units as platforms, steps, trees, columns, and similar objects are to be built; and (5) painters' elevations, which show the color of the base coat and any overpainting to be used on each unit. With the exception of the perspective sketches, all of the plans are drawn to scale so that the exact size of any object may be determined. In addition to the drawings listed above, designers may also need to provide special plans showing how the scenery is to be shifted and how it is to be stored during performance when it is not on stage.

After the plans are completed, the construction phase can begin. While designers may not be directly involved in building the scenery, they must approve all work to ensure that it conforms to the original specifications.

The setting for *Richard III* in use. Note that the setting is composed primarily of pipe scaffolding, metal grilles, and wire mesh. Directed by Jack Clay. (Courtesy of the Colorado Shakespeare Festival.)

Ming Cho Lee's set for Patrick Meyers's *K2,* the action of which takes place on the icy face of the world's second highest mountain. Essentially vertical, the setting is made primarily of Styrofoam. (Photo by Martha Swope.)

Ming Cho Lee

Ming Cho Lee is often said to be the most influential of contemporary American scene designers. Born in China, he learned landscape watercolor there before coming to the United States in 1949. After studying at Occidental College and UCLA, he went to New York, where he became an assistant to Jo Mielziner, who was then America's foremost scene designer. Most of his own early work was done for groups with limited budgets, among them the New York Shakespeare Festival, for which he was principal designer from 1962 until 1972. During these years Lee developed the style that was to influence many other designers: discarding pictorial, painted scenery in favor of defining the space with scaffolding built from metal pipes or wood and combining the scaffolding with fragments of scenery (usually heavily textured) suggesting collage. Although by 1980 Lee's designs had become more realistic, he is still usually associated with a spare, elegant, minimalist style. He has continued to experiment with innovative materials and multimedia. Though he has seldom worked on Broadway, his influence there is strong because many of its designers are graduates of Yale University's School of Drama, where Lee is head of design training. Each spring for several years, Lee has hosted the Stage Design Portfolio Review, an exhibition of work by student designers from throughout the country at which Lee and a number of other leading designers discuss and offer critiques of the students' designs. This has become a major showcase for young designers seeking to enter the profession

Lee prefers to work in regional or repertory companies because he feels that is where collaboration is most respected ("the regional theatre atmosphere invites you to behave as part of a family"), whereas on Broadway stars, directors, or producers exert too much control. Lee considers his strengths as a designer to be his sense of proportion and his understanding of the demands and restrictions of various kinds of theatrical space—arena, thrust, or proscenium. Some of his most successful work has been for arena and thrust stages. (For examples of Lee's work, see pages 238 and 371 and color plate 18.)

Basic Scenic Elements

A combination of rising costs, changing tastes, improved materials, and new equipment since 1960 has steadily diminished concern for full-stage, realistic settings. Although complete box sets are still seen occasionally, they are far less common than they used to be. A majority of settings today are composed of a few set pieces and stage properties or of steps and levels; they tend to be fragmentary and evocative rather than completely representational, many being wholly abstract. Since the 1960s, new materials (such as Styrofoam and thermoplastics) and unconventional construction methods (such as molding Plexiglas into weight-bearing forms) have encouraged innovative techniques. Traditional stagecraft practices still play a major role in most settings, however, because the built pieces (though fewer in number) are usually constructed according to time-tested procedures or variations on them.

Designers utilize a few basic kinds of units: soft, framed, and three-dimensional. Let us look briefly at each type.

Soft-Scenery Units

Soft-scenery units are typically made of unframed cloth. Usually suspended from overhead, they provide a large area of scenery that can easily be moved and stored. Most soft units can be folded up when not in use. The most common soft-scenery units are borders, drops, draperies, and cycloramas. The *border,* a short curtain or strip of painted canvas, is the most frequently used overhead masking for both interior and exterior scenes. Borders are hung parallel to the front of the stage and in a series from front to back. They may be of black cloth or of canvas painted and shaped to represent the beams of a ceiling, foliage, or some other visual element of the setting. Arena and thrust stages typically do not use borders; instead, the area above the stage is painted black and is sometimes divided into boxlike compartments within which lighting instruments may be mounted. On no type of stage is overhead masking now considered of great importance because it is no longer thought necessary to mask fully (or even partially) the space above the acting area.

Drops are used to enclose settings at the back and as surfaces on which scenes can be painted. A drop is made by sewing together enough lengths of canvas to create an area of the desired size. Typically, the cloth is attached to a wooden or metal batten at the top for support and to another at the bottom to keep it stretched and free from wrinkles. A drop may also have portions cut out so that another drop or object is visible behind it, thereby creating apparent depth and distance. Drops can be raised into, or lowered from, the fly space above the stage; they can be rolled up and stored when not in use.

Draperies may be hung parallel to the proscenium on either side of the stage in a series from front to back in order to mask the sides of the stage in the manner of wings. They may be any color. Black draperies are sometimes used to surround the acting area or to create an enclosing void for a fragmentary setting. Draperies may also be made of canvas or muslin; they may be dyed, or they may have scenes (such as a forest or a distant city) painted on them and be hung in folds to create stylized backgrounds.

Scrim, a specialized curtain made of gauze, appears opaque when lighted only from the front but is transparent when lighted from behind. It can be hung in folds or stretched tightly. It may be used initially as a background for a scene and then become transparent to show another scene behind the first one; it may be used for the appearance and disappearance of ghosts and apparitions; and it can create the effect of seeing a scene through fog or mist.

A *cyclorama* is any arrangement of curtains that surrounds the stage area on three sides. It may be composed of draperies, but typically it is a continuous, tightly stretched curtain suspended on a U-shaped pipe curving around the back and sides of the stage. It is usually neutral or light gray, so that its perceived color may be changed through lighting. It is used to represent the sky, to give the effect of infinite space, and to allow the maximum use of stage space without the need for numerous masking pieces. It is also used as a surface for projections (such as moving storm clouds or abstract, symbolic patterns).

Soft-scenery units are used more extensively on proscenium stages than on thrust or arena stages, where less masking is needed and where scenic units more easily interfere with sightlines.

Framed Units

Units are framed to make them capable of supporting themselves. They are usually relatively small in comparison with soft-scenery units but can be combined to create larger surfaces. The basic framed unit is the *flat* (a wooden frame over which canvas or muslin is stretched). Flats of almost any width or height can be made, but as they become larger, they become less stable. The height of flats usually ranges from eight to sixteen feet, and the width from one to six feet. The most common framed unit is the *plain flat*—one without an opening. Other types include the *door flat* (with an opening into which a door frame may be set), *window flat, fireplace flat,* and *arch flat* (with an opening shaped like one of the basic types of arches: Roman, Gothic, and so on). There are many variations on these basic units. Flats may be constructed with slanting sides or with edges shaped to simulate the silhouettes of trees, rocks, distant mountains, ruined arches, and the like, but most have smooth edges so that they may be combined to create larger units, such as the walls of a box set or the exterior of a castle. Other framed units include *door frames* (with or without *doors*), *window frames* (usually with some type of *window*), and *fireplace* units. Occasionally, drops are framed on all four sides.

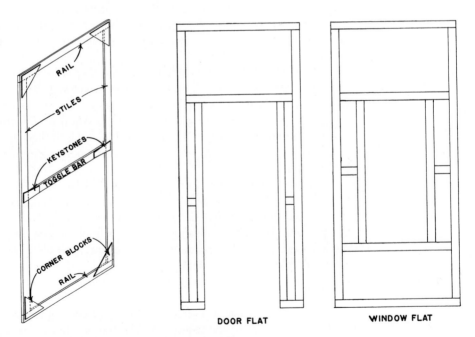

Types of flats: plain flat, door flat, window flat.

Screens have become typical framed units since the 1960s, when the incorporation of projected still or moving pictures became common. Screens may be used alone or with other screens. They may rest on the floor, although usually they are flown. Some may be relatively near the audience, others far upstage; they may be rigged so that they can be raised, lowered, or moved laterally during a performance; they may be of any shape or size and made from almost any material—wide-mesh netting, translucent plastic, textured cloth, and so on. Some of these surfaces blur images, some give texture, some permit images to bleed through onto other surfaces; on some screens, images can be projected only from the front, on others, only from the rear. Screens can be used for projected slides or moving images; they may also be used to show offstage or onstage live scenes transmitted to the screens by way of closed-circuit television. There is a wide range of uses for screens, although some options require more advanced technology than is available in many theatres.

Three-Dimensional Units

Soft and framed units are usually two dimensional. Other units, however, especially those that must support considerable weight, must be three dimensional. These include *steps, ramps,* and *platforms.* Certain other scenic pieces, though they may not always be weight-bearing, are still usually built as three-dimensional forms. These include *rocks, mounds, tree trunks,* and *columns.* Extensive use of three-dimensional

John Conklin

John Conklin (1937–   ) is one of America's most influential designers because of his work with numerous theatre and opera companies and his teaching at New York University. He began his career at the Williamstown Theatre Festival in the late 1950s. He has designed settings (and often costumes for the same productions) for the Hartford Stage, Goodman Theatre (Chicago), the American Repertory Company (Cambridge, Massachusetts), the Chicago Lyric Opera, the Metropolitan Opera, the New York City Opera, and the San Francisco Opera, as well as several European opera companies. He has also collaborated with Robert Wilson on designs for many of Wilson's pieces. His designs often select images from the different scenes of a play and combine them to create a single setting that remains unchanged throughout except for the rearrangement of a few properties or pieces of furniture. Such settings have become characteristic of much postmodern theatrical design. But his work is eclectic, some of it very realistic. In 1991, along with Mark Lamos, director, and Pat Collins, lighting designer, Conklin received the Theatre Crafts International Award for ten years of excellence and innovation at the Hartford Stage. In 1993 his play, *The Carving of Mount Rushmore,* was presented at the Actors Theatre of Louisville's new play festival. (For examples of Conklin's work, see pages 234, 281 and 300.)

units is most common on proscenium stages or in flexible spaces, but they may also be used sparingly on thrust and arena stages. Three-dimensional objects or fragments of architecture may be suspended above a thrust or arena stage to suggest what is not shown. For *Death of a Salesman* at the Arena Stage in Washington, for example, the designer Karl Eigsti hung architectural fragments overhead to create a sense of time and place (see illustration on page 287). How these various types of scenic units are constructed is beyond the scope of this discussion; the processes are described fully in books on scenic practices.

Innovative Materials and Methods

During the past two or three decades, there have been many experiments with non-traditional materials. Metal pipes and stainless steel have been joined by welding to create intricate towers and structures of various kinds. Fiberglass (treated with chemicals to make it pliable) has been molded into rocks, mounds, and other shapes

Josef Svoboda's setting for Karel Capek's *The Insect Comedy*, which looks at human behavior through the perspective of various insects. This scene concerns acquisitiveness as epitomized by the dung beetle, whose balls of dung are related to moneygrubbing through the numbers inscribed on the balls. The distinctiveness of the setting comes in part from the slanted reflecting surface (made of mylar) suspended so as to replicate endlessly the onstage people and objects. (Photo by Jaromir Svoboda.)

and allowed to harden, creating lightweight pieces capable of supporting heavy loads. Styrofoam and urethane have been incised to create the three-dimensional forms of moldings, bricks, and carvings, or sculpted to create figurines and other properties formerly difficult to construct. Vacuform molds, in which one can duplicate in plastic almost any shape (including armor, swords, or small scenic units), have also become common. Traditional and innovative stagecraft coexist and supplement each other.

The basic units discussed here are the building blocks with which designers usually work. They must decide which pieces are needed for the settings they have designed, and they must supply the working drawings for construction or indicate which pieces in existing stock are to be used. For pieces using unusual materials or construction methods, designers need to supply detailed drawings and instructions.

Assembling Scenery

After the units are constructed, they are ready to be assembled to create a setting. Some pieces may be more or less complete as built, but others need to be combined with, or attached to, other units to complete a section of the setting. The way the pieces are assembled depends in part on whether the scenery must be transported from one place to another and whether it must be shifted or stored during the run of the production. Sometimes, scenery is built in the performance space, but that is unusual. Permanent companies often build scenery in shops adjoining the stage, but for Broadway productions, the scenery is built in scenic studios far removed from the theatres in which the performances will occur. Touring companies take their scenery with them from city to city by plane or truck.

The way scenery is assembled is also determined in part by shifting demands. Once erected, sets for one-set shows may never have to be moved until the production closes. Such sets can be assembled differently from those that must be taken down and put up quickly. Another determinant is the method used to shift those sets that must be changed. For example, sets that are to be shifted manually may need to be put together in smaller units than those mounted on movable platforms. Thus, several factors influence the way a set will be assembled.

Typical methods of assembling scenery include *hinging, permanent joining,* and *lashing.* One of the most common assemblages used to create a large surface, such as a wall, utilizes hinges (mounted on the front side of the flats) to join two or more flats; the assembled unit can then be folded for moving and storage. The hinges and cracks between flats are covered with strips of muslin (*dutchmen*), and the entire assembled unit is then painted to hide the hinging. Braces, attached to the back of the assembled unit, are used to keep it from folding at the hinged points when it is in use; when the unit must be taken down, the braces are removed and the unit is folded. Hinges may also be used to hold units together temporarily. For example, loose-pin hinges (with pins that may be removed so the two halves of the hinge come apart) are sometimes used to hold platforms or steps units firmly in place and to facilitate rapid disassembly when they must be moved.

Permanent joining, done with screws, bolts, nails, or welding, is used for heavy units that do not need to be shifted, or for those that are shifted by means that do not require the units to be taken apart. Because of its greater stability, permanent joining is used whenever possible.

Lashing is a method of joining scenic units temporarily with lines or ropes drawn around cleats attached to the back of units. This method allows settings to be assembled and dismantled rapidly during performance.

Scenery is assembled in stages. The first two stages usually occur in the scene shop. First, the building-block units (flats, door frames, doors, steps, platforms, and the like) are constructed (or brought from storage). Second, these basic units are combined into larger units (the wall of a room, a door frame and door, platforms, steps, and so on). Next, the units are painted and then transported to the stage on which they will be used, and where they are assembled into complete sets.

Painting Scenery

The paint used on scenery may be created in the studio from dry pigment or bought already mixed. A scene-painting studio (or paint shop) may stock dry *pigment* in a wide range of colors that can be combined to obtain paint of any desired hue, saturation, or value. The dry pigment is then combined with a *binder*—a liquid glue-and-water solution that makes the pigment adhere to a surface after it dries. Ready-mixed paints have already been combined with a binder, usually casein, acrylic, or latex. These paints, too, may be mixed or thinned to achieve the desired palette. In addition to paint, aniline dyes (which impart color to cloth without making it opaque and without creating a surface that will crack when folded) may be used for soft-scenery units.

Newly constructed flats are usually treated with a solution of glue, starch, or alum to stretch and glaze the cloth. This process, called *sizing,* may be done before the flat is joined to others. After the larger units are assembled, they may be given a *priming coat,* which fills the cloth so that colors painted on it will not sink in and lose their brilliance. The priming coat is usually thin and neutral in hue to provide a uniform surface. Sometimes the sizing and priming coats are combined.

Next, the *base coat* is applied to provide an undercoating for the detailing that will follow. The final step usually involves some modification of the base coat through *overpainting,* which simulates textures (such as plaster, brick, or wood), conditions (peeling, mildewing, uneven fading, and the like), or patterns (wallpaper and other motifs). Overpainting may also be used to shade the upper portions of settings to decrease their prominence, to emphasize the shape and form of objects by giving emphasis to corners or curves, or to counterfeit three-dimensional details such as molding, paneling, bark, mortar, or foliage.

Scene painting makes use of a variety of techniques. The prime and base coats normally employ *flat painting* (intended to give an even surface) applied with a large brush or a spray gun. Because overpainting adds texture, shading, or details, it requires colors that provide contrast, the degree of which depends on the purpose. For example, the texture of relatively smooth plaster may be achieved by *spattering* (that is, flicking small drops of paint from a brush onto the base coat) with one color that is slightly lighter and a second that is slightly darker than the base coat,

Setting by Robert Seger for the Seattle Repertory Theatre's production of Stephen Sondheim's *Sunday in the Park With George,* which recreates a well-known work by Georges Seurat, a French master of pointillist painting. Directed by Laird Williamson. (Photo by Chris Bennion.)

creating the effect of raised and receding surfaces. Rough plaster may be simulated through *rolling,* which involves a rolled-up piece of burlap or other rough-textured cloth dipped in paint and rolled over the base coat in irregular patterns. Other common painting techniques include *sponging* (dipping a natural sponge in paint and patting it on the surface of the base coat), *scumbling* (simultaneous application and blending of more than one shade of paint on the same surface to give a mottled effect, simulating foliage or walls on which the paint is faded, mildewed, or crumbled), and *lining* (to create with line the semblance of molding, paneling, door trim, and similar details). The appropriate painting techniques are specified by the designer on the painters' elevations. The designer must also approve the finished painting.

Assembling and Shifting Scenery Onstage

After the scenery is painted, it is transported to the stage on which it will be used. In resident and university theatres, this step may involve merely moving scenery

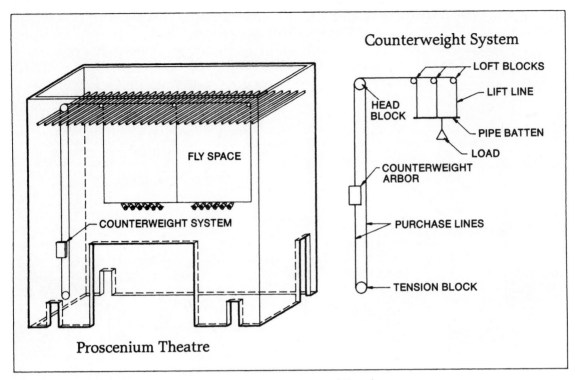

Counterweight system in a proscenium theatre. (Drawing by David Betts.)

from one part of the building to another. In the Broadway theatre, it means moving the scenery by truck from a scenic studio to the theatre.

The way scenery is assembled on stage depends on the method of shifting employed. A single setting may be set up permanently; multiple settings may need to be planned so that the individual units can be assembled quickly and quietly, moved easily, and stored economically. Several different methods are used in shifting scenery: *by hand, flying, on wagons, on elevators,* and *on revolving stages.*

The simplest method (in the sense that no stage machinery is required) involves changing all elements *by hand.* Using this method, each part of a set is moved by one or more stagehands to some prearranged storage space offstage, and the elements of a new setting are brought onstage and assembled. Parts of almost every setting must be moved manually, even when the major shifting is done by other means. Because manual shifting can be used on any stage, however simple or complex, a designer can always rely on it, though a large crew may be required to make it efficient. It is relatively slow and requires breaking the setting into small units.

Another common method of shifting is *flying*—suspending scenic elements above the stage and raising or lowering them as needed. Flying is normally reserved for drops, curtains, borders, cycloramas, screens for projections, and small units composed of flats. Flying requires a *counterweight system* composed of battens, lines, and pulleys. For such a system, a *gridiron* (a network of steel girders at the top of the stage house) serves as the weight-bearing structure. From the gridiron *steel battens* are suspended (parallel to the front of the stage and at intervals from front to back) on *wire-cable lines,* which run upward from the battens to the gridiron, pass over *pulleys,* and continue to one side of the stage house, where they pass over another set of pulleys and turn downward; these lines are then attached to the top of *cradles* (or frames), into which are placed *weights* sufficient to balance whatever is being flown. *Ropes* attached to the bottom of the cradles run downward to the *flyrail,* where they can be tied off securely when not in use and from which the entire counterweight system can be operated by stagehands. With an adequate counterweight system, a single stagehand can easily raise and lower scenic elements of considerable size and weight. Some recent flying systems use electrically controlled winches without counterweights; they may also permit battens to be rigged at various angles rather than only parallel to the front of the stage.

Another common device for shifting scenery is the *wagon* (a platform on casters). The larger the wagon, the more scenery it can accommodate, but many stages do not have sufficient wing space to store or maneuver large wagons. Some stages have permanently installed tracks that guide wagons on- and offstage with precision, but such a system has little flexibility. Wagons can be used singly, in pairs or groups, or in combination with other shifting devices. The primary advantage of the wagon is that it permits heavy or complex scenic pieces to be shifted more efficiently than by hand.

Another device for shifting scenery, the *revolving stage,* is less common in America than in Europe and Japan, perhaps because of the expense involved. In theatres with permanently installed revolving stages, a circle of the stage floor (normally larger in diameter than the proscenium opening is wide) is mounted on a central supporting pivot that can be turned by electric motors. Theatres sometimes use one or more temporary revolving stages, which are made by mounting a low circular platform on casters and attaching it at its center to the stage floor. Such temporary stages can be mounted almost anywhere in the acting space. The revolving stage is used primarily to hold two or more settings simultaneously; the individual sets are placed so that each faces the circumference of the circle. To shift scenery, the stage is revolved until the desired setting faces the audience. Settings may be changed on the backstage part while another is in use on stage. Complex arrangements of steps and platforms may also be erected on revolving stages; different views and playing areas are then revealed by turning the stage.

Still another shifting device, the *elevator stage,* raises and lowers segments of the stage vertically. In some theatres, portions of the stage may be lowered to the basement, where scenery is mounted and then raised to stage level. In other theatres, the stage is divided into several sections, each mounted on its own lift that can be raised, lowered, or tilted; the sections can then be used in combinations that create platforms, ramps, or a variety of levels without the need of building and shifting such units in the usual manner. Theatres in which the stage proper is fixed

Robin Wagner

Robin Wagner is one of America's most successful designers. He rarely designs classics or revivals, preferring to work on productions that "hold up a 20th-century mirror." In addition to his work for the stage, he has designed spectacle for rock groups, including the Rolling Stones. Wagner attended the California School of Fine Arts but had no specific training for scenic design, which he began by happenstance, first doing sets in San Francisco for opera workshops and ballet, and then for the Actors' Workshop, where director Herbert Blau involved him in the total collaborative process, a kind of involvement that he still insists on. After moving to New York, Wagner worked as a design assistant to several major designers and did Off-Broadway productions before becoming principal designer at Washington's Arena Stage for three years. His Broadway success began in 1968 with *Hair*, followed by *Jesus Christ Superstar* and *Lenny*. In the 1970s he became part of the collaborative team of Michael Bennett (director and choreographer), Theoni Aldredge (costume designer), and Tharon Musser (lighting designer) that created *A Chorus Line* and *Dream Girls*—among the most successful productions seen on Broadway. The success of these and other productions has allowed Wagner to choose only projects he likes. More recent work includes *Jerome Robbins' Broadway, City of Angels* (for which he won a Tony Award in 1990), *Crazy for You* (for which he won an Olivier Award in London in 1993), and *Jelly's Last Jam*.

Wagner's designs are sculptural, often multileveled, and functional because most of the surfaces can be used by the performers. His settings are also extremely mobile (they have been called "dancing scenery") because they are composed of a few basic pieces that can be quickly and imaginatively rearranged to create a great variety of places (in *Dream Girls* all locales were created primarily by repositioning five light towers and a light bridge). His sets are made distinctive in part by his use of nontraditional materials: mylar, chrome, Formica, tiles, and other unusual surfaces and textures. (Examples of Wagner's designs are on pages 227 and 278 and in color plate 22.)

may have a lift that raises and lowers the orchestra pit, so that it can be set below stage level for musicians, raised to the auditorium level and used for audience seating, or raised to stage level for use as a forestage.

Seldom is a single method of shifting used exclusively. Most often, two or more methods are used in conjunction. Designers must know what methods are available to them and must decide which is to be used with each unit that must be moved. These decisions are important because audiences become impatient with lengthy scene shifts. Such delays may also destroy the rhythm of a production. Few theatres now try to hide scene shifts from the audience. Efficiency and rapidity are the primary concerns.

Set Decoration and Properties

Even after the sets are assembled onstage, they are incomplete without set decoration and properties. These elements, though part of the design, are not structural parts of the setting.

Setting by Derek McLane for Harold Pinter's *The Caretaker* at the American Repertory Theatre. This setting is composed almost entirely of set decorations and properties. Directed by Ron Daniels. (Photo by Richard Feldman.)

Set decoration and properties include such items as banners, coats of arms, tapestries, window draperies, thrones, furniture, pictures, and books—anything that completes the setting. Properties may be subdivided into *set props* and *hand props*. The former is a property that either is attached to the setting or that functions as a part of the design. The latter is used by the actor in stage business. The designer is always responsible for the selection of set props and may also choose the hand props, although more frequently hand props are considered the director's responsibility because of their intimate connection with the acting. Responsibility for obtaining both types may be assigned to a property master and crew. The appropriate pieces may be bought, made, rented, or borrowed. However obtained, set decoration and properties are necessary to complete the design.

Technical Rehearsals, Dress Rehearsals, and Performances

Even after the settings are complete, they must be integrated with the other elements that make up the total production. Typically, this is accomplished during one

Projected photo as setting in *Red Fox/Second Hanging*, produced by the Roadside Theatre (Whitesburg, KY), one of a dozen of the Appalachian ensemble company's original productions that have toured the United States extensively since 1976. This production is based on the local legend of M.B. "Doc" Taylor, the Red Fox of the Cumberlands. A photo of the real-life personages serves as background for the actors (Frankie Taylor, Gary Slemp, and Don Baker). (Photo by Dan Carraco. Courtesy of the Roadside Theatre.)

or more technical rehearsals and one or more dress rehearsals. Technical rehearsals are devoted to making certain that all the "technical" elements—scenery (including scene shifts), costumes (including changes), makeup, lighting (including light levels and cues), sound (including all settings and cues), and properties (including all stage business involving properties)—are available and are functioning as they should both in terms of the action and the production concept. A technical rehearsal focuses attention on elements other than on acting (although portions of all scenes are performed) so that the various designers and technicians can see if the elements for which they are responsible are functioning properly both separately and as parts of the whole. Any difficulties revealed by a technical rehearsal are corrected as quickly as possible so that dress rehearsals can proceed as nearly like performances as possible. In complex productions, more than one technical rehearsal may be needed to make certain that any necessary adjustments have been made. It is very difficult to make major changes in scenery at this late point.

Because dress rehearsals approximate performances, they offer opportunities to see the settings as the audience will. The designer must be available for consultation and changes until the play has opened. On opening night, responsibility for the scenery passes to the stage manager and the stage crews.

The Designer's Assistants and Coworkers

Many people aid the scene designer. In the professional theatre, designers are usually members of the United Scenic Artists Union, and they are usually assisted by members of this or other unions. Established designers often employ one or more assistants who make working drawings, search for furniture and properties, act as liaison between the designer and the scenic studios—anything the designer may request.

In the nonprofessional theatre, the *technical director* is likely to perform many of these functions. In many theatres, however, the technical director's job is independent of the designer's and of equal status. When a permanent organization produces several shows a year, the designer's job may be divided into its artistic and practical aspects. The designer may then conceive the designs, and the technical director may be responsible for building, assembling, and painting them. The technical director may also purchase all materials, supervise the scene shops, and be responsible for the crews that run the shows. He or she often serves as a production manager.

The scenery is built, assembled, and painted in a scene shop (or another work space serving that function). In the professional theatre, all persons involved usually are union members. In other types of organizations, this work is undertaken by assigned or volunteer helpers under the supervision of the designer, technical director, or shop foreman.

When the scenery is delivered to the stage for rigging and shifting, scenery and property crews take over. In the professional theatre, all such persons usually are union members. A master carpenter travels with a show on tour and makes sure the scenery is in good condition. In the nonprofessional theatre, scenery and props are usually handled by volunteer or assigned crews, but in all types of theatres, during performances the heads of stage crews operate under the supervision of the stage manager. Their duties include the efficient movement and accurate placement of scenery and properties during the performance and the maintenance of units during the run of the show.

The designer's assistants frequently go unnoticed by the public because little is done to draw attention to them. Often, and especially in the professional theatre, their names do not appear in the programs. Nevertheless, they are indispensable members of the overall production team; without them the scenery would not be built and painted and could not function efficiently or be shifted during performances.

Thinking About . . .

The Scene Designer's Work

The range of scenic design in today's theatre is great. It may be realistic or abstract. It may incorporate or intermingle elements from almost any period, style, culture, or set of conventions. So much variety can be confusing. The following questions focus attention on crucial aspects of scenic design as an aid to understanding more clearly the designer's part in the performance, no matter the situation or mode in which the designer works:

1. *In what type of space was the production staged? What facilities did the space offer? How did the designer take advantage (or fail to take advantage) of them? What limitations did the space impose? How did the designer overcome (or fail to overcome) the limitations?*

2. *Did the scenery define the performance space? If so, in what ways and through what means? If not, with what effect?*

3. *How did the floor plan affect the action? Were there multiple levels? If so, how did they relate to each other, and how were they used? Were there specific entrances and exits? If so, how did their placement affect the action? Did the arrangement of furniture (or other elements) enhance or inhibit action? How did the overall arrangement affect movement and pictorial composition?*

4. *Of what sorts of units was the setting composed? What soft-scenery units were used? Framed? Three-dimensional? Other? Was the setting realistic? Fragmentary? Abstract? What was the overall effect?*

5. *Were sets (or any parts) changed during the performance? If so, by what means? How long did the changes take? How did the varied settings affect the mood, tension, and tempo?*

6. *What characteristics did the scenery embody? What did the scenery convey about the characters? Socioeconomic conditions? Period? Locale? How did it affect the play's tone? Mood and atmosphere?*

7. *Were there any unusual scenic features? Projected images? Highly distinctive effects? If so, what was the result?*

8. *How did the scenery relate to the costumes and lighting? Did they enhance and complement each other? If so, how? If not, in what ways? With what results?*

9. *Did the setting suggest any specific interpretation of the play? If so, what interpretation? How did the setting convey this interpretation? If it did not, what was the result?*

10. *How did the scenery contribute (or fail to contribute) to the total production? What would have been lost if the scenery had been eliminated?*

The relevance of each question may vary according to the particular production and setting. There are no absolute answers to many of the questions because responses are inevitably subjective. But so are most responses to art of whatever kind. Nevertheless, formulating answers to these questions forces us to go beyond our usual cursory reaction to scenery and to examine it and its function in production more specifically and critically.

Chapter 15

Costume Design and Makeup

Black Elk Speaks (based on the book by John G. Neihardt, dramatized by Christopher Sergel) as produced at the Denver Theatre Center. Andrew Roa as Red Cloud and Kenneth Martines as Commissioner Taylor. Costumes by Andrew V. Yelusich; directed by Donovan Marley. (Photo by Terry Shapiro. Courtesy of the Denver Theatre Center.)

The transformation of the human body, its metamorphosis, is made possible by the costume, the disguise. Costume and mask emphasize the body's identity or they change it; they express its nature or they are purposely misleading about it; they stress its conformity to organic or mechanical laws or they invalidate this conformity.

—Oskar Schlemmer, *Man and Art Figure*

The costume designer is concerned primarily with the visual appearance of characters. Whereas the scene designer characterizes the stage environment within which the action develops, the costume designer characterizes the players who function within that environment. Thus, the functions of the scene and costume designers interact and need to be coordinated carefully.

The Costume Designer's Skills

Costume designers need a variety of skills, many of which are pertinent to other professions, such as fashion designer, visual artist, tailor, seamstress, social and cultural historian, and actor. Like the fashion designer, the costume designer creates garments for particular types of persons to wear for particular occasions or purposes. In creating garments, both types of designers keep in mind gender, social and economic class, activity, climate, and season, as well as stylistic qualities. But unlike fashion designers, costume designers must work within circumstances dictated by the script, director, performance space, and budget. Fashion designers establish fashions, costume designers use fashions. Costume designers must be able to project themselves into any period and create garments not merely for present-day fashions but for those of other eras.

Because they communicate their ideas to others through sketches, costume designers must develop skills like those of the visual artist. They use a multitude of sketches to indicate their preliminary ideas about individual costumes and the overall look of the production. Many designers now use computers to generate sketches. However produced, sketches facilitate discussion of the costumes, their relationship to the other visual elements, and their appropriateness to character, dramatic action, and production concept. Costume designers must also be able to render their final designs in color.

Although costume designers are not always involved in the construction of the garments they have designed, they should know how the clothes will be cut and sewn. Therefore, they need to envision the garments as tailors and seamstresses would. Costume sketches should indicate how garments are shaped, the location of seams, darts, and other features that create visible lines and affect cut and fit. Such information is essential for making patterns from which the garments are constructed. Because costume designers also specify the material to be used, they need to be familiar with various fibers (cotton, wool, linen, silk, synthetic fibers) and the characteristics of each. Such information permits designers to choose cloth for appearance, durability, specific use, cost, and other pertinent factors. Designers must also be knowledgeable about weaves, textures, and other qualities because these are important to the overall appearance of a costume.

Costume designers must be well grounded in social and cultural history (including the visual arts and theatre) because clothing reflects the mores, standards of beauty, and stylistic preferences of period and place. The more designers know about daily life, occupations, class structure, and favorite pastimes of a society, the better prepared they will be to design garments that reflect the status and function of a character within a specific culture. Because much of our information about clothing of the past comes from painting and other visual arts, a knowledge of art history is helpful. Many productions today draw on theatrical conventions that were in use when the play was written; consequently, knowledge of theatre history, especially the history of theatrical costuming, may be useful to the designer.

Above all, costumes need to be suited to the characters who wear them. Costume designers must be able to analyze characters in the same way as actors do, in terms of each role's significant traits, motivations, feelings, and functions within the dramatic action.

The Functions of Costume Design

Costume design may serve several functions. It may help to establish *time and place*. If the production concept calls for a realistic approach, the costumes may be based on the clothing worn at the time of the dramatic action (fifth century B.C., Shakespeare's lifetime, present-day, and so on); they may indicate a particular country or region (ancient Rome, seventeenth-century France, southwestern United States); a particular kind of place (throne room, battlefield, hospital, farm); or a time of day or occasion (casual morning at home, formal dance).

Costumes may establish the characters' *social and economic status* by distinguishing between lower and upper classes, between rich and poor, or between more and less affluent members of the same group. Costume may identify *occupation* (nurse, soldier, policeman) or *life-style* (conservative middle class, fashionable leisure class, disaffected youth). Costumes usually indicate *gender* and may reflect *age* (by adhering to stereotypical notions of what is appropriate to each age group). Costumes may also reflect a character's *atypicality* through dress that departs from the norm. More than do settings or lighting, costumes are likely to retain some realistic qualities, probably because they are worn by actors who must be able to move effectively and appropriately in them and because actors usually draw on real-life behavioral patterns in building their characterizations.

Costumes do not always adhere to realistic standards. They may embody a *metaphor, symbol,* or *allegorical concept.* For example, in the medieval play *Everyman,* the title character is summoned to his grave by a character called Death; Everyman then tries unsuccessfully to persuade several of his companions (Beauty, Strength, and Goods among them) to accompany him. The costumes need to capture the essence of each character as indicated by its name. On the other hand, a production

The costumes used here for Shakespeare's *Titus Andronicus* place the action in the late Roman era when Romans were at war with the Goths. Costumes by Jeannie Davidson. (Photo by Hank Kranzler. Courtesy of the Oregon Shakespeare Festival.)

of *Hamlet* utilizing the metaphor of the world as prison may embody this perception in more subtle and varied ways.

Costumes may reflect *mood and atmosphere*. Winnie's neat and refined costume in *Happy Days* (see the illustrations on pages 40 and 218) contrasts sharply with her entrapped state and reinforces her determined cheerfulness. Costumes may help establish a particular *style*. In *"The Hairy Ape,"* the fashionable people on Fifth Avenue are dressed like marionettes to reinforce their mechanical behavior. Costumes may reflect formalized *conventions,* as they do in commedia dell'arte.

Costumes may enhance or impede movement. Light, flexible, and close-fitting garments (such as leotards) leave the body free, whereas heavy garments (with bustles, trains, and the like) slow down and restrict movement. Garments help to determine the amount, type, and overall pattern of movement and stage business.

Costumes can establish or clarify *character relationships*. For example, in Shakespeare's history plays, in which warring factions are significant, members of the same faction can be related to each other and contrasted with members of rival

Costume sketch by Susan Tsu for the character Chauncey DeVille in the parodistic *Dracula, a Musical Nightmare,* produced by the Alley Theatre (Houston). Directed by Doug Johnson. (Courtesy of Susan Tsu.)

factions through color schemes. Color can also be used to show a sympathetic (through compatible colors) or antipathetic relationship (through clashing or contrasting colors) among characters. Changes of color may be used to indicate an alteration in the relationship among characters.

Costume may establish the relative *importance of characters* in the action. Major characters can be made to stand out from minor ones by manipulating any or all of the elements and principles of design. For example, Hamlet is given emphasis in part through his insistence on wearing black (the color of mourning), while the others are dressed in colors more appropriate to festivities following the wedding of Gertrude and Claudius.

Costume may underline the *development of the dramatic action* through costume changes. A movement from happiness to sorrow or alterations in a character's fortunes, age, or sense of well-being may be underscored by changes in what the character wears. Costume may create both *variety* and *unity* because characters are not only individuals but are also parts of a whole. While each costume may be distinctive in some way, each must fit the total visual style of the production.

Eve in Arthur Miller's *The Creation of the World and Other Business.* Nudity is handled here cartoonishly by drawing lines on a flesh-colored body stocking. (Photo by Inge Morath/Magnum.)

Theoni V. Aldredge

Theoni V. Aldredge (1932–   ) is one of America's most successful costume designers. Born in Greece, she received her theatre training at the Goodman Theatre School in Chicago. After moving to New York, she became the principal costume designer for the New York Shakespeare Festival in 1962. She soon made her mark on Broadway as well with costumes for such productions as *Who's Afraid of Virginia Woolf?* and *Hair.* She has designed for opera, ballet, television, and film. She won an Academy Award for *The Great Gatsby*, and Tony Awards for *Annie, Barnum,* and *La Cage aux Folles.* In the 1970s, she became a part of the collaborative team of Michael Bennett (director and choreographer), Tony Walton (scene designer), and Tharon Musser (lighting designer), who created two of Broadway's most successful productions, *A Chorus Line* and *Dream Girls.* More recent work includes *Nick and Nora*, the revival of *Gypsy, Secret Garden,* and *Carmina Burana* (for the Pacific Northwest Ballet, Seattle).

Aldredge feels that she works best in a collaborative atmosphere where an extended exchange of ideas precedes the creation of designs. She believes that a good design is one the audience is not aware of because it is so much a part of the whole: "My aim is to create designs that will make people look alive and comfortable and to give a show a look of unity and inevitability." (Examples of Aldredge's designs are on pages 395 and 428.)

Costume can alter an actor's *appearance.* By manipulating line and proportion, the costumer can make a plump actor appear more slender or a thin actor stouter. Boots may disguise an actor's thin legs; color and ornament can draw attention to an actor's good features and away from weaker ones. Costume also can be used to make a handsome actor plain or misshapen. And, in many children's plays, actors may be transformed into animals, trees, or fantastic creatures.

Beginning in the 1960s, some groups questioned the need for stage costume at all. Such groups wore the same casual clothing in performance as they did in rehearsal or on the street. Since 1968, nudity has been used in some productions. But both casual clothing and nudity are variations on stage costuming because both merely extend concepts about what is dramatically appropriate.

Working Plans and Procedures

Costume designers, like other theatre artists, usually begin their preparations by becoming familiar with the script—its action, characters, themes, language, and spectacle—because the costumes must function within, and be appropriate to, the

Theoni V. Aldredge's costumes for the musical *Barnum*. The setting is by David Mitchell. (Photo by Martha Swope.)

total piece. Ultimately, designers concentrate on factors specifically related to costuming: the number of characters; the nature of each character (gender, age, occupation, socioeconomic status, likes and dislikes, goals and motivations, ethical qualities); the function of each character in each scene and in the play as a whole; the relationships among the characters; times, places, and occasions that influence costume choices; indications of changes in costume; developments in the action or changes in the fortunes of characters that might be clarified by costuming; the physical action, stage business, and movement patterns that might affect or be affected by costuming; moods and variations in mood that affect costume; form and style as influences on costuming.

Costume designers may need to do additional research. They may need to determine what clothing was in use at the time of the play's action (characteristic silhouettes, typical textures and materials, dominant colors, ornamental motifs, usual

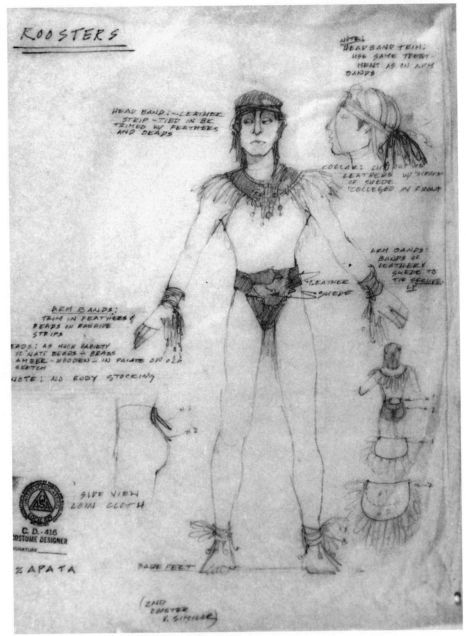

Costume design by Tina Cantú Navarro for the fighting cock Zapata in Milcha Sanchez-Scott's *Roosters*. In the scene in which two roosters battle to the death, they are played by human actors. Feathers are attached to the ankles and wrists and around the neck and head. Design for the New Mexico Repertory Theatre. (Photo by Pedro C. Ramirez. Courtesy of Tina Cantú Navarro.)

Costume design by Susan Tsu for Prospero in Shakespeare's *The Tempest* at the Oregon Shakespeare Festival, Portland. (Courtesy of Susan Tsu.)

accessories). They may also need to be familiar with the manners and customs of the time in order to understand why or when each garment or accessory was worn or used. They may explore stage costuming conventions in use when the play was written. They may need to undertake a variety of other explorations, depending upon the production concept.

Before they make sketches (and perhaps before they undertake detailed research), costume designers meet with the director and other designers to discuss the script and the production concept. The director may already be firmly settled on a production concept, or may wish to get the designers' ideas before reaching a definite decision. However it comes about, a production concept (or interpretational focus) should guide the designers' work. The costume designer also needs to know what the budget for costumes will be; the space to be used for performances; the available work space, equipment, and personnel; any special plans or demands that the director may have (specific business that will affect costuming; desired costume changes; special treatment of any character, and so on); and any plans of the other designers that will affect costume. It is also helpful (but not always possible) to

Susan Tsu's costume for Prospero in performance. The actor is Michael Kevin. Directed by Jerry Turner; lighting by Robert Peterson. (Photo by David Cooper. Courtesy of the Oregon Shakespeare Festival.)

know which actor will play each role, so that the designs may be adapted to the wearer. All of this information helps to define the limits within which the costume designer must work.

There are no standard procedures to follow in designing costumes. Because there are usually several characters, and because they appear in many scenes in many different combinations, the designer typically makes numerous tentative sketches and examines them in various combinations to see how they fulfill the needs of individual scenes, whether they sufficiently reflect the progress of the dramatic action, and how the costumes fit together as a group. There is usually a series of design conferences at which the designers show their sketches and explain their proposals. Through a process of reactions and revisions, tentative agreement is eventually reached. Before final approval is given, however, the designs usually must be rendered in color and in a manner that conveys a clear impression of the final product.

The costumer's working drawing is a color sketch for each costume (although sometimes the same basic design is used for several characters if they are part of a

OTHELLO

ROLE	I-7 (184 Lines)	I-2 (99)	I-3 (410)	II-1 (321)	II-2 (12)	II-3 (394)	III-1 (60)	III-2 (6)	III-3 (479)	INTERMISSION	III-4 (201)	IV-1 (293)	IV-2 (252)	IV-3 (106)	V-1 (129)	V-2 (371)
DUKE OF VENICE			Duke 1 Red													
BRABANTIO	1 Change to 2 add Jerkin, Hat, Gloves	Bra.	Bra.													
GRATIANO															Grat. 1 Black Gown	Grat.
LODOVICO												Lodovico 1 Gown Boots		Lod.	Lod.	Lod.
OTHELLO		Othe. 1	Othe. White & Gold	Othe. 2 Armor		3 Brown Dressing Robe		Othe. 4 Armor	Othe. 5 White Doublet		6 Dark Brown Doublet-Jerkin	Othe.	Othe.	Othe. Jerkin Off	Othe.	Othe.
CASSIO		Cas. 1	Cas. Olive & Gold	Cas. 2 Armor		Cas. Stripped of Rank	Cas.		Cas.		Cas.	Cas.			Cas.	Cas.
IAGO	Iago 1 Black Cape	Iago	Iago Black & Green	Iago 2 Armor		Iago	Iago	Iago	Iago		Iago	Iago	Iago		Iago in Shirt	Iago
MONTANO				Mont. 2 Armor		Mont.										Mont.
RODERIGO	Rod. 1 Black Cape	Rod.	Rod. Brown & Coral	Rod. 2 Armor		Rod.							Rod.	Rod.		
CLOWN				Clow.		Clow.	Clow.				Clow.					
DESDEMONA			1 Brown with Red Trim	1a Blue Gown over Brown		2 Tan Negligée			3 Rose with Tan Jacket		Des.	Des.	Des. Remove Jacket	Des.		Des. 4 Nightgown
EMILIA			Emi. 1 Green Dress	Emi.		2 Negligée	Emi.		Emi.		Emi.	Emi. Remove Over-sleeves	Emi.	Emi.		Emi.
BIANCA											1 Bian. Dk. Red & Brown	Bian.			Bian.	

A costume chart for a production of Shakespeare's *Othello*. (Courtesy of Paul Reinhardt.)

group—soldiers, for example—or members of a mob in which everyone wears variations on the same clothing). A sketch shows the lines and details of the costume as seen from the most distinctive angle. If there are unusual features, the details are shown in special drawings (usually in the margins of the sketch); and if the front, back, and sides of a garment all have distinctive features, the costume is usually shown from each of these angles. Samples of the materials to be used in constructing the garment are attached to each drawing. (See illustration on page 392.)

A costume chart may be used. It is made by dividing a large sheet of paper into squares; down the left side, the name of one character (and usually the name of the actor playing the role) is listed in each square; across the top, each scene (or act) is listed. There should be one square for each actor in each scene of the play. In the squares, the designer may indicate the costume items (including accessories) to be worn in the scene and may attach color samples of each garment. The range of colors and the overall color scheme can then be seen at a glance. The chart can also be used as a guide for dressing the actors and keeping the costumes organized for running the production efficiently. (See the accompanying costume chart.)

Patricia Zipprodt

Patricia Zipprodt (1925–) was graduated from Wellesley College and received her professional training at the Chicago Art Institute and the Fashion Institute of Technology. Since 1957 she has been one of America's most successful costume designers. She is best known for her work on musicals, among them *Fiddler on the Roof, Sweet Charity, Zorba, Chicago, Cabaret, Sunday in the Park with George,* and *My Fair Lady,* although she has designed many nonmusical plays, including *The Blacks, Waiting for Godot, Macbeth,* and *Cat on a Hot Tin Roof.* She has also designed for opera, ballet, film, and television. She has won three Tony Awards and four Drama Desk Awards. The most characteristic feature of Zipprodt's designs is texture, often created by layered paint and dye that impart vibrant, shimmering qualities to ordinary materials. She also uses lace, brocade, and other fabric to create layered, multitextured effects.

Zipprodt believes that costume design is not adequately valued. "Until the late '40s, the union didn't even offer costume designers separate exams [from scene designers]. . . . Actually it was believed that anyone could be costume designers. . . . I feel these attitudes stem from the fact that costume design is an outgrowth of dress-making and that traditionally has been women's work. . . . One of the reasons costume designers get such low pay, especially compared to set designers of equal rank, is that costume design is largely made up of women and gay men. It is a feminine and feminized industry." (Examples of Zipprodt's designs are shown on page 233 and in color plate 2.)

Realizing the Designs

Costumes may be borrowed, rented, assembled from an existing wardrobe, or made new. When costumes must be borrowed, designers look for garments that fit their needs, although they often must accept clothing that is less than ideal. Borrowed clothing can be altered only slightly because usually it must be returned in the same condition as when it was borrowed. Through the imaginative use of accessories and ornamentation, however, much can be done to alter the appearance of a garment. Borrowing clothing is restricted primarily to nonprofessional theatres and short-run productions.

Costumes from rental houses vary considerably. Some larger houses buy the costumes from a Broadway or road show when it closes and rent these costumes as a unit. Other houses employ staff designers who create costumes for frequently produced plays. In other cases, costume houses assemble a variety of costumes for each period, and from this stock the most appropriate garments are selected for any given show. When costumes are rented, the costume house assumes many of the designer's functions. The director and costumer may give detailed explanations of their interpretation of the play and request specific colors and kinds of garments, but they ultimately may not get precisely what they wanted. Sometimes a costume agency is nearby, and costumes can be selected and approved by the designer or director in person. Rented costumes normally arrive at the theatre in time for only one or two dress rehearsals, and there is seldom time to obtain replacements or make more than minor changes. The better costume houses provide dependable service, but they cannot match well-designed garments made for a specific production. Even groups that normally make their own costumes usually rent some articles (such as military uniforms and men's tailored period suits) that are difficult or costly to construct.

Permanent theatre organizations that make their own costumes usually maintain a wardrobe of items from past productions. In this way, a large stock of garments is built up over time. If garments are to be taken from stock, the play is designed with these in mind. The costumer knows what is available and can choose carefully. Existing costumes in the theatre's own wardrobe can be remade or altered to fit new conceptions.

The procedures and working conditions for creating new costumes vary from one kind of organization to another. In the Broadway theatre, the producer contracts with a costume house to make the costumes. The designer must approve the finished costumes but has little to do with the work beyond supervising fittings. The designer does not supply patterns or directions for cutting, stitching, and fitting (the costume house does this).

In resident and nonprofessional theatres, designers may supervise construction of their own costumes. If so, they must be skilled in pattern drafting, draping, and fitting. Whether or not they supervise the construction, designers should understand the techniques used to carry out designs so they will know what effects can be accomplished and by what means.

Regardless of who makes the costumes, standard procedures are involved. First, accurate measurements must be made of all the actors. (The rehearsal secretary, stage manager, or assistant director usually makes appointments for actors to have measurements taken and, later, for fittings.) Second, materials must be bought. While the designer specifies materials, precisely the right cloth or color may be difficult to find. The designer or another authorized person may need to search for the specified materials or acceptable substitutes. Next, patterns must be drafted as guides for cutting and shaping the materials. At this point, the technical knowledge of the tailor is of great value. Some costumes can be made more easily through draping than from patterns. For example, Greek garments, which hang from the shoulder in folds and are not fitted to the body, are most easily made by draping the material on a mannequin or a human body. After the patterns are completed, the material is cut and the parts basted together. The first fitting usually takes place before stitching is completed. Actors try on their costumes so the designer can check the fit and appearance. It is easy at this point to make alterations that would be impossible or troublesome later. Finally, the garment is stitched, and ornamentation and accessories are added. A final fitting is arranged to assure that the costume looks and functions as planned.

Many new costumes need to look worn, faded, or tattered. Such garments may need to be "distressed" (that is, treated in ways analogous to overpainting in

Costumes by Catherine Zuber for *Shlemiel the First,* adapted by Robert Brustein (from Isaac Bashevis Singer's Jewish/Polish folk stories for children) with music composed and adapted by Hankus Netsky. The costumes reflect the clownish, topsy-turvy world of the stories. Directed and choreographed by David Gordon. Set by Robert Israel; lighting by Peter Kaczorowski. (Photo by Richard Feldman.)

scenery). They may be washed several times, may be rolled up wrinkled to get a rumpled look, may be sprayed with paint, dye, or bleach to achieve fading or staining, may have the nap worn off the cloth with brushing in strategic places to indicate wear, or may be subjected to a variety of other processes to produce the desired effect.

The Costume Parade, Dress Rehearsals, and Performances

When the costumes are finished, it is usual to have a *costume* (or *dress*) *parade,* during which each scene of the play is covered in sequence so that the actors may appear in the correct combinations, in the appropriate costumes, and under lights simulating those to be used in performance. The actors may be asked to perform characteristic portions of each scene to make sure the costumes are functional. The costume parade allows the designer and director to evaluate the costumes without the distractions of a performance. Problems are noted and corrected before dress rehearsals begin. In the Broadway theatre, the costume parade is held at the costume house; in other organizations, it usually occurs onstage. It is normally supervised by the costume designer.

After problems are corrected, the costumes are moved to the dressing rooms in the theatre to be used for the performances. If no costume parade is held, its functions must be accomplished during the technical rehearsals. Dress rehearsals allow the costumes to be seen under conditions as nearly like those of performance as possible. There should be few changes at this time, but any that are necessary need to be made quickly so the actor is not faced with new details on opening night.

Once dress rehearsals begin, a wardrobe supervisor or costume crew usually assumes responsibility for ensuring that costumes are (and remain) in good condition and that each actor is dressed as planned. In the nonprofessional theatre, the costume designer frequently assumes these duties. In most situations, however, the designer's work is considered complete after opening night.

The Costume Designer's Assistants

The costume designer needs several helpers. In the professional theatre, costume designers usually are members of the United Scenic Artists Union, and their helpers are usually members of this or other unions. The designer's assistant, usually a younger member of the United Scenic Artists, may make sketches, search for appropriate materials, supervise fittings, act as liaison with the other theatre workers, or undertake any other assigned task.

Pattern drafters, drapers, cutters, tailors, stitchers, and fitters make the costumes. In the professional theatre, these workers usually are union members. In the nonprofessional theatre, much of this work is done by volunteer or student labor, although frequently a paid staff person supervises the construction and maintains the theatre's wardrobe.

Willa Kim's costumes for *Dancin'*, Bob Fosse's tribute to dance in Broadway musicals. Lighting by Jules Fisher. (Photo by Martha Swope.)

Willa Kim

Willa Kim, a Korean American, was born in Los Angeles and studied fashion illustration there at the Chouinard Institute of Art. She had no intention of becoming a costume designer, but while living in New York in the early 1960s she was asked to costume an Off-Broadway production and thereafter made costume design her profession. Her first Broadway show came in 1966. She has designed for numerous ballet companies, including the Feld Ballet, San Francisco Ballet, and Joffrey Ballet in the United States, and has worked extensively in Europe as well. She also designs for opera, television, and even figure skating events. Among her Broadway productions are *Sophisticated Ladies, Dancin', Long Day's Journey Into Night, The Front Page,* and *The Will Rogers Follies* (for which she won a Tony). She has won several awards for her Broadway, Off-Broadway, and television designs. Kim pioneered the use of stretch fabrics for dance costumes, and did much to popularize the use of fabric painting. She is noted for the inventiveness of her designs, described as a combination of Oriental sophistication and Western glitz.

When the costumes are finished, the wardrobe supervisor takes charge and is responsible for seeing that costumes are ready for each performance. The costumes may need to be mended, laundered, cleaned, or pressed. In long-run productions, garments are replaced when they begin to look shabby. During performances, the wardrobe supervisor is responsible to the stage manager.

Dressers help actors into and out of costumes. The number of dressers depends on the size of the cast and the number and rapidity of costume changes. Sometimes actors need little or no help, but quick changes and complicated garments may require more than one dresser for a single actor. There should be enough dressers to avoid delays, keep performances running smoothly and ensure that the costumes are in good condition at all times.

The Costume Designer and the Actor

Costume designers and actors need to cooperate because each supplements and extends the work of the other. Designers need to consider the strengths and weaknesses of each actor's figure when planning costumes. They also need to keep in mind the movement demanded of the actor. It is difficult for an actress to climb steps in a tight skirt, and an actor who must fence may be seriously endangered by billowing shirt sleeves, although these garments may enhance movement in other situations.

For their part, actors should acknowledge their responsibility to explore the potentials and limitations of the costumes they will wear. Unfamiliar garments seem awkward initially, but if actors recognize that the clothes in each period emphasize qualities that were admired at that time and allow movements that were then socially useful, beautiful, or desirable, they may use those qualities more effectively. For example, the sleeves of a man's fashionable coat in the eighteenth century would not allow the arms to hang comfortably at the sides (they had to be bent at the elbows and held away from the body), whereas the modern suit coat is cut so that the arms are most comfortable when hanging at the sides (outward and upward movements are restricted). Both garments reflect attitudes about appropriate male behavior and consequently encourage some movements and inhibit others. If designers understand the relationship between cut and movement, they can help the actors get the feel of the period by making their garments from authentic period patterns.

The designer can also aid the actors by proper attention to shoes. The height of the heel exerts considerable effect on stage movement (a high heel throws the weight forward onto the balls of the feet, while flat shoes shift weight toward the heel). Similarly, undergarments affect movement. Hooped crinoline petticoats, for example, will not allow the same freedom of movement as modern underclothing. Corsets can force the body into certain configurations and inhibit action. If costumes encourage appropriate movement, they can be of enormous help to the actor. For optimum effectiveness, however, the actor and director must be willing to explore the possibilities of garments and allow sufficient time for rehearsal in them.

Makeup

Typically, makeup has been considered the actor's responsibility, and often each actor is presumed capable of achieving any desired effect. This assumption is not always true, however, and it is especially questionable in the nonprofessional theatre. In the latter situation, makeup is sometimes delegated to the costumer, director, or another skilled person. In the professional theatre, actors are expected to create their own makeup except when it involves unusual challenges. Although the way makeup is handled varies widely, because of its intimate connection with the actor's appearance, it is treated here in conjunction with costuming.

The Function of Makeup

Makeup can serve several functions. First, makeup *characterizes*. It can indicate age, state of health, and race; within limits, it can suggest profession (outdoors versus indoors), basic attitude (through facial lines that suggest such qualities as grumpiness or cheerfulness), and self-regard (pride, or lack of it, in personal appearance). Makeup aids *expressiveness* by emphasizing facial features and making them more visible to the audience. Makeup restores *color and form* that are sometimes diminished by stage lighting. Makeup is indicative of *performance style*. In realistic plays, makeup is usually modeled on everyday appearance, whereas in nonrealistic plays it may be used to make statements, as in expressionist plays where distorted makeup may indicate distorted ideas or behavior.

The Makeup Plot

When the makeup for a production is designed and supervised by one person, it is usually coordinated through a makeup plot (sometimes supplemented by sketches). The plot is a chart recording basic information about the makeup of each character: the base color, liners, eye shadow, and powder; special features, such as a beard or enlarged nose; and changes to be made during the performance. The plot serves both as a guide for applying makeup and as a check on how the makeup of each actor relates to that of all the others. Sometimes a sketch is made of each actor's face to show how the makeup is to be applied.

Types of Makeup

Makeup effects may be achieved in two basic ways: through *painting,* and through *added plastic, prosthetic, or three-dimensional pieces.* Painting involves the application of color, highlights, and shadows to the face or other parts of the body. Plastic makeup includes the addition of such items as false noses, warts, beards, and wigs.

Painted makeup may be divided into four categories: age groups, straight or character makeup; racial/ethnic types; and special effects. *Age makeup* is of concern

Makeup, masks, and costumes create a sense of fantasy and magic in this production of Gozzi's *King Stag* at the American Repertory Theatre. Costumes, masks, and puppetry by Julie Taymor. Directed by Andrei Serban; sets by Michael Yeargan; lighting by Jennifer Tipton. (Photo by Richard Feldman.)

only when actors are to play characters whose age differs significantly from their own. As preparation, makeup artists need to be familiar with the characteristic distinctions among various age groups: typical coloration, highlights, shadows, and lines. They should be concerned not only with the face but also with hands, arms, and other visible parts of the body because if these are not made up appropriately, they may destroy the illusion created by facial makeup. A *straight makeup* utilizes the actor's own basic characteristics without altering them significantly. A *character makeup* is one that markedly changes the actor's own appearance. The change may be in age, or it may involve making the actor seem fatter or coarser, more lean and wizened, or it may emphasize some distinctive facial feature (such as a thin, sharp nose or large, soulful eyes). *Racial/ethnic makeup* emphasizes characteristic skin coloration, eye shapes, hair color and texture, along with other traits that differentiate Asian, Polynesian, Indian, African, Caucasian, and other subgroups. *Special painted effects* include clown makeup, distortions for stylistic reasons, and decorative designs painted on the face as in a tribal ritual. The effects that can be achieved by painting are almost endless.

Nevertheless, significant transformations in an actor's appearance are most easily accomplished with special three-dimensional elements. For example, a change in the shape of the nose and the addition of a beard and bushy eyebrows can mask an actor's features more completely than painting can. Prominent cheeks, hanging jowls, a protuberant forehead, fleshy jaws, warts, or large scars may be used to change the shape of the face or to give it a grotesque or unsightly appearance. Male actors can grow beards and moustaches, but these can also be made with relative ease. The appearance of the actor's hair can be changed significantly through styling and coloring, but wigs may be required for extreme changes or rapid switches. Baldness can be simulated with a "bald wig."

Makeup Materials

The materials needed for these and other effects are available from manufacturers and makeup supply houses. Most makeups begin with a *base.* Until recently (and in many places still), the most widely used base, packaged in tubes, was composed of pigment suspended in an oily solution that permitted the makeup to be applied easily and that prevented it from drying on the skin. More recently, water-based makeup has gained in popularity. Packaged in jars as relatively solid bars of pigment, it is applied after combining it with water. Base colors of either type are available in a wide range of colors: various shades of pink, tan, yellow, beige, brown, black, and white. Each color may be used alone or mixed with others to create still more gradations. The base is applied over the exposed portions of the face, neck, and ears. A wide range of colors is also available in liquid form for application to large surfaces of the body (arms, legs, and torso) if these will be visible on stage.

Used alone, a base color is likely to make the actor's face appear flat and uninteresting. Therefore, lines, highlights, and shadows are applied over the base. For this procedure, *liner* (a thick paste or solid block, usually packaged in small tins) is used. It is available in a wide range of colors, among them white, light brown, dark brown, blue, green, red, gray, and black. Like the base colors, liners may be mixed

Actors applying makeup in the makeup room of a theatre.

to create subtle gradations. Liner is used to create shadows under the eyes, hollows in the cheeks or temples, furrows in the forehead, creases that spread outward and downward from the nose, or for other highlighting and shadowing needed to emphasize facial characteristics. Red liner may be used for lipstick and rouge.

Beards and moustaches are usually made from *human hair,* available in a wide range of colors that may be combined to achieve various gradations of color or grayness. Beards and moustaches may be bought, but such ready-made products, especially beards, do not always fit the actor's face well. Beards, moustaches, and bushy eyebrows may also be made. *Liquid adhesive,* a plastic substance that solidifies but retains its flexibility when exposed to the air, is used to attach them to the face. In creating a beard, liquid adhesive is applied to the face (usually several layers are built up) to create a base on which hair can be attached in layers with additional liquid adhesive. When a beard of the desired shape and size has been completed (including shaping and trimming), the whole structure can be removed in one piece. This reusable beard can be applied for each performance by reattaching it to the face with liquid adhesive.

The shape and size of the nose can be changed through *prosthetics,* usually made from plastics or rubber latex that can be molded into the desired shape. These, too, may be purchased from makeup supply houses, but they usually are most satisfactory when made on the actors who will wear them. Similar prosthetic pieces can simulate fleshy jowls, large warts, and other protrusions. They are attached to the face with liquid adhesive and may be removed and reapplied as needed. Prosthetics are usually covered with the same base used on the rest of the face. Liners may be used for shadowing and highlighting to make the additions more realistic.

Hair coloration may be altered with *bleach* or *dye,* although this can be longer lasting than is desirable. A white liquid, frequently called *hair whitener,* may be combed through the hair to gray it, although this is not always convincing. More realistic graying can be achieved by *oiling* the hair lightly and combing aluminum *metallic powder* through it. *Wigs* are now so readily available that they often provide the easiest means of altering hair color and style. Wigs in contemporary hair styles are available in department stores; period wigs can be rented from costume supply houses or made from the type of hair used on store-window models. Wigs made from materials other than human or plastic hair are seldom satisfactory if a realistic effect is sought. For stylized wigs, various materials may be used: hemp, yarn, confetti, strips of paper, and so on.

After the actor's makeup is applied, the visible painted portions may be powdered to keep them from appearing greasy or shiny under stage lights. *Powder* comes in the same variety of shades as base paints. It is applied freely and the excess brushed off. When the performance ends, oil-based makeup is removed with *cold cream* and *facial tissues;* water-based makeup can be removed with soap and water.

Costume and makeup aid the actor's transformation into the character, although in productions that do not seek realistic effects, makeup may not be used at all; the performer is said to be "presenting" the character rather than attempting to "be" the character, and therefore there is no need to disguise the actor's own appearance. Nevertheless, makeup is still used in the majority of stage productions.

Thinking About . . .

Costume and Makeup

The range of costume and makeup in today's theatre is great. Each may be treated realistically or nonrealistically; each may reflect closely what is indicated by the script or deviate markedly from the script's specifications; or each may be largely ignored (with performers wearing their own clothing and no makeup). Costumes and makeup may make strong stylistic or interpretational statements, or they may be so unobtrusive as to be practically unnoticed. In all cases, the important issues concern why the specific choices were made and how they affect the production. Here are some questions that may contribute to a fuller understanding of choices and their results in the use of costume and makeup:

1. *In what type of space was the production staged? Did it permit close-range viewing of costumes and makeup? Were details easily visible? What was the overall effect of the space on costumes and makeup?*
2. *Did the costumes reflect a specific period, style, or production concept? If so, which? Did the approach adhere closely to the script? If not, in what ways did it depart from the script? With what effect?*

3. *Did the costumes and makeup characterize each role by clarifying specific oc-cupation or profession? Socioeconomic status? Occasion? Life-style? Age of character? Taste? Psychological traits? If so, through what means? If not, what was the effect of nonspecificity? Were some character traits ignored? If so, which and with what result?*

4. *Did costumes clarify character relationships? If so, how? With what results? If not, how did they fail to do so? With what results? Did they create ap-propriate emphasis and subordination? If so, through what means? If not, what prevented them from doing so?*

5. *Did the costumes enhance or inhibit movement and business? In what ways? With what results?*

6. *Were the costumes and makeup adapted to the actors? Did they enhance or alter each actor's appearance appropriately in terms of the role? Was the actor's overall physical appearance effective (or ineffective) for the role? In what ways was the effectiveness (or ineffectiveness) attributable to costume and makeup?*

7. *Were there costume or makeup changes? How did they relate to develop-ments in the dramatic action or alterations in the character's situation or attitudes? Did the changes in costume or makeup clarify the developments? If so, in what ways? If not, why not?*

8. *Were there any unusual, unexpected, or highly distinctive costumes or makeup? What features or means served to create these effects? Did the dis-tinctiveness enhance or detract from the overall effect?*

9. *How did costumes and makeup relate to scenery and lighting? Did they en-hance and complement each other? If so, how? If not, in what ways? With what results?*

10. *Overall, how did costume and makeup contribute (or fail to contribute) to the total production?*

The relevance of these questions will vary according to the particular pro-duction and play. To answer some of the questions about every costume or for the entire cast would be too time-consuming; for other questions, adequate an-swers may require information available only to those actually involved in the creation of the costumes and makeup. Nevertheless, attempts to answer parts or all of these questions will require us to look closely at costumes and makeup, and to evaluate their contributions to a theatrical production.

Chapter 16

Lighting Design,
Sound, and Multimedia

With Kent in the stocks, Edgar changes into his disguise as a madman as rain signals the coming storm in *King Lear* as performed at the American Repertory Theatre. Directed by Adrian Hall. Lighting by Natasha Katz. (Photo by Richard Feldman.)

Lighting is an element in itself whose effects are limitless; set free, it becomes for us what his palette is for the painter; . . . we can achieve infinite modulations. . . . [B]y means of light we can . . . materialize colors and forms . . . and can bring them alive in space. No longer does the actor walk in front of painted shadows and highlights; he is plunged into an atmosphere that is uniquely his own.

—Adolphe Appia, *Ideas on a Reform of Our Mise en Scène*

Lighting makes the other elements of theatrical production visible. But it does much more because it plays a major role in creating mood and atmosphere, in emphasizing and subordinating visual elements, and in blending the entire stage picture. It often escapes conscious notice because it is intangible, takes up no space, and is visible only when it strikes a reflecting surface. Consequently, lighting is often ignored unless it is clearly inadequate or obtrusively obvious.

The Lighting Designer's Skills

Lighting designers need a variety of skills, many of them pertinent to other professions, such as electrical or optical engineer, display designer, visual artist, electrician, social and cultural historian, and stage director. Like electrical engineers, lighting designers need to understand physics and electronics because they work with complex instruments and controlboards operated primarily by electricity. They need to know not only how the equipment works but also the physical principles involved so that they can make maximum use of the available resources and avoid their inefficient and dangerous misuse. Like optical engineers, lighting designers need to understand the principles of optics and light because they manipulate the variable properties of light when they use lamps, lenses, reflectors, color filters, and other equipment. The fuller their understanding of the principles and properties of light, the greater their potential for using light effectively for artistic purposes. Although lighting designers work in a more restricted and specialized sphere than electrical and optical engineers, all use the same base of information.

In the application of skills, lighting designers have much in common with display designers because both use the intensity, distribution, direction, and color of light to focus attention on important elements and to blend the elements into a whole that creates the appropriate mood. The lighting designer's work is usually more complex than the display designer's, however, because in the theatre one is concerned with a space that is used continuously by live, moving actors, whereas in a display the artist usually lights a fixed picture or one in which movement is created by electronically programmed elements.

Like other theatre designers, lighting designers need skills like those of the visual artist because they must be able to communicate through sketches. They may demonstrate their preliminary ideas by making many drawings, then render their final designs as sketches that emphasize light and shade—gradations in intensity, dominant direction, distribution—as well as color. Lighting designers must also be able to make various scale drawings of the stage and auditorium to show the mounting positions of lighting instruments and the areas they are to light. Many designers today use computers to create these drawings.

Although lighting designers may not perform the physical labor required to realize their designs, they must know what has to be done and supply the information needed by those who actually do the tasks. Consequently, like the stage electrician, designers must know what instruments are available, what each can do, what types of lamps, electrical cable, connectors, and the like are needed, where instruments are to be mounted and plugged in, and a host of other details. The designer's practical knowledge must be as extensive as the stage electrician's, although the designer may not be as skilled at installing and operating the equipment.

Lighting designers should be grounded in social and cultural history (including the visual and performing arts) because they often must know what role light played in various periods in the past. They need to be aware of what illuminants (candles, oil, torches, gas, and so on) were available in each period, how each was used, and what qualities of light each generated (so they can re-create or adapt these illuminants for their work as desired). Although today lighting designers normally work entirely with electrical light, they frequently must create the effects of other illuminants. They discover much of this information by studying social, cultural, and art history. Designers also need to know the conventions that governed stage lighting in each era of theatre history, in case a production requires these.

Lighting designers take an approach more nearly like that of the director than that of any other theatre artist because they must keep in mind and unify the entire stage picture. Lighting designers must be attuned to the overall needs of each scene as it develops moment by moment because light is the most flexible of all theatrical means, being instantaneously and continuously variable. The lighting designer needs to work closely with the director in realizing the production concept.

The Controllable Qualities of Light

Lighting designers achieve their goals by manipulating the four controllable qualities of light: intensity (or brightness), color, distribution, and movement.

Intensity depends primarily on the number of lamps used and their wattages. It may be increased or decreased in several ways: through the number of instruments focused on the same area or object; through the distance of instruments from what is being lighted (brightness diminishes with distance); through the use of dimmers to decrease or increase brightness; and through the presence or absence of color filters (the intensity of light decreases when it passes through a filter).

The visible spectrum of light is divided into *colors* (red, orange, yellow, green, blue-green, blue, and violet), each of which is distinguishable from the others because it is composed of light waves of a given length. We attribute color to objects because of their capacity to absorb some wavelengths and to reflect others. In stage lighting, color is controlled with filters, which function through the principle of selective transmission (that is, each color filter permits only certain wavelengths to pass through). A blue filter, for example, works by screening out other wavelengths. This process reduces the amount of light that reaches the stage. Color filters also

Strong backlighting makes a dramatic entrance for the four principal male characters in Shakespeare's *Love's Labours Lost* at the Yale Repertory Theatre. (Photo © T. Charles Erickson.)

affect our perception of color. For example, if a red object is lighted only with blue light, its apparent color will be magenta. To achieve a desired effect or to avoid unwanted distortions, light from a number of color sources can be mixed. Lighting designers may focus multiple instruments on each part of the stage to ensure control not only over intensity but also over color. Like pigment, light has primary hues from which all others may be derived by mixing them in varying proportions. The primary hues of light are red, blue, and green, which together produce white light. Various tints and shades are produced through mixing hues in differing proportions, saturations, and intensities.

Distribution depends on the direction from which light comes and the way it is spread over the performance space: All light may be directed at one area, or it may be distributed equally or unequally over the entire stage. Direction is determined by the position of a light source in relation to the area being lighted. Instruments may be mounted almost anywhere in the theatre: in the auditorium, above the stage, on the floor, on vertical or horizontal pipes, or on stands. These variations permit frontlighting, backlighting, crosslighting, downlighting, or uplighting, each separately or in various combinations.

Movement refers to perceptible alterations in any of the controllable qualities. The principal device for creating movement is the controlboard, which permits some lamps to be brightened and others dimmed to control intensity, color, or distribution. Movement allows light to change moment by moment in accordance with shifting moods and the development of the dramatic action. Its ability to move and change continuously makes lighting the most flexible of the production elements.

The Functions of Stage Lighting

By manipulating the controllable factors at their disposal, lighting designers achieve the various functions of stage lighting. First and most basically, light creates *visibility*. Apart from artistic considerations, a minimal level of intensity is essential if the performance is to be seen. Lighting also is used selectively to illuminate some parts of the scene and to conceal others. Second, lighting aids *composition*. By directing the eye to the most important elements, it creates emphasis and subordination. On the proscenium stage, the acting (or foreground) areas are usually more brightly lighted than the background, just as the level of light intensity at stage level (where the action takes place) is usually greater than on the upper parts of the setting (which are of secondary concern).

Third, lighting affects perception of *dimensionality* (mass and form). A three-dimensional structure will appear flat if all its surfaces are evenly lighted, whereas its shape will be revealed or emphasized by light that varies markedly from one surface to another. By manipulating direction (backlighting, downlighting, frontlighting, or crosslighting), intensity (degrees of brightness), and color, the lighting designer can define or alter apparent shape and dimension. This ability to influence perception of mass and form is among the lighting designer's most potent means of creating mood, atmosphere, and stylistic traits.

Fourth, lighting enhances *mood and atmosphere*. Bright, warm light is associated with gaiety and well-being, cool light with somberness. Glaring white light may create a sense of starkness or clinical probing whereas low-intensity lighting with many areas of shadow may create an atmosphere of mystery or threat. It is impossible to specify precisely the effect of each use of lighting because our response is determined by the total context and not merely by the lighting.

Sidelighting helps to create dimensionality and mood and to underscore the action in this scene from Caryl Churchill's *Mad Forest* at the Berkeley Repertory Theatre. Directed by Mark Wing-Davey; scenery and costumes by Marina Draghici; lighting by Peter Maradudin. (Photo by Ken Friedman. Courtesy of the Berkeley Repertory Theatre.)

Fifth, lighting may *reinforce style*. If the goal is realism, the lighting may establish the source of the light (sun, moon, lamps, firelight) and let the source motivate intensity, direction, distribution of light and shadow, color, and movement. Light may reflect the time of day, weather conditions, or season, and it may suggest the play's period through the lighting fixtures used on stage. If the goal is not realism, the source of the light and the way it is handled may be more arbitrary. Visible light sources may be used to distribute light evenly over the entire stage, establishing the performance space itself (rather than some fictional locale) as the place of the dramatic action. For an expressionistic play, light from very low or sharp angles may be used to distort facial features, or saturated colors may be used to indicate the dominant emotion.

Sixth, lighting may *underscore* the development of the dramatic action by reflecting the dominant feeling of each scene and the changes in mood from one scene to the next (for example, from cheerfulness to despair or regret). Light may also underscore the rhythmical patterns of scenes and changes in rhythm from one scene to another. Seventh, lighting *supports the production concept* through a combination of the other functions.

Although it serves many functions, lighting is among the most abstract of theatrical means. It works through suggestion and association rather than through concrete references (as scenery, lighting, and acting usually do). If lighting is in harmony with the other production elements, the audience may not be consciously aware of it.

The Lighting Designer's Working Procedures

Like other theatre artists, lighting designers usually begin by studying the script—its action, characters, themes, language, spectacle, mood. After gaining a sense of the whole, they may proceed to specific indications of lighting: time of day; sources of light (lamps, sunlight, and so on); changes during scenes (growing darkness, lamps being turned on); variations required for different parts of the stage (distinctions between indoor and outdoor in a divided setting, some areas lighted by lamps and other areas in relative shadow); the direction of light (moonlight through a window, light from an overhead fixture); color of light; and special effects (lightning, firelight, and the like). Lighting designers need to note carefully the dominant mood of each scene and other factors that will affect the lighting designs.

Before they make sketches (and perhaps before they undertake any detailed research), lighting designers meet with the director and the other designers to discuss the script and production concept. The director may have firm ideas about the production concept to be used, or may wish to discuss several possibilities with the designers and get their input before reaching a final decision. Whatever the process, an interpretational approach must be decided on before the designers can work effectively. Lighting designers must be sensitive to the ideas of the scene and costume designers because the work of each designer impinges on that of the others. Lighting designers also need to be aware of any specific demands of the director (such as the need to isolate areas through lighting, scenes requiring projections, specific atmospheric effects, and the like). In addition, lighting designers need to establish what performance space will be used, what the budget for lighting is, what equipment and personnel they will need, and how much working time will be available to install and focus lighting instruments and equipment. With all of these considerations in mind, the lighting designer is ready to begin.

There is no standard approach to the design of lighting. Lighting designers are in a somewhat different position from that of other theatre artists because lighting is seen only as it is reflected by the actors, costumes, setting, and performance space. Thus what they light is created by others, and frequently lighting designers must adjust their work to enhance that of others rather than proceeding as they would desire. They can make general plans, but until the floor plan and setting are agreed upon, lighting designers cannot make firm decisions about the placement and direction of lighting instruments, and until the movement pattern of each actor is established, they cannot know precisely how the light needs to be distributed.

Lighting design therefore seldom becomes as firmly fixed as other design elements do during the planning stages.

Like the other designers, lighting designers should be able to convey their ideas through sketches showing how the stage will look when lighted. These sketches emphasize mood and atmosphere or light and shadow. The number and type of sketches depend upon the complexity and variety of the lighting to be used. Lighting designers sometimes do not make sketches but instead use a *lighting score*, which breaks the play into scenes or units and indicates in a diagram the time of day, source of light, overall brightness, the desired mood, color and any other factors that will affect lighting design. Sketches or scores serve as a basis for the production team to discuss the qualities to be sought in the lighting. The designer usually attends several rehearsals to become familiar with the movement patterns and to understand the director's intentions. It is also becoming increasingly frequent for designers to try out and perfect their lighting designs in a laboratory before implementing them. However lighting designers work, they usually do not arrive at fully developed designs until shortly before the instruments are to be hung and focused.

The Light Plot and Instrument Schedule

If the sketches of lighting designers sometimes lack specificity, the same cannot be said of their two primary working plans: light plots and instrument schedules.

Light plots can be divided into two types: floor plans and vertical sections. The floor-plan plot is drawn to scale and shows, as seen from above, the layout of the stage, the setting, and the auditorium; on this plot are indicated the type, size, and position of each instrument and the area it will light. The vertical-section plot, also drawn to scale, shows the vertical arrangement of the stage, scenery, and auditorium, and the type, size, and position of each instrument and the area it will light. Together, these plots show the horizontal and vertical distribution of the light sources. It is usual to make a separate light plot for each setting and then a composite plot showing all of the settings simultaneously in order to see how the lighting for each scene relates to that of all the others. This procedure facilitates the use of the same instruments in multiple scenes. In summary, light plots specify what instruments are to be used and where each is to be mounted.

Lighting plots also take into consideration the three principal types of stage lighting: specific illumination, general illumination, and special effects. *Specific illumination* is that which is confined to a limited area. It is used principally for the acting areas, which demand the greatest emphasis and often require variety in intensity, color, and distribution. The principal sources of specific illumination are spotlights, which emit a concentrated beam that can be confined to a limited area. But because a single spotlight can illuminate only a small segment of the stage, the total acting space is usually divided, for purposes of lighting, into several smaller areas. Each area is then lighted separately. At least one spotlight is focused on each area from each side to strike it at an angle of forty-five degrees both horizontally and vertically. More typically, several instruments (mounted at varying levels and angles) are focused on each area. The lighting for each area should overlap into ad-

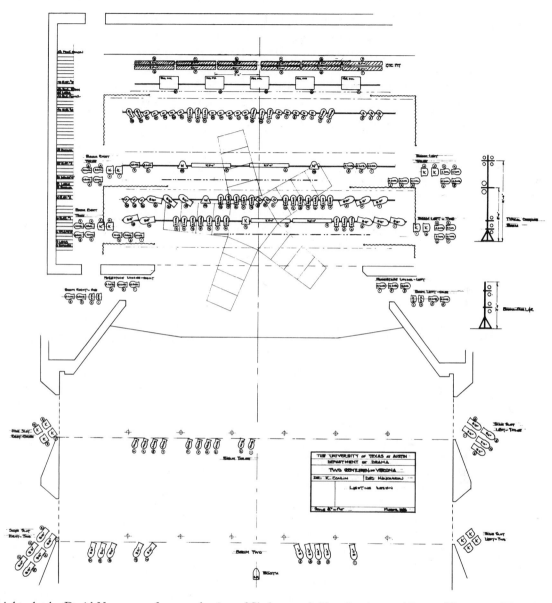

Light plot by David Nancarrow for a production of Shakespeare's *Two Gentlemen of Verona*. (Courtesy of David Nancarrow.)

jacent areas to avoid creating distracting variations in brightness and darkness as actors move about the stage.

Where instruments are mounted to achieve the desired distribution depends in part on the type of stage. In the proscenium theatre, forward acting areas cannot be lighted effectively from behind the arch, and therefore some instruments are mounted in the auditorium—in ceiling apertures, in vertical apertures at the sides, or on the front of the balcony. Upstage areas are normally lighted by instruments hung back of the proscenium—on the light bridge just behind and above the opening, on vertical pipes at either side of the stage, on pipe battens suspended over the stage at intervals from front to back, on stands, or on the floor. In the arena theatre, all instruments are usually mounted above the acting area and audience, or on vertical pipes located where they will not interfere with sightlines. Because performances are viewed from four sides, the acting areas must be lit from all directions. On the thrust stage, most of the instruments are mounted over the platform or in the audience areas, but there may be a space behind the main platform where others are hung. Because the action is normally seen from two or three sides, lighting on thrust stages is usually a compromise between that used for a proscenium and that for an arena stage. In flexible or variable performance spaces, lighting may be nothing more than normal auditorium illumination, often no more than is required for visibility. If more selective lighting is used, the instruments may be mounted almost anywhere in the performance space.

General illumination spreads over a much larger area than specific illumination. General illumination is most fully exploited on the proscenium stage, where it serves three functions: to light the background elements not illuminated by spotlights; to blend acting areas and provide a smooth transition from the higher intensity of the acting areas to the lower intensity of the background; and to enhance or modify the color of settings and costumes. General illumination is provided primarily by striplights and floodlights. Although general illumination cannot be confined to small areas, its direction can be partially controlled. Footlights point upward and backward from the floor. Borderlights are hung above the acting area and are pointed downward or tilted in one direction. Other striplights can be placed on the floor to light ground rows or cycloramas. Floodlights may be suspended on battens above the stage, mounted on vertical stands, or placed on the floor. On the arena stage, general illumination plays a minor role because usually there is no background to light and the specific illumination covers the entire acting space. On the thrust stage, general lighting may play a larger role, especially if there is a stage house. In flexible or variable spaces, all of the lighting may be general.

Special effects are out-of-the-ordinary demands—among them projections, fires and firelogs, rainbows, fog and smoke, bright rays of light (to simulate sunlight or moonlight), explosions, lightning, strobe lights, and "black" light (ultraviolet light used to pick out specially treated substances on a dark stage).

In making light plots, each type of light (specific, general, and special effects) is considered separately and then as a part of the total unit. The location of all lighting instruments is indicated on the plots.

After the light plots are completed, an *instrument schedule* is made. This is a chart that lists separately each lighting instrument with its specifications (type, wattage, lens, reflector, lamp, and any other pertinent information), mounting position, color filter, area lighted by it, circuit into which it is plugged, and dimmer to which it is connected. The schedule summarizes in tabular form all the technical information needed for acquiring and setting up lighting instruments. (See the illustration on page 421.)

THE REP. PLOT 1/91								INSTRUMENT SCHEDULE	
INV #	INST #	INSTRUMENT	POSITION	FOCUS	LAMP	CIR.	DIM.	COLOR	NOTES
1	1	ALTMAN 6X9	1ST ANTE-PRO	DOWN-L	IK	101	3	3204	
2	2	" 6X9	"	DOWN-C	"	102	2	"	
3	3	" 6X9	"	DOWN-R	"	103	1	"	
4	4	" 6X9	"	DOWN-L	"	104	6	60	
5	5	" 6X9	"	DOWN-C	"	105	5	"	
6	6	" 6X9	"	DOWN-R	"	106	4	"	
7	1	STRAND 6X9	1ST ELECTRIC	UP-L	"	15	9	3204	
8	2	KLIEGL 6X9	"	DOWN-L	"	16	15	54	
9	3	STRAND 6X9	"	UP-C	"	17	8	3204	
10	4	" 6X9	"	UP-L	"	18	12	60	
11	5	KLIEGL 6X9	"	DOWN-C	"	19	14	54	
12	6	STRAND 6X9	"	UP-C	"	20	11	3204	
13	7	" 6X9	"	UP-R	"	21	7	"	
14	8	KLIEGL 6X9	"	DOWN-R	"	22	13	54	
15	9	STRAND 6X9	"	UP-R	"	23	10	60	

A lighting instrument schedule.

Lighting Instruments, Accessories, and Controlboards

The lighting designer's materials can be divided into three basic categories: lighting instruments, accessories, and controlboards. Designers must be familiar with the characteristics of each type of instrument, accessory, and controlboard as a basis for making the light plots and instrument schedules that constitute the plans for realizing their lighting designs. Most resident and nonprofessional theatres own a supply of lighting equipment sufficient to meet the demands of their productions. They typically use buildings that have permanently installed controlboards. Many Broadway theatres, as well as many road theatres, do not have permanent controlboards or lighting equipment. Consequently, when lighting designers plan productions for such theatres, they must list (with exact specifications) every item necessary for the production. This material may be rented or bought. If the production is to tour, the lighting equipment must be transportable and easily installed.

Lighting Instruments

There are several categories of lighting instruments: spotlights, striplights, floodlights, and special lighting equipment.

Spotlights are designed to illuminate restricted areas with a concentrated beam of light. They are the primary source of specific illumination. Most spotlights have a metal housing, lamp socket, reflector, lens, color-frame guide, mounting attachments, and some means of adjusting the focus. Spotlights are normally classified according to wattage, lenses, and reflectors. They range from 100 to several thousand *watts,* the most typical being 1,000. The *lens* gathers the light from a lamp and bends it into parallel rays to create a concentrated beam. Each spotlight is designed to use a specific type of lens and will not operate efficiently with any other.

A *reflector* is placed behind or around the lamp to throw light forward that would otherwise be wasted. A reflector increases the spotlight's efficiency (the ratio of the amount of light emitted by the source and the amount of light that actually reaches the stage). Reflectors are made of metal and in various shapes, although those used in spotlights are either spherical or ellipsoidal.

Most spotlights have other features: *guides to hold color frames* (placed just forward of the lens); a *mounting* (usually a swivel C-clamp that allows the spotlight to be attached firmly to a pipe and rotated from side to side or up and down); and an *adjustable-focus* device that changes the relationship among the lamp, lens, and reflector. Some spotlights are now equipped with remote control devices that permit focus and other adjustments to be made electronically.

A *striplight* is typically a series of lamps set into a narrow rectangular trough. It is used for general illumination. Each strip is usually wired with four separate circuits. Every fourth lamp is on the same circuit, and may therefore be controlled together. All the lamps on the same circuit are covered with filters of the same color. Each strip can produce four different colors when each circuit is used alone, or it can combine circuits to produce a wide range of additional colors. Striplights are often used to "tone" (give color to) settings, costumes, and makeup. Striplights vary

---

Jules Fisher

Jules Fisher (1937–) is among the leading American lighting designers. Educated at Pennsylvania State University and Carnegie-Mellon University, he has served as producer of a number of shows and directed some short films in addition to being a lighting designer. Among his best-known designs are those for *Hair, Pippin, Jesus Christ Superstar, Chicago, Dancin',* and *La Cage aux Folles.* He has also served as a consultant on Rolling Stones tours. Fisher has been active in promoting automation and computerized lighting equipment as essential to both efficiency and creativity. He is credited with inventing the remote control spotlight. He has won a number of Tony Awards for his lighting designs, including one in 1990 for *Grand Hotel* and one in 1991 for *The Will Rogers Follies.* His recent work includes *Angels in America* and *My Favorite Year.* For more than thirty years, Fisher has been head of a theatre consulting firm. He is also a partner in an architectural lighting firm. (Examples of Fisher's designs are shown on pages 278 and 403.)

The effectiveness of the most spectacular moment in the musical *Miss Saigon*, the arrival and departure of a helicopter, depended much on David Hersey's lighting. Directed by Nicholas Hytner; production designed by John Napier. (Photo by Joan Marcus.)

in length—from those with only three or four lamps to those extending the entire width of the stage. Short lengths are most popular because they can be used alone or combined with others as needed. The development of the quartz lamp has led to a new type of striplight design that makes it possible to space striplight units as far apart as eight feet and still achieve a smooth wash of light.

Striplights can be subdivided into three categories: *footlights, borderlights,* and *miscellaneous.* Footlights are usually recessed in a slot at the front (or, in thrust stages, around the edges) of the stage. They can be used to erase unwanted shadows on the actors' faces caused by headwear or by sharp-angled overhead lighting, to enhance color, and to blend the specific and general illumination. Borderlights are hung from battens above the stage, usually in a series from front to back. They can be used for blending the acting areas and for toning the settings and costumes. Miscellaneous striplights can be placed on the floor to light ground rows and drops and around the base of the cyclorama (as "cyc foots") to create various sky or mood effects. Small strips are often used to light backings for doors and windows.

A *floodlight,* designed to give general illumination, uses a single lamp as its source. It has a housing with a large opening; there is no lens. The most popular

The combination of strong front lighting on the characters in the foreground with fog effects and sidelighting in the background creates appropriate emphasis, mood, and context for this victory scene in Shakespeare's *Cymbeline* as produced by the Huntington Theatre Company. Directed by Larry Carpenter; lighting by Marcia Madeira; scenery by John Falabella; costumes by David Murin. (Photo by Richard Feldman.)

floodlight (the "scoop") uses an ellipsoidal reflector. Wattage varies from 250 to 2,000, and a frame is provided to hold color filters. Floodlights can be used singly or in combination. They may be suspended above the stage to substitute for borderlights, or, like striplights, they may be placed on the floor to light drops or ground rows, or they may be used to light backings and other scenic units. Floodlights are frequently used to light the cyclorama (several may be used in combination to achieve a smooth, even wash over the entire visible surface).

It would be difficult to specify all the special effects that are sometimes required. Perhaps the most common special instrument is the *projector*. For still pictures, 35-millimeter slide projectors are often satisfactory. Because these projectors are not designed for stage use, however, it is usually more satisfactory to use lens projectors bought or rented from lighting supply houses or made by knowledgeable stage technicians. Some projectors are designed to use discs that project moving images of clouds, waves, rain, smoke, or fire. Motion picture projectors of various types can be used with filmed sequences. Lightning and fire effects of various types are commercially available, as is equipment to create smoke or fog and simulated explosions. These common special effects can be supplemented by personnel with a knowledge of electricity and stage-lighting instruments. Additional equipment is available from lighting supply houses.

Accessories

Several accessories—lamps, electrical cable and connectors, color frames and color media—are needed. Each instrument is designed to use a particular *lamp*. Similarly, each lamp is designed for specific purposes. Manufacturers' catalogs give details about lamps designed for stage use.

Electrical cable for the stage should be heavily insulated because it must withstand much wear. *Connectors* (plugs) used with electrical cable differ from those in household use. Made for heavy-duty use, most can be twisted to lock in place so they cannot be accidentally disconnected during performances.

Most lighting instruments are equipped for color filters. Consequently, *color frames* and *color media* are needed. A frame, usually made of metal, has an opening of the same size and shape as that of the instrument with which it is to be used. Several color media are used in stage lighting. The most common is plastic (with varying names—roscolene, cinemoid, cinabex, mylar), which is available in a wide range of hues, saturations, and intensities. It may be cut to any shape or size.

Connecting Panels and Controlboards

No lighting system is complete without some means of control. Instruments and color filters provide the possibilities for control, but before they can be exploited, a *controlboard* is needed. With a board, some instruments can be fully on while others are off or partially dimmed, and colors from several instruments can be mixed. But if a controlboard is to be efficient, a means of connecting each instrument to it must be available. This need is met by a *connecting panel* to which all stage circuits and controlboard dimmers run, making it possible to connect any dimmer to any stage outlet. In some recent installations, each circuit is permanently connected to its own dimmer.

At its simplest, a controlboard is a panel of switches for turning lights on and off. But if control is to be subtle, dimmers are required. There are many types of dimmers; the most common are *resistance, autotransformer,* and *electronic.* Each works on a different principle, but each allows a gradual increase or decrease in the electrical power reaching the lamps so that they may be dimmed or brightened. Both resistance and autotransformer dimmers are now largely outmoded, although they continue to be used in some theatres.

As the number of dimmers increases, so does the problem of control. If each dimmer had to be adjusted manually and individually, several persons would be required to operate a large bank of dimmers. Fortunately, all types of dimmerboards can be equipped with master controls that allow some or all of the dimmers to be connected so that a single lever can operate all. An efficient controlboard allows dimmers to be interconnected in almost any combination.

Although the controlboard shown here is now somewhat dated, it illustrates how a controlboard should be located so as to allow the operator an unimpeded view of the stage.

The placement of the controlboard console is important. The most common locations are at one side of the stage, at the rear of the auditorium, or in a booth built into the face of the balcony. The ideal arrangement permits the operator to see the stage from much the same vantage as the audience.

Most controlboards now in use allow dimmers to be preset; then, with a master control, lights for one scene may be faded out and others brought up simultaneously, or changes within a scene may be set on the controlboard beforehand and activated at the appropriate moment. The ability to preset controls eliminates many mistakes. All major manufacturers of controlboards now offer computerized "memory banks" capable of storing several hundred cues or preset scenes. The light levels (and changes in lighting) in each scene of a production (or several productions) can be recorded, stored, and called up as desired. Few aspects of theatrical production have undergone so many changes in the recent past as has lighting control, perhaps

Jennifer Tipton

Jennifer Tipton (1937–　) is one of today's most admired lighting designers. During much of her career she has designed for dance companies, among them those of Paul Taylor, Twyla Tharp, Robert Joffrey, and Mikhail Baryshnikov. She has also designed for Broadway, the New York Shakespeare Festival, and many regional companies, including the American Repertory Company and the Guthrie Theatre. She is especially known for her work with such avant-garde companies as Mabou Mines and the Wooster Group and with such innovative directors as Robert Wilson and Andre Serban. In 1991 she directed her first production: Shakespeare's *The Tempest* for the Guthrie Theatre. Her recent work includes lighting designs for *Martin Guerre* and *In the Summer House.* Her influence as a designer is considerable not only through her work but also through her teaching in the Yale University School of Drama. About lighting she says: "Light can change the world in a mysterious and compelling way that is not true of directing, set or costume design. . . . To me, lighting is the audience's guide to the story, and to what the production is doing. Light can confuse or clarify the issue." Examples of Tipton's work may be seen on pages 215, 250, 252, 315, 406, and in color plates 16 and 17.

because it is the one most adaptable to computerization, which continues to make possible ever more complex and subtle control.

Setting the Lights, Rehearsals, and Performances

Typically, the performance space is not available for work on lights until a few days prior to technical and dress rehearsals. Regardless of how much time is available, the tasks are reasonably standard. Using the light plots and instrument schedule as guides, the master electrician and his assistants mount each instrument and direct it toward the stage area specified in the light plot. The specified light filter is added, the instrument is plugged into the proper circuit, and is then connected to the designated dimmer. The instruments may be focused tentatively at this time, but final focusing may have to wait until the other production elements are added. Among these elements, those most likely to require adjustments in focusing are scenery and the movement or placement of actors.

To expedite these procedures, a number of aids may be used to avoid the need to refer constantly to light plots or instrument schedules. Sometimes at each instrument position the information about the instrument type, color, circuit, and so on are noted on a piece of tape and attached at the spot where the instrument is to be mounted. Sometimes the information about all the instruments to be hung on a single batten is indicated on a single card. Designers may condense much of the paperwork onto a "cheat sheet" that serves as a quick reminder of what needs to be done. Each designer and/or master electrician usually has his or her own shortcuts

The dappled background, created by lighting, helps to create the momentarily happy fantasy of the final scene in *Baltimore Waltz* as produced at the Yale Repertory Theatre. Directed by Stan Wojewodski, Jr.; lighting by Lynne Chase; costumes by Denise Hudson. (Photo © T. Charles Erickson.)

for making the complex process of mounting and focusing instruments more efficient. Although most of the work is done by others, the lighting designer is usually present to answer questions or to clarify plans.

Setting and focusing instruments can be time-consuming and sometimes disheartening, for it is difficult to confine light precisely. Unwanted lines, shadows, and bright patches may appear; and when the same instruments must be used to light more than one scene or set, an ideal adjustment for one may not be the best

Tharon Musser's lighting for the Broadway production of *A Chorus Line*. Conceived and directed by Michael Bennett; scenery by Robin Wagner; costumes by Theoni V. Aldredge. (Photo by Martha Swope.)

Female Pioneers in Stage Lighting

Jean Rosenthal and Tharon Musser have been perhaps the most influential lighting designers in America. Rosenthal (1912–1969) is often said to have created the field of lighting design. When she began working in the theatre (first with Orson Welles and John Houseman in the Federal Theatre Project in 1936), lighting was still the province of the scenic designer or master electrician. From 1938 until her death, Rosenthal was lighting designer (as well as production supervisor) for the Martha Graham Dance Company, and perhaps because light was such an essential element in Graham's pieces, Rosenthal was able to perfect lighting as a distinct artistic statement and a creator of a strong sense of mood. Largely because of Rosenthal's pioneering example, lighting design after World War II came to be recognized as a specialized field. Among Rosenthal's numerous designs for the Broadway theatre, the best known are *West Side Story* (see page 212) and *The Sound of Music*. Her views about lighting are summed up in her *The Magic of Light* (1972).

Tharon Musser (1925–   ) is often said to be America's most influential lighting designer. A graduate of Berea College and the Yale School of Drama, she did most of her early lighting work for dance companies, especially José Limon's. Her first major Broadway assignment was José Quintero's production of O'Neill's *Long Day's Journey into Night* in 1956. She went on to design for several repertory companies, among them the American Shakespeare Company, for which she lighted twenty-nine productions. Since 1971, she has lighted all of Neil Simon's Broadway productions. She has also designed many musicals, including *Mame* and *A Little Night Music*. She is perhaps best known for her collaborative work with Michael Bennett (director and choreographer), Robin Wagner (scenic designer), and Theoni Aldredge (costume designer) on *A Chorus Line* (the longest-running production ever to appear on Broadway) and *Dream Girls*. Musser has lighted more than 100 Broadway productions and has won three Tony Awards. She is credited with several innovations in lighting practice, perhaps most notably computerized lighting, which she introduced to Broadway in *A Chorus Line* (1975). More recent work includes *The Secret Garden* and *Laughter on the 23rd Floor*.

As preparation for becoming a lighting designer, Musser believes that mastery of technical skills is not enough. She is a strong advocate of liberal education as the foundation for further training. She has stated that art history courses are more valuable than lighting courses because though the lighting designer must attain adequate technical training, ultimately that training will be ineffective unless it is combined with a vision that creates paintings with light. She urges young designers to work in regional and summer stock theatres because of the variety of experience those theatres offer and because they permit the young designer to try out in a short period many ideas that help to develop craft into art. She is a strong believer in a collaborative process—she insists that she works *with*, not *for*, others. (Examples of Musser's designs are shown on page 428.)

for the others. This process may go on for hours, even days, until the desired results have been achieved.

Cue sheets—indicating the lighting at the beginning of each scene (the dimmers to be used and the intensity setting of each), any changes to be made during the scene, and the cues for the changes—must also be made. If there is a memory bank or other preset device, this information is entered into it. The cue sheets become the basis for controlling the lights during performances.

Lighting is usually integrated with the other elements for the first time during technical rehearsals. Alterations may be required at that time, and further adjustments may be made during and after dress rehearsals. This is a crucial time in the lighting designer's work, for many decisions that determine the final design are not definitely made until these rehearsals. At this time, the lighting designer is often called on to compensate for problems in other aspects of production because it is easier to adjust lights than to make a new costume or repaint a set at this stage in the production process. All necessary changes are made as quickly as possible. Some productions, especially those on Broadway, have a number of preview performances, after each of which some adjustments may be required. After the play officially opens, responsibility passes to the light crew.

The Lighting Designer's Employment and Assistants

In the professional theatre, the lighting designer usually is a member of the United Scenic Artists union, as is the *assistant designer* (if there is one). The assistant may make sketches and light plots, compile instrument schedules, locate the necessary equipment, act as liaison between the lighting designer and the rest of the production staff, and aid in putting in the lights and in compiling the cue sheets.

The *master electrician* or *lighting crew head* works closely with the designer when equipment is being installed and instruments adjusted. After the show opens, the master electrician (or crew head) must see that all equipment is properly maintained and check before each performance to see that everything is in working order. These technicians are directly responsible to the stage manager. In the professional theatre, master electricians must be members of the International Alliance of Theatrical Stage Employees union (IATSE).

The lighting crew installs, operates, and maintains all lighting equipment and shifts electrical equipment that must be moved during scene changes. The control-board console operator is of special importance because this person actually controls the lighting during performances. In the professional theatre, crews usually belong to the union (IATSE). In the nonprofessional theatre, crews are usually students or volunteers.

Sound

Like other theatrical elements, sound makes its greatest contributions when it is designed as a unit and carefully integrated with the production as a whole. Because, like lighting, sound depends on electronic means, it is treated here with lighting

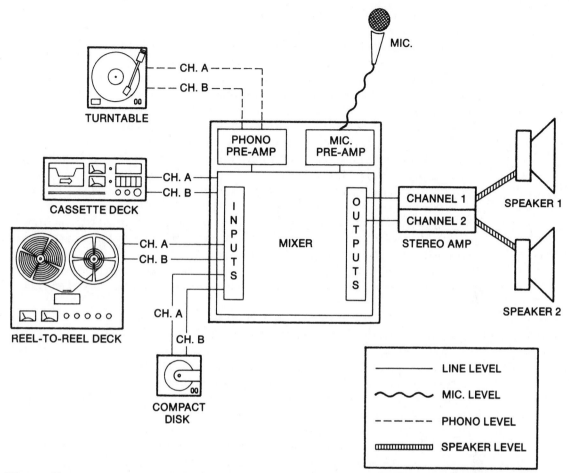

Diagram showing the elements and their relationships in a standard sound system. (Courtesy of Amarante Lucero.)

design. Sound is being increasingly acknowledged as an area worthy of separate recognition, especially because many theatres now amplify the actors' voices in every production, in addition to using a complex sound score to support the other aspects of production.

Sound may be divided into three categories: *verbal* (the actors' voices), *nonverbal* (music and abstract sound), and *realistic noises* (identifiable with recognizable sources). Because the first category has already been discussed in the chapters on directing and acting, little need be said about it here.

Sound fulfills three functions: It *evokes mood and atmosphere, reinforces the action of the play,* and *comments on the action.* An atmosphere of gaiety or somberness can be evoked by music, just as mystery or strangeness may be evoked through abstract hollow sounds. Environmental sounds, such as birds singing, may be used to suggest a quiet pastoral scene, or thunder and rain may be used to set the mood for an impending murder.

Sound may reinforce the action by preparing the audience for present or future events or by suggesting offstage events. Gunshots, crashing dishes, doorbells, telephones, and similar sounds may prepare for onstage action or indicate offstage occurrences. Certain noises may establish the time of day (a rooster crowing is usually associated with daybreak) or season of the year (sleighbells are usually associated with winter), just as others may place the action in the country or city or near a railroad or river.

Sound may comment on the action by giving audiences clues about the response sought by the director. Lugubrious music played during a long pathetic speech can make a comic or satirical comment, or the clashing of cymbals may heighten a pratfall.

Sound may be *live* or *recorded,* but in either case may be amplified. The actors create live sound, but whether or not it is amplified usually depends on the size of the auditorium, or, in the case of musicals, whether the singing voices need to be amplified to be heard above the musical accompaniment. Live orchestras are seldom amplified. Most nonmusical dramas do not demand music, but it is often added to underscore an effect, to establish the appropriate mood before the performance begins, or to bridge scenes and cover scene changes. Recorded music is most often used in these instances.

Such noises as doorbells and telephones can be produced so easily with electrical buzzers that they often are not taped. Other types of sound effects are usually created and then transcribed on tapes or compact discs. A wide range of effects is available commercially in sets of recordings often referred to as "sound effects libraries." Nevertheless, these do not always meet the specific needs of a production. Most organizations now own recording equipment and can create the effects most appropriate to their needs.

Many sound effects now make use of processed sound created through synthesizers, which can produce almost any sound. Sound can also be processed by speeding it up or slowing it down, adding echo or reverberation, mixing sound, and a number of other techniques. Almost any desired type and quality of sound can be achieved.

Effective sound requires a sound system of high quality. Some groups have only the simplest of tape recorder/playback units, while others have very elaborate systems. An effective system allows all of the controllable factors of sound—pitch (or frequency), quality (or timbre), volume (or amplitude), direction, and duration—to be varied in relation to each other and in accordance with the demands of the production. Complete flexibility in direction, for example, requires a series of amplifiers located at various spots on the stage and in the auditorium so that a sound (such as that of an airplane) can begin on one side, seem to approach, pass overhead, and pass out of hearing on the other side. Effective placement and control are made more complex by the acoustics of the space in which sound may reverberate or be reflected off various surfaces.

An efficient sound system will include the following: several recorder/playback units, so that sound may be recorded and then mixed from several sources played simultaneously; microphones, turntables, and tape/cassette or digital players for recording live sound and music and for use during performances; equipment for

Josef Svoboda's multimedia design for an adaptation of Maxim Gorki's novel *The Last Ones* at the Prague National Theatre. The various fragmentary set pieces at stage level permit multiple scenes to be played simultaneously or in sequence against projected scenes at the rear of the stage. The multiple images create a production of great complexity. (Photo by Jaromir Svoboda.)

processing and altering sound; a high-fidelity speaker system of excellent quality and versatility, so that sound at any volume can be reproduced faithfully without interference, and so that its direction can be controlled fully; a patch bay, so that sound sources (such as tapes and microphones) and amplifiers can be interconnected and mixed; and a control console, so that the entire system can be operated efficiently. Computers used for memory storage and playback are also now available.

Normally, the only working plan for sound is the *sound score,* which indicates the cue for each sound (the location in the script and length of sound), the reason for the cue (ringing telephone, desired audience response, and the like), the origin of the sound (what will need to be recorded or used to make the sound, including appropriate information about style, period, or quality), treatment of the sound (whether it needs to be distorted, enhanced, and so on), and source direction (where the speaker needs to be located).

The sound designer then begins to collect sounds to meet the needs of the sound score. When they are found, the sounds are recorded on a master tape and are edited and enhanced as desired. A tape approximating the sound that is planned

Josef Svoboda and Multimedia

Josef Svoboda (1920–   ) is among the world's best-known designers, in part because of his extensive use of multimedia. Born in Czechoslovakia and trained as an architect, he became chief designer at the National Theatre in Prague in the 1950s. Since then, he has experimented continuously with means of applying new technology and materials to scenography. He has sought to create dynamic stage environments capable of continuous alteration. In addition to his work in Czechoslovakia, Svoboda has designed for companies in the United States, England, France, Germany, Belgium, Switzerland, and many other countries.

Several of Svoboda's projects have combined filmed or closed-circuit images with live stage action. Among the most complex of these productions was Luigi Nono's opera *Intoleranza* in Boston. In addition to the live stage action, other scenes were staged simultaneously in a number of studios, some as far as three miles away from the theatre. These studio scenes were projected onto numerous screens located on the stage, thus intermingling several separately staged scenes. As Svoboda described it: "All these studios were joined with each other by audio and visual monitors, so that the actors could see the conductor in relation to themselves, the actors in the studio could see what was being played on the stage, and . . . the actors on the stage see what was played in the studios."

Svoboda has also been much concerned with the stage's ability to alter scale in ways that create emphasis and subordination comparable to that achieved by close-ups in film. In a production of Wagner's opera, *Die Götterdämmerung* in London, he placed large lenses on stage that served as scenic elements but that, when characters moved behind them, magnified those characters, making them much larger than the other live actors onstage. (See the illustrations on page 245.) The manipulation of light (in color, direction, and intensity) in relation to these lenses also created varied visual effects. Svoboda has been a pioneer in exploring the potentials for stage use of emerging technologies.

for the production is often used for some rehearsals, allowing sound designers to evaluate the effectiveness of their designs and to make adjustments.

The designer then creates a *sound plot*, which is similar to the sound score but much more detailed. It includes cue number; script page number; description and length of each sound cue; the equipment to be used (including location of speakers). On the basis of these decisions, the designer creates a *show tape* (as it will be used in the production). Sound must then be integrated into the production with all appropriate information written into the stage manager's promptbook. *Cue sheets* must be created for the persons who will operate the sound during the performances. During technical and dress rehearsals, sound levels and length of cues may need to be adjusted and the show tape altered to reflect these changes. Backup tapes are made in case anything should happen to the show tape. After the production opens, the sound designer's work is considered to be ended and responsibility passes to the stage manager and sound operator.

Mixed-Media Productions

Since the 1960s, mixed (or multi-) media productions have become common. These may combine elements from several media, but characteristically they mingle live action (which may include dance) with projected still or moving pictures and stereophonic sound and music.

Several factors explain the popularity of multimedia. First, changes in artistic taste and audience perception (probably influenced by film and television) demand that time, place, and focus shift rapidly, without long waits between scenes. This demand has led to the use of means less cumbersome than full-stage, three-dimensional settings. Second, playwrights have come to assume that time and place can be altered instantaneously, and they write accordingly. Third, computer and other electronic research has brought significant advances that have been adapted for theatrical use. Fourth, the development of computers has made it possible to program many effects and to control them with precision. For these reasons, traditional settings have been largely supplanted by those created with a few built pieces combined with effects created through light and sound. The stage has become technologically more complex, while stage settings have become less illusionistic.

A notable feature of multimedia productions has been the liberal use of projected images—often of still pictures, frequently several shown simultaneously on a number of screens. The images may be fragments of the same picture, or each may be unlike the others. All are usually chosen for their appropriateness to the mood or theme of the piece; some may suggest comparisons between the dramatic events and those of other times and places. For example, a production of Shakespeare's *Troilus and Cressida*—which takes place during the Trojan War—might project images of wars in various periods and places, thereby suggesting the similarity of all wars. Filmed sequences may be used in various ways. Footage of real events may be used to supply a context for a play's action; filmed sequences using the play's actors may be interjected into the action to give it greater scope; or filmed sequences and live sequences may be coordinated. Closed-circuit television can be used to project onto large screens close-ups of the actors' faces, portions of the action, or even of the audience. Projections (whatever the type) are often accompanied by stereophonic, directional sound or music. Performance art and the theatrical pieces of directors such as Robert Wilson are examples of multimedia productions in which nonverbal elements take precedence over a written text.

In these and other ways, multimedia productions, which depend much on the work of the lighting and sound designers, have enlarged the ways in which theatrical means are used and probably will continue to do so as new technology is developed and adapted to stage use.

Thinking About . . .

Stage Lighting

Stage lighting is among the most difficult production elements to evaluate because it usually attracts attention, not to itself, but to the actors, scenery, costumes, or directing. Unless we have difficulty seeing, are distracted by shadows on the actors' faces, are annoyed by glare, or are fascinated by some beautiful or spectacular lighting effect, we may not think about the lighting. Yet light is an essential production element both artistically and for the sake of visibility. Our understanding of any theatrical production can be enhanced by examining the lighting choices and their effects. Here are some questions that may contribute to a fuller understanding of stage lighting:

1. *In what type of space was the production staged (proscenium, arena, thrust, flexible)? How did this affect the use of lighting?*
2. *How did the lighting relate to that suggested in the script? If it departed from the script, were the changes dictated by the production concept? What overall approach governed the lighting? Did it suggest recognizable sources (sun, moon, lamps, and the like) or a specific time of day, period, or place? If so, how? With what effect? Was the lighting dictated by stylistic or interpretational considerations? If so, what was the result? Were there any unusual lighting effects? Did the lighting call attention to itself at any point? If so, how? With what results?*
3. *How did lighting affect (or help to create) mood and atmosphere? Did mood and atmosphere change? If so, how? With what results?*
4. *What was the dominant level of brightness (intensity)? Did it vary from scene to scene? If so, were the variations related to the action?*
5. *What was the dominant color (or colors) of the light? Did color vary from scene to scene? How did color relate to the action, mood, and overall interpretation? How did it affect scenery and costumes? If color was not used, what was the effect?*
6. *How was light distributed on the stage (evenly, acting areas/background, some areas isolated by light, etc.)? Did it emphasize (or deemphasize) shape and mass? Was direction other than frontlighting (downlighting, backlighting, crosslighting) evident? With what effect?*
7. *Did the lighting change? If so, frequently? What motivated the changes? How did the changes enhance (or fail to enhance) the mood, action, or production concept?*
8. *Were there special effects? If so, which? How were they handled? With what results?*
9. *How did the lighting enhance or fail to enhance the acting, scenery, costumes, and makeup? Was it unified with all the other elements? Was there sufficient*

variety? Did lighting underscore the development of the action? Was it used to build climaxes? If so, how?

10. *Overall, how did lighting contribute (or fail to contribute) to the production concept and the total production?*

The relevance of each of these questions may vary with the particular production and play. Furthermore, some of these questions may not be answerable because there is not adequate information or because the lighting cannot be isolated from other production elements or the total context. Nevertheless, attempting to answer some or all of these questions can make us look more closely at lighting and lead us to appreciate more fully its contributions to theatrical production.

Afterword

We have now looked at the theatre from several angles: the basic characteristics of theatre as entertainment and as an art form; approaches to evaluating performances; the way plays are written and structured; ways in which the theatrical experience has varied in the past and the way it continues to change in the present; how each of the theatre arts functions today and how all are combined to create the performances we see in the theatre. Taken together, these explorations provide a foundation for a fuller understanding and appreciation of the theatre.

But a foundation is just that—something to build on rather than a finished structure. What one chooses to do with the foundation is as important as the foundation itself. It can be abandoned, or it can be a basis for further growth. Whether your understanding and appreciation of the theatre will continue to develop depends upon whether you attend theatre often and enjoy the experience.

Opportunities to Work in the Theatre

An updated version of Molière's *The Misanthrope* at the La Jolla Playhouse. Directed by Robert Falls; setting by George Tsypin; costumes by Susan Hilferty; lighting by James F. Ingalls. (Courtesy of the La Jolla Playhouse.)

There are more producing groups in the United States today than ever before. Although a large proportion do not provide a living wage, there are many avenues open for theatrical talent. The professional theatre can absorb relatively few of those who seek employment. Fortunately, there are other rewarding possibilities in community theatre, education, and elsewhere.

Theatre as an Avocation

Most students who study theatre in colleges do not enter the theatre as a profession. To many, theatre is an avenue for acquiring a humanistic education, just as English, philosophy, or history are, or it is a supplement to study in some other field. Nevertheless, after graduation many continue an avocational interest in theatre either as audience members or through involvement in production. Audiences are, of course, always necessary, both in professional and nonprofessional theatres. There are also many opportunities for working in the theatre as an avocation because most nonprofessional theatre organizations rely upon volunteer personnel. The demand for actors is great, and almost anyone with interests in scenery, costumes, lighting, properties, makeup, sound, dance, or music can find opportunities to express them. There is also a need for people to work in public relations, publicity, house management, and other nonperformance areas.

Theatre in Education

Perhaps the largest number of paying theatre jobs is in education. Persons with theatre training are usually employed in schools for two purposes: to teach and to produce plays. Sometimes it is possible to specialize in directing, costuming, lighting, or some other area, but to be assured of employment one should be prepared to undertake multiple assignments.

The educational theatre may be divided into levels: *theatre for children and youth, secondary school theatre,* and *college and university theatre.*

Theatre for Children and Youth

Theatre for children and youth may operate within three frameworks: professional, community, or educational. Its distinguishing characteristic is its intended audience.

A related area is creative (or developmental) drama, although technically it is not a theatrical activity. Using creative drama techniques, children are stimulated to improvise dramatic situations based on stories, historical events, social situations, or even mathematics and science. Creative drama is used to help children feel their way into fictional and real-life situations, to make learning more concrete, to allow children an outlet in the classroom for their responses and feelings, and to stimulate imagination. It is an educational and developmental tool rather than a product intended for an audience. Normally, creative drama is handled by the classroom teacher, who should have specialized training in its techniques.

Theatre as such is seldom taught in elementary schools. Children are instead offered plays through a variety of channels. The recreation program in most large cities includes a unit that produces plays for children and young people; many community theatres, high schools, colleges, and universities produce plays for children and youth; some regional professional companies offer occasional productions for children and adolescents, and several professional organizations specialize in plays for children and young people.

There is a significant demand for persons with some training in theatre for children and adolescents and in creative drama. Some colleges and universities employ specialists in these areas; school districts may hire a person who can demonstrate and supervise creative drama; some community theatres employ a director whose sole responsibility is the production of plays for children and youth; public recreation programs often employ a specialist in this area. In addition, there are now approximately sixty professional troupes that perform for child and adolescent audiences.

Workers in theatre for children and youth need the same basic training required for any other theatre worker. In addition, they should receive some specialized instruction in child and developmental psychology and in the specialized problems of theatre for children and adolescents.

Max Bush's adaptation of *Hansel and Gretel* at the Emmy Gifford Children's Theatre (Omaha). The actors are Kevin Barratt and Laura Marr. Directed by Roberta Larson. (Photo by James Keller. Courtesy of the Emmy Gifford Children's Theatre.)

Secondary School Theatre

Almost every high school in the United States produces one or more plays each year. Still, many do not offer courses in theatre and drama, and plays sometimes are directed by persons with no theatre training at all. On the other hand, some secondary schools have excellent theatre programs. Productions are cast from high school students and are performed for an audience made up primarily of other high school students, parents, and others from the immediate community.

Secondary school teachers should understand the adolescent and usually need to be certified to teach subjects other than theatre, such as speech or English because seldom can they devote their full time to teaching theatre.

Undergraduate Colleges and Universities

Most colleges and universities in the United States offer some coursework in theatre. In most cases, theatre courses are included in the liberal arts curriculum, while the production program is treated as extracurricular, with participation open to all students.

Teachers in a liberal arts college may have an opportunity to specialize in areas such as directing or design, but often they must teach and supervise several areas of production. Undergraduate programs offering the bachelor of fine arts degree in theatre usually admit students to that degree program only after auditions, interviews, or portfolio reviews have established students' talent and commitment. Because these programs are usually oriented to the professional theatre or additional training at the graduate level, instructors should be able to set high standards through their own work. In these specialized programs, participation in production is often restricted to majors.

Graduate Schools

The graduate school, designed to give specialized training, requires a staff of experienced specialists, and employment is usually available only to those who have demonstrated ability in specialized aspects of the theatre. The graduate school is crucial to the theatre, for most practitioners now receive their basic training in colleges and universities. Graduate schools also train those who will become teachers, dramaturgs, theatre historians, critics, and scholars in the field.

University Resident Theatres

Some colleges and universities support resident theatre companies. Many of these companies are made up of students; some mingle students and professionals, and a few are wholly professional. Typically, each group produces plays of many types and from many periods.

A majority of those in such companies are actors, but a director, a few technicians, and sometimes a designer are included. Each year companies belonging to the University/Resident Theatre Association (U/RTA) hold joint auditions for admissions to the companies and/or to the graduate training programs with which they are affiliated. The number of students from each school who can audition is limited, and there is a process of elimination that occurs on the local or regional level prior to the national auditions. University resident companies that use only professional actors usually hold auditions in New York and a few other locations.

The Community Theatre

Almost every town with a population of more than thirty thousand has a community theatre. Many of these theatres are operated entirely by volunteers; others pay the director of each play and may provide a small sum for the designer and other key workers. Typically, a community theatre employs a full-time director who supervises all productions. The more prosperous groups also have a full-time designer-technician, and some hire a director of theatre for children and youth as well.

Because of their purpose, community theatres usually do not hire persons other than in supervisory capacities. The primary function of community theatre—in addition to providing theatrical entertainment for local audiences—is to furnish an outlet for the talents of adult volunteers.

Those who seek employment in the community theatre, therefore, need to be leaders. They should be diplomatic, able to cooperate with diverse personalities, and know a great deal about public relations.

Summer Theatres

There are many summer theatres scattered throughout the country. They usually perform from June until September. There is much variety in summer theatre. Some groups present a different play each week or every two weeks; during the run of a show, one or more productions are usually being rehearsed. Some companies perform a single work for the entire summer. Some specialize in plays by a single playwright, most frequently Shakespeare. Some perform only musicals. Still others employ only a nucleus company and import well-known motion picture, television, or stage actors to play leading roles. Occasionally, summer theatres try out new plays.

There are many kinds of summer companies. Some are entirely professional and hire only professional actors, designers, and directors. Others mingle professionals and nonprofessionals. (Actors Equity classifies companies according to the number of professional actors employed, minimum salaries, and working conditions.) Companies employing professional actors may hire designers and directors who are not union members. Some summer theatres are operated by educational institutions and give college credit for participation.

Many summer theatres have intern programs. Interns may receive room and board and even a small weekly salary; the pay is seldom more than enough for living expenses. Some organizations ask interns to pay a fee, but this practice is generally frowned upon.

Most hiring for professional and semiprofessional summer theatres is done in New York and a few other large cities. A few theatres send a representative to major theatre-training programs to hold auditions. Summer theatres run by colleges usually hold auditions on their own campuses. Whatever the arrangement, summer theatres provide only seasonal employment.

The Pope Theatre Company (Manalapan, FL) production of Larry Larson's and Eddie Levi Lee's *Some Things You Need to Know Before the World Ends*. The actors are Warren Kelley (top) and John Felix. Directed by J. Barry Lewis. (Photo by Debra Hesser. Courtesy of the Pope Theatre Company.)

Not-for-Profit Professional Companies

There are now more than 300 not-for-profit professional theatres in the United States. (Most theatres beyond Broadway are organized as not-for-profit, a status that makes them eligible for assistance from arts organizations, foundations, and corporations; to be granted this status under tax laws, an organization must be able to establish its purpose as cultural and community service-oriented rather than as profit-making.) Most not-for-profit theatres belong to the Theatre Communications Group (TCG), whose office in New York is a major clearinghouse for information about job openings and opportunities in the theatres affiliated with it. These not-for-profit theatres include the many regional companies outside New York as well as many Off-Broadway and Off-Off-Broadway theatres in New York.

Not-for-profit theatres are divided into categories according to their budgets and working conditions. Actors Equity Association controls the contracts for professional actors throughout the country and prescribes the percentage of actors in each company who must be Equity members. It also sets minimum wage scales.

Not-for-profit companies obtain their personnel in various ways. Most employ an artistic director and managing director on long-term contracts. Other staff (including designers, technicians, publicity directors, and box-office managers) may work on a continuing basis and may remain in their jobs for many years, but usually they can be let go on short notice. Such personnel are usually hired on the basis of portfolios, interviews, recommendations, and demonstrated aptitude or achievement. Actors are frequently hired for a single production, although some may remain for additional shows. Smaller companies, as well as large companies in sizable population centers, may hire many of their actors locally, but many still do the majority of their hiring after holding auditions in New York, Chicago, or Los Angeles. Some retain the services of casting directors. Some companies will audition applicants from colleges and universities but usually only if applicants have been carefully screened in advance.

There are now more persons employed in not-for-profit professional companies than in for-profit theatres.

Broadway

The jobs most difficult to get are those on Broadway, not only because there are few opportunities but also because of union control. Some of these conditions apply elsewhere, but seldom so fully.

Directors

The director is employed by the producer. The director must be a member of the Society of Stage Directors and Choreographers, which has standard contracts to specify the director's rights and working conditions.

Actors

Actors (including dancers and singers) must belong to Actors Equity Association. Actors Equity requires producers to devote a minimum number of hours to open interviews or auditions for each show. This screening may be done by an assistant, and few of the applicants may actually be permitted to try out. Casting directors may also handle much of the preliminary work. Many actors obtain auditions through agents, and others are invited by the producer to try out.

Stage Managers

Stage managers must also belong to Actors Equity. Most begin as performers and for extra pay take on the job of assistant stage manager; a large show usually has several assistant stage managers. If assistant stage managers prove reliable, they may subsequently be employed as principal stage managers. After the show opens, the stage manager may rehearse the cast as needed. Therefore, training or experience in directing may be an asset to the would-be stage manager.

Designers

The designers are employed by the producer. All must belong to the United Scenic Artists union, the most difficult of all stage unions to gain admission to. Applicants must pay an examination fee and, if they pass the rigorous exam, a sizable initiation fee. This union also controls design in television, films, opera, and ballet. Designers may be admitted to the union as a scenic, costume, or lighting designer, or they may qualify in two or all of these areas. All contracts must meet the union's minimum requirements. Many younger members of the union work as assistants to well-established designers.

Scenery, Costume, Lighting, and Property Crews

Members of the various crews that run shows must belong to the International Alliance of Theatrical Stage Employees. Crews are carefully separated, so that no one will perform more than one function. This union restricts admission to make sure that most of its members will be employed. Acceptance depends as much on knowing the right persons as on training.

Others

Each production must have a company manager and a press agent, who work directly with the producer. The manager aids in letting contracts, arranges for rehearsal space and out-of-town tryouts, and handles the payroll. The press agent is concerned principally with selling the show. Both must be members of the Association of Theatrical Press Agents and Managers.

Any theatrical worker may have an agent, whose job it is to market the client's services. An agent can be crucial in getting a hearing for clients who might otherwise never be able to display their talents. For these services, an agent is paid a percentage of the client's earnings on each contract negotiated. Agents customarily must be approved by the client's union.

The number of job opportunities in New York is very small in relation to those seeking employment. Usually fewer than one-fourth of the members of Actors Equity are employed at one time; fewer than twenty-five designers in each of the fields of scenery, costume, and lighting design all of the shows seen on Broadway each year; and a small number of directors direct the shows. Most designers and directors work on no more than one show each season.

Many people try to discourage would-be professionals from going to New York, but nothing can keep many from doing so. It has become common, nevertheless, for aspirants to look to theatres beyond Broadway as alternatives.

Special Employment Opportunities

In addition to the opportunities already discussed, others are available in related areas. Television and motion pictures offer additional opportunities. It has become increasingly common for actors to move from the theatre into television and film. Without these possibilities, many professionals would lead a difficult life indeed. But, because these supplementary fields have their own unemployment problems, they can merely relieve some of the pressures.

Some industrial and commercial firms stage special shows to publicize their products. Frequently, these productions are lavish, and some tour major cities. These shows normally play for invited audiences only; they pay well but provide little further recognition. Most are cast in New York.

Many municipal recreation departments employ persons trained in theatre. To be eligible, one must usually also have had some training in health, physical education, and recreation.

Theatre for the aging is an emerging field. As the average retirement age lowers and as life expectancy increases, the potential of this field will probably expand.

Theatre by and for the handicapped is another growing field. As awareness has grown of the special problems of the handicapped, theatre has sought ways to serve the needs of this group.

Theatrical techniques have been adapted for nontheatrical uses. For example, they are now used therapeutically with the emotionally disturbed. To work in such a field, training in psychology as well as in drama and theatre is needed.

When the variety of theatrical activities—in both the nonprofessional and professional theatre—is considered, there are many employment opportunities. Though there are fewer jobs than applicants, especially in the professional theatre, there is always a demand for talented and dedicated persons. The future of the theatre depends on these select few.

Glossary

Absurdism   A term used to describe certain plays of the post-World War II period. The writers of these plays believed that the human condition is absurd because the desire for clarity and order is met only by the irrationality of the universe, thus making rational or meaningful choice impossible. Absurdist plays abandoned the logic of cause-to-effect relationships for associational patterns reflecting the illogical nature of the human situation. Two of the most prominent absurdist playwrights were Beckett and Ionesco.

Acting Area   The stage space used by the actors during performance. It is usually divided into a number of smaller parts to make the blocking of stage action easier.

Antagonist   The primary opponent of the leading character in a dramatic action.

Arena Stage   Type of theatre with audience seating on all sides of a performance space; also known as theatre-in-the-round.

Backdrop   See **Drop**.

Backstage   Generally, the entire area back of the proscenium arch; more specifically, the areas beyond the visible performance space, especially the workspaces of the backstage personnel, such as designers, technicians, and stage crews.

Batten   A pipe suspended above the stage by lines that permit it to be raised or lowered; scenic pieces or lighting instruments may be hung from it. Wooden battens are attached to the top and bottom of drops to keep the cloth stretched and free of wrinkles.

Black Out   To create instantaneous and total darkness on stage by turning off all the lights.

Blocking   The placement and movement of the actors on stage moment by moment, usually planned by the director.

Border   A short curtain or piece of painted canvas hung parallel to the front of the stage and in a series from front to back used to mask the overhead space. Striplights mounted behind the borders are called borderlights.

Box Set   A set fully enclosing the acting space on three sides like the walls of a room, resembling a box with one side removed.

Business   See **Stage Business**.

Characterization   The playwright's means of differentiating one personage from another by assigning each physical, sociological, psychological, and moral traits.

Choregus   A wealthy citizen in ancient Greece chosen by lot to help finance the training and costuming of the chorus. One choregus was chosen for each competing dramatist.

Chorus   In Greek drama, a group of actors who spoke, sang, and danced in unison; the choral songs and dances, usually commenting on the action, separated the play into episodes. In Renaissance drama, a single character who commented on the action or served as a narrator. In opera and musicals, a group who sings (or sings and dances) as a group.

City Dionysia   The principal Athenian festival (held in honor of the god Dionysus) at which plays were performed.

Comedy A dramatic form based on some deviation from normality in action, character, or thought treated so as to arouse laughter or ridicule and to end happily.

Commedia dell'Arte A type of performance that emerged in Italy during the sixteenth century. Starting from a scenario that merely outlined the situation, complications, and outcome, the actors improvised the dialogue and action. Each actor always played the same stock character, which had his or her distinctive costume and mask. The most popular characters were the *zanni,* or comic servants, whose contrivances served both to create and resolve complications. Commedia companies played throughout Europe and enjoyed great popularity everywhere until the middle of the eighteenth century.

Complication Any new element that serves to change the direction of a play's dramatic action.

Controlboard Panel with switches and dimmers used to control the stage lights.

Conventions Theatrical and dramatic practices, devices, and procedures that are mutually understood and accepted by both theatre practitioners and audiences. Things seldom happen in the theatre precisely as they would in life, but audiences easily overlook and accept these deviations if they understand the conventions being used. When initially introduced, a convention may be misunderstood; it gains acceptance through continued usage. Some common conventions are Shakespeare's use of soliloquies, characters breaking into song or dance in the midst of a scene in musicals, and the rapid and visible changes that shift the action from one locale to another in many kinds of plays.

Costume Chart A chart used by the costume designer to indicate what costume items and accessories each actor will wear in each scene. It may also be used by costume crews as a guide for dressing the actors during performances.

Costume Parade A procedure used by the costume designer to make certain that costumes have been completed as designed and function appropriately. For each scene, the actors don their costumes, appear together, and perform characteristic actions under lights simulating those that will be used in performance.

Counterweight System An arrangement of battens, lines, pulleys, and weights that permits scenic pieces and lighting instruments to be suspended above the stage and lowered or raised easily.

Crew The backstage personnel who assist in mounting and running a production. There are usually separate crews for scenery, costumes, lighting, and sound.

Crisis The turning point in the action of a play, usually brought about by the revelation of those things that have been partially or entirely unknown by one or more of the principal characters.

Cue The words, actions, or other prearranged indications that serve as signals for actors to proceed to their next line or action, or for lighting, sound, or other crew members to execute some agreed-upon change.

Cue Sheet A list of cues that will serve as the basis for making changes in lights, sounds, or other production elements during the course of a performance. Cue sheets also indicate the changes to be made, along with any other information needed to carry out the appropriate action.

Cycle Plays   In the Middle Ages, a series of short plays dramatizing events drawn from the Bible, often extending from the Creation to Doomsday.

Cyclorama   Any arrangement of cloth or other material (including plaster) that curves around the rear of the stage and partially down the sides. Usually neutral in color, it is often lighted to represent the sky or used as a projection surface.

Denouement   The final portion of a play, extending from the crisis to the final curtain, that ties off the various strands of action.

Deus ex Machina   A Greek term meaning "the god from the machine," referring to the common practice of flying in a god to resolve a difficult dramatic situation. Later it came to mean the use of any unprepared-for and unexpected means of resolving an action. See **Machina.**

Dimmer   A device for altering the flow of electrical current to change the intensity of lighting instruments.

Director   The person with primary responsibility for interpreting a script, rehearsing the actors, and coordinating all elements of a production.

Directorial Concept   Sometimes called the production concept; a metaphor, dominant idea, or set of conventions used by a director to shape a production.

Discovery   The introduction of information or revelations of sufficient importance to alter the direction of the dramatic action of a play. Complications are usually initiated by discoveries.

Downstage   In the proscenium theatre, the forward part of the stage.

Dramatic Action   A play's primary focus, indicated by what the principal characters want and what steps they take to get what they want.

Dressers   Persons responsible for assisting actors with costume changes during performances.

Drop   A hanging unit made of lengths of cloth sewed together and attached at the top to a wooden batten that supports it and to another at the bottom that keeps it stretched and free of wrinkles. Scenes of various sorts may be painted on drops. Drops usually serve as backgrounds (backdrops) for the action.

Dutchman   Cloth strip used to mask the joint created when two flats are hinged together.

Eccyclema   The platform rolled out through the central doorway of the ancient Greek stage house, used typically to display the corpses of characters slain offstage.

Ensemble Playing   Performance that achieves a sense of mutual support and overall unity, as opposed to one that seems merely a collection of individual actors.

Environmental Theatre   A type of performance, especially during and after the 1960s, that intermingled acting and audience space to achieve interaction between spectators and performers. Multiple-focus and simultaneous scenes were often used.

Epic Theatre   A theatrical form that emerged in the 1920s, associated with Bertolt Brecht. Brecht sought to distance ("alienate") spectators emotionally by writing episodic scenes interrupted by songs and other devices, so the audience would watch objectively and judge what they saw. Ultimately Brecht hoped his audiences would relate what they saw in the theatre to conditions in society and would seek to alter the sociopolitical system. Brecht called his theatre "epic" because the alternation of dialogue and narration, with its frequent shifts in time and place, had more in common with epic poetry than with traditional drama.

Existentialism A philosophical position that gained popularity following World War II, especially through the writings of Jean-Paul Sartre, and carried over into playwriting by Sartre and Albert Camus. The argument of the existentialists was that there are no longer any certainties and that human beings are condemned to choose their own values and live by them, whether or not these values are accepted by others.

Exposition Imparting information, usually about events that have happened before the play begins. Typically, exposition is most abundant in the opening scene, where it is used to clarify the situation, establish the identity and relationship of the characters, and set forth the present situation, although it may occur throughout the play.

Expressionism An artistic movement that flourished, especially in Germany, from around 1910 to about 1924. Believing that the industrial age had turned human beings into machine-like creatures, expressionism sought to undermine materialist values and create "the new man," who would reshape the world in accordance with the needs of the human spirit. Expressionist drama made extensive use of distortion and grotesque imagery to portray the present human condition. Expressionism found its way into American drama, as in O'Neill's *The Hairy Ape.*

Farce A type of comic drama that usually emphasizes situation over character or idea. Coincidence, misunderstanding, ridiculous violence, and rapid pace are its typical ingredients.

Flat A basic scenic unit composed of a wooden frame over which canvas or muslin has been stretched. Of various types, the most common are plain, door, window, and fireplace flats, two or more of which may be joined to create a larger scenic surface.

Floodlight A lighting instrument without a lens designed to give a broad beam of light, typically composed of a metal housing with a reflector and a single lamp.

Focus In lighting, the direction in which a lighting instrument is aimed, or the adjustment of an instrument to alter the beam of light. In acting or directing, to concentrate on some person, object, or action.

Footlights A row of striplights mounted at floor level at the front of the proscenium stage or around the outer edges of a thrust stage.

Front Elevation A designer's plan, drawn to scale, showing each unit of a set in two dimensions from the front with indications of such features as molding, baseboards, and platforms.

Frontlighting Illumination from the front (as opposed to side or back), usually from lighting instruments mounted in the auditorium.

Front of the House That part of the theatre forward of the stage and the activities and persons associated with it: audience, ushers, box office, and the like. Often used as the opposite of *backstage.*

Gas Table The control board for a lighting system that uses gas as the illuminant.

General Illumination Stage lighting that spreads over a relatively large area, serving one or more of three functions: (1) lighting all background areas not illuminated by spotlights; (2) blending the acting areas together and providing a smooth transition between the high intensity of the acting areas and the lower intensity of the background; (3) enhancing or modifying the color of settings and costumes. The principal sources of general illumination are striplights and floodlights.

Green Room A room in the theatre where all the actors and crew members can assemble to relax or receive instructions.

Habit à la Romaine The usual costume worn by actors playing Greek or Roman heroes in neoclassical theatre; a stylized adaptation of Roman armor, tunic, and boots.

Hand Props See **Properties**.

Happenings Performance events pioneered by visual artists in the 1950s and 1960s. Multimedia events that sought to break down the barriers between the arts and between performers and spectators; to shift emphasis from creating a product to participating in a process; and to shift emphasis from the artist's intention to the participant's awareness.

Inciting Incident The occurrence that sets the action of a play in motion.

Independent Theatre Movement A trend that began in the 1880s and continues to the present, originating because major theatres would not produce certain new plays, either out of indifference or because official censors would not license the plays for production. Independent theatres, which could avoid censorship by performing only for their subscribers, were able to introduce and gain acceptance for many new plays. In the twentieth century, variations on this original plan have been used whenever the theatre has been unresponsive to new forms of writing or production. Twentieth-century independent theatres have been labelled little theatres, art theatres, fringe theatres, alternative theatres, Off-Broadway, Off-Off-Broadway, and so on.

Instrument Schedule One of the lighting designer's principal plans; a chart listing each lighting instrument with its specifications (type, wattage, lens, reflector, lamp, and any other pertinent information), mounting position, color filter, the area it lights, the circuit into which it is plugged, and the dimmer to which it is connected.

Lazzi Bits of comic business in commedia dell'arte. Many lazzi were sufficiently standardized to be indicated in the scenarios.

Left Stage The left side of the stage from the performers' point of view as they face the auditorium.

Limelight The first effective spotlight, consisting of a hood equipped with a reflector, lens, and a column of calcium (lime) onto which hydrogen and oxygen were directed, along with a gas flame, which in combination heated the lime to incandescence, creating an extremely bright light. Its frequent use as a follow spot gave rise to the phrase "in the limelight."

Lines of Business The division of acting into a few categories defined by the character types they included. Until the late nineteenth century, an actor was employed in terms of his or her line of business. Actors usually began their careers as utility actors and played supernumerary roles until they discovered the character type for which they were best suited. Most actors then continued in that line of business for the remainder of their careers.

Liturgical Play A play incorporated into or performed in conjunction with the church service or liturgy.

Living Newspaper A form that developed within the Federal Theatre Project, financed by the United States government during the 1930s to relieve unemployment. Each Living Newspaper treated a single pressing problem (such as slum housing), advocating social reform and corrective legislation to solve the problem. The Federal Theatre Project ended in 1939 when Congress, offended by the partisan stance of the Living Newspapers, refused to appropriate funds to continue it.

Ludi A Roman term literally meaning "games," referring to those religious festivals at which theatrical performances were given.

Machina A crane-like device used to simulate flying in the Greek theatre. See **Deus ex Machina.**

Mansion The basic scenic structure in the medieval theatre. As many mansions as were needed to indicate the locales of a play's action were present simultaneously on platforms or wagons. After the place of the action was indicated by associating it with a specific mansion, the performers used as much of the adjoining platform space as was needed.

Mask To conceal something (the offstage or overhead space, an action or piece of stage business, or the actor's face) from the audience. Also used to designate the covering worn over the actor's face or head to represent the character being portrayed.

Melodrama A form of drama, especially associated with the nineteenth century, based on a clear distinction between good and evil. Typically a virtuous protagonist seeks to overcome seemingly insurmountable threats created by a villain. Suspense is created and increased until the last moment, when the unmasking and punishment of the villain rescues and rewards the protagonist. Melodrama often incorporates elaborate spectacle, and originally used music to create mood and to underscore emotional responses.

Mime A short, topical, usually comic, often improvised playlet that included dialogue. A favorite theatrical form in late Rome and the first in which female performers appeared. In the twentieth century, a silent form in which story and character are presented through expressive movement and gesture.

Morality Play A type of medieval drama that treated the spiritual trials of ordinary persons, usually an allegory about the temptations besetting all human beings.

Naturalism A late nineteenth-century form of extreme realism whose chief spokesman was Emile Zola. The naturalists argued that plays should be a slice of life that demonstrated the effects of heredity and environment. Naturalism was the first artistic movement to treat working-class characters with the same seriousness accorded the upper classes by earlier movements. In the twentieth century, naturalism is often used as a label for plays that seek to re-create the details of everyday life, especially its seamy side.

Neoclassicism The set of rules, conventions, and beliefs that dominated much drama and theatre from the

Renaissance to the end of the eighteenth century. Neoclassicism recognized only two legitimate forms of drama (tragedy and comedy), arguing that the two forms should never be mixed. Tragedy should develop serious stories of kings and nobles, while comedy should treat the domestic world of the middle or lower classes. According to the neoclassicists, plays should be written in five acts, observe the unities, and uphold poetic justice in their endings.

Offstage Out of sight of the audience.

Orchestra In the Greek theatre, the space in which the chorus sang and danced. In the modern theatre, the ground-floor audience seating. Also the group of musicians who performs instrumental music in the theatre.

Overpainting Any modification of the base coat, overpainting is used to simulate textures, materials, decorations, or conditions.

Pageant Wagon In the medieval theatre, a platform on wheels (resembling a modern float) on which plays were mounted and moved from one playing place to another.

Painter's Elevation A designer's plan, drawn to scale, indicating how each scenic piece is to be painted.

Panorama A scenic element in the nineteenth-century theatre; a continuous scene painted on a long expanse of canvas that could remain fixed or be rigged to move, giving the effect that characters, though remaining on stage, were moving from one place to another.

Pantomime Originally a Roman form that was danced by one performer to the accompaniment of musicians and a chorus. During the eighteenth century, a popular entertainment in which Harlequin, usually the main character, with the help of a magic wand, transformed characters and places; it made extensive use of elaborate spectacle, music, and dance. Today, pantomime refers to any performance in which characters do not speak, communicating primarily through dance or physical movement.

Paradoi The spaces at either side of the orchestra between the skene and the auditorium in the Greek theatre, used primarily as entrances and exits for the performers, especially the chorus.

Performance Art A contemporary type of presentation, often by a solo performer, that typically intermingles elements from various arts. Performance art usually permits spectators to derive from the presentation whatever is meaningful to them.

Platea In the medieval theatre, an undifferentiated stage space in front of the mansions. After establishing the location of a scene by relating it to a mansion, as much as was needed of the platea was used as the acting area.

Plot The arrangement of a play's incidents, or overall structure of the action. It differs from the story, which may have begun long before the play opens.

Poetic Justice Making the outcome of a play fit an idealized vision of justice by punishing the wicked and rewarding the good.

Point of Attack The moment in a story when the play actually begins.

Poor Theatre Phrase introduced by Jerzy Grotowski to identify a type of theatre that discards all technological aids not essential to theatrical performance. He concluded that there are only two essential theatrical elements: the actor and the audience.

Postmodernism   Term used to describe certain contemporary artistic tendencies, among them the blurring of distinctions between dramatic forms and the mingling of elements from disparate styles, periods, and cultures.

Properties   Onstage objects of two types: (1) set properties, required to complete or decorate the set; and (2) hand properties, used by the actors in their stage business.

Producer   The person responsible for financing a production, making contractual arrangements with those involved, leasing a theatre, publicizing the show, selling tickets, and handling all other aspects relating to the business and managerial side of theatrical production.

Promptbook   A copy of the script in which the blocking and stage business of the actors, cues for lighting and sound, and all other information needed by the stage manager have been entered.

Proscenium Theatre   A type of theatre using an architectural arch to frame a raised stage.

Protagonist   The principal character in a dramatic action.

Raked Stage   A stage floor that slopes upward toward the rear.

Realism   An attempt in writing and production to represent characters and events as they are observed in real life. Scattered attempts at realism are found throughout theatre history but, as a movement, realism emerged in the 1850s, grounded in the scientific outlook and the belief that human behavior can best be explained in terms of hereditary and environmental influences. Realists argued that because we can know the real world only through direct observation, playwrights should write only about the society around them as objectively as possible.

Rear Elevation   A designer's two-dimensional scale drawing showing each unit of a setting as seen from the rear. It also indicates construction materials and methods to be used in building and assembling each unit.

Repertory   The total group of plays a company chooses for presentation. A repertory company is one that alternates performances of several productions.

Regional Theatre   A term used to designate ongoing not-for-profit theatres throughout the United States. Such theatres are sometimes called resident theatres.

Restoration   The period in English history following the restoration of Charles II to the throne in 1660, extending to about 1700. In theatre, the period is noted for its comedy of manners, which focused on the amoral behavior and witty verbal exchanges of the idle upper class.

Revolving Stage   A circular platform or segment of the stage floor mounted on a central pivot. When it is revolved, one setting comes into view as another moves out of sight.

Right Stage   That part of the stage that is to the actor's right as he or she faces the audience.

Satyr Play   A short comic or satiric play that followed each set of three tragedies at the City Dionysia in Greece. Its chorus was composed of satyrs (half man-half goat creatures), and its story usually poked fun at some Greek myth.

Scaenae Frons   The facade enclosing the back and sides of the stage in the ancient Roman theatre. It served as background for all types of plays.

Scrim A curtain or drop made of gauze-like fabric. When lighted only from the front, it appears opaque, but it becomes translucent when lighted from the back.

Set Piece A scenic piece that stands on the stage independent of other scenic pieces.

Set Prop See **Properties.**

Side Elevation A designer's scale drawing showing the units of a set in profile and indicating the thickness and shape of each unit as seen from the side.

Sightline Line of vision from any audience seat to any point on stage. Often used to indicate how much of the stage action can be seen from any part of the house.

Skene The scene house in the Greek theatre. Literally meaning a hut or tent, the name probably derives from the structure used originally as an off-stage place where actors could change costumes. It is the source of our word *scene.*

Soliloquy A speech given by a character who is alone on stage, conventionally representing the character's inner thoughts.

Specific Illumination Stage light confined to a limited area, usually produced by spotlights.

Spine The "through line" of action that holds the play together, or the dominant motivation undergirding a character's action.

Spoken Decor Locale established through speech rather than represented scenically.

Spotlight A lighting instrument composed of a metal housing, a reflector, lamp, and lens designed to illuminate restricted areas with a concentrated beam of light. The major types of spotlights are plano-convex, Fresnel, and ellipsoidal.

Stage Business Detailed action performed by the actor, such as filling and smoking a pipe or setting a table; often prescribed by the script, but may be invented by the actors or the director to clarify or enrich action or characterization.

Stage House The stage and all the space above it to the roof.

Stage Manager The individual responsible for running the show during performances, making sure that everything functions as intended.

Striplight A lighting instrument composed of a series of lamps usually mounted in a rectangular trough and used for general illumination. There are three basic types of striplights: (1) footlights, mounted in the floor at the front of the stage; (2) borderlights, hung from battens above the stage in a series from front to back; and (3) miscellaneous striplights, used to light backings, the cyclorama, or other scenic elements.

Subtext Unstated motivations, ideas, or tensions beneath the surface of a play's text. Often the subtext is more important than the text.

Summer Stock Companies that perform only during the summer, typically in resort areas, and produce a series of plays, often one each week.

Surrealism A movement, especially in the 1920s, emphasizing the importance of the subconscious. Believing that the most significant truths are those buried in the unconscious, surrealists sought to release these suppressed forces by exploring dreams, automatic writing, and stream-of-consciousness.

Symbolism A movement that emerged in the late nineteenth century, symbolism was the first of several that sought to counter the influence of realism and naturalism. Rather than seeking truth through direct observation of the world around them, symbolists argued that truth can only be intuited and that these intuitions can be expressed only indirectly through symbols.

Technical Director A position found primarily in resident and educational theatres, the technical director is usually responsible for implementing the designer's plans: purchasing materials, supervising the building, assembling, and painting of sets, and overseeing the crews that run the shows.

Technical Rehearsal One of the final rehearsals, usually immediately preceding dress rehearsals, devoted primarily to making sure that all the technical elements (scenery, costumes, makeup, lighting, sound, and properties) are ready and are functioning as planned.

Theatre-in-the-Round See **Arena Stage.**

Theatre of Cruelty Antonin Artaud's label for the type of performance he advocated to force audiences to confront the violent impulses suppressed within their unconscious minds. Although he acknowledged that such confrontations might be cruel, Artaud thought them necessary to overcome violence and divisiveness if the theatre is to fulfill its goal of "draining abscesses collectively." Artaud advocated redesigning the theatre space and finding new ways of using theatrical means to place the audience at the center of the performance, where it would be assaulted by light, music, sound, and images in ways it could not resist. Little heeded during his lifetime, Artaud later exerted major influence on theatrical practice, especially during the 1960s.

Theatron "Seeing place"; the Greek term for auditorium.

Thrust Stage A type of theatre with audience seating arranged around three, or occasionally two, sides of a raised platform. Sometimes called an open stage.

Tragedy The oldest form of drama, presenting a serious action and maintaining a serious tone, although there may be moments of comic relief. Tragedy raises issues about the nature of human existence, morality, or human relationships. The protagonist is usually one who arouses the audience's sympathy and admiration, but who encounters disaster through the pursuit of some goal, worthy in itself, conflicting with another goal or principle.

Trap An opening in the stage floor that allows performers to appear or special effects to materialize from beneath the floor.

Unities Neoclassicism demanded that three unities be observed: unity of time (which usually was interpreted to mean that all events should occur within twenty-four hours); unity of place (which typically required that the action occur in the same place); and unity of action (which usually demanded that there be only one plot). Most other movements have considered unity of action necessary, although interpreting it more liberally than the neoclassicists, but have rejected the unities of time and place.

Upstage Toward the rear of the stage, away from the audience.

Wagon Stage A platform mounted on casters that can be wheeled on or off stage, usually to shift scenic units.

Well-Made Play A term used to describe logically constructed plays following the pattern of careful exposition and preparation, a series of complications that create growing suspense and build to a climactic moment, after which all important questions are resolved. Although most of these features can be found in plays from the time of the Greeks onward, the term *well-made play* is associated with Eugène Scribe, the popular nineteenth-century French playwright who reduced these traditional playwriting techniques to a formula. Although *well-made play* is now often used condescendingly, Scribe's practice has supplied the pattern for much realistic playwriting since his time. Ibsen, among others, used the techniques of the well-made play.

Wings From the Renaissance onward, a major scenic element consisting of pairs of flats set up parallel to the front of the stage and arranged in a series from downstage to upstage. They were used in conjunction with two other major scenic elements: drops or shutters (flats that met at center back) used to enclose the rear of the stage, and borders used to complete the scene overhead. In modern times, *wings* is a term for the offstage space on either side of the stage.

Zanni The servants of the commedia dell'arte, origin of the word *zany*.

Bibliography

This bibliography lists some of the many important books on theatre. The divisions correspond to those in the text. All works are in English.

Part One

Chapter 1

The Nature of Theatre

Brook, Peter. *The Empty Space*. New York: Avon Books, 1969.
Cole, David. *The Theatrical Event: A Mythos, A Vocabulary, A Perspective*. Middletown, CT: Wesleyan University Press, 1975.
Lahr, John, and Price, Jonathan. *Life-show: How to See Theatre in Life and Life in Theatre*. New York: Viking Press, 1973.
Schechner, Richard. *Performance Theory*. New York: Routledge, 1988.
Styan, J. L. *Drama, Stage and Audience*. New York: Cambridge University Press, 1975.
Turner, Victor. *From Ritual to Theatre: The Human Seriousness of Play*. New York: Performing Arts Journal Publications, 1982.
Wickham, Glynne. *Drama in a World of Science*. Toronto: University of Toronto Press, 1962.

Chapter 2

Performance, Audience, and Critic

Cole, David. See under Chapter 1.
Esslin, Martin. *An Anatomy of Drama*. New York: Hill & Wang, 1976.
Kauffmann, Stanley. *Theatre Criticisms*. New York: Performing Arts Journal Publications, 1984.
Lahr, John, and Price, Jonathan. See under Chapter 1.
Littlewood, Samuel R. *The Art of Dramatic Criticism*. London: Pitman, 1952.
Sontag, Susan. *Against Interpretation and Other Essays*. New York: Doubleday & Co., 1966.
Styan, J. L. See under Chapter 1.
Vena, Gary. *How to Read and Write About Drama*. New York: Arco, 1988.

Chapter 3

The Playscript

Barranger, Milly S. *Understanding Plays*. Boston: Allyn & Bacon, 1990.
Barry, Jackson G. *Dramatic Structure: The Shaping of Experience*. Berkeley: University of California Press, 1970.

Beckerman, Bernard. *Dynamics of Drama: Theory and Method of Analysis*. New York: Alfred A. Knopf, 1970.

Esslin, Martin. *The Field of Drama*. New York: Methuen, 1987.

Grote, David. *Script Analysis*. Belmont, CA: Wadsworth, 1985.

Hayman, Ronald. *How To Read a Play*. New York: Grove Press, 1977.

Heffner, Hubert. *The Nature of Drama*. Boston: Houghton Mifflin, 1959.

Heilman, Robert B. *Tragedy and Melodrama: Versions of Experience*. Seattle: University of Washington Press, 1968.

Kerr, Walter. *Tragedy and Comedy*. New York: Simon & Schuster, 1967.

Styan, J. L. *The Elements of Drama*. New York: Cambridge University Press, 1960.

Weales, Gerald. *A Play and Its Parts*. New York: Basic Books, 1964.

Part Two

General Works Applicable to Part Two

Banham, Martin, ed. *Cambridge Guide to World Theatre*. Cambridge: Cambridge University Press, 1988.

Brockett, Oscar G. *History of Theatre*, 7th ed. Boston: Allyn & Bacon, 1995.

Carlson, Marvin. *Theories of the Theatre: A Historical and Critical Survey, from the Greeks to the Present*, rev. ed. Ithaca, NY: Cornell University Press, 1994.

Duerr, Edwin. *The Length and Depth of Acting*. New York: Holt, Rinehart and Winston, 1962.

Izenour, George C. *Theatre Design*. New York: McGraw-Hill, 1977.

Laver, James. *Drama: Its Costume and Decor*. London: Studio Publications, 1951.

Leacroft, Richard and Helen. *Theatre and Playhouse: An Illustrated Survey of Theatre Building from Ancient Greece to the Present Day*. London: Methuen, 1984.

Oenslager, Donald. *Stage Design: Four Centuries of Scenic Invention*. New York: Viking Press, 1975.

Oxford Companion to the Theatre, 4th ed. London: Oxford University Press, 1983.

Chapter 4

Festival Theatre: Greek, Roman, and Medieval Theatre Experiences

Arnott, Peter D. *Greek Scenic Conventions in the Fifth Century, B.C.* Oxford: Clarendon Press, 1962.

———. *Public and Performance in Greek Theatre*. London: Routledge, Chapman and Hall, 1989.

Beacham, Richard C. *The Roman Theatre and Its Audience*. Cambridge, MA: Harvard University Press, 1992.

Beare, William. *The Roman Stage: A Short History of Latin Drama in the Time of the Republic*, 3d ed. London: Methuen, 1963.

Bieber, Margarete. *The History of the Greek and Roman Theater*, 2d ed. Princeton, NJ: Princeton University Press, 1961.

Bevington, David. *From Mankind to Marlowe: Growth in Structure in the Popular Drama of Tudor England*. Cambridge, MA: Harvard University Press, 1962.

Chambers, E. K. *The Mediaeval Stage*. 2 vols. Oxford: Clarendon Press, 1903.

Collins, Fletcher. *The Production of Medieval Church Music-Drama*. Charlotte: University of Virginia Press, 1971.

Craik, Thomas W. *Revels History of Drama in English*. Vol. 2: 1500–1576. New York: Barnes & Noble, 1980.

———. *The Tudor Interlude: Stage, Costume, and Acting*. Leicester: University of Leicester Press, 1958.

Deardon, C. W. *The Stage of Aristophanes*. London: Athlone Press, 1976.

Duckworth, George E. *The Nature of Roman Comedy*. Princeton, NJ: Princeton University Press, 1952.

Hunter, R. L. *The New Comedy of Greece and Rome*. New York: Twayne Publishers, 1985.

Kitto, H. D. F. *Greek Tragedy*, 2d ed. London: Methuen, 1950.

Kolve, V. A. *The Play Called Corpus Christi*. Stanford, CA: Stanford University Press, 1966.

Nicoll, Allardyce. *Masks, Mimes and Miracles*. New York: Harcourt Brace Jovanovich, Inc., 1931.

Pickard-Cambridge, A. W. *The Dramatic Festivals of Athens*, 2d ed., rev. by John Gould and D. M. Lewis. Oxford: Clarendon Press, 1968.

Potter, Robert. *The English Morality Play: Origins, History and Influence of a Dramatic Tradition*. London: Routledge and Kegan Paul, 1975.

Salter, F. M. *Medieval Drama in Chester*. Toronto: University of Toronto Press, 1955.

Tydeman, William. *The Theatre in the Middle Ages*. New York: Cambridge University Press, 1979.

Vince, Ronald W. *A Companion to the Medieval Theatre*. New York: Greenwood Press, 1989.

Walton, J. Michael. *Living Greek Theatre: A Handbook of Classical Performance and Modern Production*. Westport, CT: Greenwood Press, 1987.

Webster, T. B. L. *Greek Theatre Production*, 2d ed. London: Methuen, 1970.

Wickham, Glynne. *Early English Stages, 1300–1660*. 3 vols. New York: Columbia University Press, 1959–1979.

Chapter 5

Creating a Professional Theatre: Elizabethan England, Italian Commedia dell'Arte, and Seventeenth-Century France

Barroll, J. L., et al. *Revels History of Drama in English*. Vol. 3: 1576–1613. New York: Barnes & Noble, 1975.

Beckerman, Bernard. *Shakespeare at the Globe, 1599–1609*. New York: Macmillan, 1962.

Bentley, Gerald E. *The Profession of Dramatist in Shakespeare's Time, 1590–1642*. Princeton, NJ: Princeton University Press, 1971.

———. *The Profession of Player in Shakespeare's Time, 1590–1642*. Princeton, NJ: Princeton University Press, 1984.

Bjurstrom, Per. *Giacomo Torelli and Baroque Stage Design*. Stockholm: Almqvist and Wiksell, 1961.

Bradley, David. *From Text to Performance in the Elizabethan Theatre: Preparing the Play for the Stage.* New York: Cambridge University Press, 1992.

Clubb, Louise G. *Italian Drama in Shakespeare's Time.* New Haven: Yale University Press, 1989.

Duchartre, Pierre L. *The Italian Comedy: The Improvisation, Scenarios, Lives, Attributes, Portraits and Masks of the Illustrious Characters of the Commedia dell'Arte.* Trans. by R. T. Weaver. London: Harrap & Co., 1929.

Gurr, Andrew. *Playgoing in Shakespeare's London.* Cambridge: Cambridge University Press, 1987.

Hewitt, Barnard, ed. *The Renaissance Stage: Documents of Serlio, Sabbattini, and Furttenbach.* Coral Gables, FL: University of Miami Press, 1958.

Hildy, Franklin J., ed. *New Issues in the Reconstruction of Shakespeare's Theatre.* New York: Peter Lang, 1990.

Ingram, William. *The Business of Playing: The Beginning of the Adult Professional Theater in Elizabethan London.* Ithaca, NY: Cornell University Press, 1993.

Lawrenson, T. E. *The French Stage in the XVIIth Century: A Study in the Advent of the Italian Order,* rev. ed. Manchester: Manchester University Press, 1984.

Lea, Kathleen M. *Italian Popular Comedy: A Study of the Commedia dell'Arte, 1560–1620.* 2 vols. Oxford: Clarendon Press, 1934.

Lough, John. *Paris Theatre Audiences in the Seventeenth and Eighteenth Centuries.* London: Oxford University Press, 1957.

McBride, Robert. *Aspects of 17th-Century French Drama and Thought.* Totowa, NJ: Rowman & Littlefield, 1980.

Mittman, Barbara G. *Spectators on the Paris Stage in the Seventeenth and Eighteenth Centuries.* Ann Arbor, MI: UMI Research Press, 1984.

Mongredien, Georges. *Daily Life in the French Theatre in the Time of Molière.* London: Allen and Unwin, 1969.

Nicoll, Allardyce. See under Chapter 4.

Oreglia, G. *The Commedia dell'Arte.* New York: Hill & Wang, 1968.

Orgel, Stephen, and Strong, Roy. *The Theatre of the Stuart Court: Including the Complete Designs . . . Together with Their Texts and Historical Documentation.* 2 vols. Berkeley: University of California Press, 1973.

Orrell, John. *The Human Stage: English Theatre Design, 1567–1640.* New York: Cambridge University Press, 1983.

Schwartz, Isidore A. *The Commedia dell'Arte and Its Influence on French Comedy in the Seventeenth Century.* Paris: H. Samuel, 1933.

Smith, Winifred. *The Commedia dell'Arte.* New York: Columbia University Press, 1912.

Turnell, Martin. *The Classical Moment: Studies in Corneille, Molière and Racine.* New York: New Directions, 1948.

White, John. *The Birth and Rebirth of Pictorial Space,* 2d ed. London: Faber & Faber, 1967.

Wickham, Glynne. See under Chapter 4.

Wiley, W. L. *The Early Public Theatre in France.* Cambridge, MA: Harvard University Press, 1960.

Worsthorne, S. T. *Venetian Opera in the 17th Century.* Oxford: Clarendon Press, 1954.

Chapter 6

From Melodrama to Realism

Antoine, André. *Memories of the Théâtre Libre.* Trans. by Marvin Carlson. Coral Gables, FL: University of Miami Press, 1964.

Bentley, Eric. *The Playwright as Thinker: A Study of Drama in Modern Times.* New York: Reynal & Co., 1946.

Bogard, Travis, et al. *Revels History of Drama in English.* Vol. 8: American Drama. New York: Barnes & Noble, 1977.

Booth, Michael R. *English Melodrama.* London: Herbert Jenkins, 1965.

Booth, Michael, et al. *Revels History of Drama in English.* Vol. 6: 1750–1880. New York: Barnes & Noble, 1975.

Carter, Lawson A. *Zola and the Theatre.* New Haven, CT: Yale University Press, 1963.

Cross, Gilbert. *Next Week "East Lynne": Domestic Drama in Performance, 1820–1874.* Lewisburg, PA: Bucknell University Press, 1976.

Davis, Tracy. *Actresses as Working Women: Their Social Identity in Victorian Culture.* New York: Routledge, 1991.

Donohue, Joseph W. *Theatre in the Age of Kean.* Oxford: Blackwell, 1975.

Glasstone, Victor. *Victorian and Edwardian Theatre.* Cambridge: Harvard University Press, 1975.

Grimsted, David. *Melodrama Unveiled: American Theatre and Culture, 1800–1850.* Chicago: University of Chicago Press, 1968.

Hunt, Hugh, et al. *The Revels History of Drama in English.* Vol. 7: 1880 to the Present Day. New York: Barnes & Noble, 1979.

Joseph, Bertram. *The Tragic Actor.* New York: Theatre Arts Books, 1959.

Koller, Ann Marie. *The Theatre Duke: Georg II of Saxe-Meiningen and the German Stage.* Stanford, CA: Stanford University Press, 1984.

McConachie, Bruce A. *Melodramatic Formations: American Theatre and Society, 1820–1870.* Iowa City: University of Iowa Press, 1992.

Meisel, Martin. *Realizations: Narrative, Pictorial, and Theatrical Arts in Nineteenth-Century England.* Princeton: Princeton University Press, 1983.

Moynet, Jean-Pierre. *French Theatrical Production in the Nineteenth Century.* Binghamton, NY: Max Reinhardt Foundation, 1976.

Odell, G. C. D. *Shakespeare from Betterton to Irving.* 2 vols. New York: Charles Scribner's Sons, 1920.

Price, Cecil. *Theatre in the Age of Garrick.* Oxford: Blackwell, 1973.

Quinn, Arthur H. *A History of the American Drama from the Beginning to the Civil War,* 2d ed. New York: Appleton-Century-Crofts, 1943.

———. *A History of the American Drama from the Civil War to the Present Day,* 2d ed. New York: Appleton-Century-Crofts, 1949.

Rowell, George. *The Victorian Theatre,* 2d ed. London: Oxford University Press, 1979.

Southern, Richard. *Changeable Scenery: Its Origin and Development in the British Theatre.* London: Faber & Faber, 1952.

Stein, Jack M. *Richard Wagner and the Synthesis of the Arts.* Detroit: Wayne State University Press, 1960.

Stephens, John R. *The Profession of the Playwright: British Theatre, 1800–1900.* London: Cambridge University Press, 1992.

Vardac, A. N. *Stage to Screen: Theatrical Method from Garrick to Griffith.* Cambridge, MA: Harvard University Press, 1949.

Waxman, S. M. *Antoine and the Théâtre Libre.* Cambridge, MA: Harvard University Press, 1926.

Chapter 7

The Modernist Temperament: 1890–1940

Appia, Adolphe. *The Work of Living Art and Man Is the Measure of All Things.* Coral Gables, FL: University of Miami Press, 1960.

Artaud, Antonin. *The Theatre and Its Double.* Trans. by Mary C. Richards. New York: Grove Press, 1958.

Bablet, Denis. *The Revolution of Stage Design in the Twentieth Century.* Paris: L. Amiel, 1977.

Braun, Edward. *The Director and the Stage: From Naturalism to Grotowski.* New York: Holmes and Meier, 1982.

Brecht, Bertolt. *Brecht on Theatre.* Trans. by John Willett. New York: Hill & Wang, 1965.

Brockett, Oscar G., and Findlay, Robert R. *Century of Innovation: A History of European and American Theatre and Drama since 1870,* 2d ed. Boston: Allyn & Bacon, 1991.

Brustein, Robert. *The Theatre of Revolt: An Approach to Modern Drama.* Boston: Little, Brown, 1964.

Clurman, Harold. *The Fervent Years: The Story of the Group Theatre in the Thirties.* New York: Hill & Wang, 1957.

Craig, Edward Gordon. *On the Art of the Theatre,* 2d ed. Boston: Small, Maynard, 1924.

Davis, Hallie Flanagan. *Arena.* New York: Duell, Sloane and Pearce, 1940.

Deak, Frantisek. *Symbolist Theater: The Formation of the Avant Garde.* Baltimore: Johns Hopkins University Press, 1993.

Gordon, Mel. *Dada Performance.* New York: PAJ Publications, 1987.

Gorelik, Mordecai. *New Theatres for Old.* New York: Samuel French, 1940.

Greene, Naomi. *Antonin Artaud: Poet without Words.* New York: Simon & Schuster, 1970.

Innes, Christopher. *Avant-Garde Theatre 1892–1992.* New York: Routledge, 1993.

Kirby, Michael. *Futurist Performance.* New York: Dutton, 1971.

Larson, Orville K. *Scene Design in the American Theatre, 1915 to 1960.* Fayetteville, AR: University of Arkansas Press, 1989.

Melzer, Annabelle. *Latest Rage the Big Drum: Dada and Surrealist Performance.* Ann Arbor, MI: UMI Research Press, 1980.

O'Connor, John, and Brown, Lorraine, eds. *Free, Adult, Uncensored: The Living History of the Federal Theatre Project.* Washington: New Republic Books, 1978.

Patterson, Michael. *The Revolution in German Theatre, 1900–1933.* London: Routledge and Kegan Paul, 1981.

Rischbeiter, Henning. *Art and the Stage in the 20th Century*. Greenwich, CT: New York Graphic Society, 1968.

Roose-Evans, James. *Experimental Theatre: From Stanislavsky to Peter Brook,* new rev. ed. London: Studio Vista, 1984.

Styan, J. L. *Max Reinhardt*. Cambridge: Cambridge University Press, 1982.

Valency, Maurice. *The Flower and the Castle: An Introduction to Modern Drama*. New York: Grosset & Dunlap, 1963.

Volbach, Walther. *Adolphe Appia, Prophet of the Modern Theatre*. Middletown, CT: Wesleyan University Press, 1968.

Willett, John. *Expressionism*. New York: McGraw-Hill, 1970.

——. *The Theatre of Bertolt Brecht*. New York: New Directions, 1959.

Chapter 8

Reevaluation, Decentralization, and Subsidization

Beauman, Sally. *The Royal Shakespeare Company*. New York: Oxford University Press, 1982.

Berkowitz, Gerald M. *New Broadways: Theatre Across America, 1950–1980*. Totowa, NJ: Rowman & Littlefield, 1982.

Bigsby, C. W. E. *A Critical Introduction to Twentieth-Century American Drama*. Vol. II: Williams/Miller/Albee. New York: Cambridge University Press, 1984.

Boardman, Gerald. *American Musical Comedy: From Adonis to Dreamgirls*. New York: Oxford University Press, 1982.

Brockett, Oscar G., and Findlay, Robert R. See under Chapter 7.

Brustein, Robert. See under Chapter 7.

Cohn, Ruby. *New American Dramatists, 1960–1980*. New York: Grove Press, 1982.

Cook, Judith. *The National Theatre*. London: George G. Harrap & Co., 1976.

Esslin, Martin. *The Theatre of the Absurd,* rev. ed. New York: Doubleday & Co., 1969.

Findlater, Richard. *Twenty-five Years of the English Stage Company*. London: Methuen, 1981.

Gorelik, Mordecai. See under Chapter 7.

Gottfried, Martin. *Broadway Musicals*. New York: Harry N. Abrams, 1979.

Hirsch, Foster. *A Method to Their Madness: The History of the Actors Studio*. New York: W. W. Norton, 1984.

Patterson, Michael. See under Chapter 7.

Rischbeiter, Henning. See under Chapter 7.

Roose-Evans, James. See under Chapter 7.

Smith, Cecil. *Musical Comedy in America*. New York: Theatre Arts Books, 1950.

Styan, J. L. *Modern Drama in Theory and Practice*. 3 vols. New York: Cambridge University Press, 1981.

Chapter 9

Contemporary Diversity

Abramson, Doris E. *Negro Playwrights in the American Theatre*. New York: Columbia University Press, 1969.

Betsko, Kathleen, and Koenig, Rachel. *Interviews with Contemporary Women Playwrights.* New York: Beach Tree Books, 1987.

Biner, Pierre. *The Living Theatre,* 2d ed. New York: Horizon Press, 1972.

Bradby, David. *Director's Theatre.* New York: St. Martin's, 1988.

Brockett, Oscar G., and Findlay, Robert R. See under Chapter 8.

Brook, Peter. See under Chapter 1.

——. *The Shifting Point: Forty Years of Theatrical Exploration, 1946–1987.* New York: Harper & Row, 1988.

Brustein, Robert. *Revolution as Theatre: Notes on the New Radical Style.* New York: Liveright, 1971.

Burian, Jarka. *The Scenography of Josef Svoboda.* Middletown, CT: Wesleyan University Press, 1971.

Byrd Hoffman Foundation. *Robert Wilson: Theatre of Images.* New York: Byrd Hoffman Foundation, 1984.

Case, Sue-Ellen. *Feminism and Theatre.* New York: Routledge, 1988.

Chinoy, Helen K., and Jenkins, Linda, eds. *Women in American Theatre,* 2d ed. New York: Theatre Communications Group, 1987.

Clum, John M. *Acting Gay: Male Homosexuality in Modern Drama.* New York: Columbia University Press, 1992.

Croyden, Margaret. *Lunatics, Lovers and Poets: The Contemporary Experimental Theatre.* New York: McGraw-Hill, 1974.

DeJongh, Nicholas. *Not in Front of the Audience: Homosexuality on Stage.* New York: Routledge, 1992.

Goldberg, Roselee. *Performance Art: From Futurism to the Present,* rev. ed. New York: Harry N. Abrams, 1988.

Grotowski, Jerzy. *Towards a Poor Theatre.* New York: Simon & Schuster, 1968.

Hill, Errol, ed. *The Theatre of Black Americans.* 2 vols. Englewood Cliffs, NJ: Prentice-Hall, 1980.

Hinchliffe, Arnold. *British Theatre, 1950–1970.* Totowa, NJ: Rowman & Littlefield, 1975.

Huerta, Jorge. *Chicano Theatre: Themes and Forms.* Ypsilanti, MI: Bilingual Press, 1982.

Itzin, Catherine. *Stages in the Revolution: Political Theatre in Britain since 1968.* New York: Methuen, 1981.

Kanellos, Nicolas. *A History of Hispanic Theatre in the United States: Origins to 1940.* Austin: University of Texas Press, 1990.

Kerensky, Oleg. *The New British Drama: Fourteen Playwrights since Osborne and Pinter.* New York: Taplinger, 1979.

Kirby, Michael. *Happenings.* New York: E. P. Dutton, 1965.

Kolin, Philip C., ed. *American Playwrights Since 1945: A Guide to Scholarship, Criticism, and Performance.* Westport, CT: Greenwood Press, 1989.

Kostelanetz, Richard. *The Theatre of Mixed Means.* New York: Dial Press, 1968.

Kumiega, Jennifer. *The Theatre of Grotowski.* London: Methuen, 1985.

Marowitz, Charles. *Prospero's Staff: Acting and Directing in the Contemporary Theatre.* Bloomington: Indiana University Press, 1986.

Marranca, Bonnie. *The Theatre of Images* [Robert Wilson, Richard Foreman, Lee Breuer]. New York: Drama Book Specialists, 1977.

Pasolli, Robert. *A Book on the Open Theatre*. Indianapolis: Bobbs-Merrill, 1970.

Pottlitzer, Joanne. *Hispanic Theatre in the United States and Puerto Rico*. New York: Ford Foundation, 1988.

Rischbeiter, Henning. See under Chapter 8.

Roose-Evans, James. See under Chapter 8.

Sanders, Leslie C. *The Development of Black Theatre in America: From Shadows to Selves*. Baton Rouge: Louisiana State University Press, 1988.

Savran, David. *The Wooster Group*. Ann Arbor, MI: UMI Research Press, 1986.

Seller, Maxine S., ed. *Ethnic Theatre in the United States*. Westport, CT: Greenwood Press, 1983.

Shank, Theodore. *American Alternative Theatre*. New York: Grove Press, 1982.

Shyer, Laurence. *Robert Wilson and His Collaborators*. New York: TCG, 1989.

Ziegler, Joseph. *Regional Theatre: The Revolutionary Stage*. Minneapolis: University of Minnesota Press, 1973.

Part Three

Chapter 10

Theatrical Space and Production Design

American Theatre Planning Board. *Theatre Check List: A Guide to the Planning and Construction of Proscenium and Open Stage Theatres*. Middletown, CT: Wesleyan University Press, 1969.

Burris-Meyer, Harold, and Cole, Edward C. *Theatres and Auditoriums*, 2d ed. with supplement. Huntington, NY: Robert E. Krieger Publishing Co., 1975.

Cogswell, Margaret, ed. *The Ideal Theater: Eight Concepts*. New York: American Federation of Arts, 1962.

Green, Peter Arthur. *Design Education: Problem Solving and Visual Experience*. London: Batsford, 1974.

Izenour, George C. *Theatre Design*. New York: McGraw-Hill, 1977.

Jones, Robert E. *The Dramatic Imagination*. New York: Meredith Publishing Co., 1941.

Maier, Manfred. *Basic Principles of Design*. New York: Van Nostrand Reinhold, 1977.

Mielziner, Jo. *Shapes of Our Theatres*. New York: Clarkson N. Potter, 1970.

Schubert, Hannelore. *Modern Theatre Buildings: Architecture, Stage Design, Lighting*. New York: Praeger Publishers, 1971.

Sommer, Robert. *Design Awareness*. San Francisco: Rinehart Press, 1972.

Chapter 11

Playwriting and Dramaturgy

Cohen, Edward M. *Working on a New Play: A Play Development Handbook for Actors, Directors, Designers, and Playwrights*. Englewood Cliffs, NJ: Prentice-Hall, 1988.

Cole, Toby. *Playwrights on Playwriting*. New York: Hill & Wang, 1961.

Richards, Gillian, and MacColl, Linda. *Dramatists Sourcebook 1994–95*. New York: Theatre Communications Group, 1994.

Savran, David. *In Their Own Words: Contemporary American Playwrights*. New York: TCG, 1988.

Smiley, Sam. *Playwriting: The Structure of Action*. Englewood Cliffs, NJ: Prentice-Hall, 1971.

Chapter 12

Directing and Producing

Ball, William. *A Sense of Direction: Some Observations on the Art of Directing*. New York: Drama Book Publishers, 1984.

Bartow, Arthur. *The Director's Voice: 21 Interviews*. New York: TCG, 1988.

Benedetti, Robert. *The Director at Work*. Englewood Cliffs, NJ: Prentice-Hall, 1985.

Bradby, David. See under Chapter 9.

Braun, Edward. See under Chapter 7.

Brook, Peter. See under Chapter 9.

Clurman, Harold. *On Directing*. New York: Macmillan, 1972.

Cohen, Robert, and Harrop, John. *Creative Play Direction*, 2d ed. Englewood Cliffs, NJ: Prentice-Hall, 1984.

Cole, Toby, and Chinoy, Helen K., eds. *Directors on Directing*, rev. ed. Indianapolis: Bobbs-Merrill, 1963.

Farber, Donald C. *From Option to Opening: A Guide for the Off-Broadway Producer*, rev. 4th ed. Wolfeboro, NH: Longwood, 1989.

——. *Producing Theatre: A Comprehensive Legal and Business Guide*. New York: Limelight Editions, 1987.

Green, Joann. *The Small Theatre Handbook: A Guide to Management and Production*. Boston: Harvard Common Press, 1981.

Hodge, Francis. *Play Directing: Analysis, Communication, and Style*, 4th ed. Englewood Cliffs, NJ: Prentice-Hall, 1994.

Jones, David R. *Great Directors at Work: Stanislavsky, Brecht, Kazan, Brook*. Berkeley: University of California Press, 1986.

Langley, Stephen. *Theatre Management in America, Principles and Practice: Producing for Commercial, Stock, Resident, College and Community Theatre*, rev. 2d ed. New York: Drama Book Publishers, 1990.

Newman, Danny. *Subscribe Now!: Building Arts Audiences Through Dynamic Subscription Promoting*. New York: TCG, 1983.

O'Neill, R. H., and Boretz, N.M. *The Director as Artist*. New York: Harcourt Brace College Publishers, 1987.

Reiss, Alvin. *The Arts Management Reader*. New York: Audience Arts, 1979.

Shagan, Rena. *The Road Show: A Handbook for Successful Booking and Touring in the Performing Arts*. New York: ACA Books, 1984.

Wills, J. Robert, ed. *The Director in a Changing Theatre*. Palo Alto, CA: Mayfield Publishing Co., 1976.

Chapter 13

Acting

Benedetti, Robert L. *The Actor at Work,* 5th ed. Englewood Cliffs, NJ: Prentice-Hall, 1990.

Berry, Cicely. *Voice and the Actor*. London: Harrap, 1986.

Chaikin, Joseph. *The Presence of the Actor: Notes on the Open Theatre, Disguises, Acting and Repression*. New York: Atheneum Publishers, 1972.

Cohen, Robert. *Acting Professionally: Raw Facts About Careers in Acting,* 4th ed. Mountain View, CA: Mayfield Publishing Co., 1990.

Cole, Toby, and Chinoy, Helen K., eds. *Actors on Acting: The Theories, Techniques, and Practices of the Great Actors of All Time as Told in Their Own Words,* new rev. ed. New York: Crown Publishers, 1970.

Hagen, Uta. *Respect for Acting*. New York: Macmillan, 1973.

Harrop, John, and Epstein, Sabin. *Acting with Style,* 2d ed. Englewood Cliffs, NJ: Prentice-Hall, 1989.

Lessac, Arthur. *The Use and Training of the Human Voice,* 2d ed. New York: Drama Book Publishers, 1967.

Lewis, Robert. *Advice to the Players*. New York: Harper & Row, 1980.

McGaw, Charles J., and Blake, Gary. *Acting Is Believing,* 5th ed. New York: Harcourt Brace College Publishers, 1986.

Machlin, Evangeline. *Speech for the Stage,* rev. ed. New York: Theatre Arts Books, 1980.

Spolin, Viola. *Improvisation for the Theatre,* rev. ed. Evanston, IL: Northwestern University Press, 1983.

Stanislavsky, Constantin. *An Actor Prepares*. Trans. by Elizabeth Reynolds Hapgood. New York: Theatre Arts Books, 1936.

——. *Building a Character*. Trans. by Elizabeth Reynolds Hapgood. New York: Theatre Arts Books, 1949.

——. *Creating a Role*. Trans. by Elizabeth Reynolds Hapgood. New York: Theatre Arts Books, 1961.

Yakim, Moni, with Broadman, Muriel. *Creating a Character: A Physical Approach to Acting*. New York: Watson-Guptill, 1990.

Chapter 14

Scenic Design

Arnold, Richard L. *Scene Technology,* 3d ed. Englewood Cliffs, NJ: Prentice-Hall, 1994.

Aronson, Arnold. *American Set Design*. New York: Theatre Communications Group, 1985.

Bablet, Denis. *Stage Design in the Twentieth Century*. New York: Leon Amiel, 1976.

Bay, Howard. *Stage Design*. New York: Drama Book Publishers, 1974.

Bellman, Willard F. *Scenography and Stage Technology: An Introduction*. New York: Harper & Row, 1977.

Burdick, Elizabeth B., et al., eds. *Contemporary Stage Design*. Middletown, CT: Wesleyan University Press, 1975.

Corey, Irene. *The Mask of Reality: An Approach to Design for the Theatre.* Anchorage, KY: Anchorage Press, 1968.

Jones, Robert Edmond. *The Dramatic Imagination.* New York: Meredith Publishing Co., 1941.

Larson, Orville K., ed. *Scene Design for Stage and Screen: Readings on the Aesthetics and Methodology of Scene Design for Drama, Opera, Musical Comedy, Ballet, Motion Pictures, Television and Arena Theatre.* East Lansing: Michigan State University Press, 1961.

Mielziner, Jo. *Designing for the Theatre.* New York: Atheneum Publishers, 1965.

Oenslager, Donald. *Scenery Then and Now.* New York: W. W. Norton, 1936.

Parker, W. Oren. *Sceno-Graphic Techniques.* Carbondale, IL: Southern Illinois University Press, 1987.

—— and Wolf, R. Craig. *Scene Design and Stage Lighting,* 6th ed. New York: Harcourt Brace College Publishers, 1990.

Payne, Darwin. *The Scenographic Imagination.* Carbondale, IL: Southern Illinois University Press, 1987.

Pecktal, Lynn. *Designing and Painting for the Theatre.* New York: Holt, Rinehart and Winston, 1975.

Smith, Ronn. *American Set Design 2.* New York: Theatre Communications Group, 1991.

Chapter 15

Costume Design and Makeup

Anderson, Barbara and Cletus. *Costume Design.* New York: Holt, Rinehart and Winston, 1984.

Barton, Lucy. *Historic Costume for the Stage.* Boston: Baker's Plays, 1935.

Corey, Irene. *The Face is a Canvas: The Design and Technique of Theatrical Makeup.* New Orleans: Anchorage Press, 1990.

Corson, Richard. *Stage Make-up,* 8th ed. Englewood Cliffs, NJ: Prentice-Hall, 1990.

Emery, Joy S. *Stage Costume Techniques,* 2d ed. Englewood Cliffs, NJ: Prentice-Hall, 1992.

Ingham, Rosemary, and Covey, Liz. *The Costume Designer's Handbook: A Complete Guide for Amateur and Professional Costume Designers.* Englewood Cliffs, NJ: Prentice-Hall, 1983.

Jones, Robert E. See under Chapter 14.

Motley. *Designing and Making Stage Costumes.* London: Studio Vista, 1964.

Payne, Blanche. *History of Costume from the Ancient Egyptians to the Twentieth Century.* New York: Harper & Row, 1965.

Russell, Douglas. *Costume History and Style.* Englewood Cliffs, NJ: Prentice-Hall, 1983.

——. *Stage Costume Design: Theory, Technique and Style,* 2d ed. Englewood Cliffs, NJ: Prentice-Hall, 1985.

Smith, C. Ray, ed. *The Theatre Crafts Book of Make-up, Masks, and Wigs.* Emmaus, PA: Rodale Press, 1974.

Chapter 16

Lighting Design, Sound, and Multimedia

Ballou, Glen, ed. *Handbook for Sound Engineers.* Indianapolis: Howard W. Sams, 1987.

Bellman, Willard F. *Lighting the Stage: Art and Practice,* 2d ed. San Francisco: Chandler Publishing Co., 1974.

———. *Scenography and Stage Technology.* See under Chapter 14.

Bergman, Gosta M. *Lighting in the Theatre.* Totowa, NJ: Rowman & Littlefield, 1977.

Burian, Jarka. See under Chapter 10.

Collison, David. *Stage Sound.* New York: Applause Theatre Books, 1990.

Gillette, J. Michael. *Designing with Light,* 2d ed. Mountain View, CA: Mayfield, 1989.

Jones, Robert E. See under Chapter 14.

Jones, Tom Douglas. *The Art of Light and Color.* New York: Van Nostrand Reinhold, 1973.

McCandless, Stanley R. *A Method of Lighting the Stage,* 4th ed. New York: Theatre Arts Books, 1958.

Palmer, Richard H. *The Lighting Art: The Aesthetics of Stage Lighting Design.* Englewood Cliffs, NJ: Prentice-Hall, 1985.

Parker, W. Oren, and Wolf, R. Craig. See under Chapter 14.

Rosenthal, Jean, and Wertenbaker, Lael. *The Magic of Light.* Boston: Little, Brown, 1972.

Warfel, William B., and Klappert, Walter R. *Color Science for Lighting the Stage.* New Haven, CT: Yale University Press, 1981.

———. *The New Handbook of Stage Lighting Graphics,* rev. ed. New York: Drama Book Publishers, 1990.

Watson, Lee. *Lighting Design Handbook.* New York: McGraw-Hill, 1990.

Appendix

Babcock, Dennis, and Boyd, Preston. *Careers in the Theatre.* Minneapolis: Lerner, 1975.

Black, David. *Actor's Audition.* New York: Random House, 1990.

Cohen, Robert. See under Chapter 13.

Greenberg, Jan W. *Theatre Careers.* New York: Henry Holt, 1983.

Henry, Mari Lyn, and Rogers, Lynne. *How to Be a Working Actor: The Insider's Guide to Finding Jobs in the Theater, Film, and Television,* 2d ed. New York: M. Evans, 1989.

Landy, Robert. *Handbook of Educational Theatre and Drama.* Westport, CT: Greenwood Press, 1982.

Thurman, Anne, and Piggins, Carol A. *Drama Activities with Older Adults: A Handbook for Leaders.* Binghamton, NY: Haworth Press, 1982.

Watson, Lee. See under Chapter 16.

Index